MY DEAR FRIENDS

—— IN ——

AMERICA

MY DEAR FRIENDS
— IN —
AMERICA

DAISAKU IKEDA

Collected U.S. Addresses 1990–1996

SECOND EDITION

World Tribune
Press

Cover photo by Daisaku Ikeda,
June 1996, Denver.

Published by World Tribune Press
606 Wilshire Blvd., Santa Monica, CA 90401

ISBN 978-1-932911-81-7

Cover and inerior design by Gopa & Ted2, Inc.

10 9 8 7 6 5 4 3 2 1

Contents

—∿∿—

Editor's Note

My Dear Friends in America is the compilation of speeches and lectures by SGI President Daisaku Ikeda given in the United States during the 1990s.

The citations most commonly used in this book have been abbreviated as follows:

- GZ refers to the *Gosho Zenshu*, the Japanese-language compilation of letters, treatises, essays and oral teachings of Nichiren Daishonin.

- LS refers to *The Lotus Sutra*, translated by Burton Watson (New York: Columbia University Press, 1993).

- OTT refers to *The Record of the Orally Transmitted Teachings*, translated by Burton Watson (Tokyo: Soka Gakkai, 2004).

- WND refers to *The Writings of Nichiren Daishonin*, vol. 1 (WND-1) (Tokyo: Soka Gakkai, 1999) and vol. 2 (WND-2) (Tokyo: Soka Gakkai, 2006).

1990

Become a Model
for the Rest of the World

—∿—

FIRST SGI-USA TRAINING MEETING,
MALIBU TRAINING CENTER, MALIBU, CALIFORNIA,
FEBRUARY 12, 1990

THIS IS MY FIRST VISIT to the United States in three years, and it gives me great joy to be reunited with my friends in America, who are so dear to me.

Originally this trip was scheduled to include three South American countries — Brazil, Argentina and Paraguay — but the importance of the United States [in terms of worldwide kosen-rufu] made me decide to change my schedule and send a representative on my behalf to South America so that I can concentrate on the United States at this particular time. I hope to meet with various Latin American leaders, including General Director Roberto Saito of Brazil, who will be in Los Angeles for the Eleventh SGI General Meeting on February 17.

When I left Japan, I was asked to convey very best regards to all SGI-USA members on behalf of Soka Gakkai President Akiya and many other top leaders. I would like to take this opportunity to give you their best wishes.

During my stay here, I am scheduled to attend the Eleventh SGI General Meeting, the First All-America General Meeting, the Second SGI Pan-American Joint Conference, training sessions for the women's division and the youth division and other events.

Furthermore, I will have discussions with Dr. Linus Pauling and Professor Norman Cousins, who are both my acquaintances. I am also scheduled to meet with Dr. Armand Hammer. I hope you will lend me your support during my stay.

The worldwide kosen-rufu movement was launched here in the United States thirty years ago. These thirty years have been the first phase. Now I would like to designate this last decade, up to October 2, 2001, as the second stage in the worldwide kosen-rufu movement. The purpose of my current visit to your country is to see that this new phase gets off to a smooth start.

All of you are together as like-minded seekers of the way from the infinite past. I hope you will advance further in harmony as wonderful companions who have a deep connection with one another, based on the Mystic Law.

All members are equal in front of the Gohonzon. You are beautiful friends sharing the same faith. I would like all of you to move forward cheerfully, amicably and with hearts and minds in unison.

A true leader is someone who protects his or her members, praising them and being tolerant toward them. In contrast, leaders who exploit their positions in the organization, rebuking people and acting in a highhanded manner, not only cause the Buddha's children to suffer but make causes for their own suffering in the future as well. If you allow that kind of leader to have control, then both parties — the leaders and the members — will end up in misery. This must be avoided at all costs. The world of faith exists for the purpose of attaining Buddhahood and true happiness in this life.

It is important to have a sufficiently elevated life-condition so that you can calmly accept whatever happens in life, always striving to put problems into proper perspective and to solve them with a positive attitude. Happiness blossoms forth from such a strong and all-encompassing life-condition.

You can forge the path to a fulfilling and enjoyable life if you have the depth of faith to regard everything as a source for creating happiness and value. Conversely, if you see everything in a negative or pessimistic light, your life will gradually but inevitably be plunged into darkness. Buddhism teaches the subtle principle of one's determination and, moreover, the power of faith.

I would like the SGI-USA to be a model for the rest of the world. I hope to make my next three weeks here worthwhile and satisfying. I intend to make an all-out effort, spending as much time as possible together with you during my stay.

Build a Solid Foundation

—◈—

SGI-USA REPRESENTATIVES CONFERENCE COMMEMORATING

THE THIRTIETH ANNIVERSARY OF THE SGI-USA, MALIBU,

CALIFORNIA, FEBRUARY 13, 1990

THE THIRTIETH ANNIVERSARY of the SGI-USA's founding is a truly significant milestone. I hope this conference will be a memorable occasion, filled with aspiration for the future.

Today I would like to talk briefly on five points that I hope you will always bear in mind.

In the first place, please advance steadily with the awareness that you are now building a foundation for the next thousand years of the kosen-rufu movement in the United States. There is no need to be impatient. Anything that is accomplished quickly and easily will not long endure. Now is the time to concentrate on the construction of a solid foundation. I hope you will complete this work slowly but surely, filled with hope and joy.

Laying the groundwork may sound tedious and lack the brilliance that attracts people's attention. However, such painstaking work is indispensable and extremely important. Once the foundation is solidified, you can construct anything on it. Please remember that the task of building the foundation of the castle of the Law, which will endure for a thousand years, is in the hands of the current generation of SGI-USA members. For my part, I will spare no effort in supporting you in any way I can.

FIND AND RAISE CAPABLE PEOPLE

The second point that I want to make is that capable people are the greatest treasure. Without capable people, neither the eternal establishment of the Law nor world peace can be achieved.

First of all, you must find capable people. Just as a miner searches for gold ore in ordinary rocks, you have to look for members who possess great potential and then work to develop their ability with your heart and soul.

Prayer is most fundamental in raising capable people. You should pray earnestly to the Gohonzon that the person you have found will become an able person important to the SGI-USA. Then, with this prayer, you take the utmost care to help that person develop.

Among the many members in Japan, there have been some who, on account of sloppiness in financial matters and other aspects of their daily lives, forsook their faith and left the pure and harmonious world of the Soka Gakkai. I have never allowed, however, anyone whom I decided to raise to fall out of the ranks. Once I have found capable people, even among older individuals who were disciples of the first and second Soka Gakkai presidents, I have done my best to thoroughly protect and develop them. The capable people I have raised are now active as pillars of our movement in all areas of society.

You should sincerely respect capable people and raise them with the determination to make them even more outstanding and capable than you are yourself. Looking down on one's juniors or exploiting them for personal gain is an offense comparable to that of slandering the Law. Please remember that one who raises capable people is great. Such a person is truly capable and important.

CONDUCT JOYFUL DIALOGUE

The third point concerns holding joyful meetings and conducting dialogue that is imbued with joy and wisdom. By making these your mottoes and living up to them, the SGI-USA can become an exemplary organization for kosen-rufu.

The raison d'etre of the world of faith is to help people become happy. In essence, ours is a gathering of supreme freedom and joy. No one has the right to reprimand and cause suffering for others, nor is anyone obliged to let him- or herself be reproved and made to feel bad.

For example, whether someone succeeds in helping others take faith in the teachings of Buddhism, the simple fact that he or she practices is in itself most praiseworthy. If you can feel heart-felt joy in expounding the Law and sharing it with others, your blessings will increase still further. Joyfully engaging in propaga-tion and other activities — this is the spirit of Buddhism.

Again, no matter what difficulties you may have, when you go to a meeting and see friends, you feel relief and a sense of joy, and your heart fills with hope. It is my sincere hope that you hold won-derful meetings of this kind — happy gatherings where friends warmly pat each other on the back, encourage one another and share their joys and sorrows.

My wish is that the SGI-USA will become an organization over-flowing with smiles, friendship and humanity. I hope that all of you, without a single exception, will lead lives of the greatest ful-fillment and joy.

Intellect will play a very important role in the coming age. By intellect I mean refined wisdom, clear reasoning, profound philos-ophy and broad-ranging knowledge. We are entering an age when the people will develop their intelligence and wisdom, infusing society with their new outlook. This is the course that [SGI organi-zations in] Japan and many other countries today are following. I ask that the SGI-USA also make efforts along these lines.

RESPECT DIVERSITY

Fourth, you must respect those who are fighting for world peace, irrespective of their race or nationality.

There are many differences, for instance, between the cultures, climates and social systems of Japan and the United States. Therefore, it is only natural that there might be differences in how kosen-rufu is advanced in the two countries.

Fundamentally speaking, however, infinite variety derives from the one Law, and the true entity of life — as described by the one hundred worlds and one thousand factors as well as "three thousand realms in a single moment of life" — is the same in all societies. From this view, it is important that we respect anyone who is struggling on the forefront of our movement. This attitude will become a great driving force behind the spread of the Mystic Law.

President Toda once said, "If you fail to respect those who are fighting for kosen-rufu, you will be unable to develop correct faith, and there will be no development in the organization that you are leading." In this sense, I ask that you receive guidance on what is important for advancing kosen-rufu.

Avoid Overexerting Yourselves

Fifth, I would like you to forge ahead, always taking good care of your health. All of you are extremely precious children of the Buddha who are dedicated to the cause of propagating this Buddhism. Nothing would be more regrettable than for you to impair your health.

Therefore, I ask that you maintain a rhythm in your daily life and get ample rest. Things that you volunteer to undertake on your own initiative aside, there is no need to overexert yourself at the expense of your health on account of organizational pressures.

I sincerely hope that you will devote yourself to peace and Buddhism while living with a correct rhythm and carrying out meaningful and enjoyable activities. Please establish a splendid life. I would like to conclude my speech with my prayers that you will open up a path for the prosperity of your families.

Cultivate a
New Common Sense

—ഝ—

FIRST SGI-USA YOUTH DIVISION TRAINING SESSION,
SOKA UNIVERSITY LOS ANGELES, CALABASAS,
CALIFORNIA, FEBRUARY 14, 1990

I AM VERY PLEASED TODAY to meet with all of you promising young people of wisdom and passion who are committed to the pursuit of your ideals. Because you are all important leaders who I trust will shoulder the responsibility for the future of humanity, I will candidly share my thoughts with you.

I deeply admire you for your energetic seeking spirit. You are pioneers who are responsible for shaping the future course of humankind and society. Also, you are forerunners of the American kosen-rufu movement and are the true successors of the SGI-USA. You are in fact envoys of the Buddha who are contributing to the development of American culture and global peace. I hope that you will become leaders throughout American society.

STUDY BROADLY, BASED ON FAITH

Today I want to share with you some of my ideas on history and life. What I desire above all is to raise leaders who are well equipped with the power of intellect. Therefore I hope that each of you will study broadly and develop your understanding of life, society and the universe, based on your faith in Nichiren Daishonin's Buddhism. This type of learning enables you to cultivate a rich state of life, or inner world, drawing forth profound wisdom and limitless leadership ability from the depths of your life.

When the long-entrenched barriers of "common sense" in people's hearts are broken down, a new common sense, borne on the wings of lively dialogue, begins to take shape. This signifies the beginning of a new era and of fundamental change in society.

Before Copernicus, the heliocentric theory was outside the realm of common sense, as was the theory of evolution before Charles Darwin. Today, however, those ideas are widely accepted. Likewise, there are currently many misconceptions and prejudices regarding Buddhism. Nevertheless, I am confident that in the future the Buddhist teachings will become a matter of common sense among all people. That will be the time of kosen-rufu.

Buddhism is so tremendously farsighted and profound a religion that, externally, it is difficult to grasp its true message. People with little understanding of Buddhism can no more discern its value than a child can understand the real value of a diamond. However, please be confident that the development of human wisdom will produce an increasing body of evidence pointing to the greatness of Buddhism.

THOMAS PAINE'S "COMMON SENSE"

During the struggle for American independence, there was a small, fifty-page pamphlet that triggered a momentous change in people's outlooks. This pamphlet altered the destiny of America and the world. That pamphlet was *Common Sense* (1776) by Thomas Paine (1737–1809).

This publication shook dispirited and cowardly people from the shackles of their accustomed common sense as colonial subjects. The author appealed to his fellow citizens to take a brave step toward freedom and independence, to never succumb to the authority and power represented by tyrannical rule and hereditary distinctions of class. He asserted that by taking one courageous step forward, they could arrive at a common sense that was new and correct.

This pamphlet sold one hundred thousand copies in only three months. Considering the difference in population size, this would correspond to roughly ten million copies today. It was truly a bestseller.

The power of the written word sometimes defies imagination. The cry for freedom in this booklet galvanized the hearts of the people.

We are now advancing toward a new century, a century of life in which all people will enjoy the benefits of equality, happiness and freedom to the fullest. The fundamental "common sense" of Buddhism and of life itself forms the basis for our activities toward this goal.

The road we walk is not level. We must climb a great mountain, a task that invariably requires painful effort. In the world of Buddhism, however, no effort is wasted. All the causes that you make will be engraved in the depths of your life; they are passages in the golden diary of your eternal existence.

Do Not Shrink in the Face of Conflict

Thomas Paine volunteered to serve in the American War of Independence. He was then thirty-nine, roughly the same age as many senior leaders of our youth division.

I always place high value on personal initiative. Spontaneity underlies the spirit of autonomy and independence; conversely, taking action only because one is told to amounts to slavery of the spirit. Our movement will be advanced by brave people armed with the spirit of independence who voluntarily strive to fulfill the vow they made in the time without beginning. Because they struggle on their own volition, they have no complaints or grievances. The greater the obstacles they face, the greater the courage, wisdom and power they muster from within.

When Paine joined the War of Independence, the American forces, led by General George Washington, were at a grave impasse. They were no match for the enemy forces, and in battle after battle, they were defeated and forced to retreat. Soldiers deserted in droves.

Paine dared to join the army at a time when its defeat seemed certain. In what Paine later called "a passion of patriotism," he poured his heart into writing a document based on his own experience in the Continental army. That tract, "The American Crisis," begins with the famous sentence, "These are the times that try men's souls." In this piece, he posed the question: Will we shrink from this moment of crisis on which the war's outcome hangs, or shall we stand firm and turn the situation to our favor?

He also wrote, "Tyranny, like hell, is not easily conquered; yet we have the consolation with us that the harder the conflict, the more glorious the triumph." Victory is not easily won. If it is, it will not be a source of pride. What gratification, for instance, could a sumo wrestler derive from defeating a child? Only when one fights and wins over dire circumstances will one's victory shine brilliantly in history.

On a cold, blizzardy day toward the end of the year, General Washington gathered soldiers who, after successive defeats, had lost their spirit and become thoroughly exhausted. The brave general had Paine's essay read to these soldiers, as though calling out to them on the front lines of the battlefield. Passion raced through their hearts, and their spirit to carry on the war for justice was revived. Paine's cry, arising from his soul as he contemplated the desperate situation, filled each soldier with the infinite power of courage and hope.

In this way, the American army righted itself and launched a great offensive. Crossing a frozen river swiftly, they crushed the enemy soldiers who had been caught off guard capriciously celebrating Christmas. This battle changed the course of the war and eventually led to victory and independence.

ENCOURAGE ONE ANOTHER TOWARD VICTORY IN LIFE

In any struggle, the critical point is how a leader inspires others. As you are leaders of kosen-rufu, I ask that you encourage friends of the Mystic Law in such a manner that the powers of faith and life force surge forth in their lives. I hope that your efforts in the struggle of faith will serve to increase the majesty and strength of the Buddhist deities.

When Shijo Kingo was unjustly persecuted on account of faith and confronted with extremely difficult circumstances, Nichiren Daishonin encouraged him, saying: "Buddhism is reason. Reason will win over your lord" (WND-1, 839). Buddhism is supreme reason. The Buddhism of Nichiren Daishonin expounds the most profound and universal common sense.

Buddhism reveals the ultimate Law of the universe and the ultimate principle of achieving happiness. Taking faith in Buddhism plants the seed of true happiness in our lives. Therefore, we must not uproot and throw away, scorch or otherwise spoil this seed of happiness by harboring hatred and jealousy against fellow believers and discarding our faith.

No matter what happens, please continue to chant daimoku in both good times and bad, irrespective of your joys and sorrows, happiness and suffering. Then you can seize victory in your daily life and in society.

To commemorate this training session, I would like to introduce several items from among the important treasures of Soka University: a collection of letters of Napoleon Bonaparte; a letter by Albert Einstein from Berlin calling for Jewish unity; an original autographed edition of Walt Whitman's *Leaves of Grass*. Please take a moment to view them later.

It is to you that I entrust the future task of kosen-rufu. I conclude by saying that I will continue to send you daimoku throughout my life, offering sincere prayers for your happiness and good health.

Profound Happiness Exists
in Efforts for Construction

—ɷ—

SECOND SGI PAN-AMERICAN JOINT CONFERENCE,
SOKA UNIVERSITY LOS ANGELES, CALABASAS, CALIFORNIA,
FEBRUARY 15, 1990

I AM OVERJOYED to see all of you at this meeting despite your busy schedules. I know that many of you must have traveled great distances to be here. With profound admiration and respect, I welcome each of you, precious children of the Buddha.

As you know, I originally planned to make stops in several South American countries. I changed my itinerary, however, because I wanted to focus my efforts on North America on this trip. I offer my most sincere apologies for this sudden change. From the bottom of my heart, I am praying for the great success of the Tenth World Peace Youth Culture Festival in Brazil and other important events soon to take place. Because I feel that this meeting is like a family gathering, I want to speak informally with you today.

All of you are noble forerunners in your respective countries and communities, and the benefits to which you are entitled are immeasurable. This calls to mind a passage from the Gosho "The Blessings of the Lotus Sutra." Although this letter was addressed to a male believer, Nichiren Daishonin's guidance is directed to his wife as well. When the Daishonin wrote to a follower, male or female, he never failed to show great consideration for the person's spouse. The Daishonin respected both men and women equally.

Where such an attitude is present — in the household as well as in the organization — there is solid growth.

The Gosho reads: "As first one person, then two persons, then a thousand, ten thousand, a hundred thousand, and then all the people throughout the country come to chant the daimoku, before you know it, their blessings will accrue to you. Those blessings will be like the drops of dew that gather to form the great ocean, or the specks of dust that pile up to become Mount Sumeru" (WND-1, 672).

As this passage indicates, although at the outset the membership in your country may be small, the Mystic Law will spread without fail when the right time arrives. Thus there is no need for you to be impatient. If you achieve something easily right from the start, you will find no sense of fulfillment or joy. It is in making tenacious, all-out efforts for construction that profound happiness lies.

You are the pioneers of kosen-rufu in your respective countries and communities. The blessings that you will accumulate are as great as the ocean or a huge mountain, and they will continue to grow limitlessly as the sphere of kosen-rufu expands. How fortunate we are, and how marvelous is the Mystic Law!

In a letter to the Ikegami brothers and their wives, who began practicing during the initial stage of the Daishonin's propagation activities, Nichiren Daishonin states, "Even if in the future other men and women become my believers, they will not replace you in my heart" (WND-1, 502). These words of the original Buddha suggest the immeasurable value of pioneers.

For pioneers, hardship and suffering are inevitable. But the fact that they have blazed a trail, and the growth that they achieve as a result, are undeniable accomplishments. This is indicated by the sutra passage "If you want to understand what results will be manifested in the future, look at the causes that exist in the present" (WND-1, 279).

There is no doubt that with the passage of time, and in lifetime after lifetime, you will enjoy immense good fortune welling forth from the depths of your life. You will enjoy both material and spiritual happiness and develop a profound state of life. Some of you may become great leaders in society, others distinguished scholars or master artists — all working to further advance kosen-rufu. In every lifetime throughout the ten thousand years of the Latter Day of the Law, you will be able to live such rich and fulfilling lives. Please be convinced of the great blessings that you will enjoy in your present and future existences. Firm confidence in this will enable you to elevate yourself to an even higher plane.

Because there are many youth division representatives present today, I want to discuss a number of points that I hope will prove of value for them as they make their way through life.

When I was a youth of twenty-two or twenty-three, my life was filled with storms of difficulty. I alone continued to follow the Soka Gakkai's second president, Josei Toda, when his business endeavors ended in failure. Around that time, I had the opportunity to speak with three people who had themselves received a great deal of assistance from my mentor.

One of them said to me: "You better stop working for Mr. Toda.... It's foolish to push yourself so hard that you damage your health." Though deeply indebted to President Toda, this individual thanklessly repaid him with such derogatory words. He later suffered from depression and lived in misery.

The second person I talked to urged me to follow him rather than Mr. Toda and to work for his company instead. At the time he was well off, but his life later took a downhill course.

The third person said to me: "This is the very time that you should support Mr. Toda. You must never harbor doubts about the Gohonzon." That person dedicated himself to the cause of kosen-rufu until the end of his life. He was right and became happy in all aspects of his life.

These three people each approached me with different words and attitudes, reflecting their own way of living and, by extension, the future course of their lives, and each thereby revealed his true colors. The human weakness and strength that I observed left an indelible impression on my mind. This unforgettable experience has influenced my outlook ever since.

On the surface, President Toda appeared to be a loser at that time; however, I had firm belief in his mission. In a sense, people's lives will be determined by the person whom they follow as youth. If you board an airplane bound for Beijing when you want to go to Los Angeles, you will never reach your destination; you cannot disembark midway once you are on board. To give up halfway in your practice of faith is like disembarking from an airplane in mid-flight.

In a letter to Shijo Kingo, Nichiren Daishonin states, "Because you did not turn against the Lotus Sutra, but showed your devotion by accompanying me [to Tatsunokuchi], you will surely become a Buddha" (WND-1, 946). With these words, the Daishonin praises this faithful disciple who, during the Tatsunokuchi Persecution, accompanied him to his would-be execution site and pledged to die at his side.

For my part, I was firmly convinced that because President Toda was the great leader of kosen-rufu, to protect him was to protect kosen-rufu and the great pure Law. In fact, because I alone remained with and supported him during that difficult time, I could expand my state of life far more than other people.

Nichiren Daishonin states in "The Farther the Source, the Longer the Stream," "Alone, Shakyamuni continued his practice and became the Buddha" (WND-1, 941). Those monks who initially practiced with Siddhartha later abandoned him, but the future Buddha concentrated on his pursuit of enlightenment.

Climbing a mountain entails difficulty, and the higher the mountain, the greater the difficulties a climber faces. But once a person reaches the summit, he or she will savor a state of mind far greater than that attained by those who handily climb lesser peaks.

I hope that all of you become people of courage who, even if you were to be deserted by others, would persevere in the way of faith that you have determined to follow to the very end of your lives, no matter what difficulties may arise. If there is even one such person of genuine faith, waves of kosen-rufu will spread far and wide.

FORMALITY IS PROVISIONAL; SUBSTANCE IS ESSENTIAL

President Toda detested formality. For this reason, as his disciple, I have tried to place foremost emphasis on substance. Formalities are important in certain cases, but mere formality that lacks substance is an evil. Formalities in and of themselves have no life, whereas substance is alive. Formality is provisional, substance essential. Formality is conventional and therefore conservative, but substance provides the impetus for progress and development.

Suppose a meeting is held. If a person is caught up with formality, concerned only about how many people attend or whether the meeting goes off without a hitch, he loses sight of substance. This a sign of failure as a leader.

Even if the participants are few, if they are convinced of the greatness of faith and feel joy, thereby deepening their confidence in the Gohonzon, the meeting is a success. In this case, you are focusing on substance. Let's say, for example, there are only three people at a meeting, but when they pray to the Gohonzon, read the Gosho and inspire one another, their lives are illuminated by the flame of faith. From the standpoint of Buddhism, such a meeting is a great success.

On the other hand, even though thousands may attend a meeting, and it may proceed smoothly and with an air of grandeur, if it does not inspire the joy of faith in the hearts of members, in the last analysis it is a vain and pointless charade.

Our meetings are held neither for the sake of leaders nor for the sake of the organization. They are intended to awaken and support the development of individual members. Both an organization and its leadership exist for the sake of individuals. This accords with the teachings of Buddhism. If, instead, individuals are manipulated to serve the needs of an organization and its leadership, the spirit of Buddhism is contradicted. In Buddhism, such a perverse relationship between the organization or leadership and the individual will block the power of the Law, stop the flow of benefits and stifle the spread of the Law. Giving warm encouragement and care to each person is the basis for victory.

The organization is a gathering of human beings, a network of individuals. If leaders feel that their organization is dull and lifeless, unable to produce remarkable results, in reality this indicates their and the individual members' states of life.

If, blinded by the mirage of an organization, a leader tries to operate by giving orders and applying pressure, nothing will change, because no spontaneous or genuine power will be generated among the people who make up that body. We must understand the subtle character of people's hearts.

It is essential that you address everyone with sincerity and compassion as an equal, carefully taking into account their individual capacities and circumstances, and seeking to give them a sense of satisfaction and assurance. As you continue making such efforts, you will definitely see great development.

The main point is to enable a single member to stand up by imparting heartfelt assurance and understanding. It is the explosion of faith in the microcosm of an individual that causes the macrocosm of the organization — a gathering of many such individuals — to commence its revolution. This is how the doctrine of "three thousand realms in a single moment of life" applies to our practice.

Put the Gosho Into Practice

Lastly, I hope that young people, with rich and apt powers of critical evaluation in all matters, will always advance toward higher and greater targets, never allowing themselves to become complacent with their present circumstances. On the other hand, as far as the fundamental teachings of Buddhism and the Gosho are concerned, I hope that, regarding them as absolutely correct, you will first and foremost strive to put them into practice. I urge you to do so because this is the shortest route to understanding the essence of Buddhism from the depths of your life.

The Record of the Orally Transmitted Teachings states, "Belief represents the value or price we attach to a jewel or treasure, and understanding [wisdom] represents the jewel itself" (OTT, 54). For example, with one dollar of belief, you can obtain but one dollar's worth of wisdom, but if you summon forth ten thousand dollars or one million dollars worth of belief, the wisdom and power you can obtain will increase in like measure. Limitless belief gives rise to limitless wisdom.

I hope that you will be people of firm belief; as such, you will never find yourself in a deadlock. At the same time, as people rich in wisdom, please live up to your mission with complete satisfaction so that you can adorn your existence with the greatest brilliance and joy.

In a very short period of practice, we create benefits and memories that will last forever. On the other hand, you can practice for a long time without seeing any results to justify your efforts. I am confident that with this gathering of the family of the Americas today, we have taken another valuable step that will shine eternally in the annals of kosen-rufu.

Every day, I earnestly pray for your happiness, good health and long lives, as well as for the peace and prosperity of your respective countries. These prayers never leave my mind. I conclude my greetings with my hope that you will lead lives of the greatest joy and contentment.

Advance With the Awareness That You Are the "SGI-USA of the World"

—⚬⚬⚬—

ELEVENTH SGI GENERAL MEETING, WORLD PEACE
IKEDA AUDITORIUM, SANTA MONICA, CALIFORNIA,
FEBRUARY 17, 1990

I AM INDEED HAPPY to see all of you in such high spirits at this significant Eleventh SGI General Meeting. The fact that all of you are in such good health means everything to me.

It is the desire of the original Buddha that each of your families is harmonious and happy. I also sincerely hope that, treasuring your lives and doing your best at your jobs, each of you without exception will lead a victorious life. It is for this reason that we carry out our practice of faith.

This is my first visit to Los Angeles in three years. The mountains surrounding the city look majestic in their fresh coat of snow. We have also had rain that seemed to purify and refresh everything. These seem almost like congratulatory messages from heaven; it is the first time I have seen the city in such a festive mood. The trees that we have planted in honor of various countries at the Soka University Los Angeles campus in Calabasas must be jubilantly sinking their roots into the soil. The person in charge of watering the plants must be exulting at all this rain! And the Buddhist gods must be dancing with joy at the events taking place here!

The First SGI General Meeting was also held in this city at the

Shrine Auditorium in 1980. I feel it is profoundly significant that now, ten years later, we are holding this general meeting here with the participation of members from fifty-four countries. Soka Gakkai President Akiya, General Director Morita and the vice presidents and other senior leaders in Japan asked me to convey their best regards to you. Similar messages have arrived from Europe, Asia, Africa and Oceania.

I also express my sincere appreciation to all those who have sent congratulatory messages, including U.N. Secretary-General Javier Pérez de Cuéllar; Dr. Henry Kissinger; Lauro F. Cavazos, the secretary of the U.S. Department of Education; Professor Bruce Merrifield of Rockefeller University; Professor Harold M. Proshansky, president of the Graduate School and University Center at City University of New York; Professor Robert H. Donaldson, president of Fairleigh Dickinson University; Professor John D. Montgomery of Harvard University and California Governor George Deukmejian.

Because this is a special occasion, and out of my deepest respect and desire to praise you, I would like to introduce some of the treasures of Soka University. I hope you will take a look at them later.

Among the letters on display are those by President Franklin D. Roosevelt and his wife, Eleanor; Marquis de Lafayette; President John F. Kennedy; President Abraham Lincoln; Richard Wagner; Bartolomeo Vanzetti; Victor Hugo; Thomas Edison; Ralph Waldo Emerson and Helen Keller.

THE DAWN OF LIBERTY

At this significant general meeting, I would like to speak about the Declaration of Independence of the United States.

Today, the deep shadows of autocracy and tyranny are rapidly receding. Historically, America's Declaration of Independence represents the first ray of democracy and the dawn of liberty. It was on July 4, 1776, that the Continental Congress of the thirteen federated states unanimously adopted the Declaration of Independence.

The Declaration sets forth the principle that all human beings are equal and asserts this to be "self-evident." It also proclaims outright that "life, liberty and the pursuit of happiness" are natural, inalienable rights of all people that no one may infringe upon. This historic declaration has much in common with the Buddhist ideal of the inherent dignity of human life.

This document preceded the French Revolution by thirteen years. In this sense, the American War of Independence was a landmark divide in world history. Fifty-six delegates representing thirteen states signed the document. Along with the Declaration of Independence, their names will live forever.

Like history itself, the lives of those who create history are everlasting. All of you have dedicated yourselves over these past thirty years to opening the hitherto untrodden path of kosen-rufu in your respective countries. Each of your names, without exception, will be remembered forever, throughout the Latter Day of the Law, and the blessings you accumulate are everlasting, indestructible and inexhaustible. This is due to the workings of the Buddhist Law; it is the promise of the Buddha.

Our first discussion meeting in the United States was held thirty years ago in Hawaii, on October 2, 1960, on the first leg of the trip with which I inaugurated my travels for worldwide kosen-rufu. There were fewer than thirty people present, including the children. I spoke earnestly about Buddhism and faith to every participant and answered each of their questions with all sincerity.

I proposed at that meeting that the first overseas district be formed. No one in my entourage had thought of this move. Today the SGI-USA has more than seventeen hundred districts. Thirty years ago, I personally saw to it that a solid core was established to open the way for future development. The only way to succeed is by first bringing to completion that which is most immediate. This principle applies in all affairs of our daily lives, our work and our families, as well as in the progress of kosen-rufu.

The statue recently erected in Hawaii of an SGI-USA woman honors the great contributions that the members of Hawaii have made as pioneers of the kosen-rufu movement in the United States.

It honors especially the members of the women's division, who bore the full brunt of the early struggles. I sincerely hope that all SGI leaders in all countries will treasure the members of the women's division and show them the utmost respect.

The United States has the honor of being the launching pad for the worldwide kosen-rufu movement, which has now spread to 115 countries [now 192]. I call on you to proudly advance with the awareness of and a sense of responsibility for the great mission you have as the SGI-USA of the world and as a model for all other countries. My wish is that the SGI-USA will eventually develop the strength to provide a lead for Japan.

The Declaration of Independence was drafted by Thomas Jefferson, who subsequently was elected the third president of the United States. The important task of drafting the document fell on Jefferson who, at age thirty-three, was the youngest of the five committee members. Replying to the great trust they had placed in him, the young Jefferson is said to have prepared the document in just a few days.

To actively promote young people of outstanding ability to positions of responsibility and allow them to give free rein to their potential accords with the spirit of Buddhism. It is also the spirit of the SGI, and it ought to be the spirit of each member-organization. The reason for this is that the dynamic activities of young people are the fundamental driving force for fresh development.

Now, what was it that Jefferson labored over? To what did he pay the closest attention? It was neither novelty nor affected formality. His sole wish was to make the Declaration of Independence the crystallization of the American spirit. Jefferson was a person who, throughout his entire life, maintained the vibrantly pulsing spirit of America.

It is the cry of the spirit from the very depths of a person's life that shakes and moves other people's hearts. Similarly, Buddhism is above all concerned with the world of the heart. It expounds the principle that enables us to manifest the infinite power of the spirit. People of faith should strive to become outstanding citizens of their respective countries. There is no need for you to try to imitate others or force yourself into following any specific pattern of behavior.

In 1800, when Jefferson was fifty-seven years old, he wrote in a letter, "I have sworn...eternal hostility against every form of tyranny over the mind of man." I feel the same way. Freedom is something that you must fight for and gain by and for yourself. It is not handed over on a silver platter.

One who has the courage to speak the truth lives a truly splendid and fulfilling life. In any sphere of society, if one loses this courage and become obsequious, one cannot resist exploitation by corrupt authorities.

The life of a person who shrinks before oppression and tries to get by with cunning strategies and falsehood is extremely pitiful. Such a life is self-defeating. Rather, by fighting against and pushing through all the evil that oppresses one, both internally and externally, one establishes a magnanimous self and a profound and happy state of life. This is the purpose of faith.

THE FOUR SUFFERINGS AND THE EIGHT SUFFERINGS

Buddhism describes the fundamental anguish that restricts the freedom of life as the four sufferings or the eight sufferings. The four universal sufferings comprise birth, aging, sickness and death. In more detail, we can describe them as follows: the suffering of living bound by the shackles of karma; the loneliness of aging; the anguish of sickness; and the fear of that most fundamental fact, death. The eight sufferings include four additional sufferings: the suffering of having to part with loved ones; the suffering of having to meet those whom one hates; the suffering of being unable to obtain what one desires, as in the case of one who wishes to become wealthy or successful; and the suffering arising from the five components, in other words, the suffering of being unable to realize harmony in the physical and spiritual aspects of one's life and of feeling heavy and depressed.

It is the sharp sword of the Mystic Law and the great power of faith that enable us to completely sever the chains of these sufferings. Therefore, I wish to make it clear that to secure eternal freedom and happiness, you must absolutely not be cowardly, especially in faith.

By coincidence, Thomas Jefferson died at the age of eighty-three on July 4, 1826, the fiftieth anniversary of the Declaration of Independence. In another example of historic coincidence, Tsunesaburo Makiguchi, the founding president of the Soka Gakkai, died on the anniversary of the Soka Gakkai's founding (November 18).

Ten days before his death, in a letter of thanks for an invitation to a ceremony commemorating fifty years of independence, Jefferson said that the Declaration of Independence would become a signal to awaken people around the world, encouraging them to win liberty by severing the chains of ignorance and superstition that had hitherto bound them. I feel that now, some one hundred sixty years later, as we contemplate the current toward a century of peace that has emerged in all parts of the world, we can see Jefferson smiling brightly in victory.

A New Philosophy To Lead People to Freedom, Equality and Happiness

The ideas espoused in the Declaration of Independence have spread worldwide. Today there is a need for a profound, reliable philosophy to support these ideals and to ensure their universal promulgation. The lack of such a philosophy is becoming an increasingly urgent issue. A new philosophy is called for to bring about the realization of freedom, happiness and equality in their most profound sense.

In our turbulent, rapidly changing society, people have begun to look with yearning toward the merciful light of the sun of the correct teaching. It is you who are playing the major role on the stage of this new era.

Every day, I offer earnest prayers for your happiness, good health and success. You each have your respective place of mission; you are all extremely precious children of the Buddha dedicated to the cause of kosen-rufu. I hope that while fostering cordial and warm relations among yourselves, you will advance as good citizens of your countries. Finally, I ask that you convey my best wishes and cordial regards to all of the members in your areas who were unable to be present today.

Become People of
True Wealth

—∿∿—

SGI JOINT TRAINING SESSION,
SOKA UNIVERSITY LOS ANGELES,
CALABASAS, CALIFORNIA, FEBRUARY 18, 1990

I AM DELIGHTED to meet with all of you who are so dear to me. Among you are many graduates of Soka University and other Soka Schools. Nothing fills my heart with more hope than knowing that Soka School alumni are vigorous and active here in America.

I offer my appreciation to the Soka Gakkai Headquarters women's Soyukai (a group of former staff members) for gathering here in high spirits; you look as lovely and youthful as ever. Also participating in this session are SGI-USA culture department and Pioneer Group members and friends from Canada and Latin America. Students of the Soka Women's Junior College visiting for a language training course are listening to today's proceedings in another room. My sincerest appreciation goes to all of you who have taken the trouble to come here on a Sunday.

We are gathered at a university, a seat of wisdom. Therefore, let me first speak about the significance of the university.

When the British poet John Masefield (1878–1967) wrote, "There are few earthly things more beautiful than a university," he was not admiring the beauty of a university's buildings or its appearance. Rather, its beauty lies in the fact that it is a "place where those who hate ignorance may strive to know, where those who perceive truth may strive to make others see."

In other words, the university is a place for the liberation of humankind. It leads people from the darkness of ignorance to the light of intelligence, from spiritual blindness to awakening, from barbarous chaos to civilized order and from slavery of the soul to its independence. To put it another way, the university is a fortress where, led by the light of reason, human beings achieve spiritual development; it is also a castle for defending civilization against barbarism, a castle founded on the love of truth. A university no doubt is in the vanguard of the effort to expel ignorance — the basic cause for all miseries — from the Earth. It is therefore aptly said that nothing in this world is more beautiful than a university. President John F. Kennedy once cited these impressive words of Masefield in an address.

Alfred North Whitehead (1861–1947), a renowned philosopher who taught at Harvard University, remarked that the "task of a university is the creation of the future." He meant that universities, in the name of reason and civilization, determine the future of humanity, that they in fact shape the future course of history.

In this sense, because we have founded a university, we have participated in the creation of a future. A university in the present is the epitome of society in the future. Therefore, please be convinced that the victory of our university will contribute to the victory of humankind.

One of the mottoes of Soka University Los Angeles is "Be a dynamic force in developing a Pan-Pacific culture." SULA will host the Second Pacific Basin Symposium this coming summer, with the participation of representatives from the United Nations University. It is argued from various angles that the twenty-first century will be an age in which Pan-Pacific nations flourish.

I hope that you study these viewpoints at school or on your own, but I will touch briefly on one aspect of the issue so as to give you food for thought.

A Soviet anthropologist, Serghei Aleksandrovich Arutiunov, once said: "It would not be an exaggeration to call the Pacific

Ocean the inland sea of Ameraustralasia [the term he coined for the North and South American continents combined with the Asian-Pacific region]. And the Pacific Ocean has played a pivotal role in this 'super-continent'.... Albeit on a different scale, the role of the Pacific could be compared to that of the Mediterranean Sea in the region of Afroeurasia (the combination of Africa and Eurasia), which shares a common destiny."

As scholars have recently pointed out, historically oceans are not great yawning abysses of division that separate people and civilizations from one another; rather, oceans connect people and cultures. Northern Africa and southern Europe, for instance, were linked by the Mediterranean. This is clear from the deep relationships that existed among the civilizations of Egypt, Greece and Rome. The Mediterranean was the mother of the civilizations of the regions surrounding it. It has continued to stimulate the development of various civilizations by facilitating the transmission of culture, people and information.

In the same way, those scholars assert, the Pacific Ocean, which links the North and South American continents, Asia and Oceania, has contributed to the development of civilizations in these regions. Although this hypothesis is yet to be verified, the concept that the Pacific Ocean is like an inland sea is an idea of tremendous scale, one that is well suited to the dawning era of global civilization.

The "eastern capital" of this inland sea would be Los Angeles. On a broader scale, we could say that the entire state of California is the "eastern capital."

The Soka University campus founded in this eastern capital is still in its stage of infancy. But we must remember that a huge tree does not immediately sprout from a seed. The question, then, is what is contained within that seed. Although SUA is still young, it has a tremendous mission and significance. I hope that all of you will help carefully nurture the growth of the seed of this school into a truly great tree.

Now I would like to talk about the meaning of success from the standpoint of Nichiren Daishonin's Buddhism.

America is the country of the success story. As Ralph Waldo Emerson put it, "America is another name for opportunity." Many people came to this country in pursuit of the American dream — the dream of success. At present, society is growing more static and constrained than in the past. Be that as it may, the American dream still draws to your shores many who seem to believe that, so long as one has wits and good luck, he can easily become a millionaire.

The word for millionaire, or wealthy person, in Japanese is *choja*. In Buddhist scriptures, however, this word has a different connotation, that of a person of virtue and influence. Based on the formulation and terminology of T'ien-t'ai, Nichiren Daishonin distinguishes three types of wealthy people in interpreting the parable of the three carts and the burning house that appears in the "Simile and Parable" chapter of the Lotus Sutra.

The first of the three categories consists of the wealthy people of the secular world — those people, such as millionaires, who are highly successful in society. Second come wealthy people who renounce the secular world, or "supraworldly wealthy people." These are Buddhist wealthy people, specifically, Shakyamuni Buddha. The third is the "mind-observing wealthy people," by which Nichiren Daishonin means common mortals who embrace the Mystic Law. The first group might be characterized as people of external achievement, while the second and third groups are people of internal achievement. There are profound differences between these two types of achievement.

Buddhist scriptures describe secular wealthy people as being of a good family, possessing wealth, having dignity, possessing profound wisdom, being pure in their actions, exhibiting proper manners and enjoying great prestige. In accordance with the teaching that "all laws are the Buddhist Law," it is worthwhile for us to strive to acquire the virtues of these people. I hope that, basing yourself on faith, you will become wealthy people of virtue and influence who are widely respected.

TRUE SUCCESS MEANS ENJOYING
AN UNRESTRAINED STATE OF LIFE

I want to add, however, that worldly success is not equivalent to true happiness. Achieving this requires that we have a profound understanding of the nature of life. There is much truth to the words of Benjamin Franklin that "success has ruined many a man." If people have wealth, they may become the target of thieves. A beautiful woman may arouse jealousy and suffer as a result. A person of public status may exploit his or her authority and end up in misery.

A person of true success is one who enjoys a free and unrestrained state of life. One who clings to the transient splendor of the world of heaven or rapture is not such a person. As Buddhism teaches, those in the realm of heaven experience the five signs of decay. The joy and success of the world of heaven will inevitably fade and wither just as the leaves of a tree scatter in autumn.

The supraworldly wealthy person is the Buddha. Attaining Buddhahood is true success; the Buddha is the eternal wealthy person. The Buddha possesses the treasure of the Law, as well as all good qualities and all virtues. He defeats all obstacles and attains all kinds of wisdom. His heart is as vast as the ocean, and he always abides in a state of limitless freedom and bliss.

In other words, the Buddha, or supraworldly wealthy person, is characterized by abundant and strong life force. It was generally taught, however, that becoming a Buddha required an incredibly long and difficult practice. Shakyamuni's teachings do not set forth a practice that anyone would be able to fulfill. This is a problem.

Third, the mind-observing wealthy people are "Buddhas who are at the same time common mortals" — that is, they are the votaries of the Lotus Sutra. This term *votary of the Lotus Sutra* specifically refers to Nichiren Daishonin, but in general it includes us followers of the Daishonin who are dedicating our lives to kosen-rufu.

Put simply, "mind-observing" means to observe one's own mind and find the world of Buddhahood inherent within oneself, or to realize that in our lives we possess the limitless treasure house of all riches gathered from throughout the universe. When we open and make free use of this treasure house, we can lead a proud and joyful life with the composure of a great wealthy person. Like the lion king, we fear nothing and are unaffected by fleeting joys and sorrows. This is what it means to be a mind-observing wealthy person. In Nichiren Daishonin's Buddhism, to "observe one's own mind" means faith in the Gohonzon. Therefore, a mind-observing wealthy person is a wealthy person of faith. Such a wealthy person is one who perceives and believes that his or her life is itself the supreme treasure house and who opens this treasure house.

In Shakyamuni's Buddhism, only special people could become wealthy people, for this was a goal beyond the reach of ordinary people. In contrast, Nichiren Daishonin taught that embracing the Gohonzon is itself enlightenment. Thus, by believing in and embracing the Gohonzon, which embodies the state of Buddhahood and the "mutual possession of the Ten Worlds," one can observe and manifest the world of Buddhahood existing in his or her life.

Some scholars compare Shakyamuni's Buddhism to aristocracy or elitism in Buddhism and Nichiren Daishonin's to democracy, because where the former can lead only a select few to attain Buddhahood, the latter addresses the needs of all. The practice of Shakyamuni's Buddhism might be compared to climbing step by step toward the summit of Buddhahood, as though attempting to reach the highest peaks of the Rocky Mountains. What's more, though people of the most advanced ability may attain the summit in this way, they will come to the end of their lives before attempting to save others or contribute to society.

Nichiren Daishonin's Buddhism, on the other hand, teaches how, in one's present circumstances, one can open up the great earth of one's life and excavate the jewel of Buddhahood existing therein. Daimoku and one's determination of faith are the key to opening the treasure house of Buddhahood. Or, to employ the metaphor of mountain climbing, the Daishonin's Buddhism could be likened to a helicopter that brings one directly to the summit of Buddhahood, from where, gazing with composure down upon the other realms of life, one can channel the invigorating breeze of Buddhahood into society.

Nichiren Daishonin teaches that whether walking, standing, sitting or lying down, the Buddha's children who dwell on the great earth of the true entity of life — that is, the world of Buddhahood — perform the actions of the Buddha. Since these are all actions of the Buddha, they are naturally carried out with supreme wisdom and virtue.

This is what Nichiren Daishonin means when he states: "The behavior of people (who base themselves on the land of the Mystic Law as children of the Buddha) is the same as the behavior of the Buddha. It is also the behavior of people of great virtue and influence (*choja*)" (GZ, 819). Neither the splendid residence of a secular wealthy person nor the special powers of a supraworldly wealthy person prove that one is a true person of wealth and integrity, or mind-observing wealthy person. The everyday actions that we carry out as children of the Buddha who embrace the Mystic Law and advance kosen-rufu are in themselves the supremely blissful actions of a great wealthy person.

While accumulating in our lives the treasures of the Law, as well as the treasures of material wealth, we dedicate ourselves to sowing the seeds of enlightenment in other people's lives, thereby creating the fundamental rhythm of peace and prosperity in society. Each day becomes a golden day, a rich and precious day of value. Such is the life of a mind-observing wealthy person.

Nichiren Daishonin also states: "Such a person (the votary of the Lotus Sutra) shall be called a Buddha. How can he not be called a person of wealth and integrity?" (GZ, 819). "Such a person" here refers to Nichiren Daishonin himself, but from a broader perspective, it also indicates all who embrace the Gohonzon. In other words, he is saying that those who persevere in the practice of Buddhism and dedicate themselves to the struggle for kosen-rufu are Buddhas; they are people of wealth and integrity.

The Daishonin concludes his teaching, "Nichiren and his followers who chant Nam-myoho-renge-kyo are the people of great virtue and influence (of whom the sutra speaks) who have gained the supreme cluster of jewels when they least expected it" (GZ, 819).

Therefore, you who have embraced this great Law are wealthy people rich in life force who possess good fortune surpassing the wealth of even the world's richest people. Material possessions cannot be enjoyed after death. But wealthy people rich in life force are able to freely make use of the treasures of the universe in life-time after lifetime and enjoy a journey of eternal happiness. That is what constitutes proof of true victory in life.

Of course, to accumulate such great good fortune, you have to persevere in Buddhist practice. When you cultivate your life in this way, you will tap an inexhaustible source of good fortune within your life. It is as though by unlocking and opening a magical trea-sure chest, you gain access to infinite treasures.

Therefore, you should never discard faith or slacken in your practice. You should never allow any obstacle to hinder your advancement. Otherwise, you will ruin the seed of Buddhahood, which is the source of all good fortune.

I earnestly hope that each of you, firmly upholding the Mystic Law, strives to produce a new success story in this country. Please be confident that we who dwell in the world of the Mystic Law will be the main players in the true story of success. With this, I conclude my speech.

Gongyo Is a Grand
and Noble Rite

—ᘏᘏ—

YOUTH DIVISION TRAINING SESSION,
SOKA UNIVERSITY LOS ANGELES,
CALABASAS, CALIFORNIA, FEBRUARY 19, 1990

I WOULD LIKE TO take the opportunity provided by today's youth division training session to present a succinct and easily comprehensible discussion of the significance of gongyo. Because of time limitations, I cannot pursue the subject in all its details, so I would like all of you to consider and explore this topic on your own afterward as well.

Nichiren Daishonin's Buddhism teaches that our existence is identical to the universe as a whole, and the universe as a whole is identical to our existence. Each individual human life is a microcosm.

The practice of gongyo is a grand and noble rite to achieve the vital communication of the microcosm of each person's existence with the universe, based on the Gohonzon.

The correspondence of each part of our bodies to parts of the universe is proof that our existence is a microcosm. Our heads are round like the heavens above us, and our eyes are like the sun and the moon. We close them and open them, like day and night. Our hair shines like the sparkling stars. Our eyebrows are like the seven stars of the Big Dipper. Our breath is the wind, and the quiet breathing from our nostrils is like the still air of the valleys and dales. There are some three hundred sixty joints in the human body, and they stand for the days of the year. The twelve major joints signify the twelve months. The warm, front side of our body — our abdomen and stomach — is spring and summer. The cold, hard back is fall and winter. Our blood vessels and arteries are streams and rivers. When we suffer a cerebral hemorrhage, it is as if a dam or dike has burst. Our bones are stones, and our skin and muscle are like the earth. Our body hair is a forest.

Buddhist scriptures discuss in detail these correspondences, including each of the internal organs, teaching that our body is indeed a universe in miniature.

There are clouds in the heavens. The wind blows, and the stars twinkle. There are oceans on Earth. Rivers flow. Volcanoes erupt. Great quantities of metals and minerals — gold, silver, copper, potassium, calcium — lie in the Earth's depths.

The activities and qualities of all of these materials are also incorporated in our bodies. The infinite elementary particles of the cosmos — protons, photons, electrons, neutrons and all the rest — microscopic animals such as bacteria, the activities of good and evil, the laws of gravity, the conservation of mass and energy and all other laws of the universe also apply in almost the same fashion to the microcosm of our bodies.

A look at the operation of our bodies suggests that they are great pharmaceutical factories. They have the capability to produce the drugs we need to preserve our health. They take in food and transform it into nourishment and energy. The human brain has the capability of a giant computer — even though we may not always be able to use it! The sixty trillion cells of our bodies work together in their established order in a perfect biorhythm. This is the original order of things.

Our existence is the universe, and its life processes are sublime. A slight change in the heat of the sun will enormously affect not only the Earth but all the other planets. If the Earth's rotation were to stop for the briefest instant, or if its axis were to tilt the slightest degree, all living things would be threatened with extinction. That is how subtle the natural order is. Furthermore, a firm and irrevocable Law of the universe exists. This holds true for the microcosm as well. Science pursues this invisible but truly existent Law, and technology means the invention of machines and other devices based on the fruits of scientific research.

Nichiren Daishonin discovered and awoke to the great Law of all existence that underlies all the partial laws governing spiritual and physical phenomena, and it was he who revealed that Law to humanity as Nam-myoho-renge-kyo. This Mystic Law applies equally to the universe as a whole and to each and every individual human existence. The universe and the individual are one in this Mystic Law.

Under certain circumstances, an invisible law takes form as a visible existence. The individual human existence, for example, emerges out of its state of fusion with the rest of the universe by taking shape in the womb and being born into the world.

A ship can be regarded as a tangible representation of the law of buoyancy, just as an airplane represents the laws of aerodynamics, and a radio or television program represents the law of electromagnetic waves. All of these objects give shape to invisible laws.

The fundamental Law of the universe and individual existence is also invisible. The Daishonin inscribed the Gohonzon as a visual representation of that Mystic Law for the people of the world. The Lotus Sutra and other Buddhist scriptures are the instruction manuals for the Gohonzon.

Josei Toda, my teacher and the second Soka Gakkai president, explained the Gohonzon in an easily comprehensible way as a "machine to produce happiness."

When we practice gongyo and chant daimoku before the Gohonzon, our individual existence is perfectly harmonized with the universe. Both the universe and our individual existence are the concrete manifestations of Nam-myoho-renge-kyo, as is the Gohonzon. That is why when we practice gongyo and chant Nam-myoho-renge-kyo with faith in the Gohonzon, our existence and the universe mesh as perfectly as two gears and, with an initial creak, begin to work together.

The single life-moment of the individual becomes one with the three thousand factors and realms of the universe and begins to produce great value. This is the concrete practice of "three thousand realms in a single moment of life."

Through this practice, we can acquire wisdom and good fortune, and glow with the energy to overcome any obstacle throughout the four seasons, 365 days a year; we can enter the way to eternal happiness and attain eternity, joy, true self and purity.

Gongyo is a practice that calls forth and activates the infinite power that the microcosm inherently possesses. It transforms your fate, breaks through any apparent dead end and converts sufferings into happiness. It creates a transformation, a revolution of the microcosm. It is a diagram in miniature of kosen-rufu in our lives.

The kosen-rufu that is our aim is a movement to transform the universe, the Earth and human society into a world of peace, comfort and harmony in accord with the rhythm of the Mystic Law.

If you let an automobile or any other machine fall into disuse, it will rust and stop working correctly. You have to use it and maintain it regularly and properly. Why, the same thing is even true of the hair on our heads: If we don't wash it regularly, we'll get dandruff!

If we don't practice gongyo, the rhythm of our lives will be thrown off kilter, just as a machine that isn't oiled will rust. Gongyo and chanting daimoku are like starting the automobile's engine every day and driving in the direction of happiness and truth. By doing so day after day, you will gradually attain perfect unity with the universe and the Law. That state is the state of the Buddha.

Once that has happened, you can enjoy yourself with complete freedom for all eternity. Your existence will be a diamond that will never perish throughout the three existences.

To attain Buddhahood in this life, the Daishonin warns us with firm concern that we must never retreat in our practice. Even though we may experience a period of sadness or depression, the principle that "earthly desires are enlightenment" teaches us that great sufferings are bound to be transformed into equally great joy, progress and value. There is nothing to fear, since the Gohonzon possesses the infinite power of the Law and the Buddha.

We often say that strong faith, valiant and untiring practice and courageous acts are important. This is an expression of the truth that without a strong will and courageous practice, it is impossible to achieve great things.

You cannot communicate with another unless you are clear and direct. If you lack the courage of your convictions and mumble vague things, you won't make any impression on your listeners or strike a chord in their hearts. And of course you will not be able to move or convince them. To do that you need to be very determined and sure.

Isn't the same thing true of love?

It's certainly true in a job interview. Unless you present your thoughts clearly and forcefully, you won't make any impression on the interviewer. In other words, mental determination and courageous actions can change any situation, and they possess a critical capability to produce happiness.

To fly, a plane needs the extra push it gets by accelerating down a runway. To get good grades in school, you need the extra push of study before a test. Whatever you do, to achieve something better, to reach a higher level, you need a push. Buddhism teaches practice for oneself and practice for others. If either one is lacking, you cannot practice properly.

The Gohonzon is the concrete manifestation of the very existence of Nichiren Daishonin, who taught kosen-rufu. Because of that, if you only practice gongyo and chant daimoku and don't take any other action for the sake of kosen-rufu or improving your own life, the Gohonzon will not have its true, full effect.

If, however, you take actions to achieve kosen-rufu, they will serve as that extra push for your own life and help you leap to higher and higher states of mind in your gongyo and chanting as well.

Moreover, it is only natural that the energy you acquire through the practice of gongyo for yourself will be channeled back into your activities for others, for kosen-rufu.

The fact is that the practice of gongyo and your actions in service of kosen-rufu will become one, and together they will unlock the infinite power of the Mystic Law in your life.

In Buddhism, practice is faith. That means action is faith, and without action, there can be no true faith. The action I speak of is the way of practice for oneself and others that is taught in Nichiren Daishonin's writings.

Action is the source of blessings and merits. In propagating the teachings, for example, whether the person you are presenting the teachings to arouses faith or not is his problem. The effects of our action of propagating will vary, depending on the person's capacities and other conditions.

There is no need at all to rejoice or lament over each effect. You can be proud that you have practiced the truest, most wonderful Law of life in the universe to the best of your ability and go forward with your head held high. One who has acted for the sake of kosen-rufu is already a great victor in life.

These words are written on the Gohonzon, "Those who vex or trouble [the practitioners of the Lotus Sutra] will have their heads split into seven pieces" (WND-2,666). This is a warning that it is wrong to seek to harm this Law of your own being. Abandoning the teachings or slandering them are self-destructive actions that are bound to split you apart.

We also find on the Gohonzon, "Those who give alms to them will enjoy good fortune surpassing the ten honorable titles" (WND-2, 666). This forceful statement tells us that the merits of one who makes offerings to the Gohonzon and spreads the teaching will be far greater than the magnificent merits of one who makes offerings to Shakyamuni Buddha. This is a promise that our personal microcosm will absorb the nourishment of all the blessings in the macrocosm, the whole universe, and be elevated to a state of existence of the highest happiness itself.

Thus we know that the children of the Buddha who strive for kosen-rufu are each guaranteed to attain the ultimate degree of happiness. There is no one who will be more blessed.

"For both the present and the future" is also written on the

Gohonzon (see WND-1, 750). For present and future — that is what faith is for, what the Buddhist Law is for. When we worship the Gohonzon, the eternal life of time without beginning wells up within us. Our faith is that every day, every instant begins from time without beginning.

We are always setting out, full of hope, from today to the future, from this moment to eternal happiness. We are always young, always beginning. My message to you is that you must be absolutely certain of this and live your wonderful lives without regret, with joy and brightness, always moving forward.

Worshipping the Gohonzon
Opens Your Life
to the Entire Universe

—⚉—

TODAY'S GATHERING is one of the true successors of the SGI-USA, the young people. In addition, many staff members who have played a large role working behind the scenes are with us.

I want our young people to study doctrine, and I also want them to test themselves in action. With that hope in mind, as well as with the great appreciation I feel for your daily efforts, I would like to discuss today several points concerning the basics of faith.

We just finished evening gongyo together and expressed our deepest prayers to the Gohonzon. It is inappropriate to discuss the Gohonzon lightly, but the history of Buddhism in the United States is short, and it is my duty as a leader to implant conviction and determined faith in your hearts to whatever extent I can. For that reason, I would like to discuss several essential points concerning the Gohonzon, though I may not be able to explain it completely.

Gohonzon means fundamental object of devotion. It is the object we devote ourselves to and have faith in as the basis of life. It is only natural, then, that our lives are fundamentally determined by the object we take as our object of devotion.

Traditionally, the objects of devotion in Buddhism were most frequently images of the Buddha. In some cases, paintings of the Buddha were used. While in early Buddhism, there were no Buddhist images, in later ages images of the Buddha were created in northwest India, in the Gandhara region, under the influence of Grecian culture. Buddhist images were one of the products of the cultural intercourse of the Silk Road.

The common people became familiar with the image of the Buddha through these statues and paintings, and they aroused faith in the Buddha and reverence for him through such works of art.

THE POWER OF WORDS

Nichiren Daishonin's basic object of devotion, however, consists of writing, of words. Rather than a graphic image, the Daishonin made the written expression of the world of the intellect — the great and lofty wisdom of the Buddha of the Latter Day of the Law — the object of highest reverence. In this one respect alone, the Daishonin's object of devotion is fundamentally different from those traditionally worshipped in Buddhism.

Words are mysterious. They have tremendous power. Take a man's name, for example. He signs it. In it is included his personality, his position in the world, his strengths, his mental and physical state, his past and the causes and effects that made him what he is.

In the word *Japan*, written with two Chinese characters, the geographical features of the country, its people, its flora and fauna — all are encompassed.

In actuality, a person and a country are always changing, moment to moment, without pause. The name of a person or country is the single word that expresses and encompasses all of those activities and functions.

Nam-myoho-renge-kyo is just like that: It encompasses all phenomena in the universe. The true aspect of all phenomena in the ever-changing universe is perfectly expressed just as it is in the Gohonzon. The true aspect of the universe is precisely the same for each of us, who are each a microcosm of the universe. Nichiren Daishonin tells us this in his writings.

That is why the Daishonin's Gohonzon embodies the basic Law of the universe; it is the true fundamental object of devotion.

Nichijun, the sixty-fifth high priest, explained that one reason the Gohonzon consists of writing is that it would be impossible to depict the "mutual possession of the Ten Worlds" in a graphic image, though they could be shown separately.

BOTH GOOD AND EVIL ARE ILLUMINATED BY THE LIGHT OF THE LAW

The universe includes both the powers of good and evil. On the Gohonzon, all of the Ten Worlds are represented, from Shakyamuni and Many Treasures, who represent the Buddha realm, to Devadatta, who represents the state of hell.

Both the representatives of good and evil powers and capacities are illuminated equally by the light of Nam-myoho-renge-kyo. Both then display the "dignified attributes that they inherently possess" (WND-1, 832). The dignified attributes of fundamental existence are manifested as the fundamental object of devotion.

When we practice gongyo and chant daimoku before the Gohonzon, the good and evil capacities of our lives begin to function as the exalted form of fundamental existence. Lives that are full of the pain of hell, lives that are in the state of hunger, lives warped by the state of anger — such lives, too, begin to move in the direction of creating their own personal happiness and value. Lives being pulled toward misfortune and unhappiness are redirected and pulled in the opposite direction, toward good, when they make the Mystic Law their base. It is as if sufferings are made the fuel for a fire of joy, wisdom and compassion. It is the Mystic Law and faith that ignite that flame.

If that is true, it goes without saying that the worlds of good — such states as Buddhahood, bodhisattva and heaven — only increase their brightness, power and glory by the power of our daimoku chanted. The sun and moon of our individual microcosms, too, shine forth with brilliant light and illuminate the darkness of life. Good and evil, all the three thousand realms of existence, merge and make a one hundred eighty-degree revolution and lead us to happiness, to a life of eternity, joy, true self and purity.

It is only natural that sometimes we fall sick, but we must see that sickness as a sickness that originally exists in life, based on the principle of the Mystic Law. In other words, there is no reason to allow yourself to be controlled by illness, for it to fill your life with suffering and distress. From the standpoint of eternal life through the three existences, your fundamentally happy self is incontrovertibly established. That realization will remove any obstacles or blocks you experience in life and will serve as a springboard for a leap to a more expansive state of being. Life will be enjoyable, and death will be peaceful, a glorious journey to the next enjoyable life.

When winter arrives, the trees and other plants temporarily lose their leaves. But those plants possess the life to send forth new, green shoots when spring comes. Human death is like that, but we possess a life force that leads us to a new life — to a new mission — immediately and without pain.

On the other hand, if the roots and even the seeds wither, no new life will spring forth. In one sense, such a life has perished. It will not send forth green leaves, beautiful flowers or fragrant fruit. You must not allow yours to become that sort of life.

Daimoku Reaches the Bodhisattvas of the Ten Directions

Next, I would like to address the question of whether there is any value in chanting daimoku and reciting sutra passages without understanding their meaning.

Of course, it is better if you understand their meaning. That will strengthen your commitment to the Law. But if you understand and yet fail to practice, it is all of no use. Moreover, you cannot understand the real depth of the teachings through reason alone.

Birds, for example, have their own language, their own speech.

People do not understand it, but other birds do. There are many examples among humans as well — codes, abbreviations or foreign languages are well understood by experts or native speakers but unintelligible to others.

In the same way, the language of gongyo and daimoku reaches the Gohonzon and the realms of the Buddhas and bodhisattvas of the three existences and the ten directions. We might call it the language of the Buddhas and bodhisattvas.

That is why the voice of gongyo and daimoku directed to the Gohonzon, whether we understand it or not, reaches all the Buddhas, bodhisattvas and heavenly deities. They hear it and say, "Excellent, excellent!" in response, rejoicing and praising us, and the entire universe envelops us in light.

The Daishonin has taught us that through gongyo and chanting daimoku, we can reach an elevated state in which, while engaged in our daily lives, we traverse the entire universe.

In his "Reply to Sairen-bo," Nichiren Daishonin writes: "Those who are our disciples and lay supporters can view Eagle Peak in India and day and night will go to and from the Land of Eternally Tranquil Light that has existed for all time. What a truly inexpressible joy it is!" (WND-1, 313).

When you worship the Gohonzon, the door to your microcosm is opened to the entire universe, the macrocosm, and you experience a great, boundless joy, as if you were looking out over the entire cosmos. You feel great satisfaction and rejoicing, a great wisdom — as if you held the entire universe in your palm. The microcosm enfolded by the macrocosm reaches out to enfold the macrocosm in its own embrace.

The Daishonin also writes, in his "Letter to Niike," "When nurtured by the chanting of Nam-myoho-renge-kyo..., [we] are free to soar into the sky of the true aspect of all phenomena" (WND-1, 1030).

In "On Offerings for Deceased Ancestors," he writes: "Though he himself is like the wisteria vine, because he clings to the pine that is the Lotus Sutra, he is able to ascend the mountain of perfect enlightenment. Because he has the wings of the single vehicle to rely upon, he can soar into the sky of Tranquil Light" (WND-I, 821).

Just as we might look down on a bright, clear scene of the world below from a lofty mountain's highest peak, we can climb the peak of the mountain of wisdom (supreme enlightenment). We can attain a state of eternal bliss, experiencing the infinite expanse and depth of life moment after moment, as if we were flying through the universe and gazing at blazing comets, the brilliantly shining Milky Way and all of the beautiful stars.

Nichiren Daishonin adds, after this passage from "On Offerings for Deceased Ancestors," the promise that we will be able to bring great fortune not only to ourselves but also to our ancestors for seven generations back and our descendants for seven generations into the future. How wonderful indeed are the enormous merits of the Mystic Law!

THE GREATEST MERITS OF FAITH ARE IN INCONSPICUOUS BENEFITS

Nichiren Daishonin writes in "The Fourteen Slanders": "'But how great is the difference between the blessings received when a sage chants the daimoku and the blessings received when we chant it?' To reply, one is in no way superior to the other. The gold that a fool possesses is no different from the gold that a wise man possesses; a fire made by a fool is the same as a fire made by a wise man" (WND-I, 756).

In other words, the benefits of the Gohonzon are completely unrelated to a person's position or wealth. They are equal for all. The Daishonin tells us that any person who chants daimoku will attain happiness.

The merits of the Gohonzon can be divided into conspicuous and inconspicuous benefits.

Conspicuous benefits reveal themselves when you have some problem with your health or with work or in some other aspect of your daily life, and you are protected, and a solution suddenly presents itself.

At the same time, you accumulate blessings and gradually establish a rich and expansive state of life, just as the waters of the sea gradually rise with the swelling tide. Once you have established that state, you will never be defeated, no matter which of life's troubles might confront you. Plus you will be able to enjoy yourself in a state of happiness not only in this existence but for all eternity.

This is the meaning of inconspicuous benefits. It is like a spring: Once you wind it up, it is always ready to be set in motion. But if the spring isn't wound, it will not work when needed. To continue this metaphor, it is faith that winds the spring, and the state of the spring when it is fully wound and has the potential to act whenever necessary is a life filled with inconspicuous benefits.

The power of the Mystic Law allows us to naturally achieve a life in which all our wishes are fulfilled and we enjoy eternal happiness. But those benefits depend upon faith. The Daishonin writes in "The Essentials for Attaining Buddhahood," "No matter how sincerely one believes in the Lotus Sutra, if one is guilty of failing to rebuke slander of the Law, one will surely fall into hell, just as a single crab leg will ruin a thousand pots of lacquer" (WND-1, 747).

The fourteen slanders are taught as the causes of evil. Among those slanders are contempt, hatred, jealousy and grudges. These mean being contemptuous of, hating, being jealous of or holding grudges against those with faith.

There are cases when we wonder why benefit doesn't reveal itself in spite of our earnest and high degree of faith. At such times, rather than entertaining doubt about the Gohonzon, it is better to ask yourself whether you are guilty of these four types of slander, because a person who harbors contempt, hate, jealousy or grudges will realize no benefits.

Of course you are perfectly free to say what must be said even to your fellow members in faith, and it is necessary to do so. But there is a difference between words spoken with real concern for your listener and those spoken with feelings of hatred or jealousy. It is extremely important to understand and observe this distinction.

All of us who gather here together before the Gohonzon in the cause of world peace are the Buddha's children, the family of the Mystic Law. That is why we must respect and encourage one another throughout our lives. Let me end today's speech by urging you to be absolutely convinced that the merits of the Gohonzon and the protection of the Buddhist deities are bound to increase for a person who does so.

Take the Next
Great Step Forward

—ᴍᴍ—

FIRST SGI-USA EXECUTIVE CONFERENCE,
SOKA UNIVERSITY LOS ANGELES, CALABASAS, CALIFORNIA,
FEBRUARY 21, 1990

CONGRATULATIONS ON the thirtieth anniversary of the SGI-USA! With persistent efforts, you have laid a firm and lasting foundation for the SGI-USA and created a brilliant history. I hope that this year you will set out to build anew on this foundation.

We have gathered today for the First SGI-USA Executive Conference. Conferences of this kind are held in each region and prefecture of Japan to provide leaders with a forum for discussing and planning activities in a democratic fashion. Various rules and procedures are also defined and approved at these conferences. All of this serves to ensure the solid and eternal progress of our movement.

It seems to me that the SGI-USA also has now entered a phase in which the rules and procedures of the organization must be further defined so as to enable members to take confident action.

It is important for leaders to be fair and impartial and to hear out opinions that differ from their own. Having the broad-mindedness to consider others' views will win you the respect of your juniors. If you have the humility to treasure members who offer good suggestions, you can raise many capable people. By giving sincere consideration to diverse opinions, you can develop a broad, flexible outlook and make stable progress. Discussing all things openly as siblings or members of a family, please proceed hand in hand, step by step, toward construction and growth. In this sense, the world of Buddhism must be a model of democracy.

Soka Gakkai Vice President Eiichi Wada has been appointed executive advisor to the SGI-USA. In this post, he will help the SGI-USA advance in a steadier and more pluralistic manner, enabling members to carry out activities more effectively.

Mr. Wada worked at my side in establishing the widely respected organization in Kansai [an area centering on Osaka, Japan's second largest city]. He is a leader of fine character and sincerity. I hope that, giving him your unreserved trust and discussing various matters with him, you will realize still further growth in a spirited and enjoyable manner.

Make Constant Efforts To Study and Grow

Without personal growth, a leader loses his appeal. Not only are the juniors of such a person affected, but the leader, too, will arrive at an impasse. People will not follow such a person, and as a result the leader will try to control them by weight of authority. Such arrogance, however, can only drive people even further away. It is a vicious circle

One of the fourteen slanders mentioned in the Gosho is that of shallow, self-satisfied understanding. This does not merely mean possessing shallow knowledge; it indicates the condition of those who have lost their seeking minds and ceased to make efforts to deepen their understanding. This signifies backsliding in faith.

If leaders make constant efforts to study hard, grow and maintain a sense of freshness, the organization will advance and be filled with dynamism. An organization will change and develop only to the extent that leaders change and develop themselves. The advancement of kosen-rufu in a community and country proceeds likewise.

In this sense, I hope that leaders continually work to polish their intellect. It is out of this desire that in my speeches, for instance, I always try to discuss broad-ranging matters pertaining to faith and society. Today also, I would like to speak on a number of such points.

In his book *The Cycles of American History*, Dr. Arthur M. Schlesinger Jr. discusses the theory that American society undergoes change at intervals of thirty years. In his view, the coming decade of the 1990s will hark back to the 1930s and 1960s in important respects.

In the 1930s, America challenged itself to realize the country's founding ideal of equality, as symbolized by President Franklin Roosevelt's New Deal.

In the 1960s, there was an effort, based on concern over human rights and on a new pioneering spirit, to prove that America was the foremost champion of the ideals of humanity, as symbolized by the New Frontier espoused by President John F. Kennedy. At the same time, there was an upsurge of counterculture movements across the country, most visibly in the form of student protests. It was a period of great change.

It is impossible to predict whether the 1990s, like the 1930s and 1960s, will be characterized by a resurgence of idealism in American society. Nevertheless, the observation that America has tended to return to the prime point of its founding ideals at intervals of thirty years is deeply thought-provoking. In human terms, thirty years correspond roughly to one generation. In a thirty-year period, one generation is replaced by the next; the order of things requires the emergence of a new, youthful generation. Herein lies one of the reasons why I heartily desire that the SGI-USA, at this milestone of its thirtieth anniversary, make a truly fresh start for the future.

A Leader Serves and Supports

Equality and human rights are the ideals of America. At the same time, Buddhism places the greatest importance on these fundamental values and seeks their practical application.

All people are equal. There are absolutely no distinctions of superior and inferior among human beings. Differences of position in an organization are temporary and provisional. They are no more than an expedient means for enabling all members to practice joyfully and become truly happy.

Therefore, a leader in an organization is not someone who stands above others but one whose role is to serve and support everyone else. This is something that Josei Toda, the second Soka Gakkai president, used to explain by saying, "Leaders are servants of the members." In a sense, true leaders of kosen-rufu are those who are determined to sacrifice themselves for the sake of the members. If leaders are under the illusion that they are somehow great or superior to others because of their position, their attitude goes against the Buddhist spirit of equality.

In this vein, I would like to emphasize the importance of fostering an atmosphere where members feel free to speak their minds to leaders and say what they feel has to be said — for we are all equally good friends dedicated to the same cause.

Buddhism teaches that "one who reprimands and corrects an offender is a voice-hearer who defends the Buddha's teachings, a true disciple of the Buddha. One who rids the offender of evil is acting as his parent" (WND-1, 286). From the standpoint of faith, to keep silent when one sees something amiss is tantamount to lacking mercy. Although to criticize and censure someone out of petty emotionalism is of course incorrect, it is necessary that constructive and valuable opinions be aired. If leaders are broad-minded enough to listen with a sense of appreciation, both they and the people voicing their views can expand their states of life.

Leaders may sometimes have occasion to call something to a member's attention in the interest of that member's growth. That is an act of compassion. But to scold someone out of emotionalism is a sign of arrogance. Leaders should never reprimand members without good cause. The human mind is infinitely delicate.

EQUALITY OF THE SEXES

Men and women are equal. People who ignore this in their behavior cannot be called civilized. If women blindly follow male leaders, both may wind up suffering in the end. Rather, Buddhism teaches that women and men should complement one another, like a bow and arrow. So that the arrow may proceed along the correct path, a correct direction for the bow must be set and, from time to time, corrective adjustments made.

In his guidance to the wives of the Ikegami brothers, Nichiren Daishonin states, "If both of you unite in encouraging your husbands' faith, you will follow the path of the dragon king's daughter and become a model for women attaining Buddhahood in the evil latter age" (WND-1, 502). This passage reflects the Daishonin's strict, yet compassionate advice to his female followers. I hope that you will take it deeply to heart.

Buddhism places the highest value on human rights and seeks to ensure that human rights are respected. In caring for a single person, we try to thoroughly protect and do everything we can for that person. One who respects and embraces the children of the Buddha in this way is a truly capable person and a true leader.

This year, which marks the thirtieth anniversary of the American kosen-rufu movement, is precisely the time for you to take the next great step forward. Where will the energy for this step come from? The new vitality of American society is produced by returning to the starting point — to the ideals on which your country was founded. Similarly, you should also reconfirm the fundamental path of faith, practice and study, and make a fresh departure based on the unity of "many in body, one in mind" — the starting point of our movement. This is the key to the reconstruction of the SGI-USA as a model organization.

ESTABLISH THE LAW AS YOUR STANDARD

In more concrete terms, united behind the great objective of realizing kosen-rufu, and viewing everything from the standpoint of faith, you should forge ahead with conviction and open the way to victory. A person or an organization that does this will enter the path to limitless happiness.

In making a phone call, if you misdial just one number, your call will not go through as desired. If even a single wire is misplaced in a sophisticated machine, it will fail to operate. How much more true is this in our practice of Buddhism, which reveals that each phenomenon, without exception, strictly possesses all of the three thousand realms of life. Unless people embrace the correct Law, maintain correct faith and carry out a correct practice, they will eventually lead many astray. This is an extremely serious offense, and those who follow such leaders are to be pitied.

In this connection, it should be pointed out that the Law, not the person, is to be regarded as the proper standard in all things. Putting the person first gives you an uncertain standard; it is to let that person's mind become your master. At some point, relations based on such a standard become like those between a paternal, godfather-like figure and those bound to him by personal loyalty.

In contrast, if you establish the Law as your standard, you will become the master of your mind. The great development that we have realized in Japan has been possible because we have exerted ourselves in the practice based on the Gohonzon and in accordance with the Gosho.

Nichiren Daishonin laments people's approach to Buddhism: "The people of our time — whether clerics or lay believers, nobles or commoners — all revere persons and do not value the Law. They make their own mind their teacher and do not rely on the sutras" (WND-1, 156). If people make their minds their sole standard, they will in due course become self-righteous. But if they carry out faith and practice based on the Law, then they are true leaders of Buddhism.

DEVELOP THE YOUTH AND WOMEN'S DIVISIONS

Something that characterizes true leaders is that they are thoroughly dedicated to raising young people. When you put all of your energy into developing the rich potential of youth, both you and the organization are rejuvenated. I hope that you will find and raise people with great potential, allowing them to steadily grow and fully engage themselves. If you create such a flow, the future will open up boundlessly before you.

Also, you should put energy into the development of the women's division. An organization where the women's division can freely conduct activities, and where its opinions are respected, is healthy and strong. Such an organization can make steady progress, and it will seldom spin its wheels in vain. As you know, the women's division has played a central role in the early development of American kosen-rufu.

The most important condition for leaders is sincerity. In contrast, an authoritarian air will only serve to alienate people, and intelligence alone may not produce anything of lasting value. Sincerity is what touches people's hearts, forges bonds of trust and imparts a sense of security. People of sincerity create a relaxed, almost spring-like atmosphere around themselves.

A verse by Walt Whitman goes, "Now understand me well — it is provided in the essence of things that from any fruition of success, no matter what, shall come forth something to make a greater struggle necessary" ("Song of the Open Road"). The SGI-USA, which has made the great land of America ring with the sound of the Mystic Law, has a history that is truly praiseworthy. Yet just as this poem states, there is never a point at which one can sit back and become complacent with the current state of affairs. To do so goes against the very essence of life.

Change, unceasing change, is one of the distinguishing characteristics of America. Change occurs more rapidly here than it does elsewhere. This could be said to be an indication of the vitality that this country possesses.

The late U.S. statesman Adlai Stevenson (1900 – 65) once said:

"There is a New America every morning when we wake up. It is upon us whether we will it or not." Similarly, Buddhism holds that everything is in a constant state of flux. Thus the question is whether we are to accept change passively and be swept away by it or whether we are to take the lead and create positive changes on our own initiative. While conservatism and self-protection might be likened to winter, night and death, the spirit of pioneering and attempting to realize ideals evokes images of spring, morning and birth.

Furthermore, Buddhism expounds the principle of "true cause." In terms of our attitude in faith, this can be understood as our spirit to always make a fresh departure. In other words, we advance with hope and youthful vitality — the vital energy of spring, morning and life — throughout our entire existence. It is in enabling us to realize this limitless improvement in our lives that the greatness and brilliance of Nichiren Daishonin's Buddhism lies.

Each of you has worked very hard to promote American kosen-rufu. You will no doubt bring your lives to a splendid completion. I hope that you will cause the great flower of happiness and virtue to bloom luxuriantly in the rich soil of your life that you have worked so hard to cultivate until today. It would be only too sad if you were to somehow end up taking a false step, thus destroying your good fortune, after many years of practice. In a sense, you have now come to a crucial point in your journey of life.

Bearing this in mind, please continue striving to attain Buddhahood in this lifetime so that you can enjoy, in one lifetime after another, a diamond-like state of life filled with overwhelming joy. I hope that, through living honorably, you will be remembered as champions of kosen-rufu whose names will forever shine in the annals of our movement.

I would like to conclude my speech at this First Executive Conference by expressing my hope that you will make a fresh determination to start anew toward the creation of a great new SGI-USA, based on beautiful unity.

Humanity Is the Essence
of Buddhism

—ⱳ—

YOUTH TRAINING SESSION,
SOKA UNIVERSITY LOS ANGELES, CALABASAS, CALIFORNIA,
FEBRUARY 22, 1990

THIS IS A GATHERING of young ladies and gentlemen. To establish meaningful lives, I hope that during your youth you will work hard to polish your intellect. Life, in a sense, is a battle of wisdom. It is the power of Buddhism that enables one to win this battle. True faith is characterized by a brilliance of intellect and depth of wisdom that result from devotion to practice.

I hope that you will strive to be leaders with such faith who also possess great warmth and humanity. That is why I would now like to take this opportunity to speak about the relationship of mother and child — or more specifically, mother and daughter.

As practitioners of the Daishonin's Buddhism, I hope you will be exemplary in showing respect to, and taking good care of, your parents. What's more, you may become parents yourselves one day.

Seventy-six years have passed since Mother's Day was instituted as a special day of commemoration. On May 9, 1914, Woodrow Wilson (1856–1924), the twenty-eighth president of the United States, proclaimed that the second Sunday of May would be designated as Mother's Day. Many countries now observe this day. I understand that in some countries, two days are set aside for the occasion: one day for celebrations at schools and clubs and the other for family celebrations. Japan started observing Mother's Day in 1949.

ANNA JARVIS — PIONEER OF MOTHER'S DAY

All endeavors start from one person, from a single pioneer. The individual who set the wheels in motion for Mother's Day was Anna M. Jarvis (1864–1948) of Philadelphia.

As a young girl, Miss Jarvis had suffered a painful disappointment in love. It is not inconceivable that, in her despair, she may have even contemplated suicide. Yet she chose to live, realizing that she should live her own life, that she had a right to become happy. Rising above her heartache and grief, she turned her affections toward her mother and her blind younger sister.

On the anniversary of her mother's death, she would hand out white carnations — her mother's favorite flower — to the people in her church congregation. The gratitude she felt toward her mother was something she could not keep to herself. One day, she came upon the idea of having a special day where everyone could show their love for their mother. She started writing thousands of letters to women's groups and influential people urging that a special day be instituted for this purpose. A groundswell of support emerged in response. Gradually, the number of people sympathizing with the idea grew. The first widely recognized Mother's Day was observed in Grafton, West Virginia, on May 10, 1908. Six years later, it became a national event, with the U.S. president issuing his proclamation.

Traditionally, if a mother is still living, her children present her with a red carnation, and if she has passed away, they wear a white carnation. This custom originated from the beautiful heart of the lady who loved, as a symbol of her own mother, the flower her mother had adored.

There are people who criticize this custom as stigmatizing those whose mothers are deceased. But mothers live on in the hearts of their children. Buddhism expounds the inseparability of life and death. Through the power of the Mystic Law, we can send waves of happiness to our mother, whether she is living or deceased.

Buddhism elucidates three types of filial piety or natural obligations to parents. Giving one's parents material goods such as clothing and food is the lowest type of filial piety. Respecting the desires of one's parents is the middle type. And leading one's parents to Buddhahood with the Mystic Law is the highest type.

A nameless woman's call reverberated throughout a city, throughout the country and eventually to the world. Why should this be so? I believe the answer is that people, regardless of nationality, cherish in the depths of their hearts a sincere love for their mothers. Anna Jarvis struck a chord in their hearts, which combined to create a beautiful cadence of sympathy and profound emotion.

When a person courageously calls out for something that touches the core of human nature, infinite waves of response appear in the ocean of the people's hearts.

Buddhism is concerned with the essential nature of humanity. Buddhism is not found somewhere separate from such beautiful expressions of humanity as appreciation toward one's mother and courtesy to others. As Nichiren Daishonin teaches "behavior as a human being" that perfectly accords with reason is what constitutes the heart of Buddhism (WND-1, 852). Therefore, our world of faith must be a gathering that is full of affection and heartfelt consideration.

When we cultivate such essential qualities of humanity and enrich our character, we will naturally touch the hearts of people. Just as Anna Jarvis had acted out of the conviction that everyone loves his or her mother, we are calling out to reach the very depths of people's lives in the belief that everyone possesses the Buddha nature.

There are various views on the origin of Mother's Day. One points to a myth in Asia Minor, and another ascribes it to a Christian holiday, such as Mothering Sunday in the United Kingdom. In actuality, however, the American account of its origin that I have cited is regarded as the only one to be supported by clear historical evidence.

THE FLAME OF LIBERTY STILL ILLUMINATES THE WORLD

The other day, I introduced to the participants in a youth division training session some of the treasures of Soka University. Among these was an autographed sketch of the Statue of Liberty by the French sculptor Frédéric Auguste Bartholdi (1834–1904). As you may know, Bartholdi conceived the design for the Statue of Liberty that stands in New York Harbor. Formally titled *Liberty Enlightening the World*, the statue was presented to the United States for its centennial by the people of France as a token of their friendship. A replica of the Statue of Liberty stands on an island in the Seine in Paris. I have often gazed upon it on my visits there.

It is said that the face of the Statue of Liberty is modeled after Bartholdi's mother. To a child, its mother's face is perhaps one of the most priceless and beautiful things. Throughout his life, Bartholdi never forgot his gratitude to his mother who, being widowed early, had to work single-handedly to raise him yet always showered him with love and affection.

Bartholdi must have long pondered how he could express his admiration for his mother. He grew to become a sculptor and eventually came to work on the Statue of Liberty. Attention was then focused on what he would do about the face. Bartholdi decided to use his mother as the model.

The Statue of Liberty holds aloft the torch of freedom in her right hand and cradles a tablet etched with the date July 4, 1776, in her left. While the statue's face is that of Bartholdi's mother, its pose he took from the image, deeply engraved in his mind, of a valiant girl whom he had seen as a youth. It was a scene that he had witnessed in 1851 at age seventeen.

At that time, the people had risen in protest against Louis-Napoleon, nephew of Napoleon Bonaparte, who as an ambitious man of power had established a dictatorial regime. Victor Hugo had also been thoroughly opposed to Louis-Napoleon. In the midst of this uprising, Bartholdi came across an unforgettable scene:

While the mass of people stood quivering in front of the enemy's barricade, gripped with indecision, a young woman suddenly appeared, breaking the darkness of night. Proudly holding high a torch, she broke through the barricade, calling out "Advance!" Just at that moment, there was a burst of gunfire, and she fell. But the torch gripped in her hand instantly set the barricade aflame.

The mass of people had shrunken in fear, daunted by the overwhelming forces of the ruling regime. Yet a lone, courageous girl marched boldly into enemy fire and died a heroine. There were no medals of honor or words spoken in praise of this nameless girl who had so selflessly dedicated her life to what she believed.

The young Bartholdi must have engraved that girl's noble and unflinching spirit deep in his life. The image of courage she embodied made him search for the meaning of liberty, which he finally crystallized in the shape of the Statue of Liberty.

The courage of that unknown girl, transcending the realm of fleeting victory or defeat, lives on as a symbol of eternal victory. The torch she bore still sheds its brilliance as *Liberty Enlightening the World*.

A Mother's Prayer Reaches the World of Buddhahood

There are many passages in the Gosho that refer to people's indebtedness to, and yearning for, their mother. I would like to cite several examples here.

At one time, Nichiren Daishonin wrote to a believer who had lost her son: "Out of its love for its child, the pheasant plunged into flames to save it. Out of her love for her child, the poor woman drowned in the Ganges River. The pheasant is now Bodhisattva Maitreya. The woman who drowned in the Ganges has been reborn as the great heavenly king Brahma. How much more will this be so of the present-day Honorable Konichi, who out of her great affection for her son became a practitioner of the Lotus Sutra? Without fail both mother and child will go to the pure land of Eagle Peak" (WND-2, 964).

The Daishonin addresses the recipient of this letter using the title of *shonin*, a title given only to a high-ranking priest, thus expressing his respect for this female lay believer. In the use of this single word, we can also see the Daishonin's exemplary sincerity and profound humanity.

The Daishonin likens the selfless love of a mother for her offspring to the compassionate actions of a bodhisattva and the majestic power of the heavenly god Brahma. He further encourages her by saying that if the mother takes faith in the Mystic Law, her love for her children will surely be communicated to the Gohonzon and enable both the mother and child to reach the world of Buddhahood.

Humanity is the essence of Buddhism. As stated in this Gosho passage, when sincere and beautiful affection, as symbolized in this Gosho by a mother's love, is nurtured by faith in the Mystic Law, we can elevate our state of life to that of a bodhisattva or a Buddha. At the same time, our children and other relatives can share in the blessings we receive.

Mothers are truly a blessing. They are priceless treasures. I sincerely hope that all of you will become people who appreciate the obligations to your mothers. In a letter written to Nichigen-nyo, the wife of Shijo Kingo, Nichiren Daishonin states: "The baby does not recognize its mother, but the mother never forgets her baby. Shakyamuni Buddha is compared to the mother, and women are compared to the baby. If two people long for each other, as a rule they will never be parted. If one person yearns for the other, but the other yearns not, sometimes they will meet, and sometimes they will not. The Buddha is like the one who yearns, and women are like the one who does not. If we yearn for the Buddha, how could Shakyamuni Buddha possibly fail to appear?" (WND-I, 315).

When she received this letter, Nichigen-nyo was then nursing her eleven-month-old daughter, Tsukimaro Gozen. The Daishonin uses the analogy of a mother and her baby to explain the compassion and great concern of the Buddha. Nothing could have been more appropriate to her situation or moved her heart more profoundly than this particular analogy. This is a perfect example that illustrates the Daishonin's characteristic attention, compassion and sensitivity to a person's state of mind in expounding the teachings of Buddhism in a manner that is most appropriate to the situation of that particular person. In his letter, he explains that we are children of the Buddha. Therefore, the Buddha, who is our parent, constantly has our welfare at heart, and thoughts of us never leave his mind. Nonetheless, like infants who do not recognize their mother's care and concern, common mortals are ignorant of the Buddha's compassion.

Please do not forget your mother's love or the hardships she has endured for you. I am convinced that while people keep the memory of their mothers' loving faces alive in their minds, they will never go far astray. Similarly, as long as we bear in mind the Daishonin's profound compassion and live in deep appreciation of it, our lives will be illuminated brightly by the light of Buddhahood. And, enveloped in the Gohonzon's great compassion, we will walk along a path that is fundamentally filled with tranquillity and immeasurable joy.

Therefore, I would ask that you take very good care of your parents — especially your mothers. A mother's love is unimaginably deep and her influence profound. If all people treasured their mothers, the world would undoubtedly be filled with peace and happiness. In closing, I would like to extend my prayers to all of you for your continued good health and future accomplishments.

Bring Forth the Great Flower of Absolute Happiness

FIRST SGI ALL-AMERICA GENERAL MEETING,
WORLD PEACE IKEDA AUDITORIUM,
SANTA MONICA, CALIFORNIA, FEBRUARY 24, 1990

I WOULD LIKE to extend my sincere congratulations to you on the thirtieth anniversary of the SGI-USA. I would also like to take this opportunity to laud the efforts of the late Ted Osaki and Fumiko Snelling — two of the SGI-USA's courageous and dedicated pioneers — and pray for their repose. This morning, during gongyo, I solemnly offered prayers for all deceased SGI-USA members who worked for American kosen-rufu.

This World Culture Center, where we are gathered today, boasts a proud history in terms of the vital role it has played from the standpoint of Buddhism.

Soka Gakkai Vice President Eiichi Wada has recently been appointed as the SGI-USA's executive advisor. Although he may look slightly non-Japanese, he cannot speak a word of English. Like me, he grew up during the last world war, when learning English was regarded as a traitorous activity in Japan. Young and innocent, we abided by the government's education decrees — hence our inability to speak English to this day. Our wartime experience shows how terrible the consequences can be when you follow misguided leaders.

Mr. Wada, however, is a man of great integrity and rock-solid faith, and he possesses a wealth of experience in practice and study. I hope all of you will welcome him as a trusted friend and advisor.

We are gathered here today for a meeting that will go down in the annals of kosen-rufu. Therefore, to begin constructing a new SGI-USA that will serve as a model organization for the entire world, I wish to discuss a few points.

Nineteen fifty-one was truly an auspicious year, in which we celebrated the seven-hundredth anniversary of Nichiren Daishonin's establishment of his teachings. That summer in Japan, a lotus seed was found among two-thousand-year-old ruins in Chiba — the prefecture where the Daishonin was born. Awakening from its long slumber, the seed gave bloom to a beautiful, pale crimson lotus flower. It was named the Oga Lotus after its discoverer, Ichiro Oga (1883–1965), and it created quite a stir among the Japanese back then.

Around the same time, right here in America, another ancient lotus seed, supposedly tens of thousands of years old, germinated and blossomed in a beautiful pale crimson. News of this was also reported in Japan, though it didn't warrant more than a small article. It did not escape the notice of my mentor, Josei Toda, however.

President Toda construed the blossoming of the two primeval lotus seeds in both the East and the West in the same year marking the seven-hundredth anniversary of Nichiren Daishonin's Buddhism as an auspicious omen for the rise of the correct teaching.

The lotus flower is invested with profound significance in Buddhism. It is thought to be the only plant that simultaneously produces both flower (cause) and seed-pod (effect). This unique trait is used to indicate the Buddhist principle of simultaneity of cause and effect.

The Daishonin explains the significance of cause and effect: All sutras other than the Lotus Sutra expound that Buddhahood (effect) can be attained only after having made good causes — that is, after practicing their teachings (cause) over a length of time.

With the Lotus Sutra, however, the very act of embracing it (cause) enables one simultaneously to become a Buddha (effect).

Such is the splendid power of the Mystic Law. It does not require that you undergo lifetime upon lifetime of practice to become a Buddha. Moreover, the Mystic Law releases us from the shackles of our past negative karma. Based upon our firm faith in the Gohonzon each day, we can enable the most precious state of Buddhahood to pulsate vibrantly in our lives every moment.

This is the Daishonin's Buddhism. In general, it expounds that followers who possess strong faith and remain committed to kosen-rufu throughout their lives are already Buddhas. Therefore, leaders who deprecate and look down on such members, in essence, despise Buddhas. And those who disparage Buddhas are naturally creating bad causes. On the other hand, we cannot praise too much an individual who is dedicated to the Mystic Law.

THE PURE FLOWER OF GOOD FORTUNE
BLOOMS IN THE MIRE

The "Emerging From the Earth" chapter of the Lotus Sutra reads, "Unsoiled by worldly things like the lotus flower in the water" (LS, 222). That is, the lotus flower brings forth pure and beautiful blooms from muddy pond waters. Just like the lotus blossom, a person who embraces this great Law can never fail to establish a vigorous and beautiful life filled with the aspects of eternity, joy, true self and purity, even in the mire of this trouble-filled world.

The Buddhism of Nichiren Daishonin expounds that we should not seek a heavenly paradise somewhere outside ourselves, nor should we seek an emotional escape from reality. The lotus flower of our own lives blooms in no other place than in actual society and in our daily existence.

Society is a place of confusion, full of contradictions and collisions of egos. It is precisely in these murky waters of earthly desires that the state of Buddhahood — in other words, the great flower of absolute happiness — fragrantly blooms forth.

Referring to the ancient lotus seeds that germinated and bloomed at the same time in both Japan and the United States, President Toda said: The great desire of the people, who are suffering in the quagmire of reality, is to see the emergence of a great Buddhism. This is the time when a great Buddhism, so sublime and righteous, strictly adhering to the law of cause and effect, and completely reliable, must spread.

"The lotus flowers bloomed simultaneously in both the East and the West, emerging majestically out of the muddy earth and awakening from a slumber of thousands of years, nay, tens of thousands of years.

"Now, the sublime Buddhism expounded by the Buddha of the Latter Day of the Law is about to burst into bloom from the troubled Japanese people as it awakes from the slumber of seven centuries — and even further back to the time of beginningless time.

"The simultaneous blooming of the lotus flowers in both the East and the West must surely be a sign for the Buddhism of the Buddha of the Latter Day of the Law to begin to blossom beautifully."

I was twenty-four years old at the time. In discussions with my mentor, I had already begun to formulate a vision of American kosen-rufu deep in my mind.

True to President Toda's great conviction that the time for worldwide kosen-rufu had arrived, I have been striving, together with you all, to bring the great flower of Buddhism to bloom not only in America but throughout the entire world.

Nichiren Daishonin states as follows: "Now, more than 700 years after Buddhism was introduced to Japan in the reign of the thirtieth emperor Kimmei, the great Law never heard of in previous ages is spreading throughout Japan. How reassuring it is to know that not only the people here, but those of India, China, and the entire land of Jambudvipa will be able to attain Buddhahood!" (WND-1, 482).

Seven hundred years after this statement, the Soka Gakkai made its advent in the world to fulfill the Daishonin's will to spread the great Buddhist Law far and wide. The Soka Gakkai has been realizing his will. The seven-hundred–year interval is no mere coincidence; indeed, Buddhism has a truly mystic rhythm. It is not hard to imagine how delighted the Daishonin would be at this present prosperity of Buddhism.

THE SEED OF BUDDHAHOOD
FOR ALL BUDDHAS

Incidentally, the sequoia trees here in California are very famous. Some of them grow more than four hundred feet, and their stumps can reputedly hold more than forty people. Some of these trees also live more than three thousand years. Even such giant redwoods sprout from a single tiny seed. One seed contains unlimited potential.

Nichiren Daishonin states in "Letter to Akimoto," "All the Buddhas of the three existences and the ten directions have invariably attained Buddhahood through the seeds represented by the five characters of Myoho-renge-kyo" (WND-1, 1015). All Buddhas attained Buddhahood through the seed of the Mystic Law. The Daishonin clarifies that the same principle, not any other special means, equally enables all people to attain enlightenment.

Now, all of us have had this same seed of the Mystic Law planted in our lives. How wonderful! When we exert the powers of faith and practice to tap the powers of the Buddha and the Law inherent in the Gohonzon, we can definitely show proof of having attained Buddhahood in this lifetime. This is a promise made by the original Buddha and absolutely never fails to materialize.

You must never be deceived by someone who does not embrace the Mystic Law, no matter how extraordinary that person may appear. Both the Great Teacher Dengyo and Nichiren Daishonin state that in the Latter Day of the Law, there will be no saints or sages who observe the precepts.

All of us are ordinary human beings. When ordinary people embrace the Gohonzon completely, we can enjoy our lives from moment to moment just as we are, savoring an inexhaustible taste of Buddhahood. In the eyes of Buddhism, therefore, all of us fellow members dedicated to the cause of kosen-rufu are indescribably precious.

COFFEE INDUSTRY OWES ITS START TO ONE SOLITARY YOUTH

Today, Brazil is famous as a leading center of coffee production. But long ago, Brazil had no coffee at all. How then was this great coffee nation born? It can be traced back to an episode in 1727, when a Brazilian explorer from the Amazon visited coffee-rich Guiana. He was the first Brazilian to learn of coffee and was burning with a desire to plant coffee in his own country. He asked the governor-general of Guiana to give him some coffee beans to take back to Brazil, but the governor-general refused because a law forbade their export. The Brazilian was not discouraged and continued to make his request time and time again. Although he was turned down each time, he still did not give up his dream.

Just as the Brazilian was wondering what he should do, the governor-general's wife, moved by his earnestness and zeal, slipped some coffee beans into his pocket as he was about to return home to Brazil. Brazil's present-day coffee industry owes its origin to this single handful of coffee beans. What a dramatic history it has!

Be it a large or small event, history always seems to be made in this way. A long river begins with a single drop of water, and a huge mountain originates from a tiny speck of dust. The promise for unlimited future development lies in first nurturing just one seed — or a handful of seeds — carefully but surely over a period of time. The success of one youth, which became the starting point for Brazil's coffee industry, in no way happened by chance.

That youth was filled with blazing integrity — never giving in, he directed himself toward his goal with passion and devotion. It is my belief that his earnest behavior moved other people's hearts and earned him their trust and friendship.

In the world of faith or kosen-rufu, too, sincerity is of prime importance. It is not schemes, orders or commanding words but sincerity that moves people. Our sincere prayers for kosen-rufu reach the Gohonzon on a profound level, thereby activating the protective functions of the Buddhist deities. In the long-range view, a sincere and honest person is always a victor. No matter how circumstances may change, no one can take away the truth in our hearts.

I have also been faithful to this course of sincerity in all actions and endeavors. Armed only with sincerity, not relying upon either authority or economic strength, I have stood in the midst of all kinds of difficulties, taking the lead of millions of people. I have done this solely out of my faithful vow to my mentor that I would devote my entire life to protecting the members and leading them to happiness. Fulfilling that vow has been my whole life.

I would like to stress that the development of the SGI-USA from now on also cannot be achieved without the sincerity and integrity of each leader. I hope that you can unite your efforts and construct a splendid organization, so that you can say, "There is no world more joyful and more reassuring than the SGI-USA." In addition, I would like to ask you to continue advancing brightly as front-runners toward the creation of a glorious human history during the next millennium.

I will end my speech on this auspicious day, praying that all of you in the United States will lead prosperous and fortune-filled lives, create harmonious households and enjoy good health and longevity.

Become a
Philosopher of Life

FIRST OF ALL, I would like to express my deep respect for all of you who have come to attend this training session on a Sunday. Originally, a reception was scheduled for today to commemorate the thirtieth anniversary of the SGI-USA's founding, and I am well aware that all of you had been involved in preparation for that event, which was to include performances of music and dance. I would like to express my deepest appreciation and offer my highest praise for your efforts.

I feel, however, that it is of greater value at this time that we conduct gongyo and study Buddhism together as we are now. We have entered an age when it is vital for us to widely expand our individual sphere of knowledge. I hope that I have your understanding on why we are holding a training session today.

There are various kinds of careers and roles that people fill in society. While each role, of course, has significance, the fundamental role that we each play as a Buddhist is that of a philosopher of life and of humanity who can impart eternal value to humankind. There are leaders in all areas of human endeavor. We are leaders of happiness and creators of peace. In this sense, our role is unique.

Please deepen your awareness of this vital role and further exert yourselves in your practice and study of Buddhism. I sincerely hope that you will grow to be leaders of a new era of the SGI-USA who combine profound wisdom and human warmth.

All of you are young. Because life is long, you should not be impatient. What matters most is that you embrace the Gohonzon throughout your life. It is vitally important to continually challenge yourself to chant even a little more daimoku and to pray before the Gohonzon for the fulfillment of your desires.

So long as you maintain this attitude in faith, the seed of Buddhahood planted in your life will continue to grow. On some occasions, you may be unable to do gongyo, or you may only be able to chant daimoku. Nevertheless, so long as you maintain faith, you will not experience negative effects on account of your occasional failure to carry out a complete practice of gongyo. While you should not take advantage of this statement or misconstrue it as condoning a lax or lazy attitude, you don't have to be overly strict or inflexible either.

Buddhism aims to make people free in the most profound sense; its purpose is not to restrict or constrain. Doing gongyo is a right, not an obligation. Because Buddhism entails practice, tenacious efforts are required, but these are all for your own sake. If you want to have great benefits or to develop a profound state of life, you should exert yourself accordingly.

If a beautiful woman goes by, men will turn their heads. Similarly, women will go out of their way to do favors for a handsome man. In the same way, when you polish your life by doing gongyo, all Buddhas, bodhisattvas and Buddhist deities will surround you, praising and holding you under their protection. In this sense, gongyo and daimoku are like cosmetics we use to beautify our lives.

Gongyo and daimoku might also be compared to the food that sustains our lives. Chanting daimoku corresponds to the main dish and doing gongyo to the side dishes. Like the main and side dishes in a meal, the two are complementary, and we need both to derive maximum joy from our practice. By having such balanced meals every morning and evening, you can activate your inherent Buddha nature and eventually establish it as your fundamental state of life.

There is a herd of deer living in the beautiful wilderness of this Calabasas campus. I came upon a group of seven the other day. Taking the chance to become friends with them, we worked out names for the seven: Manabu and Victor for the males, and Sonoko, Lisa, Annie, Sally and Tiffany for the females. The next time we meet, however, I don't think anyone will be able to recognize which deer is which.

I hope that you will be magnanimous enough to see all living beings, including deer, swans, crickets, plants and so on, as your friends.

ESTABLISH A WARM HOME OF KOSEN-RUFU

You are the true successors of the SGI-USA and future leaders of worldwide kosen-rufu. Therefore, on this occasion, I would like to confirm some basic tenets of our Buddhist practice.

The first point is that we are one big family whose members are joined by the lifeblood of faith in the Mystic Law. The organization for kosen-rufu should be a home of comfort and fulfillment in life. I hope that all members, their lives illuminated by the Gohonzon, will gather together with a feeling of relief and relaxation and a sense of energy welling up from within.

ON MEETINGS

Suppose you come back home exhausted after a hard day of work or study, and the moment you walk through the door, someone in your family barks at you: "You're late. What on earth have you been doing?" If that happens often, you will naturally feel negative and lose a sense of attachment to your home.

By the same token, sometimes members cannot be on time to certain meetings or cannot come at all. No one in the organization has the right to scold a person in this kind of situation. On

BECOME A PHILOSOPHER OF LIFE ■ 77

the contrary, leaders should warmly welcome such members. A true family is pervaded by a spirit of praise and encouragement for individual members' sincere efforts.

The same can be said about the relationship of husband and wife or parent and child. If a woman constantly badgers her husband that his salary is too low or harshly reprimands her child for low grades, to vent their frustration, the husband may think of going out and drinking and the child of going to an amusement center. My sympathy lies with them. Both the husband and the child, in this case, know their own problems, so another person pointing them out can only add to their misery.

We exert ourselves to spread Buddhism and carry out other activities in connection with our practice so that we can accumulate good fortune and become happy. We do all this for our own sake and not for the sake of the organization and most certainly not for the sake of our leaders.

Leaders should not needlessly give members a hard time. Scolding a member who is sincerely doing activities amounts to the offense of holding a fellow believer in contempt, one of the fourteen slanders.

On Propagation

Propagation is a practice that we carry out on the direction of Nichiren Daishonin. Whether people to whom you explain Nichiren Daishonin's Buddhism decide to take faith depends mainly upon their life tendency and their capacity to understand and believe in Buddhism. In any case, whether a person determines to take faith in Buddhism after listening to an explanation or decides not to take faith in it, the benefit that the believer receives is the same.

Propagation is the action of the Buddha's envoys. We should treasure and most highly respect those who carry out this noble and benevolent practice. "You've done well. You were able to plant the seed of Buddhahood in your friend's heart. That's a splendid thing." So saying, you should praise and encourage one another, sharing one another's joy like brothers and sisters.

Touched by such a family-like atmosphere, more and more people will begin to take faith in Nichiren Daishonin's Buddhism. Love and peace are the lifeblood of a home.

RESPECTING SOCIETY, YOUR JOB AND YOUR DAILY LIFE

Furthermore, faith manifests itself in daily life and Buddhism in society. By refreshing your life force through faith, you can work and study much harder than others, and you can also build a model family. People will then place their trust in you and may remark at how, as a Buddhist or as a member of the SGI family, you stand out among others. This is a kind of actual proof.

One who takes good care of his job, daily life and family is a person of deep and genuine faith. Activities are intended to be carried out in the spare time that you have from your work and family. In contrast, if on the premise that the SGI-USA is your home, no one is allowed outside, or people are dissuaded from attending to their work or study, no family can be created. Noble families are so called because they have sent many capable people into society.

In the harsh reality of society, competition and tension cannot be avoided. You may also sometimes experience clashes of ego. But once you return to the home of the SGI-USA, you can let go of your tension, relax and smile; this is where you can obtain nutrition for your life, thereby feeling refreshed and filled with energy to undertake the next day's challenges. As leaders, it is your duty to make the SGI-USA such an organization.

There may be some members who work at night or have irregular work hours and others who are extremely busy with work or studying for examinations. Such people might find it difficult to attend meetings. Yet they, too, are challenging their individual problems and trying hard to show actual proof of faith. I want you to become considerate leaders who can understand others' situations.

I hope that you will make all meetings held throughout the

country joyful, interesting, significant and filled with smiles. All Buddhas and bodhisattvas throughout the universe will watch over such harmonious gatherings of the Buddha's children.

SGI-USA MEMBERS ARE ALL EQUAL

All members of a family are equal. In terms of the organization, the father corresponds to the men's division, the mother to the women's division, the brothers and sisters to the youth division, and there are others who belong to the guidance division or who are students.

Although each member of the SGI-USA family has a different situation, they are all the Buddha's children who enjoy equal rights. In fact, the higher one's position, the heavier the responsibility one assumes. Try to imagine, for example, a family where the father alone eats good food and the children cry in hunger. This is not a home. Parents want their children to eat, even if they themselves can have nothing.

Nichiren Daishonin warmly encouraged a female disciple: "If anything at all happens, please come over here. I will welcome you. Let us die of starvation together among the mountains" (WND-1, 616). What compassion the Daishonin showed!

The family is a unit where all joys and sorrows are shared among its members. As a result, the sadness is more than halved and the happiness more than doubled. Neither orders, authority nor threats can unite a family. It is love, harmony and consideration that bind its members to one another. In a family, there is no particular need for a hero. What is needed is a strong father who can protect everyone and a mother who is impartial, fair and kind.

In a family, if one person is unhappy, then so is the entire family. Therefore, in the SGI-USA, I would like you to sincerely pray for and protect one another so that there are no people who are unfortunate and unhappy, or who will abandon their faith, and that every person will become happy. These are the kinds of humanistic bonds that give birth to true unity. Coercion or force stemming from power and authority is ineffective at critical moments.

The point is that Buddhism exists for the sake of each person's happiness. The same can be said of the organization. The organization exists for the sake of the people, not the other way around. To embrace and protect all individuals, leading them to happiness and attaining Buddhahood — this is why the organization exists.

A SHELTER FOR THE SPIRITUALLY HOMELESS

In America, the homeless problem has become a serious social dilemma. Homeless people are said to number in the millions. But I fear that the number of spiritually homeless people is even greater. These people go about searching for a comfortable place, their house of the soul, or spiritual home. The power of Buddhism provides people with a place of essential tranquility, a sweet home of life. Nichiren Daishonin states: "No place is secure. Be convinced that Buddhahood is the final abode" (WND-1, 491).

From the outset, America has been a country to which people from around the world have flocked, leaving their homelands for one reason or another. They came to this country searching for a new home. It is the task of our movement to breathe life into America's purpose of building a new home for these people. Society will become a genuine home to all only when it provides each person with absolute peace and compassionate protection.

Nichiren Daishonin states, "I, Nichiren, humble person though I am, have received Shakyamuni Buddha's royal command and come to this country of Japan" (WND-1, 331). As a disciple of the Daishonin, each one of you is an irreplaceable person who was born in this country with a unique mission that you yourself originally chose. By opening your eyes of faith, you can without fail understand your precious role.

COMPANIONS OF KOSEN-RUFU FROM TIME
WITHOUT BEGINNING

We are family not only in this lifetime. Rather, we have been brothers and sisters from time without beginning. To view our relationship only in terms of this single lifetime is extremely shallow; it is to assume the view of pre-Lotus Sutra teachings and the theoretical teaching of the Lotus Sutra, both of which held that Shakyamuni attained enlightenment for the first time in India.

To see our relationship as that of companions spanning the three existences of past, present and future is to accept the point of view of time without beginning that is expounded in the essential teaching of the Lotus Sutra. In other words, together we are carrying out an ongoing struggle, from now into the future, to advance kosen-rufu, to promote peace and culture for the sake of humanity.

I would like you to build an enviable, endearing SGI-USA family, of which those around you will say: "Those people seem truly happy. How warm the light from the window of that SGI-USA house looks!" Steadily infusing society with smiling faces and hope, please construct, with the Mystic Law as your foundation, an eternal family of peace and a happy and beautiful America.

I would like to conclude today by saying that I will watch over you throughout my life while praying for your great growth.

Live Each Day Filled With Value and Happiness

—ᶦᵚᶦ—

YOUTH TRAINING SESSION,
MALIBU TRAINING CENTER, MALIBU, CALIFORNIA,
FEBRUARY 26, 1990

THIS IS THE FINAL youth division training session. I have been touched by your efforts in faith, practice and study, and by your strong seeking spirit, and I am now confident that so long as these youthful members continue to grow, the SGI-USA's future development will be secure. In that sense, all of you have completed this training course with honors. I hope that each of you makes further efforts to become a master of faith, practice and study who has absolute conviction and outstanding ability in practice and study.

Youth is the time of continual worries. Your heart is swayed in all matters — your future direction, personality, relationships, society and life. You may often feel irresolute and restless. Some will be puzzled by the gap between ideals and reality, and others will succumb to self-hatred and behave in a neurotic fashion.

Youth is a season of unrest and agony. This is true of young people anywhere in the world. In a sense, it may be all for the best. You certainly are not suffering on your own, and since young people are all experiencing change and growth, such feelings cannot be helped.

Therefore, you should not be hasty. It is unreasonable to suppose that you can become both spiritually and socially stable in
one fell swoop. An airplane will have an accident if it tries to take
off without first building up speed. Even if a plane takes off successfully, without sufficient fuel and complete preparation, it will
not keep flying, or it may even crash.

Life is like a marathon, as is faith. Though you may lose the
lead in the midst of the race, victory or defeat is decided at the
finish line. Your training during your youth is for the purpose of
enabling you to win ultimate and true victory. Therefore, now is
the time when you must study as much as you can and chant abundant daimoku so that you can greatly increase your life force.

Please steadily advance along the fundamental path of faith
manifests itself in daily life, living in the way that best suits you.
Just as the sun rises every day, if you persistently advance based
on the Mystic Law, the absolute Law of the universe, you will definitely lead a life in which all desires are fulfilled. Please be convinced that you are now leading the most certain and valuable
youth.

COLUMBUS'S MISTAKE

For you who will grow to be leaders of wisdom and humanity,
there are a number of points that I would like to make today.

What is the origin of the name *America*, from which the United
States of America and North and South America derive their names?
It comes from the name of the Italian explorer and geographer
Amerigo Vespucci (1454–1512).

Compared with Christopher Columbus, Amerigo Vespucci is
not very well known; rather, he has long been poorly understood.
Even today, there are many differing views. Ralph Waldo Emerson, for one, branded him a thief. Over the years, people have
groundlessly voiced outrage that he should have had the gall to
name a continent after himself. As recent research has brought
more details to light, however, the extreme criticism has subsided.

There are even some who assert that it is most appropriate that the New World was named after him. Why? It is because Vespucci was the first to clarify that this land was a new continent — a New World.

Europeans regard Columbus as the discoverer. But this term is inaccurate in the sense that indigenous peoples were living there before his arrival. Be that as it may, until his death, Columbus believed that the land that he had found was part of the Asian continent. Having long searched for a sea route to India, he deeply believed that he had arrived on the eastern shore of Asia and had discovered hitherto unknown islands and peninsulas belonging to that continent. It was truly a case of seeing without perceiving.

Though a great new world lay before him, to the end Columbus remained convinced that what he saw was a part of the Old World. The tendency to be so totally caught up in old ways of thinking as to be unable to perceive new realities is one to which all people are susceptible.

In those days, Europeans' view of the world was dominated by the geography of Ptolemy, whose works had the weight of time-honored authority. According to Ptolemy, there were only three continents on the globe: Asia, Europe and Africa. Therefore, even though he had discovered an entirely new continent, a New World, Christopher Columbus could only try to locate his find on the old map; he was unable to transcend the established outlook of his day.

Nichiren Daishonin's Buddhism is unique; for many people, it is a completely new religion. Of course, just as the American continents existed since time immemorial, the Daishonin's teaching is the religion of the great Law that has existed since time without beginning.

Also, though few in number, people had inhabited the American continents since ancient times, and a unique culture had flourished. In the same way, Nichiren Daishonin's teachings have been practiced in Japan over the past seven hundred years, but it is only in the past few decades that their existence has become widely known throughout the world.

From now on as well, the number of people who seek the great Law, which ensures true freedom and equality, will continue to increase. In this sense, the Daishonin's Buddhism can be likened to a new continent.

Because the Daishonin's Buddhism is truly new to most people, the reaction it receives can be negative. When confronted by something new, people generally try to get a handle on it and classify it by applying their old, conventional "maps" — in this case, old concepts of religion — thereby seeking to reduce it to the familiar and restore a sense of security. If they cannot adapt the new thing to the framework of their knowledge, they will often abandon it completely.

In Japan as well, because the Soka Gakkai does not easily fit into any of the established concepts of Japanese society, it has at times been labeled as "leftist" and at times "fascist." People have all too often tried to categorize us by applying familiar concepts such as "conservative" or "liberal," "reactionary" or "progressive."

In fact, however, we do not fall into any of those categories on the old ideological map. Rather, ours is an unprecedented popular movement that is devoted to true humanism and to the sanctity of life.

A POSITIVE SPIRIT OPENS NEW WORLDS

Similarly, various kinds of misunderstanding or resistance may be met within any country, but such is the destiny of those who introduce something new. It is by overcoming those negative forces and replacing old maps with new ones that the movement for world peace will be carried forth.

The population of the United States is a microcosm of all humanity. The country consists of people who left their homelands and, with fresh dreams, went to America to live happily. Our mission in life is to lead people to the Mystic Law, explaining that this is the great Law for attaining true happiness and the basis of eternal peace.

What, then, is most essential for redrawing the map of the world?

What is it that led Amerigo Vespucci to be convinced that he had discovered a new continent when he arrived at an unknown land? It was his thoroughgoing spirit of positivism. It was a new spirit that placed utmost importance on experience and facts.

Vespucci was born into a prestigious family in Florence, Italy, around the time of the flowering of the Renaissance. Imbued with the refreshing spirit of the Renaissance, he applied himself to the study of geography and astronomy. Many a painter and poet visited his home. Leonardo da Vinci made a portrait of his grandfather.

In 1499, seven years after Columbus's first successful voyage west, Vespucci joined a Spanish expedition. At the time, he had in his mind a conventional map of the world, but he soon began to challenge the traditional theory that no one could live in a tropical region. Up to that time, this was a theory that, though contrary to fact, had been espoused by many scholars.

The air in tropical regions is fresh, the climate mild and the population even larger than elsewhere. In a letter from his first voyage, he stated, "Rationally, let it be said in a whisper, experience is certainly worth more than theory."

Because of his level-headed spirit of scientific inquiry, he was not limited in his thinking by contemporary views. Making use of his astronomical expertise, he calculated the Earth's circumference at the equator. His calculations are said to have been the most accurate ever made at that time, erring by only fifteen miles from modern measurements.

In 1501, Vespucci set out on his second voyage, this time aboard a Portuguese ship. He sailed southward along the eastern coast of the South American continent, off what are now Brazil, Uruguay and Argentina, almost reaching the Strait of Magellan. With great curiosity, he observed the lives of the natives and the great abundance of rare flora and fauna, recording everything exactly as he saw it. While calculating his position with painstaking accuracy, he pondered the meaning of this voyage. In so doing, he came to the following historic conclusion, "We arrived at a new

land which...we observed to be a continent." It was the first recognition ever of a fourth continent after those of Asia, Africa and
Europe.

In 1503, when Vespucci's *Mundus Novus* (*New World*) was
published, it sold far more copies than had the writings of Columbus. The New World, containing immense potential, was revealed
to people in this work for the first time. In a stroke, he changed the
way people looked at the world. Because it meant that old maps
were utterly useless, huge losses for book merchants and cartogra-
phers could result, and many were reluctant to recognize the validity of his claim. Such is human nature.

Martin Waldseemueller (1470–1518 or 1521), a German geographer who had read Vespucci's writing, published his own work
titled *Cosmographiae Introductio* in 1507. Although he and his
colleagues had originally planned to publish a book on Ptolemy,
they abandoned the idea and instead wrote this book, spurred, no
doubt, by the conviction that this discovery heralded the dawn of
a new era.

In the *Cosmographiae Introductio*, the new continent is for the
first time given a name, with Waldseemueller suggesting that it be
named "Americus" or "America," from Americus Verspucius, the
Latin name of Amerigo Vespucci.

In the maps contained in Waldseemueller's pamphlet, the map
of South America is drawn with a high degree of accuracy, and
a vast ocean (the Pacific) between Asia and the new continent is
also depicted. The name *America*, which initially referred only to
the South American continent, was used by the famous cartogra-
pher Gerardus Mercator (1512–94) [regarded as the greatest car-
tographer of the sixteenth century] to refer to the North American
continent as well. Eventually, its use with regard to both continents became widespread.

Given these accounts, it is clearly wrong to say that Vespucci
usurped the achievements of Columbus. Rather, Vespucci clarified the true significance of Columbus's achievement, of which
Columbus himself was not even aware. Thus, the name *America*

symbolizes Amerigo Vespucci's spirit of positivism. Discarding pre-conceptions, he devoted himself to diligently observing facts. That he could correctly assess America as being the New World was in no small part due to the fact that a "New World" of thought and spirit, tempered by the climate of the Renaissance, had opened up in his heart.

THE ACTUAL PROOF OF IMPROVEMENT

Truly new discoveries and innovations cannot be properly mea-sured against old, established theories. Their value is realized for the first time when they have been validated by clear evidence. This is perhaps the only way that new discoveries can gain accep-tance. For this reason, one should avoid prejudging people at all costs. Any person we meet may be an outstanding individual who possesses tremendous potential of which we have no inkling.

Since we have taken the lead in embracing this great religion to which so much of humankind still remains oblivious, above all it is important that we demonstrate the value of this Buddhism by showing actual proof in our daily lives. Seeing such proof is what enables people to realize for the first time the greatness of this Buddhism and that it is something they have never encoun-tered up to now.

Nichiren Daishonin writes, "Even more valuable than reason and documentary proof is the proof of actual fact" (WND-I, 599). Of course, when we speak of showing actual proof, it doesn't mean we have to try to put on a show of being in any way more knowledgeable or accomplished than we are. It is my hope that, in the manner that best suits your unique situation, you will show proof of the validity of this Buddhism by making steady improve-ments in your daily life and in polishing your character, and also in your family, place of work and community. In this way, you will become the kind of person who impresses others with vitality, hope and conviction, and who makes them feel reassured.

Only if you challenge your human revolution in a manner that is true to yourself will the people around you naturally begin to trust and respect you. That in itself is the greatest way of laying the groundwork for the spread of Buddhism.

HAVE PATIENCE IN PROPAGATION

There is no need whatsoever to be impatient in propagating Buddhism. Rather, I believe it is preferable that strict standards be applied when granting admission to the organization, to the extent that those eager to join will find that their wish is not so easily granted.

In a letter addressed to Nanjo Tokimitsu, Nichiren Daishonin writes: "There are a few in this province of Kai [present-day Yamanashi Prefecture] who have expressed their desire to take faith. Yet I make it a rule not to permit them to join us unless they remain steadfast in their resolve. Some people, despite their shallow understanding, pretend staunch faith and speak contemptuously to their fellow believers, thus often disrupting the faith of others" (WND-1, 800).

Here, the Daishonin laments that among his followers, some who have discarded faith and turned against him, have dragged other believers with them into unhappiness and misery. Also, one must absolutely never have an easygoing or careless attitude when it comes to allowing people to receive the Gohonzon.

A fabulous New World exists in everyone's life. The name we give to it is Buddhahood. But just as Columbus was totally oblivious that he was walking upon the soil of the New World, the majority of humankind, too, have yet to discover this New World of life.

The parable of the gem in the robe related in the "Prophecy of Enlightenment for Five Hundred Disciples" chapter of the Lotus Sutra concerns this foolishness of human beings. The story goes as follows:

Once upon a time, there lived a poor man. He had a wealthy friend who was a government official. One day, he went to visit the rich man and was treated to a sumptuous feast. Completely overcome by wine, he dozed off.

The host, however, was suddenly called to attend to urgent business and had to set out on a trip immediately. So he sewed a priceless jewel into the lining of the friend's garment; it was a jewel that fulfilled all one's wishes. He gave it to the intoxicated friend as a gift.

Totally unaware of the precious jewel given him by his departed friend, the poor man wandered through various provinces. When he was finally reunited with the wealthy friend, he had become utterly unkempt and shabby after years living as a wanderer. It was only when his friend told him of the gift given him long ago that the man realized that all along he had possessed a wonderful jewel. He became euphoric.

Shakyamuni's disciples, who had initially been satisfied with a lesser form of enlightenment, totally unaware of their potential for the supreme state of Buddhahood, related this metaphorical tale out of self-reflection and gratitude when they had realized their error. They likened a person who does not realize his inherent Buddha nature to the poor man who suffers in destitution unaware of the fact that he actually possesses a priceless jewel.

BE AMBASSADORS OF JOY TO FRIENDS STEEPED IN SADNESS

Faith comes down to the efforts we make continuously and untiringly to develop the New World of limitless power and potential existing in our lives — namely, that of Buddhahood.

The "Life Span" chapter contains the passage "Constantly harboring such feelings of grief, they at last come to their senses" (LS, 229). This passage is short yet rich in meaning. In brief, it describes how the children in the story, believing that their father had died and that they were left with no one on whom to depend, are steeped in grief. And how, as a result, they finally come to the realization that they have to take the good medicine that their father had left them. Here, ingesting the medicine represents taking faith in the Lotus Sutra.

On one level, this passage indicates how, without experiencing suffering and sadness, common mortals cannot embrace this Buddhism and manifest their Buddha nature. It may be that each of us has lived with incessant grief at one time or another before becoming a Buddhist. Also, it would be no exaggeration to say that, whether in America or in any other country, there are numerous people whose lives are steeped in such grief, bereft of any conviction or spiritual support.

Once we awaken to our Buddha nature, however, we need not grieve any longer. Our lives are filled with the greatest of all joys. A world of infinite joy blossoms in our daily lives. It is our mission to teach this to others; thus, friends of the Mystic Law are ambassadors of joy.

California is often referred to as the "Eureka State." *Eureka* is Greek for "I have found it." Legend has it that the Greek mathematician Archimedes, while taking a bath, discovered a way to measure the purity of gold in the king's crown, and was so overjoyed that he ran naked through the streets shouting "Eureka! Eureka!" What an appropriate name for the Golden State, home of the gold rush in the nineteenth century.

We have discovered our Buddha nature — a wonder immeasurably greater than mere gold or Archimedes' principle. Giving full play to that boundless joy in your youthful lives, I hope that, shouting "Eureka!" in the depths of your lives, you live each day filled with value and happiness.

With this significance, I propose that we form a new group with all the participants here today, to be called the Eureka Group. Starting with this Eureka State, let us build a current of true happiness, a current of the Mystic Law that flows throughout America and the entire world. I will come to America as many times as I can and support you to the utmost.

With my deepest prayers that all of you will lead lives filled with glory, I conclude this final youth training session.

Buddhism Is the
Clear Mirror That Reflects
Our Lives

—ЛΝ—

FIRST SGI-USA WOMEN'S DIVISION MEETING,
SOKA UNIVERSITY LOS ANGELES, CALABASAS, CALIFORNIA,
FEBRUARY 27, 1990

I SINCERELY THANK all of you for gathering here from distant places throughout the United States. My sole desire for women's division members is that they become the happiest people in the world.

What is the purpose of life? It is happiness. There are two kinds of happiness, however: relative and absolute. Relative happiness comes in a wide variety of forms. The purpose of Buddhism is to attain Buddhahood, which in modern terms could be understood as realizing absolute happiness — a state of happiness that can never be destroyed or defeated.

Nichiren Daishonin states in the Gosho, "There is no true happiness for human beings other than chanting Nam-myoho-renge-kyo" (WND-1, 681). So long as you maintain strong faith, resolutely chanting daimoku to the Gohonzon no matter what happens, then without fail you will be able to lead a life of complete fulfillment. This accords with the principle that "earthly desires are enlightenment."

True happiness lies only in establishing such a supreme state of life. In so doing, you can change all sufferings into causes for joy and contentment, and live with composure and jubilation.

Our organization exists so that each member can attain absolute happiness. Let me reiterate that the objective of this organization is your happiness.

Society and daily life are the "great Earth" for our faith and practice of the correct teaching. The steady development of world peace can be ensured only when, based on faith, we carefully attend to the affairs of society, our daily life and our families. Faith manifests itself in daily life — this is our eternal guideline.

I would like to take this opportunity to introduce to you some treasures in the collection of Soka University. This is my way of commemorating today's women's division meeting and showing my appreciation to you for your attendance. Afterward, please take a moment to look them over. Included are letters by George Washington and other American presidents, on display with their portraits; a collection of letters that Napoleon Bonaparte wrote just before his death and a letter in which he appealed for religious freedom in Italy; an autographed first edition of Victor Hugo's anthology of poems *Les Châtiments* (1853), along with some of Hugo's letters; a letter from British historian Arnold J. Toynbee to former U.S. Secretary of State John Foster Dulles appealing for peace in Pakistan; a letter in which the German composer Richard Wagner discusses the performance of his opera *Tannhäuser* (1845); a state document signed by John Hancock, a political leader during the American Revolution; and a letter written by Bartolomeo Vanzetti, dated immediately before his execution on trumped-up charges (1927), which contains a plea for a retrial. If he were executed, he wrote, the court would be guilty of murder. We can hear the cry of his soul for liberation.

These articles represent a precious, historic legacy. As part of the SGI's efforts to promote peace, culture and education, we are preserving and introducing these and other artifacts to the public. For the same purpose, we are establishing the Maison Littéraire de Victor Hugo (Victor Hugo House of Literature) in France. I am convinced that these activities will be of great significance for the future of humanity.

THE MIRROR THAT PERFECTLY REFLECTS
OUR LIVES

I hope that all of you will be cultured and graceful. Intelligent and kind people are beautiful. They inspire trust and a sense of reassurance in those around them. As you continue to deepen your faith in Buddhism, you can broaden your sphere of knowledge.

Without wisdom and sagacity, leaders cannot fulfill their mission — that is, convince others of the power of Nichiren Daishonin's Buddhism and help them attain true happiness. In this sense, I would like to speak about the correct attitude in faith through the analogy of mirrors.

A Japanese proverb has it that the mirror is a woman's soul. It is said that just as warriors will never part with their swords, women will never part with their mirrors. There would seem to be some truth to this saying, in that mirrors are prized by women the world over.

In Buddhism, the mirror is used to explain various doctrines. In one place, Nichiren Daishonin states, "There are various sayings associated with mirrors" (OTT, 51). In one of Nichiren Daishonin's writings, he states: "A bronze mirror will reflect the form of a person but it will not reflect that person's mind. The Lotus Sutra, however, reveals not only the person's form but that person's mind as well. And it reveals not only the mind; it reflects, without the least concealment, that person's past actions and future as well" (WND-2, 619).

Mirrors reflect our outward form. The mirror of Buddhism, however, reveals the intangible aspect of our lives. Mirrors, which function by virtue of the laws of light and reflection, are a product of human wisdom. On the other hand, the Gohonzon, based on the Law of the universe and life itself, is the culmination of the Buddha's wisdom and makes it possible for us to attain Buddhahood by providing us with a means of perceiving the true aspect of our life. Just as a mirror is indispensable for putting your face and hair in order, you need a mirror that reveals the depths of your life if you are to lead a happier and more beautiful existence.

Incidentally, as indicated in the Daishonin's reference to a bronze mirror in the above passage, mirrors in ancient times were made of polished metal alloys such as bronze, nickel and steel. The oldest metallic mirrors to be unearthed were found in China and Egypt. Older still are mirrors made of polished stone surfaces and those that used water. Suffice it to say that the history of mirrors is as old as that of the human race. It is perhaps an inborn human instinct to want to look at one's face.

These ancient mirrors, unlike today's mirrors that are made of glass, could only produce somewhat blurred reflections. Consequently, the first glance in a glass mirror caused a great sensation. The first time the Japanese encountered a glass mirror was in 1551. Francis Xavier is credited with having brought one with him when he came to do missionary work in Japan.

It was not until the eighteenth century, however, that the average Japanese became acquainted with this kind of mirror. Perhaps because it performed its function all too well, causing people to do nothing but gaze in the mirror all day long, the glass mirror came to be known as the "vanity mirror" among the people of the day. Many prints from this era depict Japanese beauties gazing into mirrors. Still, it was not until the latter half of the nineteenth century that glass mirrors came into wide use among the general populace.

POLISH THE MIRROR OF YOUR LIFE

Bronze mirrors not only reflected poorly but also tarnished very quickly. Therefore, unless they were polished regularly, they became unusable. This kind of mirror was popular in the time when the Daishonin lived.

In the Gosho "On Attaining Buddhahood in This Lifetime," Nichiren Daishonin writes: "This is similar to a tarnished mirror that will shine like a jewel when polished. A mind now clouded by the illusions of the innate darkness of life is like a tarnished mirror, but when polished, it is sure to become like a clear mirror, reflecting the essential nature of phenomena and the true aspect of reality" (WND-1, 4). In this well-known passage, the Daishonin draws parallels between the tradition of mirror-polishing and the process of attaining Buddhahood.

Originally, every person's life is a brilliantly shining mirror. Differences arise depending on whether one polishes this mirror. A polished mirror is the Buddha's life, whereas a tarnished mirror is that of a common mortal. Chanting Nam-myoho-renge-kyo is what polishes our life. Not only do we undertake this practice ourselves, we also endeavor to teach others about the Mystic Law so that the mirror of their lives shines brightly, too. Thus it can be said that we are masters of the art of polishing the mirror of life.

Even though people may make up their faces, they tend to neglect to polish their lives. While they quickly wash off a stain from their face, they remain unconcerned about stains in their lives.

THE TRAGEDY OF DORIAN GRAY

Oscar Wilde (1854–1900) wrote a novel titled *The Picture of Dorian Gray*, whose protagonist, a youth named Dorian Gray, is so handsome that he is called a "young Adonis." An artist who wished to preserve his beauty for eternity painted Dorian's portrait. It was a brilliant work, an embodiment of Dorian's youthfulness and beauty. Then something incredible occurred as Dorian was gradually tempted by a friend into a life of hedonism and immorality: His beauty did not fade. Although he advanced in years, he remained as youthful and radiant as ever. Strangely, however, the portrait began to turn ugly and lusterless, reflecting the condition of Dorian's life.

Making sport of a young woman's affections, Dorian drives her to commit suicide. At that time, the portrait takes on a wicked, savage and frightening expression. Dorian is filled with horror. This portrait of his soul would remain for aeons in this ugly form. Even if he died, the portrait would continue to eloquently tell the truth.

Dorian decides to obliterate the portrait, believing that if only he could do away with it, he could part with his past and be free.

So he plunges a knife into the painting. At that moment, hearing screams, his neighbors rush over to find a portrait of the handsome, young Dorian and, collapsed before it, an aged, repulsive-looking man, Dorian, with a knife sticking in his chest.

The portrait had expressed the semblance of his existence, the face of his soul, into which the effects of his actions were etched without the slightest omission.

Though cosmetics can be applied to the face, one cannot gloss over the face of one's soul. The law of cause and effect functioning in the depths of life is strict and impartial.

Buddhism teaches that unseen virtue brings about visible reward. In the world of Buddhism, one never fails to receive an effect for one's actions — whether for good or bad; therefore, it is meaningless to be two-faced or to try to put on airs.

The face of the soul that is etched by the good and evil causes one makes is to an extent reflected in one's appearance. There is also the saying "The face is the mirror of the mind." It is at the moment of death, however, that one's past causes show most plainly in one's appearance. Just as Dorian in the end revealed his own inner ugliness, so the "face of one's life" is fully expressed at the time of one's death. At that time, there is no way to conceal the truth of your soul. We carry out our Buddhist practice now so that we will not have to experience any regret or torment on our deathbed.

PERCEIVE THE BUDDHA NATURE INHERENT IN YOUR LIFE

Just as you look into a mirror when you make up your face, to beautify the face of the soul, you need a mirror that reflects the depths of your life. This mirror is none other than the Gohonzon of "observing one's mind," or more precisely, observing one's life. Nichiren Daishonin explains what it means to observe one's life in the Gosho "The Object of Devotion for Observing the Mind": "Only when we look into a clear mirror do we see, for the first time, that we are endowed with all six sense organs" (WND-1, 356).

Similarly, observing one's life means to perceive that one's life contains the Ten Worlds, and in particular, the world of Buddhahood. It was to enable people to do this that Nichiren Daishonin bestowed the Gohonzon of "observing one's mind" upon all humankind. In his exegesis on "The Object of Devotion for Observing the Mind," Nichikan, the twenty-sixth high priest of the Fuji School, states, "The true object of worship can be compared to a wonderful mirror."

Nichiren Daishonin states in *The Record of the Orally Transmitted Teachings*, "The five characters Myoho-renge-kyo similarly reflect the ten thousand phenomena, not overlooking a single one of them" (OTT, 51). The Gohonzon is the clearest of all mirrors that reflects the entire universe exactly as it is. When you chant to the Gohonzon, you can perceive the true aspect of your life and tap the inexhaustible life force of Buddhahood.

Incidentally, the glass mirrors that we have today are said to have been invented in Venice, Italy. Sources differ as to exactly when, but their appearance is traced as far back as 1279. That was also the year when Nichiren Daishonin inscribed the Dai-Gohonzon, the eternal great "mirror" reflecting the true aspect of all phenomena, for the benefit of all humanity.

At the time of the glass mirror's invention, the production technique was said to have been kept a closely guarded secret. To prevent knowledge of the technology from spreading, mirror glass craftsmen were confined to an island. Before long, however, France and other countries learned how to produce mirrors, and today mirrors made of glass have completely replaced earlier types.

These events might be construed as the "kosen-rufu of the glass mirror." Similarly, for a long time, the mirror of the Gohonzon, the source of profound beauty and happiness, was known to very few people. We are now promoting the movement to spread it widely.

The Gohonzon is a clear mirror. It perfectly reveals our state of faith and projects this out into the universe. This demonstrates the principle of "three thousand realms in a single moment of life."

One's Mind of Faith Is Most Important

In a letter to his disciple Abutsu-bo on Sado Island, Nichiren Daishonin wrote: "You may think you offered gifts to the treasure tower of the Thus Come One Many Treasures, but that is not so. You offered them to yourself" (WND-I, 299). Worshipping the Gohonzon graces and glorifies the treasure tower of your own life.

When people worship the Gohonzon, all Buddhas and bodhisattvas in the entire universe immediately respond to their prayers by lending their protection. If they slander the Gohonzon, the response will be exactly the opposite.

For this reason, one's mind of faith is extremely important. The mind of faith has a subtle and far-reaching influence.

There may be times, for instance, when you feel reluctant to do gongyo or take part in activities. That state of mind is precisely reflected on the entire universe, as if on the surface of a clear mirror. The heavenly deities will then also feel reluctant to play their part, and they will naturally fail to exert their full power of protection.

On the other hand, when you joyfully do gongyo and carry out activities with the determination to accumulate more good fortune in your life, the heavenly deities will be delighted and will valiantly perform their duty. If you must take some action anyway, it is to your advantage that you do so spontaneously and with a feeling of joy. If you practice reluctantly with a sense that it's a waste of time, disbelief and complaints will erode your good fortune. If you continue to practice in this way, you will not experience remarkable benefits, and this will only serve to further convince you that your practice is in vain. This is a vicious circle.

If you practice faith while doubting its effects, you will get results that are, at best, unsatisfactory. This is the reflection of your own weak faith on the mirror of the cosmos.

On the other hand, when you stand up with strong confidence, you will accrue limitless blessings. While controlling your mind, which is at once both extremely subtle and solemnly profound, you should strive to elevate your faith with freshness and vigor. When you do so, both your life and your surroundings will open wide before you, and every action you take will become a source of benefit. Understanding the subtle workings of one's mind is the key to faith and to attaining Buddhahood in this lifetime.

There is a Russian proverb that says, "It is no use to blame the looking glass if your face is awry." Likewise, your happiness or unhappiness is entirely the reflection of the balance of good and bad causes accumulated in your life. You cannot blame others for your misfortunes. In the world of faith, it is necessary to realize this all the more clearly.

PEOPLE WHO DO NOT KNOW ABOUT MIRRORS

A classic Japanese comedy tells the following story: Once there was a country village where no one had a mirror. In those days, mirrors were priceless. A man, returning from his trip to the capital, handed his wife a mirror as a souvenir. That was the first time for her to see a mirror. Looking into it, she exclaimed: "Who on earth is this woman? You must've brought a girl back with you from the capital." And so began a big fight.

Though this story is fictitious, many people become angry or grieve over phenomena that are actually nothing but the reflection of their own lives — their state of mind and the causes that they have created. Like the wife in the story who exclaims, "Who on earth is this woman?" they do not realize the folly of their ways.

Because they are ignorant of Buddhism's mirror of life, such people cannot see themselves as they truly are. This being the case, they cannot guide others along the correct path of life nor can they discern the true nature of occurrences in society.

MUTUAL RESPECT

Human relations also function as a kind of mirror. Nichiren Daishonin states in *The Record of the Orally Transmitted Teachings*:

"When the bodhisattva Never Disparaging makes his bow of obeisance to the four kinds of believers, the Buddha nature inherent in the four kinds of believers of overbearing arrogance is bowing in obeisance to the bodhisattva Never Disparaging. It is like the situation when one faces a mirror and makes a bow of obeisance: the image in the mirror likewise makes a bow of obeisance to oneself" (OTT, 165).

Here, the Daishonin reveals the fundamental spirit that we should have in propagating the Mystic Law. Propagation is an act to be conducted with the utmost respect for other people and out of sincere reverence for the Buddha nature inherent in their lives. Therefore, we should strictly observe courtesy and good common sense.

With the thought that we are addressing a person's Buddha nature, we should politely and calmly carry out a dialogue — sometimes, depending on the situation, mercifully correcting that person with fatherly strictness. In the course of such human interaction, the Buddha nature in that person, reflecting our own sincerity, will bow to us in return.

When we cherish that person with the same profound reverence as we would the Buddha, the Buddha nature in his or her life functions to protect us. On the other hand, if we belittle or regard that person with contempt, as though our actions are being reflected in a mirror, we will be disparaged in return.

In the inner realm of life, cause and effect occur simultaneously. With the passage of time, this causal relationship becomes manifest in the phenomenal world of daily life.

In general, the people around us reflect our state of life. Our personal preferences, for example, are mirrored in their attitudes. This is especially clear from the viewpoint of Buddhism, which elucidates the workings of cause and effect as if in a spotless mirror.

To the extent that you praise, respect, protect and care for SGI-USA members, who are all children of the Buddha, you will in turn be protected by the Buddhas and bodhisattvas of the ten directions and by all heavenly deities. If, on the other hand, you are arrogant or condescending toward members, you will be scolded by the Buddhas and others in like measure. Leaders, in particular, should be clear on this point and take it deeply to heart.

We are a gathering of the Buddha's children. Therefore, if we respect one another, our good fortune will multiply infinitely, like an image reflected back and forth among mirrors. A person who practices alone cannot experience this tremendous multiplication of benefit.

In short, the environment that you find yourself in, whether favorable or not, is the product of your own life. Most people, however, fail to understand this and tend to blame others for their troubles. The Gosho reads: "These people, failing to recognize their own rudeness, seem to think that I am rude. They are like a jealous woman with furious eyes who, unaware that when she glares at a courtesan her own expression is disagreeable, instead complains that the courtesan's gaze is frightening" (WND-1, 828). Nichiren Daishonin explains human psychology in such a clear and easy-to-understand manner.

There are people who, out of malice, have criticized and sought to oppress us who are the Daishonin's disciples. But, reflected in the mirror of the world of the Mystic Law, such people see only their own faults, ambitions and greed, and therefore slander their own reflections. To a person who is possessed by the lust for power, even the most selfless, benevolent actions of others will appear as cunning moves undertaken to gain power. Similarly, to a person who has a strong desire for fame, actions based on conviction and consideration will be seen as publicity stunts. Those who have become slaves of money simply cannot believe that there are people in the world who are strangers to the desire for wealth.

In contrast, an unusually kind and good-natured person will tend to believe that all others are the same. To a greater or lesser extent, all people tend to see their own reflection in others.

In the SGI-USA, there are a great number of people who are full of good will and intentions. In a sense, some might be even too good-natured and trusting — to the extent that I fear deceitful people could mislead them.

Say What Must Be Said

In *Père Goriot*, the French author Balzac (1799–1850) writes, "Whatever evil you hear of society, believe it...." So full of evil was the world that he perceived. He adds: "And then you will find out what the world is, a gathering of dupes and rogues. Be of neither party."

We must gain decisive victory over the harsh realities of society and lead a correct and vibrant life. This is the purpose of our faith. We have to become wise and strong.

Also, in the organization for kosen-rufu, we have to clearly say what must be said. The purpose of Buddhism is not to produce dupes who blindly follow their leaders. Rather, it is to produce people of wisdom who can judge right or wrong on their own in the clear mirror of Buddhism.

I hope that you, the women's division members, learn the correct way to practice Buddhism so that, in the event that a leader or a man does something that goes against reason, you will be able to clearly point out the error and identify the correct path to follow. Nichiren Daishonin compares men to an arrow and women to the bow. An arrow flies in the direction that the bow points it.

I would like to tell you that when the members of the women's division freely devote themselves to activities and provide a confident and strong lead for the men, that will mark the dawn of the "new SGI-USA."

To commemorate today's training session, I would like to dedicate the following poem to the SGI-USA women's division:

> *Let the flowers of the Law*
> *Bloom with beauty and purity*
> *Throughout this land of America.*

I would like to close my speech by offering my sincere prayers for the happiness of you and your families, and for the further development of the SGI-USA.

Be People of Magnanimity and Tenacity

—〰—

TRAINING SESSION FOR DIVISIONAL REPRESENTATIVES,
MALIBU TRAINING CENTER, MALIBU, CALIFORNIA,
FEBRUARY 28, 1990

I DEEPLY THANK all of you for your support during these seventeen days of my stay in the United States. Though I would like to spend more time speaking with you about the great Buddhist Law, my schedule requires that I now leave. Thank you again for everything, and please convey my best regards to those members whom I could not meet.

People tend to congregate where there is joy, while they quickly leave places that are imbued with an oppressive atmosphere. Joining a gathering of pure and sincere people enables one to summon forth a sincere seeking spirit. On the other hand, earnest people will not follow leaders who are not seriously challenging themselves.

In the course of developing, both a person and an organization will have to face various difficulties. This is reasonable and accords with the principles of Buddhism. I believe that, having now reached the thirtieth anniversary of its founding, the SGI-USA has completed one stage in its growth. By all means, please continue to advance filled with hope and confidence.

I once had a discussion with a friend about the probable causes for the rise of Christianity as a world religion. My companion, who was studying Christianity, said: "Apart from questions of doctrine and religious conviction, Christianity's rise can be attributed to the fact that those who propagated it were magnanimous and extremely tenacious. Also, they were always gentlemen, conducting themselves in a polite and courteous manner. This was the main reason for the worldwide spread of Christianity."

What he said was historically accurate and no doubt played an important role in the religion's spread. Of course, we, as Buddhists, must be strict in distinguishing the higher religions from the lower and the profound from the shallow, but at the same time we must learn from human history, drawing important lessons to fuel our further progress and improvement.

Therefore, I sincerely hope that SGI-USA members will always conduct themselves as people of magnanimity, tenacity and gentleness in their respective communities and in society.

Above all, I hope that the SGI-USA will be pervaded by warm bonds of trust and friendship. An organization that is filled with trust and friendship is strong; it grows, and its members are happy. Where individuals are on bad terms with one another, there is conflict and suffering. In all certainty, such an organization will at some point self-destruct.

A world filled with affection and warmth is beautiful. An elegant flower garden is produced when the flowers bloom in harmony with one another. If the flowers are broken, twisted, turned in disorder or all bloom at different times, the flower garden will not be so impressive.

Being on good terms with one another means to live in a world of harmony. By way of analogy, we maintain our health and can conduct vigorous activities when our internal organs and bodily systems are all working in harmony. If this internal physical harmony is lost, diseases result, possibly even leading to one's death.

Therefore, it is my heartfelt desire that you, the SGI-USA members, basing yourselves on faith in the Gohonzon, always live as a harmonious family of the Mystic Law, embodying the spirit of "many in body, one in mind." No matter what happens, I hope that you will continue to advance, directing your hearts toward unity and friendship.

Fundamental to Buddhism is the Law. The foundation for advancing kosen-rufu is always the Gohonzon. It is the person — human beings who are responsible for the organization that correctly upholds and spreads the Mystic Law.

In essence, the most important point regarding central figures is that they base themselves on faith in the Gohonzon. If the central figure forgets this vital point and tries to skillfully control and direct the members by exerting authority, a very dangerous situation results. Such a person could even destroy the beautiful world of the Mystic Law. Therefore, we must always watch that central figures base themselves on and cherish the Law above all else.

The other day, Soka Gakkai Vice President Eiichi Wada was appointed executive advisor of the SGI-USA. In that capacity, Mr. Wada will soon travel to New York to give guidance.

Mr. Wada, the SGI Women's Division Leader Eiko Akiyama, and the newly appointed SGI-USA Women's Division Chief Secretary Tomoe Kudamatsu, I assure you, are excellent leaders. In particular, Mrs. Kudamatsu is an outstanding woman, who, were she in Japan, would surely now have become the leader of the young women's division or women's division. I am very happy for the SGI-USA that you have such a superb leader as she.

As long as my schedule allows, and as many times as possible, I hope to come here to support you. Though I now return to Japan, I will always offer my most sincere prayers for the success of your vigorous activities.

1991

Equality Is the Lifeblood
of Buddhism

—m—

U.S.–JAPAN EXCHANGE TRAINING MEETING,
SOKA UNIVERSITY LOS ANGELES, CALABASAS, CALIFORNIA,
SEPTEMBER 23, 1991

CONGRATULATIONS on holding this U.S.–Japan exchange training meeting, a gathering based on faith and wisdom.

We have just recited gongyo together. The ceremony of gongyo is, in a sense, an exchange between the microcosm of our own lives and the macrocosm of the universe. Through the power of the Mystic Law, we are physically and spiritually invigorated from the very depths of our beings, our inner balance is restored, and we gain energy and vitality. We thus begin to sing life's song of joy. In response to the sound of our voices chanting daimoku, all of the Buddhist deities, bodhisattvas and Buddhas existing throughout the universe are activated and begin spiritedly working to protect us.

Every day, we groom ourselves and take care of our personal hygiene; we straighten our rooms; we keep ourselves fit through exercise; and we eat to maintain energy. Similarly, by carrying out a consistent practice of gongyo, we can gradually establish a correct rhythm in our lives, thereby actualizing the principle of faith manifesting itself in daily life. I hope that year by year, you will enjoy increasingly good health and lead lives of ever greater joy and fulfillment.

THE IMPORTANCE OF CONTINUING IN FAITH

The Mystic Law's fundamental beneficial power is inconspicuous. When you pray for something, even though signs of your prayers being fulfilled may not be immediately apparent, the result will definitely appear in time. Underground water eventually comes to the surface. A seed that is planted waits until springtime to produce flowers. A certain time is required for a sapling to develop into a great tree.

By the same token, continuing Buddhist practice is very important. Buddhism is reason, after all. Even though people might have practiced faith with a fiery, almost fanatical fervor at one time, if they fail to continue, they cannot savor the true benefit of the Mystic Law.

On the other hand, even if, for instance, there are days when it is just not possible for you to do gongyo, you need not feel that you have been remiss in your practice. So long as you cherish the mind of faith, your good fortune will stay with you. Even chanting just one daimoku yields great benefit. The important thing is that you practice with strong and tenacious faith throughout your entire life.

I believe that those who continue to study throughout their entire lives can continually advance and realize victory in life. If you lose the spirit to advance and improve yourselves, you will stagnate, backslide and ultimately experience failure in life.

THE PLACE WHERE YOU ARE IS THE LAND OF TRANQUIL LIGHT

Bryan Wilson of the University of Oxford, a world-renowned sociologist of religion with whom I have published a dialogue (*Human Values in a Changing World*), cites the quality of "being practically applicable in any place" as one of the prerequisites for a world religion. He points out that if one must go to some distant place to practice a teaching, then ultimately only a limited number of people will be able to take faith in it.

Nichiren Daishonin's Buddhism teaches that "'Holy Peak' [Holy Eagle Peak] refers to the Gohonzon. It also refers to the place where Nichiren and his followers, who chant Nam-myoho-renge-kyo, dwell" (OTT, 135). Again, since wherever the Daishonin and his followers who embrace the Mystic Law live is the Land of Tranquil Light, the Daishonin teaches, "It is not that he leaves his present place and goes to some other place" (OTT, 192).

You can accumulate good fortune here in this land of the United States. Confident that the area where you live and make your home is itself the Land of Tranquil Light, you should strive to make it shine as such. This is the correct way of practicing Nichiren Daishonin's Buddhism, which is truly a world religion.

On Guidance

The mission of a leader is to guide all people, both individually and as a group, to victory. This is the purpose that guidance serves.

The main point in giving guidance is to elevate the state of mind or determination of the other person. A change in your determination will cause a change in the prayers that you offer and the actions that you take. According to the doctrine of "three thousand realms in a single moment of life," subtle and imperceptible changes in your determination or state of mind affect everything immensely. One who can help raise another person's state of mind is an outstanding leader. Those who merely issue orders or give directions — to say nothing of those who just scold and lord it over others — do not qualify as leaders.

To illustrate what I mean, I would like to relate an episode from the history of Great Britain, a country with which America shares deep ties.

One of the most enduring popular figures among the British is the one-eyed, one-armed naval commander Horatio Nelson (1758–1805). Nelson won two major naval victories over the French, in Egypt (1798) and at Trafalgar (1805), thereby thwarting Napoleon's ambition of conquering Great Britain.

In Egypt, Napoleon had occupied Alexandria in an attempt to cut lines of communication between Britain and India. In the end, however, his forces were destroyed by ships under Nelson's command, with the result that his Egyptian campaign ended in failure.

The night before the decisive Battle of Trafalgar, Nelson revealed his strategy to his subordinate, a Captain Berry. Berry, when he understood the scope of the plan, was filled with excitement, exclaiming, "If we succeed, what will the world say?"

"There is no 'if' in this case," Nelson replied, calling him to task. The admiral's voice became harsh: "That we shall succeed is certain: Who may live to tell the story is a very different question.... Before this time tomorrow, I shall have gained a peerage or Westminster Abbey [where the English bury famous people]."

The admiral's determination and that of his subordinate officer were different. Through this officer, the admiral's intent was conveyed to the other officers and the crew. On the following day, they seized nine French ships and almost completely destroyed the remainder of the fleet, thus winning a great victory. The admiral was a person of great perception who deftly sensed the irresolute attitude of his subordinate and very effectively changed it.

I hope all of you will attain excellence in giving individual guidance and become "excellent doctors" of human existence and of life's inner dynamics. The human heart is very vulnerable. You should continually ask yourself: How can I give others confidence and enable them to advance with courage and strong determination?

Problems that arise are many and diverse, varying from person to person and from one situation to the next. Furthermore, people have greatly differing characters. For this reason, to give effective guidance, you yourselves must accumulate rich experience, develop your understanding of Buddhism and polish your faith. I hope you will lead others with wisdom, all the while praying for their happiness with the spirit of compassion. One who can win the heart of even a single person can win the hearts of ten thousand. Cultivating such humanity is the essence of Buddhism.

FULFILLING ONE'S DUTY

Horatio Nelson lost his life in the Battle of Trafalgar. Just before the battle was about to begin, shortly after eleven in the morning, Nelson had a set of signal flags hoisted high on the mast of his flagship. These flags bore the famous message "England expects that every man will do his duty." They remained raised throughout the entire course of the battle, arousing a fighting spirit in the British.

Even after sustaining injuries that would prove fatal, Nelson continued to lead his forces with all of his might. Seeing such a display of courage, his men could not help being roused to valor.

Before long, the British forces won a great victory, which was reported to Nelson, then dying of his wounds below deck. Upon hearing the news, he cried out, "Now I am satisfied, . . . I have done my duty." Shortly thereafter, he breathed his last.

His victory had been complete. Without the loss of a single allied ship, his forces had captured twenty enemy ships and destroyed one. As a result, Napoleon's naval power was irreparably damaged.

"Duty!" Human worth derives from thoroughly carrying out the duties with which one is charged. Nelson was never disheartened by any enemy he faced. He never retreated out of fear. His sense of responsibility was such that he would carry out his duties no matter what. Therein lay his true worth.

While it is wrong to hound others out of impatience to achieve a victory, having the compassion to help others win is a necessary qualification of leaders.

People will follow a leader who is always victorious — about whom they feel that if they advance together with that person, they can definitely win. To be such a leader, you must be unmatched in earnestness, consideration for others, eloquence and action.

THE SACRIFICE OF MAHANAMA

I would now like to turn to events that occurred in ancient India. The massacre of the Shakya clan by King Virudhaka was one of Shakyamuni's nine great ordeals.

Virudhaka was a king of Kosala in the days of Shakyamuni Buddha. He was humiliated by the Shakyas because he discovered that his mother had been a servant of a lord of the Shakya tribe, and he vowed to take revenge. Later, he seized the throne from his father and immediately led an army against the Shakya kingdom, virtually annihilating the clan.

The Gosho states, "A king named Virudhaka, incited by Ajatashatru, put hundreds of Shakyamuni Buddha's clan to the sword" (WND-I, 799).

A Buddhist scripture relates an episode that occurred during this tragic incident. Just as the entire clan was about to be put to death, an old man approached the king. It was Mahanama, who was the king's blood relation. [Another source says that Mahanama was a cousin of Shakyamuni. In any event, he was a lay follower of devout faith.]

"Your majesty, I beg of you to honor my one request," he said. "Please allow all of them [the remaining Shakya members] to flee for the interval of time from when I immerse myself in the water until I rise to the surface."

Reluctantly the king agreed to the request of the old man, to whom, as kin, he was bound by a sense of obligation. He thought to himself that the old man could probably hold his breath underwater only for a few minutes at most and that he could just as well round up again those who had escaped.

The old man jumped into a pond, whereupon the Shakyas fled through the gate. One minute passed. Then another. Meanwhile, more and more people escaped.

The king grew increasingly anxious. "Hasn't he come up yet?" he asked.

"Not yet? Not yet?" he repeated.

The old man simply did not reappear.

"Go find him!" the king shouted, losing his patience.

His subordinates entered the pond. There they found that the old man had tied his hair to the underwater roots of a tree so that his body would not float up to the surface. He was already dead.

It was a heroic death. The old man had sacrificed himself to buy time, thus saving many others.

True leaders exercise great forbearance and buy time for the sake of those who follow. Such people sacrifice their lives to protect others. Many leaders, however, sacrifice others to protect themselves.

A leader, especially a Buddhist leader, absolutely must not be an oppressive authoritarian who exploits others. Rather, Buddhist leaders should, with selfless compassion, protect and praise the Buddha's children, laying down their lives if necessary to make others happy. I hope each of you will be keenly aware of this fundamental difference.

Those who devote themselves for the sake of the Buddha's children will accumulate great blessings and merit. Leaders who look down on the Buddha's children, on the other hand, commit a great offense.

To Deny Equality Is To Deny the Lotus Sutra

The great desire of Nichiren Daishonin, the Buddha of the Latter Day, is to enable all people, without any favoritism or discrimination, to attain Buddhahood equally.

"Nichiren declares that the varied sufferings that all living beings undergo—all these are Nichiren's own sufferings" (OTT, 138). Every time I read this passage, I am moved by the infinitely vast and immeasurable compassion of the original Buddha, who sought to save all people of the Latter Day from life's numerous sufferings. I am filled with a profound sense of appreciation.

The purpose of Buddhism is to bring out the Buddha nature that all people inherently possess, to awaken people to it and enable them to attain Buddhahood. Moreover, the Lotus Sutra does not allow for any discrimination; all people are equally entitled to salvation. Thus, to deny equality is to deny the Lotus Sutra.

The Daishonin writes, "There should be no discrimination among those who propagate the five characters of Myoho-renge-kyo in the Latter Day of the Law, be they men or women" (WND-1, 385).

The Gosho in which this passage appears was written 718 years ago, in May 1273. In the feudal era of the Middle Ages, the Daishonin was already expounding the equality of the sexes based on the Law.

Looking at gender equality on a worldwide scale, though, it is not until the seventeenth and eighteenth centuries that the concept of the equality of the sexes gained prominence, while it is only in the nineteenth century that women's suffrage movements began to emerge. And it is much later that women actually obtained equal voting rights on par with men in national elections. Women's suffrage was first won in New Zealand in 1893. It was won by the United Kingdom in 1918, the United States in 1920 and Japan in 1945.

This history only serves to bring home again how far ahead of his time the Daishonin was. As early as the thirteenth century, he expounded the equality of the sexes, revealing the profound nature of the egalitarian and humanistic principles of Buddhism.

A WORLD RELIGION FOR REALIZING TRUE DEMOCRACY

Nichijun, the sixty-fifth high priest, was one of the greatest scholars in the priesthood in modern times. He praised the Soka Gakkai, convinced it was an organization that would spread the Daishonin's Buddhism for the people to the entire world.

Once, in a discourse on "Democracy and Religion," Nichijun remarked: "This world is the world of religion. Consequently, in the world of democracy, religion must form the foundation and should be stressed at all times. What I mean by *religion* here is not religion in general. What is termed *religion* often takes a variety of forms: Many arise out of ignorance, some are developments that have incorporated theory or practice to justify their existence, while some are merely corruptions of existing religions.

"These religions are essentially irrational, for they ignore reason and the intellect. As a result, they either have no doctrine or, if they do, then it is merely deluded doctrine. They only serve to keep the people in ignorance and darkness. That which is irrational is an enemy to individual development. Democracy is said to be rational. In modern times, issues concerning science and religion are constantly debated, but this debate arises because religion is irrational.

"While confirming that the world of democracy must be based upon religion, we must at the same time courageously strive to remove irrational religions as enemies of democracy. When viewed in this light, we must adopt only the religion of Myoho-renge-kyo as the religion for the present and future. For it is a unique doctrine that, in a correct and rational manner, elucidates and actualizes the freedom, equality and dignity of the individual, while revealing that all people possess the Buddha nature and the potential to attain Buddhahood" (October 1949 *Dai-Nichiren*).

Nichiren Daishonin's Buddhism is the great teaching that enables all people to develop their inherent Buddha nature and attain Buddhahood. It is the supreme teaching that elucidates individual freedom, equality and the dignity of life in a logical, realistic manner, enabling people to manifest them in the reality of their daily lives and in society.

This is what prompts Nichijun to state unequivocally that the Daishonin's Buddhism is the world religion that will form the foundation for realizing true democracy. He also points out that "irrational teachings" keep people in ignorance, obstruct the development of individual potential and are enemies of democracy.

Worldwide, we now see a trend toward an era of democracy and an era of the people. We must not allow this dramatic change in the course of human history to be set back by confusion and countermovements. That would be a tragedy we cannot afford. Many educated people have begun to recognize the need for a universal humanism, religiosity and spiritual values capable of providing the foundation for an era of the people.

The time has at last arrived when Nichiren Daishonin's Buddhism is sought by people around the world, and its greatness is being proven to all. The times are moving toward Buddhism. Please be convinced that the time of full-fledged worldwide kosen-rufu has arrived.

In this day and age, religions or ecclesiastics who oppress the people and expect unconditional obedience to authority from them are anachronistic; they will eventually bring about their own downfall. How much graver then would be the offense of anyone behaving in this manner while professing to uphold the Mystic Law, for they would be turning their backs on and going against the Daishonin's spirit of compassion and equality. As indicated by Nichijun, such people would be irrational and would be enemies of humankind out to destroy democracy.

THE SGI MOVEMENT FOSTERS DEMOCRACY

The noted American scholar of education, Dayle M. Bethel of the International University, Osaka, Japan, has observed: "During the nineteenth and early twentieth centuries, democracy became the great hope of the world's peoples. The democratic current that swept through the world during that period whispered to people everywhere that they, as individual human beings, had the ability and the potential to be the salvation of themselves and their families....

"What people all over the world are having to face up to during the final quarter of this century is that democracy...has failed....

"Throughout the world at the present time, people are reacting to this failure of democracy by placing their hope in various types of religious fundamentalism. In these fundamentalist perspectives, hope for salvation, for the possibility of improving conditions for oneself and one's family, rests not in oneself and in democracy but in the authority of a deity or in the clergy or in political leaders who profess to speak for the deity. The dangers for individuals and for societies stemming from such blind following of absolutist religious authority are, I think, obvious.

"As I observe the Soka Gakkai organization, I see it as running counter to this fundamentalist trend of the times. It is a movement that seeks to develop people who can think and discern for themselves; a movement that rejects authoritarianism because it impedes human growth. Two general types of religious organizations can be observed in the world: dogmatic religions that seek to gain the allegiance of the people through authority and blind faith, and those that seek to develop people who are free-thinking and self-determined. For the sake of humanity's future, this latter type of religious organization is most important. . . .

"It is important, therefore, that the people of . . . religious organizations engage in periodic reflection and examine themselves and the organization of which they are a part from the standpoint of their original purpose. . . .

"When activities and ways of thinking that were once fresh and unique and effective in serving people become taken for granted and routinized, they, ironically, wind up eventually restricting and controlling the very people they were supposed to serve. Secretive actions and oversensitivity to suggestions and criticism signify the stiffening and bureaucratization of an organization" (*Issues Between the Nichiren Shoshu Priesthood and the Soka Gakkai*, vol. 2, pp. 137–41).

As Professor Bethel points out, self-righteous religions obsessed with making the people yield to their authority demand blind obedience from their followers and try to restrict and control them.

The original purpose of religion is to serve humanity and lead people to happiness. Toward this end, Nichiren Daishonin's Buddhism is the ultimate teaching that espouses humanity and delivers freedom and dignity equally to all human beings, refusing to bend to any authoritarian power or force.

If anyone who embraces Nichiren Daishonin's Buddhism looks' down on the Buddha's children and creates discrimination among believers, then that person shall not deserve to be called the Daishonin's follower.

The history of the Soka Gakkai, as Professor Bethel remarks, has been a continuous battle against authoritarianism, which hinders human growth. In its course, we have taken our movement promoting true democracy to all parts of the world. For this, we have been the target of constant criticism and persecution. Therefore, we must have keen perception to see through devilish functions and continue to wage our battle against evil without retreating an inch. This is the way we can protect the correct teaching, faith, the Buddha's children and democracy.

"RESIST MUCH, OBEY LITTLE"

Walt Whitman, the great American poet whose name is synonymous with democracy, wrote these lines to his country: "Resist much, obey little, / Once unquestioning obedience, once fully enslaved" (from "To the States" in *Leaves of Grass*). Believers who blindly follow religious authority end up becoming spiritual slaves and risk having their personal freedom and dignity trampled upon.

Buddhism is win or lose. I hope all of you will join me in advancing the kosen-rufu movement even more vigorously than before, in accordance with the Daishonin's teachings.

Please have no doubt in your mind that Nichiren Daishonin and the Dai-Gohonzon are aware that we are the ones who are working earnestly for, and are on the most correct course toward, kosen-rufu. In contrast, the Daishonin's harsh admonishment is bound to await those who would become enemies of the Mystic Law and the people.

The present situation [with the Nichiren Shoshu priesthood] is an opportunity to deepen our faith and accumulate good fortune, a chance to experience on a more profound level the greatness of the Daishonin's Buddhism. I hope you will continue to advance cheerfully and confidently based on this conviction.

I would like each of you to enjoy a life of victory and great benefit, to remain steadfast in the face of obstacles so that we can achieve an era of true democracy.

Worldwide kosen-rufu is the mandate of Nichiren Daishonin, and it is the SGI that has begun making this a reality. I am determined to keep blazing new paths and extending existing ones out into the world, opening them ever wider.

The United States above all serves as an all-important stage for the whole world. It is an exciting and dynamic stage of vast dimensions. My wish is to give you my all-out support in your efforts.

I would like to conclude this first training session by saying: "Congratulations, steadfast SGI-USA! I foresee great future development for you!" Thank you once again for taking time out of your busy schedules to attend today's meeting.

The Age of Soft Power

—ഝ—

HARVARD UNIVERSITY,
CAMBRIDGE, MASSACHUSETTS, SEPTEMBER 26, 1991

IT IS AN HONOR to be here today, but I feel especially privileged to have been invited to speak at this time, when Harvard University is commemorating 355 years of an illustrious history. I want to thank Professor John D. Montgomery of the John F. Kennedy School of Government for making this occasion possible and professors Joseph Nye and Ashton Carter for their comments, among all the many people who have so kindly welcomed me here.

The recent political changes in the Soviet Union have shaken the world, calling attention to a momentous and unstoppable trend. It has been hailed as the rise of soft power. In the past, the driving force of history all too often depended on the hard power of military might, political authority and wealth. In recent years, however, the relative importance of hard power has diminished, slowly giving way to knowledge and information, culture, ideas and systems — the weapons of soft power.

Although the conduct of the 1991 Gulf War might appear to be a classic example of the application of hard military power, the guns and tactics of the coalition forces first needed the soft power of United Nations support and positive world opinion to allow their use in the first place. I believe we have a historical obligation to encourage the steady reduction of the use of hard power while ensuring the permanent substitution of soft power in its place.

I propose that self-motivation is what will open the way to the era of soft power. While systems depending on hard power have succeeded by using established tools of coercion to move people toward certain goals, the success of soft power is based on volition. It is an internally generated energy of will created through consensus and understanding among people. The processes of soft power unleash the inner energies of the individual. Rooted in the spirituality and religious nature of human beings, this kind of energy has traditionally been considered in philosophical themes. But without the support of a philosophical foundation to strengthen and mobilize the spiritual resources of the individual, the use of soft power would become nothing more than "fascism with a smile." In such a society, information and knowledge would be abundant but subject to manipulation by those in power. A citizenry without wisdom would fall easy prey to authority with self-serving goals. For these reasons, the burden of sustaining and accelerating the trend toward soft power lies with philosophy.

RELIGION AND INDIVIDUAL CONSCIENCE

Let me offer an example to illustrate what I mean by self-motivation. In his *Les Provinciales* (Provincial Letters), Blaise Pascal attacks the elaborate system of "precedents for the conscience" that were established by the Jesuits to facilitate missionary work. The nature of his attack sheds light on the fundamental difference between internally generated motivation and that which is imposed from without. The Jesuits had developed a highly elaborate system for the propagation of their faith. When expedience demanded, they went so far as to permit Christians to worship non-Christian deities. As a Jansenist, Pascal emphasized the importance of the individual conscience. He denounced the use of Church authority to establish and impose predetermined standards and precepts for the conscience. Pascal describes the practice: "This plan they followed in the Indies and in China, where they permitted Christians to practice idolatry itself, with the aid of the following ingenious contrivance: they made their converts conceal under their clothes an image of Jesus Christ, to which they taught themselves to transfer mentally those adorations which they rendered ostensibly to the idol [of Shakyamuni or Confucius]."[1]

Pascal does not condemn the way of faith in other countries; he acknowledges that there might be times when there is no choice but to engage in such an approach. The decision to do so, however, can only be reached through a process of contemplation, self-questioning and soul-searching, which add up to the workings of the individual conscience. If a preestablished standard or precedent for such a decision is provided from without, this painful process of self-examination is avoided. Instead of developing, the conscience atrophies. For Pascal, what the Jesuits called "precedents for the conscience" were nothing more than a servile surrender to the desire for easy answers. For him, they represented the suicide of the conscience, one's inner moral guidance. Pascal's criticism reaches beyond its particular historical context to address the universal question of the nature of human conscience.

Nineteenth-century America, while perhaps not evincing the level of purity that would have satisfied Pascal, provides one of history's rare cases when an emphasis on the inner workings of the soul set the tenor for an entire society. Visiting the United States a half century after its founding, Alexis de Tocqueville was impressed above all by the simplicity of American religious practices and, at the same time, by their sincerity and depth of feeling. With analytical acuity, Tocqueville conveyed his impressions in *Democracy in America*, which contains the following passage: "It then became my object...to inquire how it happened that the real authority of religion was increased by a state of things which diminished its apparent force...."[2]

The Catholic Church in France had visual and artistic impact, characterized by elaborate formality and complex ritual. Often, the effect was to fetter and restrain the spirit. Tocqueville had, therefore, assumed that any reduction in the church's "apparent force" — its formalities and its rituals — would free people from its external control, resulting in weaker faith. In America he found that the opposite was true. To quote him again: "I have seen no country in which Christianity is clothed with fewer forms, figures, and observances than in the United States; or where it presents more distinct, more simple, or more general notions to the mind."[3]

At first glance, it may appear that Alexis de Tocqueville is simply comparing the formalism of French Catholicism with the flourishing spirit of Puritanism in America. On a deeper level, however, I think that he is really praising the intensely personal religious nature that was generated from within and that, refined into its purest form, had become this country's defining spiritual tone.

All religions that leave a lasting mark on human beings and society must operate on both personal and institutional levels. All great religions are based on an absolute entity or truth and transcend differences of race, class or social standing. They teach respect for the individual. However, as religious convictions evolve into religious movements, organizational demands emerge. In my view, these institutional aspects of religion must constantly adapt to the changing conditions of society. Furthermore, they should support and give primary consideration to the personal, individual aspects of belief. The unfortunate truth, however, is that few religious movements have been able to avoid the pitfall of organizational ossification. The development of a religion's institutional features ends up shackling and restraining the people whose interests it originally intended to serve. The external coercive powers of ecclesiastical institutions and associated ritual stifle the internal and spontaneous powers of faith, and the original purity of faith is lost. Because this is such a common occurrence, we tend to forget that it actually represents a reversal of the true function of religion.

Tocqueville considered it important that such abuses had been largely avoided by the Christian communities in America. He believed that the American people had preserved an essential purity of faith. This purity, and the degree to which religion was regarded as a matter of the inner life, is noted in remarks delivered by Ralph Waldo Emerson at Divinity College, Cambridge, Massachusetts, in 1838: "That which shows God in me, fortifies me. That which shows God out of me, makes me a wart and a wen."[4]

In one viewpoint, the broad-minded, optimistic view of religion taken by Emerson and his contemporaries was only a momentary, happy respite in the spiritual affairs of modern times. Preceding it was an age of collusion between established religion and political authority; following it is an age of secularization that has reduced spiritual matters to private concerns, stripped of any larger implications. It is not justified, however, to place this special period and its fruits completely in the past. The traditions of an inwardly directed spirituality live on in the depths of the American historical experience and awareness.

BUSHIDO AND SELF-CONTROL

If we turn to modern Japan, it is not easy to find there meaningful examples of this type of spirituality. After opening the country to the rest of the world in the mid-nineteenth century, Japan plunged headlong into the task of catching up with and overtaking the industrial nations of the West. The great Japanese author Soseki Natsume characterized that effort as an externally imposed process of civilization. He was right, in the sense that all of the goals and models for modernization came from outside. In their rush to catch up, the Japanese of that period did not feel that they had the time to work out the concepts associated with modernity for themselves.

Here, I would like to introduce an episode from the life of Inazo Nitobe, the Meiji-period educator and pioneer of Japanese American friendship. Discussing religion with a Belgian acquaintance, Nitobe was asked whether the Japanese system provided for spiritual education. After careful consideration, Nitobe answered that, from the early seventeenth through the nineteenth centuries, it was *bushido*, or the way of the samurai, and not religion per se, that had shaped the spiritual development of the Japanese people. In 1899, Nitobe published an English-language book entitled *Bushido, the Soul of Japan: An Exposition of Japanese Thought.*

There are a number of points in common between the spirituality of *bushido* and the philosophy of Protestantism and Puritanism. In part, this accounts for the enthusiasm with which the writings of Benjamin Franklin were received in Meiji Japan. More important here, however, the spiritual development of the Japanese people, guided in part by the ideals of *bushido*, was largely inwardly directed. Inner motivation implies self-control; one acts in a correct and responsible manner not because one is forced to but spontaneously and on one's own volition. During the Edo period, the incidence of crime and corruption was relatively low; this may be evidence of the concrete influence of an inwardly directed spirituality on the workings of Japanese society. It is interesting to consider similar implications in Tocqueville's observation that "in no country is criminal justice administered with more mildness than in the United States."[5]

Because the Japanese people of that period were motivated from within, they were able to attain a high degree of self-control and self-mastery. These qualities are among the best expressions of humanity, insofar as they help to create smoother social relations and less anxiety in personal contacts. Self-control and inner motivation as social ideals gave birth to a culture of distinctive beauty in Japan. It was noticed by many, among them Edward S. Morse, a graduate of Harvard and pioneer in archaeology in Japan. He wrote prolifically about the surprising beauty he found in the life and ways of ordinary Japanese. Walt Whitman was likewise struck by the air of dignity he sensed in the Japanese emissaries he saw walking the avenues of Manhattan.

With the growth of Japan's economic strength in recent years, contemporary Japanese American relations, while still essentially friendly, have been strained by increasing disharmony. The stresses of the relationship were revealed at a deeper level in the Structural Impediments Initiative talks of 1990. Those discussions revealed frictions that were more cultural than economic. Cultures do not always respond amicably toward one another. Intercultural contacts that probe and question deeply rooted, daily-life practices can provoke aversion or hostility. The need for restraint and self-control is never so necessary as when people are confronted with the confusion and tensions brought about by a collision of cultures. True partnership cannot be attained unless the effort to create it is based on mutual self-control at this inner, spiritual level.

The necessary inwardly generated self-control has been conspicuously lacking in modern Japan. Without it, Japan has tended to swing widely between extremes of overconfidence and timidity. Sometimes the nation has seemed unnecessarily obsequious in its relations with other countries, in particular with the West. Now we see an oddly resurgent arrogance based on nothing more than the most recent Gross National Product statistics. The approaching fiftieth anniversary of the Japanese attack on Pearl Harbor is a painful reminder of the enormous horror and destruction that the absence of self-control can cause.

Incidentally, Nitobe's *Bushido* played a very constructive role in the Portsmouth Conference at the end of the Russo-Japanese War in 1905. Soon after hostilities began, the Japanese government dispatched Kentaro Kaneko, a member of the House of Peers, to the United States to enlist the good offices of President Theodore Roosevelt in negotiating a settlement. Kaneko had been a classmate of Roosevelt at Harvard, and the two had maintained and strengthened their contacts in the intervening years. When the president requested a book that would explain the driving force behind the Japanese character and spiritual education in Japan, Kaneko gave him a copy of *Bushido*. A few months later, Roosevelt thanked Kaneko; the book, he said, had given him a clearer understanding of the Japanese character. Armed with this knowledge, he willingly took up the task of mediating the peace negotiations. In the far-from-peaceful history of modern Japanese American relations, this episode is a refreshing example of mutual understanding.

The task that confronts us now is to revive the innate sources of human energy in a world marked by a deepening sense of spiritual desiccation. This task will not be an easy one, either for Japan or for the United States. Much depends on the attitudes we take. In that respect, the Buddhist doctrine of dependent origination, which shows how profoundly and inextricably our fates are interwoven, can make an important contribution.

ACTIVATING THE WILL TO HARMONY

One of the most important Buddhist concepts, dependent origination holds that all beings and phenomena exist or occur in relation to other beings or phenomena. All things are linked in an intricate web of causation and connection, and nothing, whether in the realm of human affairs or natural phenomena, can exist or occur solely of its own accord. Greater emphasis is placed on the interdependent relationships between individuals than on the individual alone. As astute Western observers like Henri Bergson and Alfred North Whitehead have noted, however, overemphasis on interdependence can submerge the individual and reduce one's capacity for positive engagement in the world. Passivity, in fact, has been a pronounced historical tendency in Buddhist-influenced cultures. The deeper essence of Buddhism, however, goes beyond passivity to offer a level of interrelatedness that is uniquely dynamic, holistic and generated from within.

We have noted that encounters between different cultures are not always amicable. The reality of opposing interests and even hostility must be acknowledged. What can be done to promote harmonious relationships? An episode from the life of Shakyamuni may help. Shakyamuni was once asked the following question: "We are told that life is precious. And yet all people live by killing and eating other living beings. Which living beings may we kill and which living beings must we not kill?" To this simple expression of doubt, Shakyamuni replied, "It is enough to kill the will to kill."

Shakyamuni's response is neither evasion nor deception but is based on the concept of dependent origination. He is saying that, in seeking the kind of harmonious relationship expressed by respect for the sanctity of life, we must not limit ourselves to the phenomenal level where hostility and conflict (in this case, which living beings it is acceptable to kill and which not) undeniably exist. We must seek harmony on a deeper level — a level where it is truly possible to "kill the will to kill." More than objective awareness, we must achieve a state of compassion transcending distinctions between self and other. We need to feel the compassionate energy that beats within the depths of all people's subjective lives, where the individual and the universal are merged. This is not the simplistic denial or abnegation of the individual self that Bergson and Whitehead criticize. It is the fusion of self and other. At the same time, it is an expansion of the limited, ego-shackled self toward a greater self whose scale is as limitless and unbounded as the universe.

The teachings of Nichiren Daishonin include the passage "Without the body, no shadow can exist, and without life, no environment" (WND-1, 644). In other words, Buddhism regards life and its environment as two integral aspects of the same entity. The subjective world of the self and the objective world of its environment are not in opposition nor are they a duality. Instead, their relationship is characterized by inseparability and indivisibility. Neither is this unity a static one in which the two realms merge as they become objectified. The environment, which embraces all universal phenomena, cannot exist except in a dynamic relationship with the internally generated activity of life itself. In practical terms, the most important question for us as individuals is how to activate the inner sources of energy and wisdom existing within our lives.

Let me illustrate this idea in relation to the previous discussion of conscience. I am sometimes asked to advise couples who are considering divorce. Divorce is a private matter whose final resolution rests with the two people involved. I encourage unhappy couples to remember that, from the Buddhist perspective, it is impossible to build personal happiness on the suffering of others. Such situations sometimes require painful reflection and forbearance. But through that pain, one can strengthen and discipline the internal workings of the conscience — something Pascal understood very well. Ultimately, those concerned are able to minimize the destruction of human relationships that might otherwise result.

Our society today urgently needs the kind of inwardly directed spirituality to strengthen self-control and restraint. It is a quality that deepens our respect for the dignity of life. In a world where interpersonal relationships are becoming increasingly tenuous, greater self-control and discipline would also help restore and rejuvenate endangered feelings, including friendship, trust and love, for without them there can be no rewarding and meaningful bonds between people.

It is my hope and my conviction that we will see a revival of philosophy in the broadest, Socratic meaning of the word. An age of soft power with its source in this kind of philosophy will bear true and rich fruit. In an age when national borders are breaking down, each of us will need the integrity of an internalized philosophy to qualify us for world citizenship. In that sense, those great standard-bearers of American thought, Emerson, Thoreau and Whitman, were all citizens of the world.

In closing, let me share with you this passage from Emerson's poem "Friendship," which was a particular favorite of mine in my youth.

> *O friend, my bosom said,*
> *Through thee alone the sky is arched,*
> *Through thee the rose is red,*
> *All things through thee take nobler form*
> *And look beyond the earth,*
> *The millround of our fate appears*
> *A sunpath in thy worth.*
> *Me too thy nobleness has taught*
> *To master my despair;*
> *The fountains of my hidden life*
> *Are through thy friendship fair.*[6]

Notes

1. Blaise Pascal, *Provincial Letters (Les Provinciales)*, Letter V, March 20, 1656, in Robert Maynard Hutchins, ed., Pascal, *Great Books of the Western World* (Chicago: Encyclopedia Britannica, Inc., 1952), 33:28.
2. Alexis de Tocqueville, *Democracy in America* (1835), trans. Henry Reeve (New York: Alfred A. Knopf, 1980), 1:309.
3. *Democracy in America*, 2:27.
4. Ralph Waldo Emerson, *The Complete Writings of Ralph Waldo Emerson* (WM. H. Wise & Co., 1930), 1:41.
5. *Democracy in America*, 2:166.
6. *The Complete Writings of Ralph Waldo Emerson*, 2:912.

Freedom and Equality Are the Hallmarks of Buddhism

—⚏—

FIRST SGI-USA BOSTON GONGYO MEETING,
BOSTON COMMUNITY CENTER, BOSTON, MASSACHUSETTS,
SEPTEMBER 27, 1991

FIRST OF ALL, I would like to express my most profound gratitude for the efforts you have made to ensure the success of my visit to Boston. I am deeply indebted to you all. With your great support, we have left another glorious page in the history of kosen-rufu. Thank you once again.

As an expression of my appreciation, I would like to present to you a poem I composed this morning. [Here SGI President Ikeda read his poem "Flagbearers of Human Renaissance."]

"Flagbearers of Human Renaissance"
To my friends of *Jiyu* in Boston, American Athenaes

O what refreshing blue skies!
What dazzling sunlight!
What lush, green forests!

A fresh, invigorating morning,
When all living things
Seem reborn.

The prayers
Of my beloved Bostonian friends
Have crystallized in
A performance of nature —
In the majestic and dignified
Beauty of New England.

O my dear Bostonian friends!
My visit to Boston,
Enveloped in your sincerity
And smiling faces,
Will stay an unforgettable memory,
A page of golden history,
Throughout my life, nay, eternity.

Our great city of Boston
Is the home of noble ideals —
Pioneering spirit,
Freedom and equality.
The courageous and stalwart
Mothers and fathers of America,
Cast off the heavy chains of the Old World,
And with their own hands,
Carved out and defended
Their own New World.

Constrained by nothing,
Dependent on no one,
They cheerfully sang rousing songs
As they built their city.

From its historic red-brick streets,
From the avenues of shady elms,
The strains of those spirited tunes
Of construction still linger.

Now my beloved Bostonian friends,
In this great city,
Where you have desired to live
Since the remote past,
Together with other
Bodhisattvas of the Earth
Of time without beginning,
You are building your own world —
One where human beings can enjoy their existence
To the fullest,
Living humane lives.

Never allow those who
Harbor dark jealousy toward us
To interrupt our joyous advance.

Our religion exists for the sake of human beings,
Our faith for the sake of daily life,
Our organization for the sake of happiness.

Advance along this solid course
Boldly and wisely,
Without doubt or hesitation.

0 Boston,
The city of the great American Renaissance!

Emerson and Thoreau
Raised their voices high
In songs of praise of the human being.

Thoreau wrote:
"Direct your eyesight inward, and you'll find
A thousand regions in your mind
Yet undiscovered. Travel them, and be
Expert in home-cosmography."

You, my friends,
Are the ones who will fulfill the dreams
Inherited from your forerunners,
Who aspired for this wisdom of the East.

You are kings and queens of the heart,
Who, through the philosophy of "three thouand realms
in a single moment of Life,"
Can travel freely and confidently through
Your inner universe of life —
A realm vaster than the sea
And wider than the sky.

My beloved Bostonian philosophers of the Mystic Law!
Bring forth a new Soka Renaissance
That shines with strong and dazzling splendor.

Our Boston is the "Athens of America,"
A seat of intellect
That is central to the world,
And a capital of education
That ranks first in the globe.

The pioneering founders
Established Harvard University out of a desire
To prevent ignorant leaders
From stifling the future development of the New World.

After 355 years,
Their aspiration
Still deeply moves us.

My heart filled with the memory of
The Soka Gakkai's first and second presidents,
Who championed humanistic education,
I made a historic step

In this venerable seat of learning.

Confident that an unceasing flow
Of wise Bodhisattvas of the Earth
Will continue to issue forth vigorously
Like the Charles River.

O the beautiful eyes
Of my beloved Bostonian friends
Shining with intellect —
I will never forget this sight.

O dear friends!
Let us travel the path of hope, cheerfully,
With a spirit as bright and clear,
As the wide, blue sky,
Always,
And forever.

TEACHERS ARE REPRESENTATIVES OF HUMANITY AND CULTURE

The exhibition "Humanity in Education: The Soka Education System," organized by the SGI-USA culture department, will commence at the SGI-USA Headquarters on September 29. Scheduled to tour leading cities around the country, the exhibition will be held here in Boston, the capital of education and intellect, next year. Today, therefore, I would like to speak about education.

The Soka Gakkai, as most of you probably know, began as the Soka Kyoiku Gakkai (Value-Creating Education Society), at which time it was mainly composed of educators. Both our founding president, Tsunesaburo Makiguchi, and our second president, Josei Toda, were educators. Education has been my life's great work as well.

Throughout his life, the French poet and philosopher Charles Péguy (1873–1914) constantly urged people to become defenders of humanity. Humanity is not something that develops on its own or is sustained without effort. Unless humanity is actively cultivated and maintained, it soon begins to wither. The same applies to peace and culture.

Péguy also said to teachers that they must not give in to the pressures or temptations of authority. Teachers at elementary schools, he asserted, were representatives of humanity, not of government authorities. The French philosopher said that elementary school teachers should represent the large majority in their cities, towns and villages — not the prime minister, no matter how important this individual might be. He held that teachers should be unique and outstanding representatives of those who help form and support the humanity of poets, artists, philosophers and scholars. Péguy urged teachers to be steadfast representatives of culture.

There are probably a number of reasons why Péguy turned his focus on elementary school teachers. President Neil L. Rudenstine of Harvard University, whom I met with yesterday [September 26], also stressed the importance of early, basic education.

According to Péguy, so important are teachers as defenders and representatives of humanism and culture that no poet, artist, philosopher or scholar could compare to them. Certainly, the work of teachers — who have a direct hand in molding the character of human beings — forms the foundation for all cultural endeavors.

For this reason, Péguy strongly emphasized the need for teachers to study. Having a big mission means that one's responsibility is equally big. The French thinker remarked that the most outstanding individuals were those who had continued, and would continue, to study and improve themselves. Nothing worthwhile could be attained without hard work, he believed, stating that life was a process of never-ending study. Education, he insisted, was not something handed down arbitrarily from above but something conveyed from one person to another through individual effort.

In other words, the level of culture that teachers themselves have attained in the depths of their lives through their own efforts is conveyed from one human being to another, from teacher to child. Education should not be something that is imposed upon students by authority. Consequently, teachers' inner growth contributes to children's happiness and educational and social advances.

HUMANISTIC EDUCATION IS A BAROMETER OF CIVILIZATION

The French philosopher also asserted that a crisis in civilization and society indicates a crisis in education. Civilization is placed in jeopardy when humanity is jeopardized or crushed by political force or religious authority. Since teachers are the representatives of humanism, education provides the key to overcoming a crisis in this area. As a result, protecting education is protecting civilization; transforming education, meanwhile, serves to transform society. Indeed, the extent to which humanistic education flourishes is the barometer of civilization.

On the other hand, if education represents not humanity but authority and economic supremacy at all costs, then no matter how it may flourish, it is only an index of an uncivilized culture.

In this regard, Victor Hugo wrote that those who open schools close down the prisons. It was his way of expressing symbolically the significance of education. The opening of schools sheds the light of humanity on society and does away with the need for prisons, which symbolize darkness.

Hugo believed that social evils arose from a lack of education and lamented that most criminals had not willingly become what they were. He held that poverty, discrimination and the biased and repressive education of the times twisted and distorted people.

I cannot help feeling that his contrast between schools and prisons represents the confrontation between humanity and authority. And I am stirred anew by the lofty conviction of Tsunesaburo Makiguchi, who, exemplifying great humanity, died in that symbol of authority — prison.

IGNORANCE IS THE ORIGIN OF ALL DECLINE

Helen Keller (1880–1968) believed that the existence of youth made it impossible for culture to regress.

John Amos Comenius (1592–1670), the Czech educational reformer, declared, "If the corruption of the human race is to be remedied, this must be done by means of the careful education of the young."

Comenius was incensed at the evil in the world, writing: "Instead of mutual love and purity, reign hatred, enmity, war and murder. Instead of justice, we find unfairness, roguery, oppression, theft and rapine; instead of purity, uncleanliness and audacity of thought, word and deed; instead of simplicity and truth, lying, deception and knavery; instead of modesty, pride and haughtiness between man and man."

He deplored how barbarous acts inflicting pain and suffering on people continued to be carried out in the name of religion, when religion should have been for the sake of people's happiness. This is a truly frightening aspect of religion. Comenius strove to heal the ravages of the religious wars through education.

At first, he was motivated by a desire to help his country, Moravia [part of the former Czechoslovakia], and his church, but this eventually burgeoned into a wish to help all humankind and the entire world.

Why do things degenerate? Comenius is not alone in asking this question. We, too, are forced to deplore many phenomena in our own environment.

Comenius believed that ignorance is the origin of all decline. Thus he endeavored to save society from corruption in three different areas: in learning (the relationship between people and things), in government (the relationship between people and other people) and in religion (the relationship between people and an absolute being) by means of "the light of universal wisdom." He asserted that learning, government and religion that lack the light of reason grow dark and that in darkness "devilish things" proliferate.

As long as youth polish their wisdom and intellect, civilization will not regress. Neither youth nor education allow the flow of culture to reverse. On this one point alone, I would like you to be convinced of the correctness of our SGI movement, which, through promoting peace, culture and education based on Buddhism, imparts its universal light to others. Globally, we are moving toward an era of true respect for the autonomy and rights of human beings. We must never allow this flow to be turned back.

True Harmony Entails Sharing Both Sufferings and Joys

Incidentally, many professions are thought of as "holy" in that they entail rendering selfless service to others. These professions include those of doctors, teachers and priests.

Physicians in the United Kingdom are known to use such expressions in addressing their patients as "How are we doing today?" and "We will cure our ailment," rather than saying "you" or "your." The underlying assumption here seems to be that curing an illness is an effort that requires the cooperation of the physician and the patient. The ideal is that the physician should regard the patient's disease as his or her own problem, responsibility and suffering.

I also understand that schoolteachers in the United Kingdom speak in terms of "our examination" and "our passing"; and they generally avoid using such expressions as "your examination" or "your answers." Whether the pupil can get good marks on an exam is in a sense a test of the teacher. The teacher's proficiency, in other words, is also being tested. Good results are a victory for student and teacher alike.

In the cases of both physicians and teachers, we see examples of people fulfilling their roles with compassion, with a sense of responsibility and human warmth. Fundamentally, the role of those practicing such "holy" professions is to share sufferings together with, live alongside and advance together with the people.

This is also the spirit of Buddhism. Bodhisattvas of Mahayana Buddhism vow to save others, even putting off their own attainment of Buddhahood until all others have attained the Way. To have the attitude that one alone is a Buddha and is great, that others are insignificant, goes against the spirit of Buddhism. In contrast, the lifeblood of Buddhism is pulsing and alive where there is a unity of people committed to sharing both the sufferings and joys of others.

Thus, in a letter to his lay follower Shijo Kingo, Nichiren Daishonin wrote, "If you should fall into hell for some grave offense, no matter how Shakyamuni Buddha might urge me to become a Buddha, I would refuse; I would rather go to hell with you" (WND-1, 850).

Again, to another follower, Oto Gozen, he wrote: "If anything at all happens, please come over here. I will welcome you. Let us die of starvation together among the mountains" (WND-1, 616).

Revering the Daishonin's immense mercy and compassion, we in the SGI have developed a great circle of human solidarity in perfect accord with this fundamental spirit of Buddhism. This one point makes it clear that the SGI is correctly carrying out the practice of the Daishonin's Buddhism. For this reason, its members receive true benefit.

Both good and evil exist in the world. If the people tolerate evil, good will languish and decline. Evil always tries to conceal its true nature. But if we exercise keen powers of discernment, relentlessly pursue and attack evil, and lose no time in confronting it with one question after another, its false skin — its veneer of goodness and justice — will crack and fall away.

A Buddhist scripture contains a tale about a village of cattle thieves. The people of one village steal a valuable cow belonging to a person in another village, and together they feast on it.

The owner of the stolen cow follows the cow's hoofprints, which lead him to the village. There, he corners one of the villagers and begins to question him.

"Do you live in this village?" he asks.

"Village? Don't be absurd!" the person replies. "There is no village here."

"There is a pond in this village, and next to it you killed and ate my cow, didn't you?" continues the injured party.

"There's no pond here," the villager retorts. The thief's conscience is uneasy, so he tries to conceal the truth by giving nonsensical answers.

"There is a tree next to the pond, isn't there?" insists the cow's owner.

"There are no trees here," the thief returns.

Infuriated, the owner pursues his line of questioning relentlessly, at last getting straight to the point, "You and others went from this village to the east, and there you stole the cow, didn't you?"

"No," comes the reply. "There is no east here."

The thief's lies begin to become patently obvious.

"You stole my cow during the daytime," the bereaved owner pronounces.

"No," the villager replies. "There is no daytime here."

The thief's replies are utterly ridiculous.

Finally, the cow's owner explodes in rage: "Don't lie! To claim that there is no village, no pond, and no tree is one thing, but to say that there is no east and no daytime is going too far! Where on earth could such a place exist? Everything you have said up to now has been lies. You have as good as confessed your guilt. You're the one who stole the cow, aren't you?"

The thief, his guilt discovered, can only hang his head in shame.

While this might seem like a humorous tale, the scripture then adds: "Those who destroy the Buddhist Law are just like this. Even though they might try to conceal their offense, when they die they will fall into hell without fail. They cannot conceal their guilt from the Buddhist deities, who observe everything with their heavenly vision."

This tale teaches that it is the cattle owner's anger directed toward injustice and his determined efforts to stamp it out — his adamant attitude of refusing to just stand by and suffer the loss of his cow — that strengthens the protective functions of the Buddhist deities.

Since it is a fact that evil has been committed, the alibis of the guilty party are certain to fall apart if they are subject to careful scrutiny.

Up to this time, there have been many instances where the schemes of evil persons — who, motivated by jealousy, have sought to destroy the SGI's movement for kosen-rufu — have come to light. There have been those who, like thieves, have tried to steal the fruit of our industrious labors. Such people are active even now. We must not be the least reserved or accommodating toward such thieves.

Time and again, the Daishonin teaches that we should not tacitly acquiesce to or permit the existence of evil. Calling into action the protective functions of the Buddhist deities by taking confident action to root out evil, we must solemnly fight to clarify where good and evil, truth and falsehood, lie.

YOU CAN SEE EAGLE PEAK WITHOUT TAKING A SINGLE STEP

I would now like to read from a letter Nichiren Daishonin wrote in exile on Sado Island. This letter was sent to Sairen-bo, a learned priest formerly of another school who had become the Daishonin's follower. Highly educated, Sairen-bo can be thought of as having something in common with all of you who live in and benefit from the intellectual richness of this city of Boston.

The Daishonin writes: "Wherever we dwell and practice the single vehicle, that place will be the Capital of Eternally Tranquil Light. And, without having to take a step, those who are our disciples and lay supporters can view Eagle Peak in India and day and night will go to and from the Land of Eternally Tranquil Light that has existed for all time. What a truly inexpressible joy it is!" (WND-I, 313).

Nichiren Daishonin states that the desolate island where he resides is the "Capital of Eternally Tranquil Light." This capital does not exist off in some distant land. The Daishonin does not teach that to attain Buddhahood we must venture from where we are to some other place. Without having to take a step, the place where we live and attain Buddhahood becomes the land of eternal happiness. This is Nichiren Daishonin's teaching.

This point is of great significance. One meaning that derives from it is that the Daishonin's teaching directly opposes evil authoritarianism.

It is said that distance gives rise to authority. This adage assails the foolish tendency of human beings to regard as respectable people or things so distant or at such height as to make them inaccessible.

The Gosho states: "As a rule, people in the world value what is distant and despise what is near, but this is the conduct of the ignorant. Even the distant should be repudiated if it is wrong, while what is near should not be discarded if it accords with the truth" (WND-1, 155–56).

While this passage is speaking of things near and distant in a temporal sense, the same principle holds true in terms of space. People tend to overlook the value of things close at hand. In Buddhism, however, the reality of the present and of the place where we live is of the utmost importance.

To those who must travel to some special place, others who are closer to that place come to possess greater authority. Thus a hierarchy of authority evolves among people according to their relative proximity.

In a religion that teaches belief in an external deity, often the clergy, in serving as a bridge connecting the people with the distant deity and its world of heaven, comes to possess special authority.

By contrast, Buddhism teaches that the people themselves are the entity of the Buddha. The Buddha exists not in some distant other world but in the inner realm of people's lives, and where they live becomes the Land of Eternally Tranquil Light. Among all the Buddhist sutras, the Lotus Sutra places particular emphasis on this teaching.

Viewed from this standpoint, it becomes clear that Nichiren Daishonin's Buddhism is no place for authoritarianism. Only the Gohonzon, the world of Buddhahood, is to be solemnly revered.

The Buddha exists right at this moment, in the very place where we are.

"Never seek this Gohonzon outside yourself," Nichiren writes. "The Gohonzon exists only within the mortal flesh of us ordinary people who embrace the Lotus Sutra and chant Nam-myoho-renge-kyo. The body is the palace of the ninth consciousness, the unchanging reality that reigns over all of life's functions" (WND-1, 832).

The Daishonin's words about the Land of Eternally Tranquil Light, in this letter addressed to Sairen-bo, set forth the fundamental guidelines for the age of worldwide kosen-rufu and the age of establishing the identity of each locality. Wherever you are, that place is the stage for worldwide kosen-rufu. Wherever you are, that place is the Land of Eternally Tranquil Light.

I hope all of you members who live here in Boston will make your lives shine with blessings, confident that this city, the community where you live and your homes are all the capital of eternal happiness. Also, I hope that, ever joyful, ever cheerful and ever exercising your good common sense, you will enjoy the happiest of lives. I would like to ask husbands to cherish their wives; wives to cherish their husbands; parents to cherish their children; and children to cherish their parents. The correct Buddhist way of life is to make such steady, down-to-earth efforts, focusing on showing actual proof of faith. Herein lies the way to a life filled with good fortune and blessings.

Thank you for all the hospitality and kindness you have extended us here over these four days. I am most grateful to you all. I pray that each of you will lead the greatest life possible and create the happiest of homes.

See you again!

Note

1. One Hundred Parables Sutra. Translated from Japanese.

Pioneer the Ultimate Frontier of Life and Death

—∭—

FIRST SGI-USA GENERAL MEETING,
WORLD PEACE IKEDA AUDITORIUM, SANTA MONICA,
CALIFORNIA, SEPTEMBER 29, 1991

CONGRATULATIONS on this truly high-spirited, first general meeting of the new SGI-USA!

I would like to speak informally with you today in a relaxed manner, as though we were having a family gathering or looking up at the stars and enjoying a cosmic melody or conversing among flowers, because Buddhism exists in warm, heart-to-heart communication.

PIONEERS WHO OPENED THE PATH OF WORLD PEACE

On this occasion of the start of the new SGI-USA, my thoughts are filled with the smiling faces of many precious and unforgettable friends who pioneered the organization, building the foundation that we have today. People like Harry Hirama of Hawaii; Arizona's Ted Osaki and his wife, Keiko; Dallas's Aileen Vaden; Fumiko Snelling of Washington, D.C.; and many others. All of them were courageous comrades who dedicated themselves to spreading the Law, steadfast and loyal to the very last. I will remember these pioneering members eternally. I hope that one day their names will be engraved on a bronze plaque alongside their photographs and be displayed for posterity.

The pioneers who opened the untrodden frontier of kosen-rufu in the United States were heroic, ordinary people who put everything they had into their pioneering mission. We must never allow the flower garden of the Soka Gakkai, which is the crystallization of their sweat and tears, to be trampled upon by mean-spirited individuals who are strangers to hard work and utterly lacking in gratitude.

WINTER NEVER FAILS TO TURN TO SPRING

The original Buddha, Nichiren Daishonin, more than anyone, warmly recognized people's hardships and efforts. In a well-known letter to the lay nun Myoichi, who had suffered the loss of her husband, he writes: "Those who believe in the Lotus Sutra are as if in winter, but winter always turns to spring. Never, from ancient times on, has anyone heard or seen of winter turning back to autumn. Nor have we ever heard of a believer in the Lotus Sutra who turned into an ordinary person. The sutra reads, 'If there are those who hear the Law, then not a one will fail to attain Buddhahood.'

"Your husband gave his life for the Lotus Sutra. His entire livelihood depended on a small fief, and that was confiscated because of his faith in the Lotus Sutra. Surely that equals giving his life for the Lotus Sutra. The boy Snow Mountains was able to give his body for half a verse of a Buddhist teaching, and Bodhisattva Medicine King was able to burn his arms as an offering to the Buddha because both were sages, and it was like pouring water on fire. But your husband was an ordinary person, so it was like putting paper in fire. Therefore, he must certainly have received blessings as great as theirs" (WND-1, 536).

In this passage, the Daishonin asserts that those who selflessly dedicate themselves for the sake of Buddhism will definitely become Buddhas just as winter unfailingly turns into spring. No matter what problems we may now be facing, we SGI members, who embrace the Mystic Law, will not be defeated and will definitely become happy. The spring of happiness and hope will definitely arrive.

"Then not a one will fail to attain Buddhahood" [LS, 41], declares the Daishonin, citing the Lotus Sutra. Here he is explaining that Shakyamuni Buddha expounded the Law [the Lotus Sutra] to enable all people without exception to attain Buddhahood. It is therefore inconceivable that the children of the Buddha, who earnestly practice this Law, could not become Buddhas. He assures his lay follower Myoichi that those who have been persecuted because of their faith in the Lotus Sutra will receive the greatest blessing — that of attaining the state of Buddhahood.

As lay believers, we, too, may encounter persecutions or unpleasantness from others because of our correct practice of Nichiren Daishonin's Buddhism. But by overcoming these kinds of obstacles, we can develop great good fortune of a magnitude that truly defies the imagination. Viewed in this light, I hope you will be convinced that the current problems [with the Nichiren Shoshu priesthood] have profound significance for the further great advance of the SGI.

The Daishonin continues in the same Gosho: "[Your husband] is probably watching his wife and children in the heavenly mirrors of the sun and moon every moment of the day and night. Since you and your children are ordinary persons, you cannot see or hear him.... But never doubt that he is protecting you" (WND-1, 536).

This passage is extremely profound. The friends of the Mystic Law belonging to the SGI family will continue their deeply meaningful and valuable journeys of life eternally while freely interacting with one another, transcending life and death. I cannot help feeling that the great pioneers of American kosen-rufu, whom I mentioned just a moment ago, are watching over this gathering today with serene, smiling faces.

THE FUTURE IS DETERMINED BY OUR PRESENT CHOICES

Two days ago [on September 27], in what is a truly historic decision, U.S. President George Bush announced a program of sweeping reductions of nuclear arms stockpiles. The reductions include the destruction of all ground-launched battlefield nuclear weapons and the removal of all nuclear cruise missiles deployed at sea or underwater — a move that would free U.S. submarines from carrying nuclear weapons in peacetime.

Only the day before, I delivered a speech titled "The Age of Soft Power" at Harvard University. It is vital that soft power — knowledge, information, culture and systems — replace hard power — military might, political authority and wealth — as the mainstream in the post–Cold War world order. President Bush's announcement was symbolic of this momentous trend.

This move is a great source of joy to me personally, as someone who has been traveling throughout the world to carry out the mission I inherited from my late mentor, Josei Toda — to work for the abolition of nuclear weapons.

In his address to the nation announcing the arms reductions, President Bush said: "Perhaps we are closer to that new world than ever before. The future is ours to influence, to shape, to mold.... It has been said, 'Destiny is not a matter of chance, it is a matter of choice; it is not a thing to be waited for, it is a thing to be achieved.'... Let them say [of us], that we led where destiny required us to lead — to a more peaceful, hopeful future. We cannot give a more precious gift to the children of the world."

He is saying that the future is determined by our present choices. I could not agree more.

Mr. Toda cried of the need to "rip out the claws that lie hidden in the very depths" of the nuclear arms issue (see *The Human Revolution*, 1780). Choosing the desire for peace over the devilish nature of nuclear weapons is the path that humankind has continued to pray for and now, at last, has reached the start of (see *The Human Revolution*, 1781).

The era of soft power is an age of the spirit, culture and human beings. And it is we who are the leading players in this era. Let us advance even more vigorously our movement to spread a future of hope throughout this great land of the United States of America and the world.

I would now like to focus on how religions, in a general sense, change in character and grow authoritarian.

The original purpose of religion is to help people find happiness. But we find quite frequently that religions, abandoning their doctrines, act in a way that generates unhappiness. We see teachings of love turn into evil behavior, compassionate creeds become the rationale for atrocities — all of which causes people to suffer. Why is it that religion undergoes this kind of evil transformation?

Paul Tillich (1886–1965), a renowned philosopher and Harvard University professor, said: "Affirming the finite in the name of the holy as the majesty of the ultimate, as the Divine, is called demonization. If the finite were elevated to the level of ultimate, then it would strive to subjugate all other finite things. And if it found it impossible to do so, it would seek their destruction."

In Nichiren Daishonin's Buddhism, "the ultimate" corresponds to the Gohonzon. If, for example, people who are of finite existence should raise themselves to the same level of dignity as the Gohonzon and declare that they were "one and the same [as the Gohonzon]," we could say that the "demonization" of our religion has started. Once this happens, such people assume a condescending attitude toward all others and try to force people to submit to their control. This is truly an abuse of authority. Then they try to destroy anyone who refuses to yield like slaves to them. I hope that this helps you understand the causes of the insane behavior [among Nichiren Shoshu priests] of disrupting the harmonious unity of believers working to achieve kosen-rufu.

Tillich especially stresses the threats posed by demonization of the church and clergy, naming examples such as belief in the infallibility of the pope. He says that such institutions only "convey the holy" or are "symbolic of the holy."

He continues: "It is for this reason that an institution which is demoniacally destructive will attack all other institutions and conflicting cultures. Similarly, individuals who engage in profanization become fanatical."

Asserting that [singing "Ode to Joy" in] Beethoven's *Ninth Symphony*, which was performed earlier at this meeting, is slanderous [as the priests have done] is a typical example of this kind of attack on culture.

Born in Prussia, Tillich was driven from University of Frankfurt for his outspoken criticism of the Nazi regime. In deifying and investing absolute power in Hitler, a finite being, and in the Third Reich, a finite regime, the Nazis had turned into demons, just as Tillich outlines. The concentration camp at Auschwitz bears stark testimony to this.

With its worship of the state and worship of an individual, Nazism could be termed a kind of religion. Perhaps in Tillich's mind as he expounded his theory of the "demonization of religion" was the recurring thought of the tragedies that had visited his country. We must absolutely never allow such a tragedy to be repeated.

THE HUMANIZATION OF THE WORLD

The author Elie Wiesel, with whom I met the other day [September 25], said in relating his experience in Nazi concentration camps that it is essential that religion contribute to humankind. I sensed his fervent conviction behind these words.

In contrast, the belief that people should serve religion leads to fanaticism and the creation of hell. I believe that this was the professor's sentiment when he told me of his experience. Professor Wiesel said: "The original purpose of religion is to unite, not separate, people. At the same time, however, we must not forget the fact that, during the past few centuries, religion has perpetrated a history of bloodshed in the name of God. For that reason, religion now requires a rehumanization."

I believe that the world is seeking a rehumanization of religion. As long as human beings exist, there will always be some kind of religious spirit. For this reason, the humanization of religion must form the core for the humanization of the world.

Let us continue to spread the ideals of humanism throughout the world through our open activities of promoting peace, culture and education based on Buddhism. The time has come when humankind must choose hope toward humanizing the world.

What, then, is fanaticism? Dr. Tillich once described the psychological foundation of fanaticism as the "suppression of doubt," saying: "Those who choose or prefer the repression of their questions to their uncertainty are referred to as fanatic. Led to the frontier of other thinking or belief, they fall back on old certainties. Thus they show aggression toward autonomous thought, aiming to bring into subjection new possibilities."

To illustrate, it is like the case of people who, while inwardly aware that the SGI is correct, suppress that awareness, not wanting to acknowledge it. Instead, they attack those who outwardly express support for the organization.

Such people hate most of all those who show outward support because they disturb their unstable and unconfident state of mind. In fact, such people feel anger and revulsion toward their own inner awareness of what is correct.

Thus fanatics attack other people, seeking to make them like themselves, or, where this is not possible, trying to destroy them. I think that Tillich's analysis shows profound insight.

A glimpse at the psychological makeup of such people reveals that they are deeply unhappy and to be pitied. Such people caustically attack the children of the Buddha, seeking to bend them to their will. If unable to do so, they then attempt to destroy our conviction and undermine our confident advance.

Also, fanatic people are characterized by their refusal to enter into dialogue. Discussion is impossible for fanatics. If they were to earnestly discuss contested issues, their repression of their own questions would become untenable.

In other words, because inwardly they are highly unstable, like a tottering structure made of building blocks, they spurn the company of, and have no desire to talk to, persons who may upset their inner balance. Correct faith, however, can be cultivated only in the kind of atmosphere where anything at all may be openly discussed.

THOSE WHO DISREGARD THE LAW DESTROY BUDDHISM

In Buddhism, the Law is absolute. Nichiren Daishonin always revealed through his example the necessity of practicing in exact accord with the Buddha's teachings. In all of his actions, the Daishonin conducted himself as the votary of the Lotus Sutra. This is of great significance.

From the standpoint of Buddhism, if there is someone who disregards the Law and claims an absolute status for himself, the actions of such a person are those of the devil.

In the Gosho, Nichiren Daishonin cites a passage from the Nirvana Sutra that reads, "If there is any person who does not abide by the expositions of the Buddha, you should understand that this person is a servant of the devil" (WND-2, 6).

In his four dictums, Nichiren Daishonin denounces Zen as the "invention of the heavenly devil." Adherents of the Zen school ignore the teachings of the sutras and make their own minds their master. Failing to carry out a correct practice, they hold that the mind, just as it is, is the Buddha. The devil king easily finds a home amid such arrogance.

Should someone forget the Daishonin's oft-repeated admonition to "become the master of your mind rather than let your mind master you" (WND-1, 486), that person will begin to career away from the correct path of faith, becoming the scion of devils and demons.

If any followers of Nichiren Daishonin should slight the importance or deny the validity of the Gosho, the basic scripture of the Latter Day of the Law, and instead make personal feelings and interests the foundation of their practice, their actions can aptly be described as those of the devil king.

Tillich visited Japan in 1960. That was the year I visited the United States for the first time, taking the first step for worldwide kosen-rufu.

In Japan, Tillich made some comments on Buddhism. One of the principal points he made came in the form of the question "Is Buddhism a living religion?" He questioned the significance of the established Japanese Buddhist schools that had long been reduced to mere shells.

In Japan, the Soka Gakkai has created a history in which religion has been revived as a moving force of society and as a guideline for the contemporary world.

At the time of his visit, Tillich was quick to point out that the practice of Zen, which is relatively well known in the West, poses the danger of plunging the practitioner into the "arrogance of regarding himself as absolute."

He also identified two methods whereby the "demonization of religion" can be warded against. The first way is secularization, or denying religion itself. In modern times, this trend has been rapidly promoted by persons who have had firsthand experience of conflicts involving religion. The drawback of secularization, however, is that it poses the danger that spirituality itself may become lost and that human beings may be reduced to mere machines.

The other method that he mentioned is that of establishing a path whereby individual believers can gain personal and direct contact with "the ultimate" without any mediating parties. The Buddhism of Nichiren Daishonin is the great teaching that enables all people, wherever they may be, to carry out the highest practice of faith and gain the supreme benefit of attaining Buddhahood. It is the teaching that enables each person to cultivate the greatest wisdom, lead the most respectable of lives and attain the greatest happiness.

Because of these qualities, authoritarianism can never take hold; the "demonization of religion," which oppresses human beings, has no connection to the Daishonin's Buddhism. If there should appear any people who, while purporting to be followers of the Daishonin, demonstrate such evil tendencies, such people are definitely not true followers of the Daishonin. This I resolutely declare.

At any rate, in Buddhism, if you can recognize a devil for

what it is, you can definitely defeat it through faith. I hope that, in light of the Gosho and the sutras, in light of reason and common sense, and with the eye of faith, you will wisely and unerringly discern the true nature of the current problem [with the priesthood].

LIFE AND DEATH: THE ULTIMATE HUMAN FRONTIER

In his poem "Life and Death," which I fondly read as a youth, Walt Whitman, the poet of democracy, sings:

> *The two old, simple problems ever intertwined,*
> *Close home, elusive, present, baffled, grappled.*
> *By each successive age insoluble, pass'd on,*
> *To ours to-day — and we pass on the same.*

No matter how much wealth, authority or fame a person may possess, the problem of life and death is a fundamental issue that absolutely no one can avoid. Still, at no time in history have people been able to arrive at a solution to this problem of life and death. Even Walt Whitman, after earnestly grappling with the issue of death, could find no recourse other than to leave its solution to future generations.

All of you who embrace faith in, practice and study the Buddhist Law are great pioneers who are challenging this ultimate human frontier of life and death.

Dr. Linus Pauling and I discussed the notion that the twenty-first century would be a Century of Life. The focus of the world's foremost thinkers is now beginning to turn to the problem of life and death and to the nature of life itself. Currently, I am also preparing a dialogue on the theme of life and health with Dr. René Simard (an authority on cancer research), vice rector of the University of Montreal in Canada. [This was eventually published as *On Being Human*.]

Nichiren Daishonin states: "Today, when Nichiren and his followers recite the words Nam-myoho-renge-kyo, they are illuminating the darkness of birth and death, making it clear, so that the wisdom fire of nirvana may shine forth. . . . [When Nichiren and his followers recite Nam-myoho-renge-kyo], they are burning the firewood of earthly desires, summoning up the wisdom fire of bodhi or enlightenment" (OTT, 10–11). This passage explains the principles of "the sufferings of birth and death are nirvana" and "earthly desires are enlightenment."

While saving a detailed discussion for another occasion, I want to say that when I studied this passage under President Toda during my youth, I had the sense that I was awakening to the lucid, great philosophic principles of the Buddhism of Nichiren Daishonin, who revealed his teaching for the sake of all humankind.

Through my practice over the course of the forty-four years since my conversion, I have grown steadily, ever more strongly and profoundly convinced that every single teaching of the Daishonin is true and valid.

It is not true that because we practice faith in the Mystic Law our lives will be free of worries. And of course, it is certain that we will eventually die. Nevertheless, through our mind of faith, we can illuminate our lives with the brilliant light of wisdom and the flame of happiness shining forth from the depths of our lives.

For this reason, no matter what happens, as long as you embrace faith, you will never be deadlocked; you have nothing to fear. Turning everything into a source of energy to advance still further, you can continue vigorously climbing the hill of growth and hope in life. By challenging your circumstances with composure in this fashion, you can perfectly establish a vast and eternally unshakable inner state as if you were kings and queens of life.

About his follower Nanjo Tokimitsu's father, Nichiren Daishonin states: "When he was alive, he was a Buddha in life, and now he is a Buddha in death. He is a Buddha in both life and death" (WND-1, 456). This also applies to the great seniors in faith whom you yourselves have known. In life, great good fortune, and in death, great satisfaction — in fact, a single person can enact an infinitely respectable drama of life and death in this world. I hope that you will continue making tenacious efforts based on the three pillars of faith, practice and study, all the while cherishing lofty pride in being philosophers who embrace the great Buddhist Law. Those who do so will realize unparalleled victory and will lead lives of unparalleled happiness.

TOWARD THE NEW WORLD!

Lastly, I would like to read from another of Whitman's poems ["Pioneers! O Pioneers"]:

> *For we cannot tarry here,*
> *We must march my darlings, we must bear the brunt of*
> *   danger,*
> *We the youthful sinewy races, all the rest on us depend,*
> *Pioneers! O pioneers!*

We can rest at ease so long as the United States, the pioneer in the advancement of worldwide kosen-rufu, is strong and healthy. It was with this thought in mind that thirty-one years ago, in opening the path of worldwide kosen-rufu, I came to this country first.

The advance of America is the advance of the world. An inch of growth for America is an inch of growth for the rest of the world. I am convinced that, in the future, America will of necessity become the central stage for the SGI movement.

Whitman's poem continues:

> *All the past we leave behind,*
> *We debouch upon a newer mightier world, varied world,*
> *Fresh and strong the world we seize, world of labor*
> *   and the march,*
> *Pioneers! O pioneers!*

We, too, are cheerfully advancing toward a new world. To create an age of the people, of freedom and of equality — in short, an age of the human being — we must compose a history of pioneering, all the while speaking out with courage and hope.

Whitman also calls out to the mothers, wives and daughters:

> *O you daughters of the West!*
> *O you young and elder daughters! O you mothers and you*
> *   wives!*
> *Never must you be divided, in our ranks you move united,*
> *Pioneers! O pioneers!*

I hope that, no matter what happens, all of you friends within the SGI-USA will continue advancing — always harmoniously, always cheerfully, always wisely and always in beautiful unity.

I hope that the members of the men's and young men's divisions will always respect the views of the members of the women's and young women's divisions.

I hope that those of you who are wives will cherish your husbands, that those of you who are husbands will cherish your wives, and that, throughout your lives, you will strive to create at home and in your friendships an atmosphere that is pervaded with a sense of mutual respect and mutual encouragement.

The paths of faith manifesting itself in daily life and of firmly establishing indestructible good fortune in your life lie amid the seemingly mundane reality of your daily lives and amid the actions you take based on simple common sense.

May the great country of America flourish and prosper! Commence your advance with pride in knowing that you have the central role to play in worldwide kosen-rufu! With these words, I conclude my speech on this brilliant day.

Common Sense, Steadiness and Character Are the Basis for Development

—m—

JOINT CONFERENCE FOR LEADERS OF THE SGI ORGANIZATIONS
IN THE UNITED STATES AND CANADA, SOKA UNIVERSITY
LOS ANGELES, CALABASAS, CALIFORNIA, SEPTEMBER 30, 1991

I EXTEND A HEARTY WELCOME to all the Canadian members who have traveled so far, and I offer my warmest thanks to all the leaders of the SGI-USA for their continuing efforts.

Since today is a meeting of representatives, I hope you will regard my speech as part of your training as leaders. When the leaders grow, the organization moves forward and produces capable people. Strides made by the organizations in the United States and Canada represent progress for the entire world.

Leaders must learn all kinds of things. So long as you polish your intellect and character, your juniors will continue to benefit from you. I hope you will recognize that common sense, steadfastness and character form the foundation for great development.

PERCEIVING THE TRUTH WITH COMMON SENSE

Lafcadio Hearn (1850–1904) [an American writer and aficionado of things Japanese] was a journalist who worked for several publications in the United States before moving to Japan, where he eventually became a citizen and took the name Yakumo Koizumi.

Mr. Hearn lived in a number of places in Japan, including Matsue in Shimane Prefecture, as well as in Kumamoto, Kobe and Tokyo. He played an instrumental role in opening cultural exchange between Japan and North America — between East and West.

Among the many Japanese folktales that he documented is one called "Common Sense." It is the tale of how the common sense of an ordinary person saves a priest who has been deceived by an apparition.

As the story goes, there once lived an erudite priest in the mountains somewhere in Kansai. This priest had almost no contact with the secular world. One day, a hunter came to make offerings at the temple. The priest told him that Bodhisattva Universal Worthy, who is described in the Lotus Sutra, had begun appearing at the temple every night. The priest believed that this wondrous occurrence was a benefit of his having practiced diligently for long years. He urged the hunter to stay the night so that he could see the noble bodhisattva.

The hunter readily agreed to stay, but he remained dubious about the priest's story, for the more he thought about it, the more unlikely it seemed. The hunter also spoke to a young acolyte at the temple who also claimed to have seen the bodhisattva on a number of occasions. The hunter's feeling that something was amiss grew stronger.

Together, they waited for the dead of night. Then, in the east, there appeared a dazzling white light, like a star, that grew rapidly. After a moment, the light began to take shape, and Bodhisattva Universal Worthy appeared, riding a snow-white elephant with six tusks — just as he is described in the sutra. The priest and his young assistant prostrated themselves before the image and began to pray desperately.

Without warning, the hunter stood up with his bow in hand and fired an arrow at the bodhisattva. There was a tremendous noise like a thunderclap, and instantly the white light vanished.

The priest was beside himself with despair and anger. Tears streaming down his face, he cursed the hunter: "O miserable man! O most wretched and wicked man!"

"Reverend sir, please try to calm yourself and listen to me," said the hunter, quietly.

"Let me now assure you..." he continued. "That what you saw was not Bodhisattva Universal Worthy but a goblinry intended to deceive you — perhaps even to destroy you. I beg that you will try to control your feelings until daybreak. Then I will prove to you the truth of what I have said."

As the dawn began to break, they discovered a thin trail of blood. Following this trail, they found the carcass of a great raccoon dog shot by an arrow. The raccoon dog had transformed itself into the apparition.

How had the hunter known that it was the work of this mischievous creature? He was deeply perceptive, realizing that if the real Bodhisattva Universal Worthy had chosen to make an appearance, he would surely have done so only to someone who had been practicing the Lotus Sutra assiduously. But the young acolyte, whose practice was far from advanced, and even the hunter himself had been able to see the apparition quite clearly. This convinced the hunter that his suspicions were correct.

Surely, he thought, in Buddhism, benefit is dependent on the state of one's practice. Should the result appear irrespective of whether one practices, then, he reasoned, it could not have anything to do with Buddhism, the teaching based on the law of cause and effect, but was merely the trickery of a malicious demon.

Mr. Hearn concludes the story: "The priest, although a learned and pious person, had easily been deceived by a raccoon dog. But the hunter, an ignorant and irreligious man, was gifted with strong common sense, and by mother-wit alone he was able at once to detect and to destroy a dangerous illusion."

This is an old Japanese folktale and is not related to Nichiren Daishonin's Buddhism. Nevertheless, it is a story that highlights in a simple, straightforward manner the dangerous potential religions have for making people ignorant and foolish. No matter how much knowledge we may possess, we cannot use it properly if we lack sound common sense.

REASON WINS OVER AUTHORITY

Common sense has also played an indispensable role in U.S. history, when the nation was founded and when its independence was established.

Without common sense, religion eventually develops into blind belief and fanaticism, which have no place in Buddhism. The Daishonin writes: "Buddhism is reason. Reason will win over your lord" (WND-1, 839). In other words, reason will win over authority.

There is a saying that the truth is simple. In contrast, never will one find so much argument for argument's sake as in the words of those who, in order to pass off some falsehood, deliberately set out to make an issue complex and difficult. Like the raccoon dog that changed itself into a bodhisattva, such people are skillful at embellishment. It is merely ignoring the law of cause and effect if, for example, people claim to be superior on the basis of their position in Buddhism without making efforts to propagate the Law with the spirit of laying down their lives. This is not Buddhism. Such talk resembles that of an evil spirit appearing as a bodhisattva.

Only if your practice is "one and inseparable" from the Buddha's does your status become "one and inseparable" from the Buddha's, too. From the standpoint of reason and the common sense of Buddhism, this is self-evident. If you are armed with this understanding, you will not be deceived.

Consider the following statements:

"Just are those who actually advance kosen-rufu."

"People of questionable character have questionable faith, too."

"That they keep changing their story proves they are lying."

"They are highhanded and refuse to enter into a dialogue because they are trying to hide something."

Such statements are clear. All we need to do is recognize reason and have common sense when we view the problem with the Nichiren Shoshu priesthood. What is judged as peculiar by the standards of the average person's common sense is just that—peculiar.

Moreover, since we possess the "clear mirror" of the Daishonin's writings, we must use his teachings to illuminate the truth and absolutely never follow something that is amiss.

NICHIREN DAISHONIN'S WRITINGS ARE OUR STANDARD

If things are left unexplained, many people may fail to understand even that which is crystal clear. So today, I would like to say a few words regarding the traitorous acts committed by Mimbu Niko [one of the five senior priests] and Hakiri Sanenaga [the steward of the Minobu area] against their mentor, Nichiren Daishonin, after his death.

Some priests are now going around branding the Soka Gakkai as having committed the "slander of Hakiri."

What is the standard for the Daishonin's disciples? It is nothing other than his writings. If we always bear in mind and base ourselves on this extremely clear and explicit principle, everything will become crystal clear.

The Daishonin strictly admonishes us, "To forget the original teacher who had brought one the water of wisdom from the great ocean of the Lotus Sutra and instead follow another would surely cause one to sink into the endless sufferings of birth and death" (WND-1, 747). To follow the Daishonin, who is the "original teacher," is the very meaning of our faith.

Nikko Shonin, the second high priest, revered Nichiren Daishonin as the original Buddha and strictly upheld his teaching. The other senior priests, by contrast, forgot the teaching of the original teacher and transferred their allegiance elsewhere They haphazardly concocted false doctrines to accommodate persons of power and authority, whom they feared, and succumbed to the allures of the secular world.

In "Reply to Lord Hara," Nikko Shonin describes in detail the actions of Mimbu Niko, who went against the Daishonin's teaching. Although Nikko Shonin repeatedly pointed out with strict compassion this priest's serious mistakes, his warnings were not heeded. This led to Nikko Shonin's departure from Mount Minobu.

At the conclusion of the lengthy "Reply to Lord Hara," Nikko Shonin states: "Needless to say, you should clearly understand that the Daishonin's teaching tells us that if we do not disavow those [evil] teachers who go against Nichiren Daishonin, we will be committing an offense ourselves. You should consider, in particular, how the Daishonin must feel at this turn of events" (*Hennentai Gosho*, p. 1734).

Nikko Shonin makes it clear that if someone follows priests who have turned against Nichiren Daishonin and who have become enemies of the correct teacher who strictly upheld the Daishonin's teaching, then that person is guilty of the same offense as those evil priests.

It goes without saying that correct teachers are those who conduct themselves in accord with the Daishonin's teaching, and evil teachers are those who act contrary to it. To say that we should follow someone who goes against this principle just because he is a priest, or a priest of high rank, contravenes Nikko Shonin's precept.

Citing T'ien-t'ai's *Profound Meaning of the Lotus Sutra*, the Daishonin writes, "All assertions that lack scriptural proof are to be branded as false" (WND-1, 56). If some think that anything they say or do out of personal interest and emotionalism should be accepted and followed because of their authority, in the absence of any documentary proof as well, such people are evil teachers of the same ilk as Mimbu Niko.

Where, for example, is it written that destroying the unity of believers is permissible?

The Gosho and the sutras make it clear that destroying the unity of believers is one of the five cardinal sins in Buddhism (see WND-2, 251). Nittatsu, the sixty-sixth high priest, once emphatically directed priests not to encourage members to leave the Soka Gakkai and join temple groups, and Nikken himself once clearly remarked, "Promoting such a movement is the wrong way to spread the teaching."

Nichiren Daishonin teaches that those who follow teachers who go against the sutras will fall into the hell of incessant suffering. He emphasizes: "T'ien-t'ai said that to accept and put faith in the doctrines of evil teachers is the same as drinking poison. You should deeply consider this and beware!" (WND-1, 61).

According to the same Gosho, the evil teachers to whom he is referring are priests who "despise, hate, envy, or bear grudges against" those who correctly embrace the Lotus Sutra (WND-1, 61). Such persons, in other words, while saying that they revere the Law, in fact despise and hate those who are actually spreading and propagating faith in it. The Daishonin says that to follow and place faith in such evil priests is the same as drinking poison.

Nichiren also says, "Just as all the different kinds of plants and trees come forth from the earth, so all the various teachings of the Buddha are spread by persons" (WND-1, 61). It is because there are people who spread the teaching that the power of the Law becomes manifest.

SLANDERING THOSE WHO SPREAD THE LAW IS SLANDERING THE LAW ITSELF

Nichiren teaches, "To speak ill of that person is to speak ill of the Law, just as to show contempt for the child is to show contempt for the parents" (WND-1, 61). The "person" here, in the specific sense, refers to Nichiren Daishonin. In a broad sense, however, it indicates his followers, we Soka Gakkai members who are promoting kosen-rufu. To speak ill of those who are propagating the Law even at the cost of their lives is to speak ill of the Mystic Law. To show contempt for the Buddha's children is to show contempt for the Buddha.

We can regard this as documentary proof that to speak ill of and look down on the SGI members who are opening a great path of global kosen-rufu is to speak ill of and look down on the Gohonzon and Nichiren Daishonin himself.

Nichiren writes: "How can they fail to be ashamed of such actions! The pains of hell are frightful indeed. Beware of them! Beware of them!" (WND-1, 61). Regarding the current priesthood situation, the truth of the matter is certainly known to the original Buddha. The Daishonin states that such people should be ashamed of their actions and should fear the sufferings of hell.

One must not allow teachers who go against the Daishonin to carry on in their ways — this is the fundamental spirit of Nikko Shonin. It is the spirit with which he abandoned Mount Minobu, where the pure flow of faith had become polluted due to the actions of Hakiri Sanenaga, who had been misled by the evil teacher Niko.

In this way, he took the first step toward accomplishing the will of Nichiren Daishonin — that of establishing the "sanctuary. . . of Hommon-ji temple. . .at Mount Fuji" (WND-2, 993) — and toward the realization of worldwide kosen-rufu.

Ultimately, whether we practice in exact accord with the Daishonin's teaching or we turn against it alone determines whether we are disciples of Nikko Shonin or followers of Niko and Hakiri. When we make this our standard of judgment, it becomes perfectly clear that we SGI members are faithfully following the three treasures of the Buddha, the Law and the Buddhist Order.

Nittatsu [the sixty-sixth high priest] once lectured [in 1969] on the circumstances that prompted Nikko Shonin to leave Mount Minobu. He said, "Niko returned to Minobu in 1285, the year after the third memorial service for the Daishonin." Nikko Shonin was extremely happy to see him and appointed him chief instructor of the priests at Minobu.

"As time passed, however," Nittatsu continued, "Hakiri gradually became very close to Niko and, influenced by the latter's lackadaisical attitude in faith, eventually committed four acts of slander."

The four slanderous acts committed by Hakiri were as follows:

First, he built a statue of Shakyamuni as an object of worship. As to the aspersions being cast that the Soka Gakkai is acting like Hakiri, it should be pointed out that on no occasion has the Soka Gakkai done anything of this kind. On the contrary, it is the SGI that has spread faith in the Gohonzon to people in as many as 115 countries worldwide [now 192].

Second, Hakiri visited Shinto shrines for worship. The only places to which Soka Gakkai members have gone to pay homage are Nichiren Shoshu temples, and the number of visits Soka Gakkai members made to the head temple, Taiseki-ji, comes to an astounding total of seventy million. To claim that the Soka Gakkai is like Hakiri would be to say that Taiseki-ji is a heretical temple.

Third, Hakiri erected a Nembutsu monument in Fukushi, and, fourth, he built a temple for the Nembutsu school. These last two offenses entailed making donations to slanderous teachings. Nichiren Shoshu is the only sect to which the Soka Gakkai has made donations. Never in the seven hundred years since the Daishonin's advent, and never in the history of Buddhism, has there been a lay body that has made larger contributions for the sake of the Law. This is not something I say out of pride; rather, it is a plain fact.

To compare the Soka Gakkai to Hakiri would imply that the contributions made to Nichiren Shoshu constitute slander. In that case, wouldn't the priesthood themselves be asserting that their head temple is slanderous? In fact, just as the Daishonin states that to speak ill of the "person" is to speak ill of the Law, so to slander us in this way is to slander the Mystic Law we have been spreading.

Nittatsu went on: "Nikko Shonin cautioned [Hakiri] three times, but the letter failed to heed him. Unable to put up with [Hakiri's slanderous actions] any longer, Nikko Shonin, in accord with the Daishonin's words, 'If the steward violates my teacher, I will no longer dwell here.' Nikko Shonin left Minobu and moved to Mount Fuji."

Many people have pointed out that if the Soka Gakkai is to be likened to Hakiri, then, logically speaking, the priesthood should take its leave of all [356] temples donated by the Soka Gakkai, saying that the Daishonin's life does not dwell there.

Nittatsu continued: "Abandoning Minobu and coming to Fuji with the Daishonin's ashes and the Dai-Gohonzon of the sanctuary of the essential teaching, which was inscribed on October 12, 1279, Nikko Shonin established Taiseki-ji thanks to the donations of Nanjo Tokimitsu, the steward of the Ueno area. And now, as a result of the great aspiration of Daisaku Ikeda, head of all Nichiren Shoshu lay organizations, the sanctuary of the essential teaching will be completed in the year 1972."

Nittatsu referred to the Grand Main Temple as the "santuary of the essential teaching." While these remarks were made before the structure's completion, I wonder what the present leaders of the priesthood think about these words by their late mentor.

Incidentally, recent scientific studies conducted by the Japanese Ministry of Education's Bureau of Statistics concluded that "On the Receiving of the Three Great Secret Laws" (in which Nichiren Daishonin entrusts the construction of the sanctuary of the essential teaching to his disciples of later generations) is genuine beyond any doubt. While for us, this conclusion is only natural, there are those who have long claimed this writing to be a forgery. We must call into question, therefore, what these persons — who include adherents from all other Nichiren schools — have done to realize the Daishonin's will for the establishment of the sanctuary of the essential teaching. [The Grand Main Temple was destroyed by Nikken in 1998–2000.]

Nittatsu praised the Soka Gakkai's sincere efforts for kosen-rufu as comparable to those of Nanjo Tokimitsu, who contributed the land for and promoted the establishment of Taiseki-ji. At the ceremony for the dedication of the newly rebuilt main hall of Myoren-ji temple in 1974, Nittatsu stated: "Now, in 1974, exactly 642 years after Nanjo Tokimitsu's death, there is an outstanding individual of great devotion who has embraced the spirit of Nanjo Tokimitsu. This is Daisaku Ikeda, head of all Nichiren Shoshu lay organizations. Thanks to the efforts of this person, both at the head temple and at branch temples, old buildings have been reconstructed, new temples have been built, believers have been increasing daily, and in one great leap Nichiren Shoshu has become known throughout the world as a major religion. This is by virtue of Daisaku Ikeda's profound faith and his meritorious accomplishments. Indeed, he may be called the Nanjo Tokimitsu of our age."

Although I have no wish to praise myself, I have taken the liberty of mentioning the late high priest's words today merely to set the record straight from the standpoint of Nichiren Shoshu history. Nittatsu himself even went to the trouble of having his remarks on this occasion engraved on a monument to remain as an eternal reminder.

The priesthood's current leaders disparage the person Nittatsu called the "Nanjo Tokimitsu of our age," calling him another Hakiri. Neither the Soka Gakkai nor I have changed in any way. What has changed is the priesthood's view. Haven't the members of the priesthood turned against their late mentor, Nittatsu?

In retrospect, the decadent priest Niko, who accommodated much slander, did not carry out the practice of propagation. Moreover, he was fond of drinking and conducted himself disgracefully. He went so far as to slander Nikko Shonin for indulging in reading non-Buddhist literature. As a result, the pure flow of the Daishonin's teaching ceased to exist at Minobu.

I will explain the unwarranted charge that Nikko Shonin indulged in reading non-Buddhist literature on another occasion [see "The Mystic Law Gives New Life to All Knowledge," page 177]. But suffice it to say that to follow a teacher who attempts to destroy the teaching of Nichiren Daishonin is tantamount to turning against the Daishonin, Nikko Shonin and their successors who correctly revered the Law. We must be absolutely clear on this point.

A DICTATOR LABELS, THEN LIQUIDATES, HIS ENEMIES

The fraudulent misinterpretation and manipulation of facts and circumstances have been part of the standard repertoire used by dictators throughout history. Take the Soviet dictator Joseph Stalin, for example. The purges conducted under his regime claimed untold lives — some believe tens of millions. Certainly millions were imprisoned, tortured and executed on trumped-up charges.

The father of my close friend Chingiz Aitmatov, the Soviet author (formerly a member of the Soviet Presidential Council), and the husband of Natalya Sats, president of the Moscow State Children's Musical Theater, were victims of the mass executions.

Stalin's reign was one that saw the Soviet citizens turning against one another and Communist Party members stabbing one another in the back. To retain his grip on power, the Soviet dictator with impunity inflicted cruel suffering on the citizens who believed in and trusted him. Such insanity has rarely been seen in the pages of history.

I will not go into detail here, but suffice it to say that Stalin's typical method of operation was to falsely label those whom he wanted out of his way.

Former Soviet premier Nikita Khrushchev wrote, "The mass repressions at this time were made under the slogan of a fight against the Trotskyites [anti-Leninists]." In other words, Stalin ordered his underlings to go out and execute people he claimed were out to "destroy the teachings of Lenin." This is comparable, for example, to calling someone a slanderer or a present-day Hakiri and meting out summary punishment. Once stamped with this label, Soviet people were executed without a trial. Facts were utterly irrelevant.

Khrushchev continues, "Stalin thought that now he could decide all things alone and all he needed were people to fill the stage; he treated all others in such a way that they could only listen to and praise him." This perfectly illustrates the diabolical nature of authority. In Buddhist terms, we would say that a devil had entered the Soviet leader's body.

In terms of his humanity, this despot was indeed the exact opposite of Lenin. Khrushchev continued, "[Stalin] discarded the Leninist method of convincing and educating, and he abandoned the method of ideological struggle for that of administrative violence, mass repressions and terror." Once Stalin had decided that certain individuals were anti-Leninist, he would have them tortured until they confessed to his charges. His motto was "Beat, beat and, once again, beat." Instructing his underlings in these methods, he oversaw the torture and execution of his fellow citizens.

It is common for tyrants to think that if they continue their relentless oppression, the people will eventually be beaten into submission and throw themselves on the tyrant's mercy. This is the ultimate expression of contempt toward human beings. It exemplifies a demonic arrogance.

Purging Those of Distinguished Service

The whole country had turned into a living hell. Stalin executed many of those who had rendered distinguished service to the cause of the Soviet Revolution. One eminent person wrote with great poignancy: "There is no more bitter misery than to sit in the jail of a government for which I have always fought.... I have not been guilty of even one of the things with which I am charged, and my heart is clean of even the shadow of baseness.... My whole case is a typical example of provocation, slander and violation of the elementary basis of revolutionary legality."

Thus, the ideals of the Revolution were destroyed at the very roots. Despotic leaders still operate this way today.

The failed coup d'état in the Soviet Union last month [August 1991] clearly highlighted for the entire world the folly and absurdity of the remaining Stalinist elements in Soviet politics.

Stalin, by instigating an insane witch hunt among his fellow citizens under the pretext of disciplining anti-Leninist forces, betrayed Lenin more than anyone, for Stalin was the one responsible for the ultimate failure of the Revolution.

Buddhism and Communism, however, are two entirely different things. In Buddhism, we must absolutely never allow despotic authority to prevail. We cannot permit kosen-rufu to be reduced to an empty dream by persons who would arbitrarily condemn us, for example, as guilty of the same offenses as Hakiri. Although the current situation is most regrettable, there is no alternative for us but to stand up and fight to protect the flow of kosen-rufu.

The biggest difference between Lenin and Stalin was their distance from the masses. A historical appraisal of Lenin says that he "always was close to the people; he used to receive peasant delegates and often spoke at factory gatherings; he used to visit villages and talk with the peasants."

By contrast: "Stalin separated himself from the people and never went anywhere. This lasted decades.... How then could he have known the situation in the provinces?"

Irrespective of the comparative depth or correctness of the ideology, an essential requirement of leaders is that they go among the people and advance together with them. Buddhist leaders such as Shakyamuni, Nichiren Daishonin and Nikko Shonin without exception always personally met and interacted with the people.

Highhanded and authoritarian leaders cut themselves off from the people and live in ease and comfort as if they were on a higher, more exalted level than ordinary people. This is the fundamental difference between humanistic leaders and authoritarians.

Not only did Stalin betray the ideals of the Revolution, but in the process, he executed many of those who had worked ardently for its realization. For Stalin to carry out his insanity, it was necessary to affix anti-Leninist labels on his enemies — without any factual basis or evidence — and summarily execute them without giving them an opportunity to deny or affirm the charges against them.

As he went about in this manner, Stalin declared himself to be the present-day Lenin, claiming, as it were, that he and Lenin were "one and the same."

I think this will give you a good idea of what the labeling of the Soka Gakkai as acting like Hakiri implies. We must not allow such a great tragedy of history to be repeated.

The Daishonin writes: "It is a time…when truth and error stand shoulder to shoulder, and when Mahayana and Hinayana dispute which is superior. At such a time, one must set aside all other affairs and devote one's attention to rebuking slander of the correct teaching. This is the practice of shakubuku" (WND-1, 126). Here, the Daishonin says that it accords with the time to "set aside all other affairs" and rebuke slander of the Law, and that this is the way to attain Buddhahood. Those who stand up to the enemies of Buddhism and kosen-rufu, to protect and propagate the Mystic Law, will receive the greatest blessing of attaining Buddhahood.

WE ARE DIRECTLY RELATED TO THE ORIGINAL BUDDHA

Let us now consider things from a different angle. In many writings, Nichiren Daishonin cites this passage of T'ien-t'ai's *Profound Meaning of the Lotus Sutra*: "Originally one followed this Buddha and for the first time conceived the desire to seek the way. And by following this Buddha again, one will reach the stage where there is no retrogression" (WND-1, 748). This passage explains the principle of relationship [one of the ten mystic principles that T'ien-t'ai employs to explain the significance of the Chinese character *myo* of Myoho-renge-kyo]. What this passage indicates is that the followers of a Buddha are born into the world through their original relationship with that Buddha.

Also, in the *Annotations on "The Words and Phrases of the Lotus Sutra,"* Miao-lo reiterates, "In the beginning one followed this Buddha or bodhisattva and formed a bond with him, and so it will be through this Buddha or bodhisattva that one will attain one's goal" (WND-1, 748). The Daishonin summarizes this principle as follows, "The Lotus Sutra is like the seed, the Buddha like the sower, and the people like the field" (WND-1, 748).

Just as a seed is planted and raised, and its harvest reaped by the same person, people attain Buddhahood due to the efforts of the Buddha or bodhisattva who plants the seed of enlightenment in their lives and raises it to fruition.

The *Annotations on "The Words and Phrases of the Lotus Sutra* also says: "Forming a bond with a Buddha represents the process of birth, while the maturing of one's Buddhist practice represents the process of upbringing. If the Buddha with whom one forms a bond and under whom one's practice matures is different [from the Buddha of this saha world], then one cannot establish the father and son relationship with the Buddha" (WND-2, 1040). Thus, in Buddhism, the original relationship that one forms is very important; such a relationship is maintained over the three existences of past, present and future.

Citing passages from these commentaries, the Daishonin indicates that he himself is the "original teacher" whom all people should follow. This point is also clarified in "Reply to Sairen-bo" and other writings.

We are the followers of the original Buddha and shall always remain so. All of you here today are people who initially aroused faith, have developed and grown, and are steadily advancing toward attaining Buddhahood thanks to the Soka Gakkai and the SGI organizations that appeared in accordance with the will and decree of the original Buddha. As such, this is a gathering of people who share a truly profound relationship with the original Buddha.

Embraced in the infinite compassion of the original Buddha, we have developed in the soil of the Mystic Law that has spread throughout the world; let us therefore continue practicing in this great earth so that we may realize the full fruition of our efforts. In light of the Gosho, this is clearly the correct path for us to follow. We live, die and are reborn in this world to advance kosen-rufu. The ties uniting true friends of the Mystic Law are eternal and everlasting.

Nichiren Daishonin quotes T'ien-t'ai's *Profound Meaning of the "Lotus Sutra"*: "How. . . could those who formed a bond with the Buddha fail to come into his presence? Just as all the hundred rivers flow into the sea, so is one drawn by one's connection with the Buddha and born in company with the Buddha" (WND-2, 1041).

In lifetime after lifetime, we can be reborn and carry out activities in the world of the original Buddha, in the world of kosen-rufu. With a sense of complete fulfillment and satisfaction, we can lead lives of great good fortune and merit over the three existences of past, present and future. What could be more fortunate? What could be a greater cause to rejoice?

Therefore, if we have the firm realization that we SGI members are friends whose relationship spans life's three existences, it will solidify the path on which we are advancing toward attaining Buddhahood. All we need to do is continue straight along this fundamental path.

Buddhism exists for everyone's happiness. The organization exists to enable each of you to practice with peace of mind and satisfaction. I pray that all of you, in the United States and in Canada, will continue advancing in harmonious unity and with heart-to-heart bonds of shared affection, as the happiest of all SGI families.

The Mystic Law Gives
New Life to All Knowledge

—〜〜—

YOUTH TRAINING MEETING,

SOKA UNIVERSITY LOS ANGELES,

CALABASAS, CALIFORNIA, OCTOBER 1, 1991

A FAMOUS PASSAGE from the Lotus Sutra states, "If you see a person who accepts and upholds this sutra, you should rise and greet him from afar, showing him the same respect you would a Buddha" (LS, 324).

President Toda would often say: "The coming era belongs to youth. We have to cherish young people as though greeting the Buddha. By openly discussing any subject with them, we must pass on all our thoughts and ideas, so that they will carry on our mission." These are my exact sentiments as I address you today.

In the forty-four years since I took faith in the Daishonin's Buddhism at age nineteen, I have walked unswervingly along the path of kosen-rufu, following my convictions and sense of justice.

When I was still a new member, I did not like the Soka Gakkai as it was at that time. I could not accept the behavior and bearing of my seniors. Learning of my honest feelings, President Toda said to me: "If that's how you feel, Daisaku, then what you have to do is make the Soka Gakkai into the kind of organization you can be truly happy with. Work really hard and fight earnestly to build a Soka Gakkai that matches your ideal!"

His answer was extremely clear; it also showed his incredible broad-mindedness and generosity. Following my mentor's words, I subsequently went on to build a new Soka Gakkai. I would now like to present my mentor's words to all of you.

CHANGING THE KARMA OF HUMANKIND

On another occasion, I asked President Toda why we had to practice faith with the spirit of not begrudging our lives. This is what he said in response: "Around the world, soldiers vie to kill one another. Economics is based on the survival of the fittest and does not necessarily lead to human happiness. Among the ranks of doctors, lawyers and government officials — who are supposed to serve the people — are many who look down on people and exploit them. We can see this trend in other areas, too — politics, science, education and religion.

"Call it the karma of humankind if you like, but society is complex — a mass of contradictions lacking a fundamental path leading to people's happiness. Only the Daishonin's Buddhism shows us the fundamental way to change people's karma. It teaches us the path toward eternity, happiness, true self and purity, and toward the eternal fulfillment of all desires. This is the supreme path of life. Therefore, only by practicing this faith without begrudging our lives can we be completely free of all regrets."

His words made perfect sense to me. Convinced that what he said was true, I advanced with the spirit of not begrudging my life. I believe this is the attitude that youth should possess.

THE MYSTIC LAW PROVIDES A HOLISTIC VIEW OF LIFE

I also asked President Toda: "When there are so many religions around, how can we say that the Daishonin's Buddhism is the most correct? Isn't this a dogmatic assertion?"

President Toda, delighted that I had asked this question, remarked, "That is a natural question for a young person to ask." And giving another very clear response, he said: "Many of the world's religions and philosophies expound only a partial view of life. If we use the analogy of the body, it is like expounding only an arm or a leg, or the eyes and the ears, or the torso — in other words, they expound only part of the whole. In contrast, the Daishonin's Buddhism comprehensively and holistically explains the true aspect of life. For this reason, it is an unsurpassed philosophy. When based on the Mystic Law, the intrinsic worth of all other positive teachings comes to the fore."

He also said: "No one can avoid the four sufferings of birth, aging, sickness and death. The only thing that enables us to come to terms with the four sufferings is the Mystic Law."

In a similar vein, regarding the inevitability of death, the French poet and author Victor Hugo declared that we are all "under sentence of death but with a sort of indefinite reprieve."

True happiness is impossible unless one can solve this fundamental problem of existence. This is what makes kosen-rufu, the widespread propagation of the Mystic Law, such a necessity.

I have countless fond memories of the time I shared with my mentor — memories I regard as priceless treasures. I, too, will do my best to pass on all my thoughts and hopes to you by talking with you young people as I am today.

I want you to work in tight unity to create an SGI organization that will be the best in the world, in both name and reality, for I am convinced that in the future the United States will become the central stage for the SGI's worldwide activities. Let us work on this task together, with painstaking care and patience, aiming at the twenty-first century! I am determined to support and encourage your efforts in any way I can, visiting your shores more often and, if possible, for longer periods of time.

THE ARDENT WISH OF A MOTHER

Before the lecture I delivered at Harvard University on September 26, I met and talked with University President Neil L. Rudenstine, and I joined SGI-USA members who are students and graduates of the university in a commemorative photo. We then enjoyed a very pleasant interlude strolling around the Harvard campus.

One of the buildings we passed on the way was the Harry Elkins Widener Memorial Library — a building that projects a sense of the quiet dignity of its almost eighty years. The library owes its existence to the beautiful and noble drama of a mother and her son.

Until the beginning of this century, the library facilities of Harvard University were very poor, with inadequate room to house all its books. The library director and others sympathetic to the cause of building a magnificent, new library exhausted all possible avenues to realize this wish. They called on private corporations and the alumni for financial assistance but had little success in bringing their dream any closer to reality.

Then a woman unexpectedly appeared who offered to finance the entire project of constructing a new library. She had lost her beloved son in the tragic sinking of the *Titanic* in April 1912. Her son, Harry Elkins Widener, who died at age twenty-seven, had been a graduate of Harvard University and a youth of much promise.

The young Widener had a great passion for reading and had lovingly collected many books. He cherished a beautiful dream to leave his collection one day to the alma mater that he held so dear. In fact, he had just successfully completed a book-buying trip in London when he boarded the *Titanic* together with his mother and father for their return voyage to America — a voyage that was to be his last.

The youth was a loving son to his mother — a gallant and heroic gentleman. Seeing his mother safely into a lifeboat, the young Widener stayed behind with his father on the sinking ship; until the very last, he watched over his mother's progress, praying for her safety.

The youth's collection of more than three thousand valuable volumes were bequeathed to Harvard University in accordance with his wishes.

An Eternal Monument

Harvard had no library to accommodate his vast collection, however. This prompted his mother to propose that a new library be built. Her offer was completely selfless; she was driven only by a desire to fulfill her son's wish. She is said to have donated between $2 million and $3.5 million to the project — a monumental sum by the standards of the day.

Owing to her selfless devotion, a magnificent library was completed in June 1915. Harvard University, by naming the library in memory of Harry Elkins Widener, pays eternal tribute to this lofty drama of mother and child, passing it on from one generation to the next.

Furthermore, Mrs. Widener, out of a fervent wish to reduce accidents at sea even a little, also proposed that swimming lessons be made compulsory at Harvard University — a proposal that was accepted and implemented. No doubt, she regarded all the students who followed in her son's footsteps at Harvard as irreplaceable treasures.

Buddhism lists the suffering of parting from one's loved ones as one of the eight types of suffering. In life, we will encounter separations of inexpressible sadness. But those who overcome such grief and continue to live their lives with strength and courage will be cherished and respected by their juniors as kings and queens of life. There is no more lofty life than that of one who surmounts personal tragedy and leaves behind some achievement for future generations.

Niko's Slander of Nikko Shonin

Yesterday, at the conference for leaders of the United States and Canada, I talked briefly about the reasons for Nikko Shonin's departure from Mount Minobu.

The fundamental cause for his departure lay with the decadent priest Mimbu Niko [one of the five senior priests], who tolerated and even encouraged slanderous actions on the part of

Hakiri Sanenaga, the steward of the area. This caused the area of Minobu [where Nichiren Daishonin spent the latter years of his life] to become defiled.

Among Niko's perverse views were his accusations that Nikko Shonin indulged in non-Buddhist interpretations.

Non-Buddhist literature here indicates Brahman writings of India, the Confucian and Taoist works of China, and general, secular and literary works. In some cases, the term is used to indicate scholarly writings and the Chinese classics, which at the time were considered the basic foundation of all learning.

Nikko Shonin strictly upheld the spirit of Nichiren Daishonin as revealed in "On Establishing the Correct Teaching for the Peace of the Land." Based on this spirit, he instructed Hakiri that for him to make pilgrimages to Shinto shrines was [against the Daishonin's teaching and therefore] impermissible.

Hakiri thereupon sought the counsel of Niko. Niko told Hakiri, "Being a person who indulges in non-Buddhist literature, Nikko reads 'On Establishing the Correct Teaching for the Peace of the Land' from that perspective, and so he fails to grasp its more profound meaning." He thus undermined Hakiri's trust in Nikko Shonin.

Nikko Shonin cites Niko's words in the letter "Reply to Lord Hara": "[Mimbu Ajari Niko answered Hakiri's queries, saying,] 'That the tutelary benevolent deities have abandoned this country is written in "On Establishing the Correct Teaching for the Peace of the Land." However, Byakuren Ajari [Nikko Shonin], basing himself on non-Buddhist scriptures, reads it in a biased manner and so is incapable of understanding its true intention'" (*Hennentai Gosho*, p. 1731).

Niko contradicted the Daishonin's teaching in telling Hakiri that it was therefore all right to visit Shinto shrines. Furthermore, he told him to visit shrines as often as he wished on the grounds that the Buddhist gods would gather at a shrine if a person who embraced the Lotus Sutra went there to pray.

Hakiri placed his complete trust in this false teaching, which allowed him to do as he wished. "Niko is a priest who can be reasoned with," Hakiri probably thought with delight. Almost invariably, a lay person's deviation from the Daishonin's teaching can be traced to the influence of a decadent priest skilled at accommodating the demands of lay people [regardless of what is correct from the standpoint of Buddhism].

To Hakiri — who had lost his faith — the admonitions of Nikko Shonin, who strictly protected the Daishonin's teaching by staunchly refuting slander, had already become little more than a source of irritation.

Nikko Shonin declared Niko's tolerance of slander to be the "workings of the devil king," a "betrayal of the late mentor" and an "[offense equal in gravity to committing] the seven cardinal sins." If someone who is charged with responsibility for protecting and spreading the Daishonin's teaching willfully distorts and arbitrarily alters the teaching, then the actions of such a person certainly represent the workings of the devil. They are the actions of a priest of the greatest evil, who is guilty of betraying the mentor and committing the seven cardinal sins. This is what Nikko Shonin taught.

These historical facts contain an important lesson.

First of all, those who betrayed the mentor [Nichiren Daishonin] after his death all sought to justify themselves by making reference to some "more profound meaning" contained in his teaching, despite all documentary proof to the contrary.

In Buddhism, the offense of betraying the mentor is extremely grave. It amounts to destroying the very life of Buddhism. People who do so try to win acceptance for their false views by saying, "You should listen to what I say, irrespective of what my mentor wrote." And if someone presents them with written proof that shows their words or actions to be wrong, they try to gloss over the contradiction by saying: "That is a superficial level of interpretation. The true meaning is found elsewhere."

In exactly this manner, the Nichiren Shoshu priesthood is contradicting the Gosho and the guidance given by the successive high priests, desecrating them and attempting to consign them to oblivion.

A contemporary example of this is found in the priesthood's abrupt denial of High Priest Nittatsu's view on the significance of the Grand Main Temple. This view had served as a fundamental guideline for both priests and lay believers of Nichiren Shoshu for more than twenty years. Yet now the priesthood claims that "the former high priest's true intention is not contained in his official statements but is found elsewhere."

"ALTHOUGH THE MENTOR HAS DIED, HIS WRITINGS REMAIN"

Nikko Shonin came to learn that Hakiri, in a quandary over whether it was permissible for him to make pilgrimages to Shinto shrines, had been making such remarks as "The priests in the Kamakura area (followers of the five senior priests) say it is all right for me to go, but Nikko Shonin of Minobu has told me that I must not. Whom should I listen to now that the Daishonin has died?"

Thereupon, Nikko Shonin strictly instructed him: "Although the mentor has died, his writings remain. This is in 'On Establishing the Correct Teaching for the Peace of the Land'" (*Hennentai Gosho*, p. 1731). When the Daishonin is no longer in the world, it is his writings that we should make our mentor. So long as we continue practicing in accordance with the Gosho, what possible cause for confusion can there be? Here, Nikko Shonin teaches the fundamental attitude for the Daishonin's followers.

What a remarkable contrast between the attitude of Nikko Shonin, who made the Gosho his foundation, and that of Niko, who based himself on his own personal views and neglected the Gosho!

We in the SGI are advancing in perfect accord with the teaching of Nikko Shonin, who represents the treasure of the Sangha, in that we make the Gosho our foundation. At the same time, we are now witnessing the appearance of the followers of Niko within Nichiren Shoshu.

PEOPLE LOOK DOWN ON THE CORRECT TEACHER DUE TO IGNORANCE

We must also bear the following lesson in mind: People who betray their mentor criticize those who strictly observe the mentor's teaching and interpret that teaching themselves in a biased manner as being non-Buddhist. In disparaging the correct interpretation as being "similar to non-Buddhist literature" or a "superficial reading," such persons, in their arrogance, suggest that they themselves have grasped the ultimate teaching of Buddhism when in fact they have not.

Thus, SGI members, too, while faithfully observing the precept that they must strictly admonish slander, have come to be accused of "revering non-Buddhist teachings." We can regard this as an honorable badge of proof that we are indeed heirs to the legacy of Nikko Shonin.

Niko went so far as to brand non-Buddhist literature per se as evil. Nikko Shonin refutes this extreme and distorted view, saying: "The Daishonin's 'On Establishing the Correct Teaching for the Peace of the Land' was written based on the style of non-Buddhist literature. The letter sent in the eighth year of Bun'ei was likewise written in the style of non-Buddhist works. In addition, the Lotus Sutra was written by the people in China most well-versed in non-Buddhist literature, and for this reason it stands out among all of the Buddhist sutras for its style.

"In expounding this doctrine now, I would like to have someone who is well versed in non-Buddhist literature commit it to writing. Without an understanding of both Buddhist and non-Buddhist writings, I believe it will be extremely difficult to establish the Buddhist Law and to secure the land' (*Hennentai Gosho*, p. 1734).

Not only does he refute Niko's accusations about his "indulging in non-Buddhist literature" and about "non-Buddhist literature being false," but Nikko Shonin goes on to state that unless one incorporates the literary style and knowledge of non-Buddhist writings in attempting to introduce people to Buddhism, it will be impossible to "establish the Buddhist Law and to secure the land."

The fifty-ninth high priest, Nichiko, commented on the mistaken views of Niko: "His views certainly arose from a sheer lack of knowledge, and no doubt there were many priests and lay believers of little understanding who sympathized with him. In other words, I assume that his notions were based on the vulgar conventionalisms of the dark age [in terms of literature] of the Kamakura period, and that he simply used such accepted ideas to put down the teacher Nikko" (From *Fuji Nikko Shonin Shoden* [Detailed Accounts of Nikko Shonin of the Fuji School]).

In other words, Niko's defamatory remarks and false views were either due to his own lack of knowledge or were employed as part of an attempt to attack Nikko Shonin by appealing to the ideas of the uneducated masses.

We must cultivate in ourselves the light of intelligence. We must positively bring an end to the current "dark age" [of Nichiren Shoshu].

CAPABLE PEOPLE MUST MASTER BOTH BUDDHIST AND NON-BUDDHIST TEACHINGS

Just as Nikko Shonin states, without an understanding of both Buddhist and non-Buddhist writings, neither realizing peace ("securing the land") nor accomplishing kosen-rufu ("establishing the Buddhist Law") will be possible. In addition, Nikko Shonin indicates that capable people who are well versed in both realms of Buddhist and secular knowledge are necessary.

In particular, young people, basing themselves on Buddhism, must study hard, avidly seeking to expand their grasp of the knowledge and wisdom of the world.

In Article Eight of "The Twenty-six Admonitions," Nikko Shonin states, "Those who, lacking a thorough understanding of Buddhism, are bent on obtaining fame and fortune are not qualified to call themselves my followers" (GZ, 1618).

The failure of Nichiren Shoshu priests to observe this admonition is no doubt one of the factors underlying the current situation. Moreover, these priests have practically no knowledge about the world and lack the desire to study.

They nevertheless imperiously command us to show them greater respect (fame) and increase the amount of our donations to them (wealth). Just whose disciples are they anyway?

NIKKO SHONIN'S SPIRITUAL HEIRS ARE INCLUDED IN THE TREASURE OF THE SANGHA

"The Twenty-six Admonitions" also states, "Until kosen-rufu is achieved, propagate the Law to the full extent of your ability without begrudging your life" (GZ, 1618). We SGI members are putting this admonition into practice.

In the postscript to these "Twenty-six Admonitions," which were originally set forth as guidelines for priests, Nikko Shonin clearly states, "A person who violates even one of these articles cannot be called a disciple of Nikko" (GZ, 1619).

By following Nikko Shonin, who is the true treasure of the Sangha, the members of both the priesthood and laity, in a broad sense, are included within the treasure of the Sangha. It is only too obvious, therefore, that any priests who go against Nikko Shonin's admonitions are naturally *not* to be regarded as representing the treasure of the Sangha.

If priests, while calling themselves the Daishonin's disciples, demonstrate a blatant willingness to accommodate slanderous practices, belittle the value of the Gosho and, while calling themselves disciples of Nikko Shonin, conduct themselves in exactly the same manner as Niko, then they are destroying the three treasures of Nichiren Daishonin's Buddhism.

In any event, it can be definitely stated that the poorer people's breadth of study, the more prone they will be to brand those who are earnestly striving to promote kosen-rufu as persons who "indulge in non-Buddhist teachings."

BE PASSIONATE AS YOUTH; TAKE ACTION
AS BUDDHISTS

Niko, revealing his superficial understanding of Buddhism, pro-
faned Nikko Shonin by calling him a non-Buddhist. Nikko Shonin,
on the other hand, thoroughly understood Buddhism and strongly
urged his disciples to study non-Buddhist teachings as well.

This highlights two contrasting attitudes toward Buddhism: one
that confines Buddhism to a limited, esoteric realm for the benefit of only a small number of specialists, and one that takes the
broader view that all laws and phenomena of the universe are part
of Buddhism.

Simply put, Niko's was a dead Buddhism, while that taught by
Nikko Shonin was a living Buddhism. We of the SGI are perpetu-
ating the orthodox lineage of a dynamic, vibrant Buddhism.

How can one propagate the Daishonin's Buddhism without
knowing about various other teachings that exist in the world?
Just as I explained at the beginning — by quoting President
Toda — when based on the Mystic Law, all laws of the world and
society begin to function in their most valuable way. All endeavors in human society — politics, economics, learning and so
on — become revitalized. They come to display their full potential and attain new life. The lifeblood of Buddhism pulses within
society. If it is cut off from secular affairs, Buddhism's full validity
cannot be revealed.

Niko might also have been jealous of Nikko Shonin's extensive
knowledge and learning. The Danish philosopher Søren Kierkegaard (1813–55) claimed that when action and passion disappear,
the world is dominated by jealousy. This argument was the heart
of his criticism against the modern world — against evil wisdom
that strives to pull everything down to the same level [irrespective
of its excellence or baseness].

BUDDHISM GAINS LIFE ONLY IN CORRECT FAITH

Buddhism's mission must be to impart dynamism to the society and the age in which it is practiced and to the people who practice it. In one of his lectures, President Toda fielded this question: "You said Buddhism became extinct in India and China, yet many sutras still exist in these countries, don't they?"

President Toda spoke forcefully: "There may be sutras, but sutras are by no means Buddhism. They are just books! For without faith, sutras are nothing more than books. No matter how many sutras and temples there may be in these countries, their Buddhism is already dead."

For example, even though a temple may possess original writings in the Daishonin's own hand, if that temple embarks on a heretical course, then it does not possess the lifeblood of the Daishonin's Buddhism. The lifeblood of Buddhism exists only in the correct faith actually manifested in people's lives. Correct faith — the lifeblood of Buddhism — is transmitted through the mentor–disciple relationship. Only when we follow the teachings of Nichiren Daishonin and Nikko Shonin can we perpetuate the pure flow of the Daishonin's Buddhism for eternity. Should we follow the corrupt stream of Niko, who betrayed his mentor's teachings, we would commit the serious offense of destroying the heart of Buddhism.

The traitorous Niko attempted to destroy the Daishonin's Buddhism in many ways. Nikko Shonin, meanwhile, though having to endure the insult of being called a non-Buddhist, strictly abided by his mentor's teaching and protected the lifeblood of Buddhism. This contrast is a mirror that reflects the truth, now and always.

I sincerely hope that you, my young friends, will develop the SGI organization in the United States into the foremost in the world. Please take good care of this center of the worldwide kosen-rufu movement. Thank you and congratulations on today's gathering.

Conduct Enjoyable Meetings and Meaningful Discussions

—m—

GONGYO MEETING COMMEMORATING
WORLD PEACE DAY, SOKA UNIVERSITY LOS ANGELES,
CALABASAS, CALIFORNIA, OCTOBER 2, 1991

ON THIS DAY thirty-one years ago, here in the United States, I took the first step toward the achievement of worldwide kosen-rufu. I am very glad to celebrate the anniversary of that day together with all of you.

Live eternally like the phoenix,
Soaring across the vault of the sky.

My mentor, Josei Toda, gave this poem to me in July 1953. I have lived my life based on its spirit, spreading my wings throughout the world.

"To protect my beloved friends, the SGI members! To spread the Mystic Law! To give people hope and courage and help them accumulate the treasures of life!" These have been my only desires for these thirty-one years.

The time has now come for the full-fledged realization of worldwide kosen-rufu and for the spread of peace, with America at the forefront.

Today, I would like to briefly go over the main guidelines for leaders:

First, never be haughty. Leaders must be modest through and through.

Second, never reprimand others. You should always treat others gently. In the Gosho we find the statement "One who rids the offender of evil is acting as his parent" (WND-1, 286). Naturally, it will sometimes be necessary for you to admonish or encourage others with a spirit of compassion. But you must not scold people in a fit of emotion.

Third, never raise your voice with fellow members. Leaders should be people of reason who always seek to win others' understanding through discussion.

Fourth, do not lie. Because we are common mortals, we make mistakes. There is no reason to feel that we have to cover up these errors. The world of faith is a world where things can be discussed frankly, without any concealment. Honest people will win the trust of those around them.

Fifth, never betray the privacy of another individual. In the organization, leaders are often called upon to counsel members with personal problems. Those who betray this trust and fail to safeguard individual privacy demonstrate irresponsibility — as leaders, as people of faith and as human beings. Leaders must be discreet, sincere people who respect the rights of others.

Sixth, do not look down on others. Leaders who have an inflated sense of self-importance, who look down on and discriminate against others, will eventually reach an impasse in life. All people are equally precious, regardless of their position. Excellent leaders have a heartfelt respect for everyone.

Seventh, do not be unfair. All of the members — whether rich or poor, prominent or lacking in social standing — are irreplaceable children of the Buddha. I hope all of you will become impartial and just leaders.

Eighth, never overly strain yourselves or force members to push themselves beyond reasonable limits. You cannot maintain such a pace for very long. Pushing yourselves too hard is not necessarily a reflection of strong faith. Members can fully display their abilities only if they are allowed a certain amount of latitude.

The last two items I want to mention are included in the qualifications I have just outlined.

Ninth, do not be arrogant. Arrogance undermines humanity and destroys faith.

Tenth, do not be unkind. Spiteful leaders make members miserable. On the other hand, those who can warmly support their juniors — to the point of enabling their juniors to eventually surpass even themselves in ability — are great leaders.

I hope you will become leaders who possess common sense, sophistication, conviction, sympathy and the spirit to encourage others. I hope you will be people who have warm affection for others, able to share their sorrows and pains; who are brimming with confidence and can instill hope and courage in others; who are always vivacious and give an indescribable sense of peace of mind and courage to those they meet. With leaders such as this, members can carry out vigorous activities and realize prodigious growth.

As we bear these points in mind, making a fresh start toward the goal of the SGI-USA becoming the foremost organization in the world, I would like to suggest that "Enjoyable meetings and meaningful discussions" be adopted as the new motto for the American organization.

Every meeting should be lively and cheerful, the type of gathering where everyone leaves feeling: "That was fun. I'm glad I came."

Significant discussions that foster mutual understanding are much more valuable than the self-complacent pronouncements of one person. Please conduct discussions that deeply penetrate the hearts of the participants — the kind that make them want to say: "That was really refreshing. I have so much hope now. That gave me confidence. I now have the strength to advance."

We advancing together for kosen-rufu are in a sense brothers and sisters traveling together aboard the one ship of the Mystic Law. No matter what happens in the course of the journey, the ship will unfailingly reach the shore of eternal happiness. I hope you will advance cheerfully and majestically, fully convinced of this fact.

I would like to express my heartfelt gratitude to all of you for your support during the past two weeks. Thanks to your sincere daimoku, all the events during my stay in the United States have been a great success. To conclude, I would like to reiterate my sincere desire that you should work together to create an SGI-USA that is the No. 1 organization in the world.

1993

Let Us Strive Together Toward Even Greater Development

—⚬—

SECOND SGI-USA GENERAL MEETING
AND FIRST INTERNATIONAL KANSAI GENERAL MEETING,
WORLD PEACE IKEDA AUDITORIUM,
SANTA MONICA, CALIFORNIA, JANUARY 27, 1993

CONGRATULATIONS on this brilliant departure for a "New America"! I offer my most heartfelt felicitations on the holding of this Second SGI-USA General Meeting. Members in sixty-two locations around the United States and in the Caribbean [via live satellite hookup] are taking part in this momentous general meeting today.

My congratulations also on the holding of the First International Kansai General Meeting — a meeting that is symbolic of Kansai's world standing. I welcome my beloved members of Kansai from the bottom of my heart. [Kansai is a region of Japan that includes Osaka, Kyoto, Nara, Wakayama, Hyogo and Shiga.]

Opening in October 1991, the SGI-USA exhibition "Humanity in Education: The Soka School System" has been held in a total of ten U.S. cities. The exhibit has so far been displayed in Los Angeles, San Francisco, Seattle, Denver, Chicago, Washington, Philadelphia, New York, Boston and Atlanta, with future showings in Dallas, Phoenix and Honolulu scheduled.

The pioneering ideals of Soka pedagogy, the value-creating

educational philosophy espoused by first Soka Gakkai president Tsunesaburo Makiguchi, and the SGI's endeavors to develop and widely apply his concepts to modern society in the realms of culture and education have won high acclaim among many leading U.S. scholars and thinkers. I offer my deepest gratitude to all those who worked so hard to make the exhibition a great success.

Mr. Makiguchi, our mentor, once said: "Teachers must not instruct students with the arrogant attitude of 'Become like me!' It is far more important for teachers to adopt the attitude 'Don't satisfy yourself with trying to become like me. Make your model someone of higher caliber.' True teachers, therefore, are those who have the humility to advance together with their students."

Education must never be coercive. The heart of education lies in the process of teacher and pupil learning together, the teacher drawing forth the pupil's potential and raising the pupil to surpass the teacher in ability.

In the same way, I ask that all of you who shoulder the future of the new SGI-USA be warm and compassionate leaders who thoroughly respect and cherish each member. I hope you will be wise leaders who can activate the unlimited potential known as Buddhahood in each person's life and help him or her become even more capable and happier than yourselves.

COMPASSION IS THE SOUL OF BUDDHISM

One winter, concerned about the illness of a dedicated follower's wife, Nichiren Daishonin wrote the following words of encouragemen: "I am as concerned about the illness of your wife, the lay nun Toki, as though it were I myself who is ailing, and day and night I pray to the heavenly gods that she will recover" (WND-2, 666). In this short passage, we can sense the Daishonin's infinitely profound compassion. Compassion is the very soul of Buddhism.

To pray for others, making their problems and anguish our own; to embrace those who are suffering, becoming their greatest ally; to continue giving them our support and encouragement until they become truly happy — the Daishonin's Buddhism lives and breathes in such humanistic actions.

Why have we, the SGI, achieved such remarkable development? Because we have wholeheartedly treasured each member as a child of the Buddha, in exact accord with this compassionate spirit of the Daishonin.

The Nichiren Shoshu priesthood is the exact opposite. Its priests view believers as nothing but a means for lining their own pockets. They are always arrogant and highhanded. Theirs is a truly frightening betrayal of the founder, Nichiren Daishonin.

Today, our friends from Kansai are celebrating their brilliant general meeting. Josei Toda once declared: "I want to rid Kansai of sickness and poverty. Indeed, I am determined to do so!" These words remind us again of how he put his heart and soul into giving guidance and encouragement to the members.

Exactly forty years ago, on the occasion of the First Osaka Chapter General Meeting, President Toda proclaimed, "The purpose of our practice of faith is for all of us to become truly happy" and "We embrace faith to secure our happiness throughout the infinite future."

The purpose of faith is certainly not to subjugate oneself to the authority of temples or clergy but, as my mentor clearly stated, to enable every person to attain happiness that endures eternally throughout the three existences of life.

President Toda also often said: "Those of you who have problems or sufferings, pray earnestly! Buddhism is a deadly serious win-or-lose struggle. If you should [pray with such an earnest attitude] and still have no solution forthcoming, then I will give you my life!"

This invincible conviction on which Mr. Toda was willing to stake his life inspired the members. By faithfully carrying on and practicing in accord with this spirit, we have built a global organization — the SGI.

Buddhism means putting the teachings into practice. Practice equals faith. With sincere prayer and action, our desires cannot possibly fail to be fulfilled. When you continue to apply yourselves to your Buddhist practice toward kosen-rufu, solidifying and gaining mastery in your faith, you will find that all your prayers will definitely be answered.

An expert archer can accurately hit a target with a single arrow. I hope all of you will become masters of faith and masters of life who will realize the complete fulfillment of all your desires. I also pray that you will be leaders of unshakable conviction who proudly open up a new age of hope for kosen-rufu and the world.

In nature, there are mountains and oceans; there are languidly flowing rivers and flowers that bloom according to the season. In the same way, the speeches made by leaders and the format of meetings should not become monotonous. Great leaders are flexible, broad-minded, innovative; they put people thoroughly at ease and inspire trust and confidence in them.

You must not be leaders who are like a dried-up, barren wasteland. Such people can shout themselves hoarse, crying "Advance, advance!." But when they turn around to look behind them, they'll probably find that no one's following!

Please be leaders who possess both charm and wisdom.

New SGI-USA General Director Fred M. Zaitsu [appointed in November 1992] is a person of integrity and sincere commitment. I hope you will work together with him in solid unity to build a wonderful new SGI-USA upon the pioneering achievements you have made thus far.

Today, members are gathered all around the United States. I would like to say a few words of greeting to the members at the major centers.

How are all the visiting Kansai members at the Universal Amphitheatre in Los Angeles? Are all the performers well? Thank you to all the Los Angeles members!

To the members in San Francisco, thank you for your wonderful hospitality to the exchange delegation from Kansai. More exchange groups, with members from Chubu, Shikoku, Saitama and Chiba, will be on their way in March, so I hope you will extend them an equally warm welcome.

To the members in Seattle, congratulations on the thirtieth anniversary of the founding of your first chapter. Don't let those eighty-mile-per-hour winds defeat you! All of you are great!

Howdy to the members in Dallas! Congratulations on Dallas making it into the Super Bowl. Please live as champions of kosen-rufu!

To the members of Atlanta, congratulations on hosting the 1996 Olympics. Let's aim to become gold medalists of faith!

Good evening to the members in Washington, D.C.!

And my warmest thanks to all the members of Puerto Rico and St. Maarten in the Caribbean.

To the members of the Big Apple, New York, congratulations on your lively gathering.

Good evening to the members of Boston, the capital of learning and culture. Thank you for your great hospitality two years ago [when President Ikeda gave his first lecture at Harvard University].

My appreciation to the members in Chicago for braving bitterly cold winds to attend this meeting. Please take care not to catch cold.

My heartiest welcome to the members of Alaska — land of the aurora borealis, land of dreams — who are themselves as lofty as Mount McKinley.

Aloha to the members of Hawaii! Congratulations on your native son, Akebono, winning the New Year Grand Sumo Tournament in Japan and being promoted to the highest rank of grand champion [the first non-Japanese sumo wrestler to attain this title]. My congratulations also on the new Hawaii Culture Center, scheduled for completion next year, as well as the grand culture festival that will be held there. [The grand culture festival was held in Hawaii in January 1995 with President Ikeda in attendance.] A number of exchange delegations from Japan will be the beneficiaries of your hospitality next year. Mahalo! Thank you very much.

To commemorate today's historic general meeting, I wish to dedicate a poem to the members of Los Angeles. It is titled "The Sun of *Jiyu* Over a New Land."

Kansai is the heart of the kosen-rufu movement in Japan; Los Angeles, in America; and America, in the world. I would like to present this poem with my infinite hopes and expectations for the members of Los Angeles and the United States. Although this poem is dedicated to the Los Angeles members, it goes without saying that its message is relevant to all SGI-USA members.

In the coming weeks, I will be traveling to various countries in South America to continue my efforts for the sake of peace and kosen-rufu. Let's meet again! Thank you very much for today.

"THE SUN OF *JIYU* OVER A NEW LAND"

To my treasured friends of Los Angeles, the city of my dreams.

A brilliant, burning sun
rises above the newborn land,
aiming toward a new century,
raising the curtain on a new stage
of humanity's history.
Shedding its light equally on all things,
it seeks the sky's distant midpoint.

In this land wrapped
in the limitless light
of the morning sun,
my splendid American friends
make their appearance;
bearing the world's hopes,
with power and vigor they commence
their progress anew.
To my beloved and treasured friends I say:
"Long live America renewed!
Long live the SGI-USA reborn!"

Ah! This enchanting city, Los Angeles!
Land of freedom and pioneering spirit!

From jagged mountain ranges
to the Pacific Ocean,
variegated nature changes ceaselessly —
rich agricultural lands
nurtured by the sun's dazzling rays,
and the groundbreaking efforts
of those who came before.
Downtown, clusters of buildings soar
    skyward.

To think that this vast metropolis
could grow from a single aqueduct
stretched across the barren desert
from beyond the distant mountains!

It is said that in America
new winds blow from the west.
And indeed, the fresh breezes
of new ways of thinking,
new styles of living,
have arisen in California
and spread to the entire United States.
So many stories of the silver screen,
created here in Hollywood,
have delivered bountiful gifts
of romance and dreams
to the world's people.

This rich spiritual soil,
this great earth alive with the diversity
of peoples and traditions —
giving rise to new culture,
a new humanity.

Los Angeles is a city pregnant with future,
a city where, in the words of one writer,

you can set new precedents
with your own energy and creativity.

And more, Los Angeles is a bridge
linking East and West,
a land of merging and fusion
where cultures of the Pacific
encounter traditions of the West.

Ah, the Pacific that opens before our eyes!
The boundless, free and untamed sea
for which the great Melville
voiced his respect and praise:
"It rolls the mid-most waters of the world.
...the tide-beating heart of earth."

Once, the Mediterranean
was inland sea and mother to the
civilizations of the surrounding regions —
Europe, the Middle East and Africa.

In like manner, the Pacific's depths
must not divide —
but be the cradle of a new civilization,
an enormous "inland sea" connecting
the Americas North and South,
the continents of Asia and Australia.

This is my firm conviction —
California will be the energy source
for the Pacific region
in the twenty-first century
and Los Angeles its eastern capital.

In October 1960, I took my first steps on
the American continent

in California, the Golden State.
The honor and glory of becoming
the first chapter established in North America
belong to the Los Angeles Chapter.

Since then, this city has been
the core and center of kosen-rufu
in the United States, the starting point
for worldwide kosen-rufu.
My dear friends, never forget
this mission which you
so decidedly possess.

In the thirty-three years since that time,
I have visited Los Angeles seventeen times.
Kansai is the heart
whose beating drives the movement
for kosen-rufu in Japan;
Los Angeles plays this self-same role
for the entire world.
For this reason, on each visit,
staking all, I drove in deep
and deeper
the pilings of construction.

In 1980,
the first SGI General Meeting was held,
and in 1987, Soka University of America
opened its doors.

Ah, February 1990!
I postponed my visit
to South America and for seventeen days
gave myself heart and soul
to the work of encouraging
my beloved fellow members

here in Los Angeles!
Those impassioned, consuming days of
unceasing toil and action
are the collaborative
golden poems of shared struggle.

Nor can I ever forget
the spring of 1992 —
even now my heart is rent with pain
when I recall how the
tragic news of the civil unrest in Los Angeles
raced around the world.

Heartrending images
of the evening sky shrouded in black smoke,
of buildings collapsing in flames,
once peaceful streets shattered by riot,
the entire city gripped
by a battlefield tension.
People standing lost in confusion,
a woman holding an infant cried out
— What has become of the ideals of this country?
What are we supposed to teach our children? —
Her woe-filled words tore
like talons at my heart.

I received continuous reports,
extended prompt relief.
And, putting everything aside,
I sat before the Gohonzon and
single-mindedly prayed —
for the safety of my treasured friends,
for the immediate restoration of order,
for a world without violence and discrimination.

Ah, America, land bringing together
so many different peoples!
A republic of ideals
born beneath the lofty banners,
the uniting principles of
freedom and equality.
As this century draws to its close,
the soul of your idealism
grieves at the stark realities of racial strife.
What is to become of the
spirit of your nation
fostered by so many people of
wisdom and philosophy?

My treasured friends,
There is no question that
your multiracial nation, America,
represents humanity's future.
Your land holds secret stores
of unbounded possibility, transforming
the energy of different cultures
into the unity of construction,
the flames of conflict
into the light of solidarity,
the eroding rivulets of mistrust
into a great broad flow of confidence.
On what can we ground
our efforts to open
the horizons of such a renaissance?

It is for just this reason,
my precious, treasured friends,
that you must develop within yourselves
the life-condition of Jiyu —
Bodhisattva of the Earth.

As each group seeks its separate
roots and origins,
society fractures along a thousand fissure lines.
When neighbors distance themselves
from neighbors, continue your
uncompromising quest
for your truer roots
in the deepest regions of your life.
Seek out the primordial "roots" of humankind.
Then you will without fail discover
the stately expanse of Jiyu
unfolding in the depths of your life.

Here is the home, the dwelling place
to which humankind traces
its original existence —
beyond all borders,
beyond all differences of gender and race.
Here is a world offering true proof
of our humanity.

If one reaches back to these fundamental roots,
all become friends and comrades.
To realize this is to "emerge from the earth."

Past, present, future...
The causes and effects of the three existences
flow ceaselessly as the reality of life;
interlinked, they give rise to all
differences and distinctions.
Trapped in those differences,
human society is wracked by
unending contention.

But the Buddhism of True Cause,
expounded by the Daishonin whose

teachings we embrace,
enables us to break the spell
of past karma, past causes and effects,
and to awaken to the grand humanity
— the life of Jiyu *—*
that had lain dormant in our hearts.

My mentor, President Toda,
taught us that when one embraces
the Mystic Law,
all intervening causes and effects
ebb and retreat, and there emerges
the common mortal of beginningless time.

This, another name for Bodhisattva of the Earth,
is the greatness and splendor
of the human being writ large,
after all false distinctions and adornments
have been removed.

Awaken to the life of Jiyu *within!*
When the bright sun of True Cause rises,
the stars and planets of
past cause and effect grow dim,
and the supreme world of
harmonious unity emerges —
the unity of friends and comrades
each manifesting the life-condition
of Bodhisattva of the Earth,
offering timeless proof that, indeed,
"The assembly on Eagle Peak has not yet
*   dispersed."*

Ah, my treasured friends,
whom I so deeply love and respect!
It is critical for you now

to directly perceive
the web of life that binds all people!

Buddhism describes
the connective threads of
dependent origination.
Nothing in this world exists alone;
everything comes into being and continues
in response to causes and conditions.
Parent and child.
Husband and wife.
Friends. Races.
Humanity and nature.
This profound understanding
of coexistence, of symbiosis —
here is the source of resolution for
the most pressing and fundamental issues
that confront humankind
in the chaotic last years of this century.

The Buddhist scriptures include
the parable of "Two Bundles of Reeds,"
aptly demonstrating this relation
of dependent origination.
Only by supporting each other
can the two bundles stand straight —
if one is removed, the other must fall.
Because this exists, so does that;
because that exists, so does this.

For several brilliant centuries,
Western civilization has encouraged
the independence of the individual
but now appears to be facing
a turbulent twilight.
The waves of egoism

eat away at the shores of
contemporary society.
The tragedy of division
wraps the world in a thick fog.
Individuals are becoming
mere scraps, mere fragments,
competing reed bundles of lesser self
threatened with mutual collapse.

My friends!
Please realize that you already possess
the solution to this quandary.
First you must break the hard shell
of the lesser self.
This you must absolutely do.
Then direct your lucid gaze
toward your friends, fellow members.

People can only live fully
by helping others to live.
When you give life to friends,
you truly live.
Cultures can only realize
their further richness
by honoring other traditions.
And only by respecting natural life
can humanity continue to exist.

Now is the time for you to realize
that through relations
mutually inspiring and harmonious,
the greater self is awakened to dynamic action,
the bonds of life are restored and healed.
And blossoms in delightful multitude
exude the unique fragrance
of each person, of each ethnicity,

in precise accord with the principle of
cherry, plum, pear and damson.

Our goal —
the Second American Renaissance.
Holding high the standard of humanity,
we advance —
from divisiveness to union,
from conflict to coexistence,
from hatred to fraternity.
In our struggle, in our fight,
there cannot be
even a moment's pause or stagnation.
My beloved friends,
Bodhisattvas of the Earth
readying yourselves
for the new century's dawn!
With your own efforts
bring about a renaissance here,
in this "magnetic land"!

The certain signs of America reborn,
Los Angeles rejuvenated,
are to be found within your hearts.
With this pride and conviction,
be victorious in your daily life,
overcome your own weaknesses every day.
Never forget that it is only through
relentless challenge
— one step following another —
that you can steadily transform
your ideals into reality.

Buddhism is reason.
Therefore, always maintain self-control.
Be the master of your actions.

Exercise common sense in society.
Keep a smiling countenance at home.
Be courteous to your friends and fellow members,
like a warm spring breeze to the suffering.
Reason exhaustively with the confused.
But, when you deal with the arrogant ones,
be bold and fearless like the Lion King!

Look!
Seen from the Malibu Training Center,
the Pacific Ocean's unbounded expanse
is bathed in radiant California sun.
An ocean of peace across whose surface
innumerable waves murmur and dance.

Beloved Los Angelenos!
I want you each to be
like the California sunshine,
showering on all people
the bright light and warmth
of your compassion.
Be people who extend hope and courage,
who inspire respect and gratitude
wherever you go.

Buddhism teaches us the means
to overcome life's fundamental pain
— the sufferings of birth, aging, sickness and death —
which none can escape,
and which no degree of wealth and fame
can relieve in the slightest.

Everyone, anyone —
when returned to
their solitary human existence,
is but a karma-laden "reed,"

trembling before the onslaught
of the four sufferings.

Seeking eternity within impermanence,
crossing over delusion to nurture confidence,
building happiness from anguish,
rush forward from today
toward tomorrow
in the prodigious battle that is
our human revolution!
For you are the Buddha's emissaries
upholding the ultimate philosophy of life!

Comrades!
Fellow Bodhisattvas of the Earth!
Born here, gathered together here in Los Angeles
that you might fulfill your mission —
Raise your voices in songs of praise
for freedom, democracy and humanity!
Wave the banners of culture and peace!

Ah, Los Angeles!
Here is to be found SUA,
a palace of intellect for
the Pan-Pacific era of the twenty-first century.
Here is located the World Culture Center,
dynamo of American kosen-rufu.
And here rises the splendid form
of the future site of the SGI Headquarters —
which will become the mainstay
of the grand endeavor of worldwide kosen-rufu.
Truly a new wind will blow from the west!
Los Angeles, the stage on which
you act with such freedom and vigor,
is the launching site for world kosen-rufu,
the cornerstone that links East and West.

Walt Whitman, giant of
the American Renaissance, penned these words:
"Come, I will make the continent indissoluble,
I will make the most splendid race
the sun ever shone upon,
I will make divine magnetic lands,
With the love of comrades,
With the life-long love of comrades."

Ah, Los Angeles!
The sun rises beyond the Rockies,
spreading its light over the wide Pacific.
Now! In its luminous beams,
let friend and friend pull together
in perfect unity, rowing into the seas —
embarking on a new leg
of our journey of kosen-rufu!

Grip the rudder,
hold firm to your course —
the Stars and Stripes,
the tricolor flag of the SGI,
ripple as a hopeful breeze fills our sails.
The lapping waves beat out their message
of congratulations upon our ship's bow!
Our destination —
America's distant future,
the lights and colors
of a Century of Life,
the brilliant glory of human harmony.

Our Value As Human Beings Is Determined By Our Actions

—ᴍᴍ—

SGI-USA CULTURE AND SCIENCE EXECUTIVE CONFERENCE,
LOS ANGELES, CALIFORNIA, JANUARY 28, 1993

TODAY'S CONFERENCE is a gathering of individuals of intellect and character. To commemorate this significant meeting, and for the sake of posterity, I would like to share one perspective on the American spirit.

If I were to make an analogy, thought and philosophy would be like the heart or respiratory system of the human body. When the heart is sound, the whole body can maintain healthy activity. This same principle applies to both the individual and society.

The SGI has a mission to serve as the heart that ensures the healthy functioning of society. Consequently, taking good care of the SGI allows the fresh, life-giving blood of humanism to flow to and nourish all areas of society, including culture, politics and the economy, to name but a few.

Nourishment, both mental and spiritual, is also vital to the individual. This is why I take every possible opportunity to speak about matters of faith from different perspectives.

When America made its departure as a new nation, the world wanted to know, "What kind of country is it?" Benjamin Franklin provided this answer: "People [in America] do not enquire concerning a Stranger, *What IS he? but What can he DO?* If he has any useful Art, he is welcome; and if he exercises it and behaves well, he will be respected by all that know him" (from *Information to Those Who Would Remove to America*).

Actions are far more important than status or social standing. Ranks or titles or distinctions in position, such as those between priesthood and laity, are of little importance. What truly matters is: What have you actually done, what can you actually do, and what are you actually trying to accomplish? Our value as human beings is determined by our actions.

Do Not Become a Parasite

Franklin continued, "But a mere Man of Quality, who on that Account [his birth or social position] wants to live upon the Public, by some Office or Salary, will be despis'd and disregarded." People who hold high status or live lives of luxury solely by virtue of their birth or position are "living off" society. This was the prevailing sentiment in America, the republic of the people.

In Buddhism, those who have in actuality advanced kosen-rufu are worthy of greatest respect. In contrast, those who crave personal fame and profit, while not making the slightest exertion themselves [for the sake of the Law or the believers], are parasites who live off Buddhism. The Nichiren Shoshu priesthood is the most pernicious example of this.

Franklin also said with a touch of humor, "In Europe it [birth] has indeed its Value, but it is a Commodity that cannot be carried to a worse Market than to that of America."

Yours is a country that questions not a person's status or birth but his or her actions. The United States should indeed become a model for the Soka Renaissance — a reformation based on the ideals of humanism.

Revitalization Through Human Revolution

The famous French aristocrat, Lafayette, sympathizing with the ideals of the American Revolution, traveled across the Atlantic to fight alongside the American colonists. In a letter addressed to his wife back in France, he wrote: "The happiness of America is linked to the happiness of all humankind. America will become a haven of virtue, integrity, generosity, equality and peaceful liberty." He is saying that when these values are imperiled elsewhere, the United States will be a sanctuary where they will continue to thrive.

Today, too, the renewal of the United States is linked to the renewal of the world, and the revitalization of the American people, awakened to a new humanism, must become the basis for the revitalization of the country. The SGI's movement of human revolution is the most fundamental contribution we can make to the renewal of the United States and the world.

In terms of kosen-rufu, the new departure of the United States is directly linked to a fresh departure for the worldwide kosen-rufu movement. The magnificent future of global kosen-rufu rests on the shoulders of all of you SGI-USA members.

A Pioneer of U.S.–Japan Exchange

Yesterday, members of the visiting exchange delegation from Kansai participated in the SGI-USA general meeting. Some representative Kansai members and SGI-USA members who are originally from Kansai are also attending today's executive conference. Therefore, I would like to talk a little about a person from the Kansai area who pioneered in forging ties between the United States and Japan.

At the end of the Edo period (1600–1868), when Japan was still pursuing its policy of seclusion from the rest of the world, one open-minded person worked actively to build links between the two countries. His name was Hamada Hikozo, a native of Harima province (present-day Hyogo Prefecture in Kansai), who is commonly known as "America Hikozo" among the Japanese.

At age thirteen, Hikozo, the son of a ship's captain, was sailing back from Edo (present-day Tokyo) when his ship was wrecked, casting him adrift on the open sea for fifty-two days. Suffering unbearable agony and convinced that he was going to die, Hikozo was finally rescued by an American ship and taken to the United

States. There, he received an education in San Francisco and eventually acquired American citizenship, the first Japanese to do so. His American name was Joseph Heco.

XENOPHOBIC JAPAN

He returned to Japan after nine years, as the interpreter for the American consulate. At that time, a storm of xenophobic sentiment raged in his homeland.

Even in the world today, the spreading wave of exclusionism — as evidenced by the emergence of neo-Nazi movements in some countries — is cause for grave concern.

In America, the castaway Hikozo was warmly welcomed and given the chance to obtain an education and legal citizenship. In contrast to America's openness, Japan's doors were firmly closed. The isolationist policy of the Japanese nation seeped into the hearts and minds of its people, bringing about a drastic disparity in openness between Japan and the United States.

During his life, Hikozo met three U.S. presidents: Franklin Pierce, James Buchanan and Abraham Lincoln. Details of these encounters are featured in Hikozo's autobiography. He was astonished at how open and receptive the presidents were. All three, he said, were genuinely warm and considerate toward him.

"EVEN THE PRESIDENT SPOKE TO ME AS AN EQUAL"

When he met President Pierce, Hikozo was a bundle of nerves, having been told the president was the most powerful person in the country. Much to his surprise, the president spoke to him as an equal, without any affectation whatsoever.

One can imagine his bewilderment: "What's happening here? In Japan, even an official of the smallest municipality is surrounded by a host of retainers, and it is virtually impossible to approach him without observing an elaborate code of etiquette. Not to mention what one has to go through when meeting a samurai lord! And yet the leader of a great country like the United

States, without any awesome display of authority, came over to me with such easy familiarity; he sat down with me and spoke to me as an equal! Can he really be the head of state?"

The less true ability people have, the more they are concerned with formalities and displays of authority. The grandiloquent rituals observed in the domain of priests were all created in later ages [after the originator of the particular religious teaching had died].

Encountering the youthful American spirit of valuing people for their real ability or substance, Hikozo was astonished and deeply moved that this country should be "totally void of unnecessary formalities."

With the new open-mindedness he had learned and acquired in the United States, Hikozo [on his return to Japan] threw himself into efforts to open Japan's doors and bring about its modernization. He also began publishing Japan's first regular newspaper, *Kaigai Shimbun* (Overseas News).

"'To Open' Is Another Name for Faith"

The American tradition of dispensing with formality strikes a chord with the Kansai spirit. It also has close parallels with the original spirit of Buddhism and the SGI's way of value-creative living.

In *The Record of the Orally Transmitted Teachings*, Nichiren Daishonin says, in reference to attaining Buddhahood, "'Attain' means to open or reveal" (OTT, 126). Attaining Buddhahood means opening our lives to their fullest potential and revealing our innate Buddhahood. This is the purpose of Buddhism.

Nichiren Daishonin says of the phrase "Opening the door of Buddha wisdom," which appears in the Lotus Sutra: "'Opening' here is another name for the mind of faith" (OTT, 28).

Faith is the sole means by which to open our lives and our inner state of Buddhahood. Faith is the most open state of mind of all. Infinite clusters of good fortune spill forth from this unbarred treasure house of life.

Intellect and Faith Line
the Royal Road of Humanity

Faith is the ultimate essence of intellect. Through the practice of correct faith, the intellect comes to shine.

Intellect without correct faith lacks a firm anchor in the soil of life and eventually becomes disordered. This prompted Tsunesaburo Makiguchi to remark that many modern thinkers were suffering from what he termed *higher psychosis.*

Faith without intellect, meanwhile, leads to blind faith and fanaticism. Faith or intellect alone — one without the other — is unhealthy.

All of you here at this conference possess both faith and intellect, and you are applying them in your activities to promote peace, culture and education based on Buddhism. This way of life accords with the Middle Way, the loftiest path that human beings can follow; it is the royal road of humanity.

I close today's speech with my prayers that your lives will shine with ever greater splendor with each passing year.

Radicalism Reconsidered

—⚍—

CLAREMONT MCKENNA COLLEGE,
CLAREMONT, CALIFORNIA, JANUARY 29, 1993

IT IS WITH a feeling of exuberance that I join you today, sensing the vigor, energy and intellectual vitality of Claremont McKenna College. I am honored to have been invited to speak, and I extend my greetings and grateful thanks to President Jack L. Stark, the members of the faculty and students.

NEW PRINCIPLES OF INTEGRATION

Only a few years remain before we begin the twenty-first century, and our world seems to be sliding deeper into the malaise and disorder so often associated with *fin de siècle*. Among its constant features, history has demonstrated cycles of coming together and breaking apart, integration and disintegration, but now we face the prospect of pitching into a level of global chaos from which there may be no recovery. I refer to the extremely potent disintegrative forces of national and ethnic fundamentalism, which, in the wake of the Cold War, are emerging to fill the vacuum left by the abandonment of ideology as the ersatz principle around which our world was ordered and integrated.

At each important juncture in recent history — the liberation of Eastern Europe, the peaceful birth of a reunified Germany and the end of the Gulf War — we have heard discussions of the need for a vision on which to base a new international order. But dreams have rapidly faded, and still we are searching blindly for the out-lines, having achieved only a general agreement that whatever form a new order takes, the United Nations will play a central role.

Our world can be likened to the scorched earth that is left after a brush fire. If we are to sow this desolate bed with the seeds for new growth, we cannot depend on the old guidelines. We must put our full energies into the task of discovering new principles of integration for our world.

Peoples and nations have only just begun to awaken from their long intoxication with ideology. Several of my friends from the former Soviet Union have used the parable of Procrustes's bed to describe the domination and victimization of people by ideology.[1] When we pause to think of the enormous sacrifice and the toll of human suffering that have been the price of attachment to ideol-ogy, it is clear that the search for integrating principles must be conducted with great caution. This search cannot be transcendent but must be entirely human in scale, directed at our inner lives. For the essence of our quest is the recovery and revival of the total-ity and unity of human experience that are being so disastrously eroded by accelerating fragmentation.

In an interview published in the Soka Gakkai's daily newspa-per, the *Seikyo Shimbun*, pioneer researcher in psychopharmacol-ogy Joel Elkes astutely observed: "Healing is a restoration to the whole.... The words *healing, whole* and *holy* all derive from the same root. To be holy is to be complete, connected as a person and with other persons, connected with the planet. Pain is a sig-nal that the part has become loose from the whole."[2] This obser-vation applies not just to physiological pain but to all that ails our contemporary civilization, whose fundamental pathogenesis can be found in the breakdown of human wholeness.

It has been some time since expressions such as "the totality of humanity" have ceased to summon a vivid image to our minds. "Human wholeness" might be conceived as a generic term embrac-ing our potential for wisdom (*homo sapiens*), our entrepreneurial skills (*homo economicus*), our ability to work transformations (*homo faber*) or our playfulness (*homo ludens*). But this is little more than an array of definitions and as such is too simplistic to capture the essence of "human wholeness."

START WITH THE SUN

In the final chapter of his admonitory work *Apocalypse*, D. H. Lawrence repeats his frequent appeal for a restoration of wholeness, delineating the problem with great clarity: "What man most passionately wants is his living wholeness and his living unison, not his own isolated salvation of his "soul".... What we want is to destroy our false, inorganic connections, especially those related to money, and reestablish the living organic connections, with the cosmos, the sun and earth, with mankind and nation and family. Start with the sun, and the rest will slowly, slowly happen."[3]

What Lawrence expresses with such poetry has a remarkable parallel in the words of Eduard Heimann, whose macroscopic analyses of social dynamics have invited comparison with Marx and Schumpeter. Mr. Heimann advances the idea that the term *organic growth* can be applied to those modalities of social development in which the wholeness of the person and the unity of life are left intact. "If we may be permitted for present purposes the use of a dangerous analogy, 'the organism' of society lives and evolves, growing and changing while maintaining its identity."[4] Needless to say, modern society has drifted far from any semblance of healthy, ideal "organic growth."

"Human wholeness" refers to that vibrant state of being where we can absorb and embody the immanent rhythms of cosmic life in new patterns of action and activity, and in so doing, give vital meaning to history and traditions. The experience of human wholeness is one of deep fulfillment, enabling us to manifest the qualities — such as composure and generosity, tolerance and consideration — that have been considered virtues since ancient times. Conversely, people who sever themselves from history and tradition, from others and the cosmos, are fated to an uncontrollable process of degeneration and loss of self, leading to nervous torment, instability and, finally, madness.

It is sometimes suggested nowadays that Nietzsche's "last man" is the image of modern humanity, yet the very idea itself is but another aspect of instability and loss of self. The "last man" is anything but history's victor. He seems inescapably trapped within the "false, inorganic connections, especially those related to money," of which Lawrence warns. If this is the contemporary *homo economicus*, what a long and sad decline from the independence and dynamism of the original economic man portrayed by Adam Smith! The transformation in this single aspect conveys incontrovertible evidence of human wholeness sundered, as we advance into modernity.

How can we restore wholeness to the human condition without jeopardizing the benefits of modernization, among them the work being done to eliminate hunger and disease? It is my belief that balanced, steady gradualism will allow us to rein in the terrible momentum of disintegration and develop new principles of integration. Such an approach may strike some as circuitous, but in the long run it represents the most direct and fundamental way to provide lasting solutions for the ills of our age. As we take on the challenge of this daunting task, there are a number of points to consider, the first of which is the importance of the gradualist approach to change.

CASE FOR GRADUALISM

The year before last, the seventy-year experiment of communism in the Soviet Union culminated in abject failure. Some observers remarked that the Russians had ended the process started by the French Revolution. In other words, the dissolution of the Soviet Union thoroughly undercut attempts to view history as a linear, causal process in which, for example, the bourgeois revolution in France must inevitably lead to a proletariat revolution in Russia. To me, such a diagnosis of the failure of what might be called the "radical rationalist approach to history" is convincing.

The historiographical premise behind that approach is the a priori existence of a blueprint for the rational development and advancement of history; it is a method that judges and seeks to remake reality against a single theoretical model. This approach reflects the unquestioning faith in reason that swept through nineteenth-century intellectual history. As it relates to the question of human wholeness, it exalts the single faculty of reason to the exclusion of all others. It was this mistaken sense of having mastered immutable laws of history that produced the repulsive intolerance and heady arrogance characteristic of so many modern revolutionaries. The sad irony is that most of them were originally motivated by good intentions.

There is a natural relation between rationalism and radicalism. If all events can be understood by rational processes, from which the blueprints for a rationalist utopia can be drawn, theoretically they can be sped up, and the sooner the utopia is realized, the better. Equally natural is the quick resort to force in dealing with counterrevolutionary elements who refuse to adopt this utopian vision as their own.

This kind of radicalism does not necessarily have general appeal. Consider, for example, the words of the Kyrgyzstan-born novelist Chingiz Aitmatov, one of the leading lights of contemporary Russian literature. In the introduction to the dialogue he and I have carried on over the past several years, Aitmatov has written: "Some fatherly advice: Young people, do not put your faith in social revolutions. For a nation, a people and a society, revolution is riot, mass disease, mass violence and general catastrophe. We have found that out to the fullest. Seek ways of democratic reform, like bloodless evolution and the sequential transformation of society. Evolution demands more time, patience and compromise. It is the organization and augmentation of happiness, not its forceful establishment. I pray to God that the younger generations will learn from our mistakes."[5]

Interestingly, Aitmatov's trenchant critique of revolutionary radicalism echoes the charges Edmund Burke and Goethe leveled at Jacobinism.

Not only revolutionary radicalism but any worldview that bases itself on "historical inevitability" fundamentally denies the human capacity to create our own destiny through our own efforts. We must always resist the temptation to treat individual lives or history as mere objective things or facts; their truth can only be known through active, living engagement and participation. To be of real and lasting value, change must be gradual and inspired from within. The application of external, coercive force will always destroy some aspect of our total humanity and compromise the balance and integrity of life.

In this regard, there is considerable validity in the economist Friedrich A. Hayek's analogy of a gardener to describe the attitude a true liberal takes toward society. The growth of plant life is both spontaneous and gradual. At most, the gardener can create conditions propitious to growth. In the same way, Hayek urges, we must utilize the "spontaneous forces of society."[6]

Coincidentally, the gardener analogy also leads us to consider the need to respect diversity within society. One of the most critical questions today is how, after the fashion of a skilled gardener, we can create a harmonious garden from the manifold human talents and qualities, while respecting the unique and sacrosanct individuality of each person. By adopting an inner-directed and gradualist approach, we can find ways through which the diversity of our experience can become a source of creative energy. The tradition and experience of Americans, I believe, qualify the United States to assume a special mission to demonstrate a pattern for the entire world.

Let me also stress that just as radicalism is fated by its nature to resort to violence and terror, the most potent weapon in the arsenal of the gradualist is dialogue. In Socrates, we see the steadfast commitment to dialogue, to verbal combat from which there is no retreat, and an intensity that is, in some literal sense, "death-defying." Such dialogue can only be sustained by resources of spiritual energy and strength far greater and deeper than will be found among those who so quickly turn to violence.

DISCIPLINE AND DIALOGUE

It is only within the open space created by dialogue — whether conducted with our neighbors, with history, with nature or the cosmos — that human wholeness can be sustained. The closed silence of an autistic space can only become the site of spiritual suicide. We are not born human in any but a biological sense; we can only learn to know ourselves and others and thus be trained in the ways of being human. We do this by immersion in the ocean of language and dialogue fed by the springs of cultural tradition.

I am reminded of the beautiful and moving passage in *Phaedo* in which Socrates teaches his youthful disciples that hatred of language and ideas (misology) leads to antipathy toward humanity (misanthropy).[7] The mistrust of language that gives birth to a misologist is but the inverse of an excessive belief in the power of language. The two are different aspects of the same thing, which is a frailty of spirit unable to cope with the stresses of human proximity brought about by dialogue. Such spiritual weakness causes a person to vacillate between undue trustfulness and suspicion of other people, thus becoming easy prey for the forces of disintegration.

To be worthy of the name *dialogue,* our efforts for dialogue's sake must be carried through to the end. To refuse peaceful exchange and choose force is to compromise and give in to human weakness; it is to admit the defeat of the human spirit. Socrates encourages his youthful disciples to train and strengthen themselves spiritually, to maintain hope and self-control, to advance courageously choosing virtue over material wealth, truth over fame.

While we cannot regard modern mass society in terms of the values of ancient Greece, we must not overemphasize the differences between them. In his classic study *Public Opinion*, Walter Lippmann, for one, repeatedly calls for Socratic dialogue and Socratic individuals as the keys to the more wholesome formation of public opinion.[8] When I recently met in Tokyo with President Jack L. Stark, we agreed fully on the primacy of education among social values. Education, based on open dialogue, is far more than the mere transfer of information and knowledge; it enables us to rise above the confines of our parochial perspectives and passions. Institutes of higher learning are charged with the task of encouraging Socratic world citizens and spearheading the search for new principles for the peaceful integration of our world.

Incidentally, Shakyamuni, who is often mentioned with Socrates as one of the world's great teachers, spent the last moments of his life exhorting his grieving disciples to engage him in dialogue. To the very end he, also, continued to urge them to question him on any subject, as one friend to another.

CHARACTER AND HUMAN WHOLENESS

My final point is the central importance of character, another name for human wholeness or completeness. The integrating principles to which I have been referring are not just abstractions but something that must be sought inwardly by people striving to grow in character. It is character that, in the end, holds together the web of integrating forces.

Almost contemporaneous with the establishment of Claremont McKenna College, my mentor in life and second president of the Soka Gakkai, Josei Toda, emerged from a two-year imprisonment imposed by the forces of Japanese militarism to initiate a new humanistic movement in Japan. In his efforts, he always focused on raising people of character, one person at a time, from among the populace. I have many fond memories of this compassionate man, whose love for youth knew no bounds and who encouraged us to be great actors on the stage of life. Indeed, the power of character is like the concentrated energy of an actor who has given himself or herself entirely over to the performance. A person of outstanding character will always, even under the most difficult circumstances, retain an air of composure, ease and even humor, like an accomplished actor playing a part. This is nothing other than the achievement of self-mastery or self-control.

Goethe, who was an outstanding stage director in addition

to his other talents, responded when asked what he looked for in an actor: "Above all things, whether he had control over himself. For an actor who possesses no self-possession, who cannot appear before a stranger in his most favourable light, has, generally speaking, little talent. His whole profession requires continual self-denial. . . ."[9]

Goethe's idea of self-control corresponds to the concept of moderation in Platonic philosophy. Self-control is not only an essential quality for actors but is arguably the foremost prerequisite for the development of character.

One of the central teachings of Buddhist philosophy bears directly on the question of character formation. Buddhism classifies the states of life that constitute human experience into ten worlds or realms. From the least to the most desirable they are: the world of hell, a condition submerged in suffering; the world of hunger, a state in which body and mind are engulfed in the raging flames of desire; the world of animality, in which one fears the strong and abuses the weak; the world of anger, characterized by the constant compulsion to surpass and dominate others; the world of humanity, a tranquil state marked by the ability to make reasoned judgments; the world of rapture, a state filled with joy; the world of voice-hearers, or learning, a condition of aspiration to enlightenment; the world of cause-awakened ones, or realization, where one perceives unaided the true nature of phenomena; the world of bodhisattvas, a state of compassion in which one seeks to save all people from suffering; and finally the world of Buddhahood, a state of human completeness and perfect freedom.

Within each of these ten states or worlds is likewise to be found the full spectrum of the Ten Worlds. In other words, the state of hell contains within it every state from hell to Buddhahood. In the Buddhist view, life is never static, but is in constant flux, effecting a dynamic, moment-by-moment transformation among the states. The most critical point, then, is which of these ten states, as they exist in the vibrant flow of life, forms the basis for our own lives? Buddhism offers a way of life centered on the highest states, those of bodhisattvas and Buddhahood, as an ideal of human existence.

Emotions — joy and sorrow, pleasure and anger — are of course the threads from which life's fabric is woven, and we continue to experience the full span of the Ten Worlds. These experiences, however, can be shaped and directed by the pure and indestructible states of bodhisattvas and Buddhahood. Nichiren, whose Buddhist teaching is the basis of our SGI organization, did more than merely preach this doctrine; he lived it, providing a remarkable model for the future. When, for example, he was about to be executed by the iniquitous authorities of the time, he reproached his lamenting disciples, "What greater joy could there be?" (WND-1, 767). After overcoming the greatest trial of his life, he even had sake brought for the soldiers who had been escorting him to his execution.

Because of these qualities, I am confident that Buddhism can deeply affect the formation of character, which is the key to the restoration of human wholeness. As a practitioner of Buddhism, it is my hope that, together with our distinguished friends gathered here today, we will set off on a courageous journey in search of those new principles of integration that will determine the fate of humankind in the coming century. I would like to close by quoting a passage from a poem by Walt Whitman, whose poetry I have read and loved since my youth.

> I see male and female everywhere,
> I see the serene brotherhood of philosophs,
> I see the constructiveness of my race,
> I see the results of the perseverance and industry of
>   my race,
> I see ranks, colors, barbarisms, civilizations, I go
>   among them,
> I mix indiscriminately,
> And I salute all the inhabitants of the earth.[10]

Notes

1. Procrustes was a mythical Greek robber who stretched or lopped off the limbs of his "guests" in order to make them fit the size of his bed.

2. From an interview with Dr. Joel Elkes, *Seikyo Shimbun*, July 8, 1992, p. 3.

3. D. H. Lawrence, *Apocalypse* (New York: Penguin Books, 1976), p. 125.

4. Eduard Heimann, *Soziale Theorie der Wirtschaftssysteme* (Hamburg: J.C.B. Mohr Tübingen, 1963), p. 36.

5. Chingiz Aitmatov and Daisaku Ikeda, *Ooinaru tamashii no uta* (Tokyo: Yomiuri Shimbunsha, 1991), p. 81.

6. Friedrich A. Hayek, *The Road to Serfdom* (Chicago: The University of Chicago Press, 1972), p. 17.

7. Scott Buchanan, ed., *The Portable Plato*, trans. Benjamin Jowett (New York: Viking Press, 1973), p. 238.

8. Walter Lippmann, *Public Opinion* (New York: Macmillan, 1938), p. 402ff.

9. Johann Peter Eckermann, *Conversations with Goethe*, trans. John Oxenford, ed. J. K. Moorhead (London: Everyman's Library, 1972), p. 100.

10. Walt Whitman, *Leaves of Grass* (New York: Random House, 1950), p. 116.

The Desire for Kosen-rufu Is the Wellspring of Happiness

—◆◆◆—

MEETING FOR VOLUNTEERS, WORLD PEACE IKEDA AUDITORIUM,
SANTA MONICA, CALIFORNIA, JANUARY 31, 1993

My sincere appreciation to all the Los Angeles members who have been working so hard behind the scenes this past week. I am greatly indebted to all of you. Los Angeles is the cornerstone of the worldwide kosen-rufu movement, and I am determined to return to this city again many times in the future. Earlier today, I enjoyed a delightful exchange with several hundred youngsters, the future heirs of the SGI-USA. I am truly overjoyed to see their vibrant and spirited growth.

Lighting the Path for Others

Some Japanese diplomats stationed here in the United States recently said to me that there is no place where the volunteer spirit to help others is more firmly rooted than in America. I agree. Moreover, all of you are exerting yourselves tirelessly every day for others, for society and for the Law.

Nichiren Daishonin writes, "If one lights a fire for others, one will brighten one's own way" (WND-2, 1060). Please be confident that the higher your flame of altruistic action burns, the more its light will suffuse your life with happiness. Those who possess an altruistic spirit are the happiest people of all.

FAITH IS THE SECRET OF HAPPINESS

We are currently facing a serious worldwide recession. The Daishonin teaches that those who embrace faith in the Lotus Sutra can change calamities into good fortune (see WND-2, 669).

Faith is the secret of happiness for all people. When you truly forge your mind of faith, you will become an eternal victor throughout the three existences of life — past, present and future. Strong faith enables you to display your wisdom appropriately so that you can take advantage of change and move forward in the direction of victory and hope. You can definitely show actual proof and benefit in accord with the passage "Those who now believe in the Lotus Sutra will gather fortune from ten thousand miles away" (WND-1, 1137).

Your new general director's name, Zaitsu, which literally means "harbor of wealth" in Japanese, conjures images of a vast and luxuriant expanse of treasures and riches. [Fred Zaitsu served as SGI-USA general director from November 1992 to December 1999.] The name inspires economic confidence! I hope, therefore, that, together with General Director Zaitsu, you will build a prosperous SGI-USA overflowing with the world's greatest fortune and benefit, wisely implementing the principle that faith manifests itself in daily life.

THOSE FREE OF COMPLAINT POSSESS WISDOM AND ABUNDANT GOOD FORTUNE

In another Gosho, the Daishonin writes: "Do not go around lamenting to others how hard it is for you to live in this world. To do so is an act utterly unbecoming to a worthy man" (WND-1, 850).

If you practice faith yet have an attitude of complaint, you will destroy your good fortune in direct proportion. Those who are full of complaint are not respected by others. From both Buddhist and secular perspectives, their behavior does not befit a wise or worthy person.

Everything is determined by oneself, by one's inner resolution. Let us assume, for example, that after exerting yourself diligently in your practice of faith, you have finally accumulated a solid store of good fortune. But then you start complaining, "I'm sick of being so busy" or "I really wanted to watch that TV program today [instead of doing activities]" or something similar. The moment you start grumbling or complaining or harboring ill feelings toward your fellow members, you immediately forfeit a substantial portion of all the good fortune you have worked so hard to attain!

You erase more good fortune when you allow yourself to become discouraged over, for example, losing an argument with your spouse. But when you resolve to challenge the situation by chanting daimoku, you add a hefty increase to your accumulated store of fortune. The sum of all these additions and subtractions, gains and losses, represents the final balance of your happiness.

Therefore, if you are practicing faith, you stand to gain far more when you do so willingly, joyously and with a sense of gratitude.

Victory Lies in Continuing

The Gosho does not specify the current format for doing gongyo nor does it specify the amount of daimoku we should chant. While it goes without saying that doing a complete gongyo and chanting abundant daimoku are ideal, what matters most is our mind of faith.

As long as our mind of faith is connected to the Gohonzon, our benefits will never disappear. That is why it is vital for us to persevere in our Buddhist practice throughout our lives, no matter what, even if on some days our physical condition or other circumstances prevent us from doing gongyo and chanting daimoku to our full satisfaction. Those who continue to challenge themselves to the end savor ultimate victory.

THE SGI — AN ORGANIZATION OF
BOUNDLESS BENEFIT

To emerge victorious, it is important never to cut ourselves off from the SGI, the organization dedicated to the achievement of kosen-rufu. No one who has left our organization has achieved happiness.

The mind of faith is invisible. So, too, are radio waves. TV broadcasts are electromagnetic waves that travel through space to reach their destinations. The communications between NASA and space shuttles are highly sophisticated and impressive. If the receiver is broken or turned off, however, radio waves from even the most powerful transmitter will not be picked up.

The SGI is the sole organization directly connected to Nichiren Daishonin. It is a wondrous gathering that has "emerged from the earth," carrying out activities in accord with the Buddha's decree. Those who link up and advance together with this organization dedicated to kosen-rufu and pervaded by benefit will evolve the correct mind of faith that matches the time. With this mind of faith, they can fill the canvas of their lives with portraits of happiness in which all their wishes are fulfilled.

SHOWING WOMEN THE HIGHEST RESPECT

All of you are the standard-bearers of the new American Renaissance. Ralph Waldo Emerson, one of the leaders of the original American Renaissance, declared that "speech is power" (*Letters and Social Aims*, 1917, p. 92). Nichiren states, "The voice carries out the work of the Buddha" (OTT, 4). A voice that rings with deep conviction derived from faith in the Mystic Law functions as an instrument to carry out the Buddha's work — whether it be in encouraging and praising others, engaging in dialogue, trying to impart understanding and peace of mind or saying what has to be said.

Emerson also goes on to say that women reign supreme when

it comes to the art of conversation. He extols the remarkable conversational power of women as being "better than song, and carr[ying] ingenuity, character, wise counsel, and affection" (*Letters and Social Aims,* 93).

The renowned poet and thinker continues: "They are not only wise themselves, they make us wise. No one can be a master in conversation who has not learned much from women…" (p. 93).

The conversation of women of keen perception, who are sensitive to the feelings of others, has the power to open even the most heavily barricaded heart. And it is invariably women's cries for justice that move people to action and change the times.

We of the SGI must learn from women, defend their rights and, more than anywhere else in the world, accord women the highest respect and consideration [in our organization]. Men who scold women out of emotionalism are contemptible. I suspect that many such men may feel a sense of inferiority to their own wives, and that is why they feel the need to vent their frustrations.

Bringing Happiness to All Humankind

Josei Toda called on the Soka Gakkai members to "bring an inexhaustible wellspring of happiness to the people of the world." He did so because it was also the desire of Nichiren Daishonin.

The Nichiren Shoshu priests, in contrast, have not even a fragment of such compassion. Rather than praying for the happiness of humankind, they exploit the Daishonin and the faith of the believers to satisfy their cravings for lavish feasts and sumptuous lifestyles in a most base and despicable manner, like so many hungry demons. Theirs is a world rampant with devilish forces — one that is poles apart from the pure world of the Daishonin.

Be that as it may, the future of the sacred task of accomplishing worldwide kosen-rufu rests on the shoulders of you members of the new SGI-USA.

Each day I fervently pray for the health, longevity, safety and good fortune of all you who are so dear to my heart. Wishing that you, my friends, enjoy glory and happiness and always be full of good cheer, I conclude my speech of thanks today. Thank you very much for everything.

Respecting Those Dedicated to Kosen-rufu Is the Ultimate Message of the Lotus Sutra

—⟋⟍—

SGI-USA REPRESENTATIVES CONFERENCE,
MIAMI, FLORIDA, FEBRUARY 2, 1993

MY MOST SINCERE THANKS to all who have worked hard to maintain the grounds and facilities of the Miami Training Center in such splendid condition.

I would like to take this opportunity once again to express my sympathy to all those who suffered loss or damage in the devastation wrought by Hurricane Andrew here in Florida last summer. I am deeply grateful for the efforts of all who worked tirelessly to restore this and other local centers affected by the hurricane.

When I viewed the gardens here at the training center, I noticed that, not surprisingly, the trees with the strongest and most solid roots are still standing. It is the same with human beings. We must put down firm roots; we must be strong. Inner strength is a prerequisite for happiness, a prerequisite for upholding justice and one's beliefs.

One of the Buddha's titles is "One Who Can Endure" (WND-1, 41). The Buddha is the ultimate embodiment of the virtue of forbearance — the ability to courageously endure, persevere and overcome all difficulties. The power of faith gives us the strength to weather and survive any storm. Perseverance is the essence of a Buddha. Nichiren Daishonin, the original Buddha, is the epitome of this quality.

CULTIVATE PHYSICAL, INTELLECTUAL AND SPIRITUAL STRENGTH

Following in the Daishonin's footsteps, the first and second Soka Gakkai presidents, Tsunesaburo Makiguchi and Josei Toda, endured imprisonment. Even during the thirty-odd years since I became Soka Gakkai president, I have endured all imaginable persecutions, intrigues and treachery.

Unless we are strong, we cannot win in life, nor can we accomplish kosen-rufu. The essence of our human revolution is to become as strong a human being as possible.

President Toda used to say, "Become individuals who are strong physically, intellectually and spiritually." To be strong in all three areas is the ideal. Many people may be strong in one or two of these areas, but only when all three are combined can we enjoy a well-balanced life, a life of resounding victory. Those who cultivate such all-round strength are never defeated.

If your physical health is poor, both you and your family will suffer. Without sound mental capabilities, you cannot see the truth and thereby will be too easily deceived by evil. Nor can you create any great value in society. It is imperative that you have wisdom. For that reason, it is vital that, based on chanting daimoku, you study diligently, starting with the Daishonin's teachings. It is essential that you develop and strengthen your intellect.

Furthermore, it is our minds that put our bodies and intellect to work. No matter how healthy, intelligent or affluent we may be, if our minds are weak, then our happiness also will be frail and brittle. Our minds of faith, moreover, enable us to bring out the full potential in all things and situations, so it is crucial that we strive to forge our minds of faith.

You cannot win in your daily lives or in society if you are weak-minded or given to quick despair or complaint. Only in our daily lives and in society can we prove the validity of Buddhism. Please strive to become exemplary children of the Buddha and SGI members endowed with physical, intellectual and spiritual strength.

I hope you will build, and help others build, solid lives filled with unshakable happiness, while protecting the weak and the suffering. Also, I ask that men always remember to show the utmost respect to women.

In *The Record of the Orally Transmitted Teachings*, in which the Daishonin explains profound Buddhist doctrines, is the phrase "The foremost point [the Buddha] wished to convey" (OTT, 192), referring to a passage from the Lotus Sutra.

To expound the Lotus Sutra is the reason Shakyamuni made his advent in the world. It is the highest of all his teachings. What, then, were Shakyamuni's last words therein? "If you see a person who accepts and upholds this sutra, you should rise and greet him from afar, showing him the same respect you would a Buddha" (LS, 324).

"A person who accepts and upholds this sutra" — in other words, a votary of the Lotus Sutra — specifically refers to Nichiren Daishonin. In a broader sense, however, it indicates all those who, directly linked to the Daishonin, are devoting their lives to the widespread propagation of the Mystic Law.

The likes of those [of the Nichiren Shoshu priesthood] who appear to embrace the Gohonzon yet in reality abuse faith to serve their own ends are totally undeserving of respect.

Nichiren teaches, "With just these eight characters ['you should rise and greet him from afar, showing him the same respect you would a Buddha'] he [Shakyamuni] summed up the message of the entire sutra" (OTT, 193).

"Respect the children of the Buddha; respect and cherish the practitioners who dedicate themselves to the widespread propagation of the Mystic Law as you would a Buddha!" This sums up Shakyamuni's last words, or final testament. It is also the underlying spirit of the entire Lotus Sutra — a spirit the Daishonin decreed to be the "foremost point."

The true inheritors to whom the Buddha conveyed the teachings are those who exert themselves to the utmost in its practice. Those who, more than anyone else, respect and treasure the SGI members — the present-day votaries of kosen-rufu — understand the foremost point conveyed by the Buddha.

On this point alone, it is obvious that Nikken has not truly inherited the teaching from Nichiren Daishonin. The behavior of the Nichiren Shoshu priesthood is diametrically opposed to the Lotus Sutra and the Gosho.

In the seven hundred years since the founding of the Daishonin's Buddhism — and indeed in Buddhism's entire history — it is only with the appearance of the SGI that the Buddha's mandate of worldwide kosen-rufu is now becoming a reality. Far from treasuring us SGI members, the Nichiren Shoshu priesthood cruelly exploited us to the hilt, allowing their greed to run rampant; they tormented and bullied us and then callously disposed of us. It is all too clear that the current priesthood has inherited nothing from the Daishonin.

Details of their profligate ways have recently been featured in the Soka Gakkai youth division's newspaper, *Soka Shimpo*, confirming the priests of Nichiren Shoshu to be "animal[s] dressed in priestly robes" (WND-1, 760).

They take the sincere offerings made to the Mystic Law and the Daishonin by the children of the Buddha and squander them on idle, pleasure-seeking pursuits. In light of the Gosho, it is evident that they are destroyers of the Daishonin's Buddhism, enemies of the Buddha and anything but its legitimate heirs.

THE SPIRIT OF THE LOTUS SUTRA HOLDS THE KEY TO WORLD PEACE

The priests of Nichiren Shoshu despise the children of the Buddha; they hold human beings in contempt. The Daishonin, in contrast, teaches respect for the children of the Buddha and for all people. He espouses reverence and respect for the inherent Buddha nature of all human beings.

When this spirit of the Lotus Sutra — that is, to respect others — finally spreads and prevails, there is no doubt that true world peace will be achieved. Humankind will then be united, not by authoritarian power, military force or economic might but by the Law of life. Since the Law is eternal, the bonds that are formed on this basis will also be everlasting.

Consequently, in urging us to respect all people, the Daishonin also teaches us the secret, or key, to attaining world peace. We of the SGI are the only ones who have received the foremost point and are putting it into action.

BEAUTIFUL MIAMI

The southern part of the United States, the area covered by the Atlanta Joint Territory, has produced many famous literary works, such as *Gone With the Wind*. America's South is also the home of such pioneering civil rights champions as Martin Luther King Jr. and Rosa Parks. President Bill Clinton and President Jimmy Carter are also both from southern states, Arkansas and Georgia, respectively. The South is blessed with wonderful natural landscapes and a diverse array of able and talented individuals. Miami, in particular, is the envy of the world for its warm weather and natural beauty.

As an expression of my deep appreciation to all of you members here in Miami, I propose that a tree be planted for each chapter of the Atlanta Joint Territory — a total of thirty-eight in all — in the soon-to-be-opened Soka Bodhi Tree Garden in India.

I am always earnestly praying for your good fortune, excellent health, longevity and safety. Please advance with the utmost confidence and assurance.

Thank you very much!

Raising Children To Be Capable Leaders of the Twenty-first Century

—⟋⟍—

SGI REPRESENTATIVES CONFERENCE,
MIAMI, FLORIDA, FEBRUARY 3, 1993

I AM SURE that the just-announced decision to found the SGI-USA future division[1] will shine with increasing significance as time goes by. My most heartfelt congratulations.

Nearly thirty years ago in Japan I founded the senior high school division [1964], the junior high school division [1965] and the boys and girls division [1965], and I devoted my full energies to the cultivation of these young members.

Today, the former members of these divisions are active in Japan and around the world. They are diplomats, government officials and leading figures in industry. They are scholars, doctors and lawyers, and they are leaders of our esteemed Soka Gakkai. Friends committed to kosen-rufu work in every field.

I also believe that in the same way, or to an even greater extent, humanistic leaders will emerge like a glittering galaxy of stars from the future division of the SGI-USA in the twenty-first century. I firmly believe this.

THE JOY AND GOOD FORTUNE
DERIVED FROM RAISING SUCCESSORS

The other day (January 30), I met Rosa Parks, the highly respected civil rights activist, at Soka University's Calabasas campus. Mrs. Parks said that she derives her greatest pleasure from working with and for youth. Let us, too, joyfully and wholeheartedly exert ourselves in the task of nurturing the messengers of the future, our precious youth.

Those who will be responsible for the new divisions will have much work to do, but the law of causality guarantees that all your efforts will definitely adorn your own future with blessings and good fortune. Please also be assured that your benefits will be passed down generation after generation to your descendants.

Let me now say a few things that are on my mind concerning what we should teach our children in the home. I have observed many families and experienced many situations, and what I offer are my own conclusions. I will be most gratified if they are of some use to you.

STUDY FIRST

First, the members of the future division should make study their first priority. It goes without saying that faith is important, but faith is something we practice throughout our entire lives. There is a certain period and age when we should study. If we do not work hard during that period, we may fail to acquire important knowledge and skills, and we may come to regret it deeply later.

Faith manifests itself in daily life. For the members of the future division, faith manifests itself in their studies. During this period, to devote themselves to study represents an important part of their practice of faith.

It is certainly not right for them to use faith as an excuse to neglect their studies, saying they are too busy doing gongyo or attending meetings.

Sometimes your children may not be able to do gongyo, but there is no reason for parents to become overconcerned or agitated about this. There are times when chanting only three daimoku is sufficient.

To continue practicing is far more important. What matters is that the children maintain their connection to the Gohonzon and the SGI for their entire lives. They can make gradual improvements in their practice. Parents should be broad-minded on this matter. They might even sometimes reassure a child who is busy with studies by saying, "Don't worry, I'll do gongyo for you today."

In fact, putting too much pressure on children to practice may only alienate them from faith. I hope you will lead them wisely so that they will mature in the best direction and in a relaxed and natural manner.

COMMUNICATE WITH YOUR CHILDREN

Next, I would like to request that, no matter how busy you may be, you find the time to get together and talk with your children. The length of time is not important. What matters is that parents use their wisdom.

When you have to be away from home for some reason, try to leave a note for your children or call them on the phone when you have a chance. The important thing is to make sure that you stay in communication with them in some form.

Say your children come home, and there is no one there. They do not know where their parents are. No message is waiting for them. Naturally, they are bound to feel lonely, to feel emotionally insecure. This is a heartless way to treat children. You must not subject them to such loneliness.

Even if it is only a brief meeting, give your children a hug when you see them. Touch them, talk to them. Try to make time to listen to what they have to say. As long as you have love and compassion, you will find the wisdom to make this work.

Faith manifests itself as wisdom. The purpose of our faith is to become wise so that we can live wisely. The desire to save others becomes merely an abstract goal if those who practice faith cannot communicate with their own children or build strong and happy families.

The good fortune that accrues to parents who apply themselves diligently to SGI activities will protect their children without fail. Nonetheless, you must still make positive efforts to open and sustain dialogue with your children, not allowing yourselves to neglect them, claiming that you are too busy or it cannot be helped or telling yourselves that somehow things will be taken care of. Unless you exert yourselves in this way, you are irresponsible parents who lack compassion.

Outward appearance is not important — what counts is what is inside our hearts. Are there heart-to-heart bonds? Some families may always be together physically but be estranged at heart. Other families can only get together for brief periods but manage to enjoy concentrated and lively heart-to-heart communication at such times.

Families that share bonds of closeness based on day-to-day efforts are ones in which the members feel comfortable and at ease with one another, no matter where they are or what they are doing.

I ask that parents continually strive to improve themselves together with their children, in the way that best suits their individual families.

A Child Is a Person

A child is a person, an individual with his or her distinct personality. Sometimes children can be even more keenly perceptive than adults. That is why we must be careful how we behave in front of them. For example, couples should never argue in front of their children. If you must fight, go off where they cannot see you! Children are saddened when their parents fight. They go off to school with heavy hearts, and they will not forget the incident for a long time.

According to one psychologist, in many cases when children

witness their parents fighting, they are shaken to the core of their being and experience fear and anxiety as if the ground had given way beneath them. Tall trees grow from secure and solid ground. Please give your children a home where they can enjoy tranquillity and peace of mind.

FATHERS SHOULD NOT SCOLD

Sons tend to rebel when scolded by their fathers, while they are more likely to listen to their mother's scolding. The worst thing is for the father and the mother to gang up on and together scold the child. This leaves the child with no one to whom he or she can turn.

Fathers tend to have a soft spot for daughters and, consequently, are too easy on them. Mothers and daughters, meanwhile, often share a deep, natural understanding as women. That is why it is often better for mothers to discipline their daughters as well.

President Toda said: "When fathers grow angry, they alienate their children. But even when a mother gets angry, her children stay close to her." This wisdom is based on the laws of human behavior, the laws of life and psychology. Of course, there are always differences among cultures and among households, but I hope these remarks provide some sort of guidelines for you.

DISCOVER AND PRAISE A CHILD'S STRENGTHS

Parents must be fair. They must never favor one child over another because one is smart or good-looking or whatever. A parent's single thoughtless remark can often deeply wound a child and give him or her a sense of inferiority. How much worse the damage will be if children are always being compared to their siblings and treated unfairly! They will be starved for affection and feel lonely and hurt. Under these circumstances, they cannot mature in a healthy fashion. This is not good for either child or parent. It is a senseless way to behave.

Children who may be suffering a disadvantage compared to

their peers need our encouragement all the more. Watch over these children with affection and encourage them. Discover their strengths and praise them for those, building their confidence. Become their unfailing ally, support them, shower them with love and believe utterly in their potential. Respect each child's individuality. That is a parent's role.

Our society and our schools may operate on a cold, unemotional principle of competition, judging and selecting people by their abilities and appearance. That is precisely why it is important for the family to be a fair and equitable place where each member is valued for being the unique individual he or she is.

Telling Our Children About the Joy of Faith

One of the most essential ingredients in raising children to become fine adults is that parents get firmly in tune with their children and grow together with them, marching forward as one.

We SGI members devote ourselves to serving the Law, serving humanity. Ours is not an egocentric life. That is why we are busier than others and perhaps do not have as much opportunity for relaxation with our families. Nevertheless, we continue to devote ourselves to others.

Ours is the most noble way of life. We must make sure our children can understand and respect our beliefs, our way of life and our dedication. It is a mistake to assume that they will somehow come to know we love them or to understand our commitment to kosen-rufu on their own, without us having to say anything. We must make conscious efforts to verbalize and communicate our thoughts and feelings to them — and to do so wisely, in a relaxed and open manner, without undue haste. Finding the wisdom for this task is an expression of our faith.

Men and women are completely equal. Working from that assumption, we can still identify certain tendencies exhibited by members of each sex. I would like our men to be brave and upright individuals, capable people who can protect others. I would like our women to be blessed above all with happiness and good fortune. To achieve that, they must have pure hearts. "A pure-hearted woman is an angel; a foul-hearted woman is a witch," goes a saying. The only difference between these two extremes is a person's heart.

I have heard that the breakdown of the family has become a major social problem in the United States. The same tendencies are emerging in Japan. In light of this situation, and also prompted by the announcement of the upcoming establishment of the SGI-USA future division, I have shared with you several points that came to mind on this topic.

One of the SGI's eternal guidelines is for its members to create happy and harmonious families through faith.[2] Visualizing the day when the youngsters produced by your warm and delightful families grow to become outstanding leaders of the twenty-first century, who will illuminate America and the entire world like a brilliant constellation of stars or the dazzling sun, I conclude my speech.

Notes

1. Future division: Shortly after this announcement, the name of the group was expanded and changed to reflect its focus: junior high school division and high school division. Several months later, the SGI-USA boys and girls group was established, which later was renamed the elementary school division.

2. In December 2003, SGI President Ikeda announced five eternal guidelines of faith (February 6, 2004, World Tribune, p. 3). They are: 1) Faith for a harmonious family; 2) Faith for each person to become happy; 3) Faith for surmounting obstacles; 4) Faith for health and long life; and 5) Faith for absolute victory.

A Renaissance of Spirit
Based on Friendship

—⚹—

SGI-USA REPRESENTATIVES CONFERENCE,

MIAMI, FLORIDA, FEBRUARY 5, 1993

ATLANTA WILL BE the site of the 1996 Summer Olympic Games and is the focus of much attention now. The climate and natural setting of the American South, starting with Miami, are also wonderful, and all of you who live here are truly blessed.

Let me take this opportunity to express my gratitude to all of you who worked behind the scenes to ensure the success of the various events held during the past week.

The day of a new American Renaissance is dawning, and every one of you is a standard-bearer for that new age. I want you to march forward, carrying high the Stars and Stripes and the tricolored SGI flag as symbols of your diamond-strong solidarity, cheerful progress and brilliant victory.

A NEW AMERICA, DAY BY DAY

I would like to talk a little today about the spirit of renaissance that beats in America's heart.

The previous American Renaissance in the nineteenth century also took place in an age of change. A new America was being born day by day. Ralph Waldo Emerson was one of the leaders of that glorious American Renaissance.

Emerson was a great thinker, a masterful poet and an unrivaled speaker and writer. He was a philosopher who endeavored to bring to light a new spirit sought by humanity.

As a youth, I read his writings avidly. In the desolation that followed World War II, I turned to them again and again as nourishment for my starved soul. My mentor, Josei Toda, always encouraged me to read Emerson.

The other day, I met with some representative alumni of the Soka Schools, and they presented me with one of Emerson's original, handwritten letters. It is a letter to Henry David Thoreau, in which Emerson expresses his feelings of friendship. It is also an important historical document, the complete contents of which have not yet been made public. I will ensure that it is preserved as one of the treasures of Soka University.

An Inner Revolution
Is the Ultimate Revolution

As you all know, Emerson battled fiercely against religious authority. He declared, "The faith that stands on authority is not faith. The reliance on authority measures the decline of religion, the withdrawal of the soul."

Religion exists first and foremost for the sake of human beings. Buddhism in particular is thoroughly humanistic, based as it is on the philosophy of human equality and the sanctity of life. Whatever their position, those who claim to wield authority over others cannot be termed Buddhists. Reliance on authority is, in fact, eloquent testimony to a person's corruption and weakness.

Where can we find the royal road to reformation and change? Emerson declared: "Not he is great who can alter matter, but he who can alter my state of mind." He strongly urged us to undergo an inner reformation. How much more strongly does Buddhism urge this, with its teachings of "three thousand realms in a single moment of life" and "the oneness of life and its environment."

I want you to be assured that the challenge to which we set

ourselves day after day — that of our human revolution — is the royal road to bringing about a reformation in our families, local regions and societies. An inner revolution is the most fundamental and, at same time, the ultimate revolution for engendering change in all things.

THE WARMING RAYS OF FRIENDSHIP

Emerson also spoke of the power of affection: "Let our affection flow out to our fellows; it would operate in a day the greatest of all revolutions. It is better to work on institutions by the sun than by the wind."

Our hearts change others' hearts. Friendship changes people. Travelers who pull their capes over their shoulders and brace themselves determinedly against the cold wind naturally relax and change their outlook and actions when warmed by the sun. The SGI is an organization of friendship. I hope that, with the warmth of the sun, you will shower one another with friendship and spread waves of camaraderie and affection throughout society.

BECOMING HAPPY TOGETHER

In *The Record of the Orally Transmitted Teachings*, referring to "The Benefits of Responding With Joy" chapter of the Lotus Sutra, Nichiren Daishonin says, "'Joy' means that oneself and others together experience joy" (OTT, 146).

Joy is not simply your personal, egoistic happiness, nor is it making others happy at the expense of your own happiness. You and others delighting together, you and others becoming happy together — this is the Mystic Law and the wondrous thing about our realm of kosen-rufu.

The Daishonin also states, "Both oneself and others together will take joy in their possession of wisdom and compassion" (OTT, 146). To possess both wisdom and compassion is the heart of our human revolution. If you have wisdom alone and lack compassion, it will be a cold, perverse wisdom. If you have compassion alone and lack wisdom, you cannot achieve your own happiness or give happiness to others. You are even likely to lead them in the wrong direction.

As we advance together in the pursuit of our human revolution — on the path of unsurpassed joy and self-improvement — we deepen both our wisdom and compassion with the passing of time. This is our way of life in the SGI.

OUR PRAYERS FOR OTHERS' HAPPINESS ARE THE DRIVING FORCE FOR DEVELOPMENT

Each of you developing wisdom, making joyful progress with open and generous hearts and spreading waves of joy into society and the world — this is the Daishonin's Buddhism.

Faith means infinite hope, and infinite hope resides in the SGI. As long as your faith is sincere, infinite glory, boundless good fortune and endless victory will unfold before you. You will never find yourselves at a dead end.

FROM COMPASSION SPRINGS WISDOM TO BRING OTHERS HOPE AND JOY

Leaders must bring happiness and hope to their fellow members.

When people are joyful, they act with courage and initiative. When they move toward the future with hope, they demonstrate the great things of which they are capable. And in this process, the natural rhythm of improvement and victory will take hold.

That is why leaders must love the members as if they were their own children and why they, more than anyone else, must pray for their happiness. In this single determination for the members' happiness lies all the power needed for development. The wisdom to bring hope and joy to others springs from this compassion. Please march forward as ever-victorious leaders who possess both wisdom and compassion, enveloped in happiness for both yourselves and others, setting your sights on May 3, Soka Gakkai Day, of the year 2001.

Let me close my speech by conveying my profound gratitude to all of you once again for your dedicated daily efforts.

Our Attitude
Changes Everything

—⚏—

SGI-USA REPRESENTATIVES CONFERENCE,
MIAMI, FLORIDA, MARCH 9, 1993

I AM TRULY DELIGHTED to be back with all of you here in Miami after my thirty-day tour of South America, during which I traveled to five countries and six cities.

Thank you for the sincere daimoku you chanted for my visit's success, and my humble appreciation for your deep understanding in regard to the change of venue for the SGI General Meeting from the United States — where it was originally scheduled — to Brazil.

Your fellow members in Latin America asked me to convey their best regards to you, members of the great SGI-USA.

I am also profoundly grateful for your hospitality toward the friendship exchange delegations from Japan that are currently visiting Los Angeles and San Francisco. I have received detailed daily reports that confirm that the delegation members are in extremely high spirits.

At today's meeting are representative members from throughout the United States, along with friends from the Dominican Republic, who have traveled from afar to be with us. We are sure to enjoy a truly memorable gathering of the Soka family today. To mark this occasion, let me share a few words with you.

FLOWERS THAT NEVER FADE

Buddhism expounds the concept of the "mystic function of one's mind," which refers to the wondrous workings of the human mind. Life is a visible manifestation of the invisible workings of the mind.

The alumni of a certain girls school gathered for a thirty-year class reunion. On their way home after the event, one woman said to her friend: "Those who were quite unremarkable when they were young looked far more beautiful today than those who were pretty in their youth. Why is that, I wonder?"

I think what she implies is this: Those who have been told they were beautiful from an early age tend to enjoy lives of ease, without having to put in any great effort of their own. Their beauty, however, only lasts while they are young because, with time, their attitudes and the lives they have lived are revealed in their faces.

Indeed, there is truth to this, I believe.

Noh is one of the leading traditional dramatic arts in Japan. The work *Fushi kaden* (The Transmission of the Flower Acting Style) by Zeami [the brilliant actor, playwright and critic who established Noh as a classic theatrical art] is said to describe the quintessence of Noh.

In this writing, he discusses the difference between seasonal flowers (youthful beauty that fades with time) and true flowers (mature and enduring beauty that has been refined through discipline and training).

Only those who ceaselessly polish themselves can bloom as true flowers that never wither as time goes by.

THE THUS COME ONE WHO IS AWAKENED TO THE MIND

William James, an American pioneer in the field of psychology, discovered in essence that people could change their lives by changing their attitude. This is remarkably similar to the Buddhist teaching of the "mystic function of the mind."

Nichiren wrote: "This mind that is beyond comprehension constitutes the core teaching of the sutras and treatises. And one who is awake to and understands this mind is called a Thus Come One" (WND-2, 844). The Thus Come One — that is, the Buddha — is one who has awakened to the "mystic function of the mind." In other words, to the mind's wondrous workings and its infinite power. The Thus Come One is the gifted physician who can cure the deluded minds of sentient beings.

Mahatma Gandhi once said that people become the people they expect themselves to be. Your minds determine your future, your lives.

BELIEF AND THOUGHT ALTER REALITY

The British essayist William Hazlitt was an acute observer of human psychology. He wrote that if we believe we can win, we can, asserting that confidence is a prerequisite for victory. The belief that you will win without fail summons all your strength, even that which is normally latent, and makes your triumph a reality.

The human brain has been called a microcosm. Some believe that billions of nerve cells can be found in the brain. When all their interrelated combinations are taken into account, the number becomes astronomical. The potential of the human brain remains an unknown. We do not know what powers it holds.

But one thing is certain: The power of belief, the power of thought, will move reality in the direction of what we believe and how we conceive it. If you really believe you can do something, you can. That is a fact.

When you clearly envision a victorious outcome, engrave it in your heart and are firmly convinced that you will attain it, your brain makes every effort to realize the mental image you have created. Then, through your unceasing efforts, that victory is finally made a reality.

ENERGY RISES FROM CONVICTION

The other day, I spoke at Claremont McKenna College near Los Angeles (see p. 222). Before that (on January 13), I spoke with the president of the college, Jack L. Stark, in Tokyo. The subject arose of Andrew Carnegie — the great American industrialist and a relative of Donald McKenna, the college's first director.

Carnegie was born into a family so poor that they could not afford to call a midwife to assist at his birth. But by his death, he had accumulated $400 million. It is difficult to calculate the equivalent value today.

Carnegie believed in returning his earnings to society. He contributed $60 million to the creation of public libraries and $78 million to improving the educational system. When all his contributions are totaled, they amount to $365 million. This is equivalent to a daily contribution of $1 million for an entire year!

For kosen-rufu and the SGI, I, too, have worked unstintingly, giving my all on every front.

Incidentally, Carnegie's philosophy of victory was that a cheerful personality is more important than wealth. The human heart, he insisted, is just like the body. It should not remain in the shade but should move to a place in the sun. When we face difficulties, we should laugh at them. Carnegie called on everyone to walk out into the sunshine.

Always turning our hearts to the sun — that kind of life will bring victory, according to Carnegie. As a child, he would often say to his impoverished mother: "Mother, I promise that someday I will buy you a silk dress. I will make sure that you have servants and your own carriage to go out in."

This determination, this mind of Carnegie's, became a force for invincible effort and infinite wisdom in his life. His mother also believed in her son's future, believed without the slightest doubt. "I know you'll become a great person," she said to him.

Carnegie never dreamed failure possible. That is why he could march forward without fear. His energy and confidence were contagious. A story of victory unfolded around Carnegie, with him as its central character.

THE POSITIVE LIFE VIEW FOUND WITHIN A SINGLE MOMENT OF LIFE

You are the playwright of your own victory. You are also the play's hero. Shakespeare wrote, "All the world's a stage, / And all the men and women merely players" (*As You Like It*, act II, scene vii, line 139).

Buddhism teaches us that the individual writes and performs the script for his or her own life. Neither chance nor a divine being writes the script for us. We write it, and we are the actors who play it. This is an extremely positive philosophy, inherent in the teaching of "three thousand realms in a single moment of life."

You are the author and the hero. To perform your play well, it is important to pound the script into your head so thoroughly that you can see it vividly before your eyes.

You may need to rehearse in your mind. Sometimes it helps to write down your goals (for example, to pass an examination or to improve at your job), copying them over and over until they are burned into your heart.

Once, there was a young boy who had an accident that left one of his legs shorter than the other. But his parents never, under any circumstances, discouraged him by saying things like "You can't do that" or "That's too hard for you."

They treated him like any other child and encouraged him to play sports. They taught him that he could do whatever he believed he could, and that if he failed it was because he had decided to fail before he tried.

The boy became a star football player at school, and after graduation he succeeded in society as well. His life is a perfect demonstration of the assertion made by Russian writer Maxim Gorki that talent is believing in yourself, in your own power. This is not some abstract speculation or theory about the triumph of the will. It represents a belief in the latent potential of the human being.

TO THE COWARD,
EVERYTHING IS IMPOSSIBLE

Sir Walter Scott, the great Scottish novelist, wrote that everything is impossible to the coward. Why? Because he sees everything as impossible.

The attitude that "This is impossible" or "It's no good" makes things impossible and no good. If your parents are always saying, "You're a worthless child," you can come to believe it and actually become worthless.

This autumn, an exhibit titled "Napoleon Bonaparte: The Man" will be held at the Tokyo Fuji Art Museum. Among other things, Napoleon is famous for the remark "You write to me that it's impossible; the word is not French."

By this, Napoleon was not boasting of his great deeds, saying "Nothing is impossible for me." Rather, he was saying that it was precisely because he so firmly believed that nothing was impossible for human beings that he had achieved such great accomplishments.

In other words, this famous remark is not an expression of his victorious results but of their cause. Nichiren cites the Flower Garland Sutra in one of his writings: "'The mind is like a skilled painter, who creates various forms made up of the five components. Thus of all the phenomena throughout the entire world, there is not a single one that is not created by the mind. . . . Outside of this mind there is no other phenomenon that exists" (WND-2, 844).

When we read Nichiren's letters, we are struck by the way he always refers to examples and passages from the scriptures that are appropriate for the recipients, to somehow change their hearts, strengthen their determination and give them confidence and conviction.

He always radiates hope and encouragement, like the sun. This is because he fully understood that changing our mental attitude changes everything.

Is There Any Place Without Worries?

Many people ascribe others' victories to luck. Such people are likely to think, "If only I had that" or "If only I didn't have this problem to deal with." But those are nothing more than excuses. There is no one who does not have his or her own problems.

A certain Japanese businessman said to his friend: "You're always complaining about having so many problems. I know a place where there are at least ten thousand people, but not one of them has even a single problem or worry. Should I take you there?"

His friend said, "Yes, please do!" And guess where the businessman took him? To the cemetery.

He was teaching his friend that as long as we live, we will have to deal with problems and sufferings. How do we tackle our problems? This challenge is what makes for a rich life.

Buddhism teaches that "earthly desires are enlightenment." The greater our sufferings, the greater happiness we can transform them into through the power of daimoku.

Shakyamuni's Compassion Toward a Grief-stricken Mother

In Shakyamuni's day, there was a woman who had lost her beloved child through illness. Half insane with grief, she wandered around the town clutching her dead child to her bosom and beseeched all those she encountered, "Please give me medicine for my child."

Finally, taking pity on her, someone took her to see Shakyamuni. When he heard her story, he said: "Do not fret. I will give you good medicine. Go into the town and bring me back a white poppy. However, it must be a white poppy from a house where no one has lost a loved one."

In her quest, the woman walked all over the town, going from door to door. But there was not one house that had not lost a loved one. Finally it dawned on her. All human beings die. She was not alone in her suffering. To gain insight into the eternity of

life, she became a follower of Shakyamuni, and she later came to
be respected as a saint.

By sending her out to find medicine, Shakyamuni freed and
restored peace to the heart of this woman who had been wrapped
up in her own grief. He awakened deeper wisdom in her, based
on the eternity of life.

GENEROUS HEARTS INVITE GREAT HAPPINESS

The most important thing is to develop our state of life. When
human beings think of nothing but themselves, they increasingly
become entrenched in small-mindedness and their small, lesser
selves.

In contrast, those who work toward a great and all-encompassing
objective — for the sake of the Law, for others, for society — can
forge generous hearts and great, magnanimous selves through the
mystic function of their minds. Those with big hearts are assured
of savoring great happiness.

By developing your life-condition in this way, sufferings that
may have been a heavy burden when you had a lesser state of
mind will appear minor, and you can calmly rise above them. I
hope all of you will lead lives in which you show splendid proof
of this mystic function of the mind.

Finally, as you depicted on the wonderful hand-drawn world
map that greeted me on my arrival at the Miami Training Center,
my travels for peace have now taken me to fifty countries.

I need not tell you that the very first step on this vast journey
was taken here in the United States [on October 2, 1960]. America
is the starting point [for worldwide kosen-rufu].

From this land where all my journeys began, together with all
of you with whom I share such profound bonds, I would like to
open new doors of history.

I conclude today's speech with my prayers for the magnificent
renewal of the United States, for the great development of the SGI
and for the vigorous endeavors of all SGI members, each of whom
has a precious mission for kosen-rufu.

Faith Means To Manifest
Supreme Humanism

—⚭—

SGI-USA REPRESENTATIVES TRAINING SESSION,

MIAMI TRAINING CENTER,

MIAMI, FLORIDA, MARCH 11, 1993

FIRST, PLEASE ALLOW ME to express my sincere appreciation to all of you, the members of Miami and the Southeastern Region, for your wonderful hospitality both before and after my visit to South America. You gave us a warm send-off when we left and a warm welcome when we returned. I will cherish memories of this time with all of you for as long as I live.

I found our friends in Latin America industriously exerting themselves and achieving great development. They have won the shining trust and approbation of society. The SGI has truly become the world's foremost international organization.

I hope that the SGI-USA will lead the way in this dramatic age of change with even greater vigor.

A SATISFYING AND INVIGORATING GONGYO

Nichiren teaches that the object of fundamental devotion (the Gohonzon) exists within our lives. The Daishonin inscribed the Gohonzon so that we common mortals may bring forth the brilliance of this inner object of devotion.

We must never forget this basic point. We ourselves hold the fundamental key, every one of us. We practice faith so that we may proudly hold our heads high and, in our respective spheres, lead the most valuable lives, in which all our desires are fulfilled.

By reciting the sutra during gongyo, we humbly praise the Buddha, which means we are automatically praising and reinforcing to the utmost our own Buddhahood.

Chanting daimoku allows us to accumulate the supreme treasure of the universe in our lives day by day. The origin of the universe is Nam-myoho-renge-kyo, our lives are Nam-myoho-renge-kyo and the Daishonin's name is Nam-myoho-renge-kyo. Chanting daimoku enables us to tap this supreme power in our own lives and, at the same time, make it resonate powerfully in our surroundings. Therefore, we need fear nothing.

In "Offering Prayers to the Mandala of the Mystic Law," the Daishonin writes that the four great bodhisattvas will surround and protect those who embrace the Mystic Law, walking by their side at all times on the journey through life (see WND-1, 415).

Formality is not important. There are no rigid formalities for gongyo laid down in the Daishonin's writings. What counts is that gongyo refreshes and invigorates your lives.

Just as a morning walk or jog may be pleasantly exhilarating for both the body and the mind, please do a gongyo that is personally satisfying to you — one that leaves you feeling refreshed and uplifted both mentally and physically.

A Narrow-minded Religion Oppresses Human Beings

In recent weeks, the media have been filled with reports of an ongoing standoff between U.S. federal agents and a religious cult in Waco, Texas. The antisocial, narrow-minded and intolerant characteristics of a cult led by a fanatical leader are truly fearful and barbarous.

The aberrant behavior of the Nichiren Shoshu priesthood has also inflicted suffering on a great number of people. The Daishonin writes, "All phenomena that exist are manifestations of the Buddhist Law" (WND-2, 844).

Buddhism is not a closed or insular teaching; it applies to and is open to all of society. The Daishonin also states, "A person of wisdom is not one who practices Buddhism apart from worldly affairs" (WND-1, 1121).

The path of correct faith is to value society, daily life and humanity to the utmost.

Let us in the SGI contribute even further to the world and to humanity through our activities for peace, culture and education, based on the correct teaching.

CHERISHING THOSE AROUND US

Nichiren strongly desired that his followers play an active part in society, while treasuring others with open, magnanimous hearts. In a letter to Shijo Kingo, he writes: "I am most grieved over your lord's illness. Although he has not professed faith in the Lotus Sutra, you are a member of his clan, and it is thanks to his consideration that you are able to make offerings to the sutra. Thus, these may become prayers solely for your lord's recovery" (WND-1, 848).

Though this passage refers to Shijo Kingo's lord, it should by no means be taken to imply that Buddhism encourages feudalistic mores and values. Worthy of greatest respect is our humanism with which we pray ceaselessly for the health and happiness of all with whom we have a connection, whether or not they practice Buddhism. Our practice of faith enables us to illuminate everything in our environment with the sunlight of unlimited fortune and benefit.

While in Rio de Janeiro, I met a woman pioneer who had contributed greatly to the development of kosen-rufu in that country. She was accompanied by her husband, who was not a member. I said to him: "I hope you will make your business even more successful and that you will cherish your wife even more dearly. This in itself represents faith." I made this remark based on the aforementioned Gosho passage.

There is absolutely no need to feel constrained or ill at ease because some members of your family are not practicing. I hope you will lead your families wisely and cheerfully toward harmony and happiness.

As good sons and daughters, we should take care of our parents whether or not they practice faith. It is the same in our relationships with our partners. We practice faith so that we may become exemplary children, partners and parents.

In stark contrast to this spirit of generosity is the elitist mentality that rejects those who are not practicing and the self-righteous logic that asserts, "I'm practicing, so anything I do is perfectly fine." Nikken is the ultimate example of this.

THE DAISHONIN'S PROFOUND COMPASSION
TOWARD LAY BELIEVERS

How immense was the compassion with which the Daishonin embraced his followers! He always showed the utmost consideration for and understanding of each individual's circumstances and position in society.

In a letter he wrote to one of his lay followers, Misawa Kojiro, the lord of a domain who was persevering in faith under difficult circumstances, the Daishonin states: "Even if you should abandon your faith in the Lotus Sutra, how could I regard as strangers the people who, if only for a day or even for a moment, have helped me survive?... You have less knowledge of Buddhism than I, and moreover, you are lay believers with lands, wives and children, and retainers. Therefore, it may be extremely difficult for you to sustain your faith throughout life. This is why I have always told you that, because of your position, it would be better to feign ignorance of this teaching. No matter what may happen in the future, be assured that I will never forsake or neglect you" (WND-1, 895–96).

The Daishonin's Buddhism is a stranger to fanatical dogmatism. Human beings do not exist for the sake of religion. Religion must always serve the needs of human beings.

In this passage, the Daishonin's intention is certainly not to sanction backsliding in faith or acts of betrayal by his followers. It is to compassionately embrace and reassure his followers, who struggle courageously with many difficulties, by saying: Even if by some chance you cannot persevere with your faith to the end, I will resolutely protect you because you have helped me, even if just for a moment. We must thoroughly engrave in our hearts the profound compassion revealed by the Daishonin in this passage.

By inflicting suffering and pain on the children of the Buddha, trampling on the sincerity of the SGI members who for many years have made unprecedented efforts to protect the priesthood, Nikken has utterly transgressed the Daishonin's spirit. He is an enemy of the original Buddha.

I hope all of you, as leaders of kosen-rufu, will warmly embrace, protect and encourage the members, who are the precious children of the Buddha.

You must never make unreasonable demands upon or burden the members. You must not get angry with them. There is a big difference between training people and behaving in an arrogant, highhanded manner. A leader constantly takes pains to make the members feel confident and at ease.

Encouragement is important. The Gosho states: "When praised highly by others, one feels that there is no hardship one cannot bear. Such is the courage that springs from words of praise" (WND-1, 385).

Those who praise and protect the Buddha's children are praised and protected in like measure by the Buddhas and heavenly deities throughout the universe. In contrast, those who abuse and torment them will incur in same proportion the anger of these protective forces, and they will suffer as a result.

GLORIOUS SUNSHINE STATE

Florida, which is home to Miami, is truly the glorious Sunshine State. It overflows with the sun's blessings. It is also a pivotal gateway to Latin America, Canada, Europe and Africa. And, what's more, there are no earthquakes!

Excitement is mounting in Atlanta, where the next Olympic Games will be held in 1996, marking the centennial of the modern Olympics.

Let us contribute further to the prosperity and development of the southeastern part of the United States. Plans for the Florida Nature and Culture Center are only the beginning. When the new center is finally opened, I hope you will treasure it as you would your own homes. The care you put into looking after the castles of Buddhism — our SGI centers — translates into your own good fortune.

Please strive to live with a heart so rich that, should you quarrel with your partner, after the storm has blown over, you can say: "Honey, let's go to the palace of hope. Let's visit the castle of eternity!" and then walk hand in hand to this golden abode.

The Land of Eternally Tranquil Light (the Buddha land) does not exist in some distant place nor is it imaginary. It is to be realized in our actual lives and in the actual land in which we dwell.

I propose that, when the new center is completed, trees be planted in honor of all those here today.

With broad-minded and generous hearts as wide as today's expansive blue skies, may all of you who reside in this wonderful paradise further extend our network of friendship.

Praying for your increasing good health, longevity, wealth, freedom from accidents and abundant happiness, I close today's speech. Thank you very much.

Leaders Must Yearn for the Welfare of the People

—ᗰ—

SGI-USA EXECUTIVE CONFERENCE,
SAN FRANCISCO, CALIFORNIA, MARCH 13, 1993

NOTHING GIVES ME GREATER JOY than to be back here in San Francisco, reunited with so many old friends on this, my fifth visit to the city, my first in thirteen years. [President Ikeda's first visit was on his first trip to America, in 1960.]

San Francisco is extolled as one of the most beautiful cities in the United States, and it was also an important starting point for the American kosen-rufu movement. Thus it is my unbounded delight to meet here with top SGI-USA leaders from throughout the country and make a new start with all of you. Thank you for traveling all the way to attend this meeting.

I also wish to express my deep appreciation to the San Francisco members for the great hospitality they extended to the large exchange delegations of more than nine hundred people from Japan.

I have received a deluge of letters from the Japanese members expressing their gratitude for your kindness.

SAN FRANCISCO'S GREAT DEVELOPMENT

The development of the kosen-rufu movement in San Francisco is truly remarkable.

In this city of rich diversity, you have forged beautiful and harmonious bonds of unity, centering on San Francisco #1 Joint Territory Leader Daniel Nagashima and Women's Division Leader Kay Rood, #2 Joint Territory Leader Ed Horan and Women's Division Leader Miki Sasai, and vice joint territory leaders Bob Hanson, Frank Williamson and Bruce Williams, as well as other leaders.

You are also leading in your endeavors to expand the circle of friends who support and understand our activities, sending out a growing wave of friendship from this region. The members here overflow with the courageous spirit to protect the SGI; in other words, with the dynamic energy to advance the widespread propagation of the Mystic Law.

I have also heard of the outstanding contributions that San Francisco members, including those who belong to the culture department, have been making in various spheres of society. I wholeheartedly praise these efforts.

The Birthplace of the United Nations

San Francisco, incidentally, is also the birthplace of the United Nations. Representatives from fifty countries gathered here to sign the Charter (in June 1945).

This year is the United Nations' International Year of the World's Indigenous People. It is interesting to note that the wisdom of North America's indigenous people is said not only to have played an important part in the realization of the early federation of thirteen American states but also to have influenced the drafting of the Charter of the United Nations. I am referring to the wisdom of the Iroquois League, a confederation of five (later six) Native American nations.

From around 1000 to 1450, five nations of Native Americans in the northeastern woodlands of the United States mutually agreed to end dispute among themselves and adopted a constitution known as the Great Binding Law. It sparkles with brilliant gems of wisdom.

Some SGI-USA members kindly sent me reference material on this subject, so I would like to share with you today some of the great wisdom of the Native Americans.

THE POWERFUL RIGHTS OF WOMEN

For example, although the chiefs of each nation in the Iroquois League were men, it was the women who chose them. In other words, from a relatively early period in their history, women had voting rights. The women of these nations also had the right to rebuke any chief who transgressed the Great Binding Law and even to remove him should he fail to rectify his behavior.

Also, our SGI woman here in the United States and other parts of the world have dealt a decisive blow against the current aberrant high priest of Nichiren Shoshu, Nikken Abe.

STRENGTH OF CHARACTER DEMANDED OF LEADERS

The Great Binding Law of the Iroquois League spelled out the qualities it required of leaders as follows: "The chiefs of the League of Five Nations shall be mentors of the people for all time. The thickness of their skins shall be seven spans, which is to say that they shall be proof against anger, offensive action and criticism."

This requirement for tolerance and forbearance corresponds to the Buddhist concept of the "armor of endurance" (WND-1, 392). The Great Binding Law continues: "Their hearts shall be full of peace and good will and their minds filled with a yearning for the welfare of the people of the League. With endless patience, they shall carry out their duty. Their firmness shall be tempered with a tenderness for their people. Neither anger nor fury shall find lodging in their minds and all their words and actions shall be marked by calm deliberation."

Each of these points is equally applicable to the leaders of kosen-rufu as well.

It would appear that the chiefs of the League endeavored to

lead not by controlling their members with orders or through coercion but through the power of dialogue and character.

According to one historian, when the Native Americans met in a group, it was immediately clear who the leader was. Why? It was certainly not because he was the one putting on the biggest airs. In fact, it was the exact opposite. The chief was the most unassuming and modest in demeanor, generously distributing all that was his among the people.

I hope that all of you will also thoroughly treasure the members.

LEADERS MUST BE MODEST

The second Soka Gakkai president, Josei Toda, said: "It is a mistake to consider yourself of special importance because you have been designated to a position of leadership. The correct attitude, I believe, is for all of us as common mortals to be willing to give and receive guidance from one another. Should there be any leaders who think they are special, send them to see me! …

"Filling your hearts with the Buddha's compassion, please give sincere and enthusiastic guidance, showing the same caring attitude toward the members as you would toward your own partners or children. Leaders are not automatically entitled to others' respect. If leaders are respected, it is a benefit from the Gohonzon, and as such we must be truly humble. If this sentiment of profound gratitude permeates our chapter, district, group and unit leaders, then it will communicate itself to the Gohonzon.

I hope that all of you, striving to be leaders who are loved and respected by the members, will build a garden of peace and harmony that rings with the sound of joyful laughter."

"WE ARE RIGHT NOW IN THE VERY MIDST OF KOSEN-RUFU"

I will never forget my visit here to San Francisco in August 1965, when I accompanied the sixty-sixth high priest, Nittatsu.

Immediately upon his return from this visit, High Priest Nittatsu spoke at a Soka Gakkai Headquarters Leaders Meeting. Though he referred to me, I wish to introduce his comments on that occasion as part of our history of kosen-rufu.

He said: "I have just returned from a tour of the United States, Mexico, Hawaii and other locations, with President Ikeda leading the way.

"I have come today to report to you on that trip and to express my greetings to Mr. Ikeda: Thanks to his boundless care and solicitude, I splendidly fulfilled all my duties without the slightest worry or anxiety. I would like to express my profound appreciation."

High Priest Nittatsu and the current high priest, who is implicated in the Seattle incident, are as different as night and day. High Priest Nittatsu was also concerned about the shameful conduct of Nikken while the latter was on foreign soil.

The sixty-sixth high priest ended his address on the aforementioned occasion by saying: "There is no true Buddhist Law other than Nam-myoho-renge-kyo, which the Daishonin embodied since the remotest past. Today no organization other than the Soka Gakkai is spreading this Law throughout the world. This marks the start of kosen-rufu of the Latter Day of the Law. And, indeed, I am convinced that we are right now in the very midst of kosen-rufu. Visiting the United States, Mexico and other places for the first time has only deepened this conviction."

I am sure that High Priest Nittatsu would have been thoroughly delighted to see the great development of the kosen-rufu movement here in San Francisco today.

The Great Binding Law of the Iroquois League also states the following: "Look and listen for the welfare of the whole people and have always in view not only the present but also the coming generations, even those whose faces are yet beneath the surface of the ground, the unborn of the future Nation."

Tomorrow, you will hold the First SGI-USA Youth General Meeting and formally establish the junior high and high school divisions. I hope you will further develop the path of successors, using your wisdom and energy.

The SGI's Mission: Securing the Eternal Welfareof Humanity

Finally, I would like to quote from the Gosho. The Daishonin warns us: "Strengthen your faith day by day and month after month. Should you slacken in your resolve even a bit, devils will take advantage" (WND-1, 997).

I feel that my efforts for kosen-rufu thus far have been small [compared to my vision]. I am determined to exert myself with even greater energy from now on.

In closing, I pledge together with all of you to always advance courageously for the sake of the eternal future, striving to live up to President Toda's declaration that "the Soka Gakkai's mission is to secure the eternal welfare of humanity."

The Key to Humanity's Fundamental Problems

—ᴍ—

FIRST SGI-USA YOUTH GENERAL MEETING,
SAN FRANCISCO CULTURE CENTER, SAN FRANCISCO,
CALIFORNIA, MARCH 14, 1993

FAR MORE than meeting with eminent figures, I derive my greatest joy from meeting with you, the SGI-USA members.

I have also been asked to convey messages of congratulations to you on holding this meeting, from SGI youth leaders around the world, including Japan and South American countries.

New Future Division Members — Thirty Years From Now

Today marks the historic founding of the SGI-USA's junior high and high school divisions. My most sincere congratulations. To the representatives of these divisions here today, thank you so much for all your efforts!

The Japanese organization established the junior high and senior high school divisions almost thirty years ago. Today, like great legendary birds, the young people of these divisions have grown to adulthood and soar unlimitedly in the glorious realm of global kosen-rufu and in various fields of society.

Daniel Nagashima, who is fulfilling a leadership role here in San Francisco as a joint territory leader [in 1999, he became the

SGI-USA general director], is also a member of the first graduating class of the senior high school division in Japan.

My heart is filled with excitement at the thought of what great leaders the first class of both the SGI-USA junior high and high school divisions will assuredly grow into thirty years from now.

I ask that the leaders responsible for these divisions, as well as those of you who are seniors in faith, nurture these infinitely precious treasures of the future with all your heart.

TRANSCENDING THE SUFFERINGS OF BIRTH, AGING, SICKNESS AND DEATH

What is the purpose of life? It is to become happy. What, then, is true happiness? Can fame, wealth or social position, no matter how great their magnitude, bring us true happiness? It is very doubtful.

Such qualities alone do not create lasting happiness at life's deepest realms. Nor can they solve the most fundamental sufferings of existence — birth, aging, sickness and death. For this very reason Nichiren expounded his teachings.

Birth — the pain that goes with being born and of living. There are innumerable sufferings in life. Also, there is our karma to deal with. There are accidents we cannot anticipate. There are divorce, problems with our children, frustrations at work. The question is, how do we overcome these and other sufferings?

Aging — the suffering of growing older. Right now you are all young; you are all healthy and possess the beauty of youth. But you will all age into old men and women. There is no inoculation against this, and the most expensive medicine will not cure you of old age.

Sickness — the suffering of illness. Some suffer from cancer, some from AIDS. Others suffer from spiritual illnesses. Life is a battle against myriad diseases. The second Soka Gakkai president, Josei Toda, often said that there is an illness called poverty, just as there is an illness called bad temper. He also asserted that the karma of being hated by others and ending life in defeat can be termed an illness. The power of the Mystic Law cures these illnesses of body and mind at a fundamental level.

Death — the most uncompromising of the four sufferings. None of us here today will be alive in a hundred years. The French literary giant Victor Hugo declared, "We are all under sentence of death but with a sort of indefinite reprieve."

There are many ways of dying as well. Some die by their own hand, others are murdered. Some suffer unspeakable agony before they die.

What should our attitude be toward this inescapable fate? How can we overcome the suffering it causes? This is the most basic theme facing each of us.

And what happens after death? Do we still exist? Or is there nothing? If we do exist, in what state do we exist? Such things are beyond common mortals.

The sufferings of birth, aging, sickness and death are universal to humankind. They are the basic issues we face in our unending search for happiness. Yet almost all leaders sidestep them. They furtively avert their eyes from the very issues that any leader who feels a sense of responsibility for the welfare of the people cannot possibly neglect. This is a great misfortune for the people.

The SGI confronts these fundamental problems head on. And Nichiren reveals the means for resolving them completely.

He elucidates the Mystic Law, which enables us to serenely overcome the four sufferings and all other kinds of hardship and obstacles, and in fact even use our sufferings as an impetus to propel us forward as we live lives pervaded by the four virtues of eternity, happiness, true self and purity.

BEING VICTORIOUS IN LIFE

All of you here have embraced the Mystic Law at an early stage in your lives. I hope that in the future, the men, each in his respective way, will prove themselves in society and that the women will lead lives that bring them such unparalleled happiness that they may wonder, "Is it possible to be any happier?"

Buddhism enables us to make this a definite reality. If this were not so, our practice of faith would have no meaning.

Life is a struggle. Reality is a struggle. Nichiren teaches that Buddhism is about winning. He exhorts us to be victorious. So we must win in life. To embrace the Mystic Law is to grasp the sword of victory. We can triumph over all. We can triumph and enjoy our lives. A "person of faith" is synonymous with a "person of victory."

Therefore, I hope all of you will be victorious in your lives. Live your lives so that you can each declare: "I have no regrets. I enjoyed my life. I encouraged many others and gave them hope. It was a good life."

The original Buddha, Nichiren, promises us that this will be the result if we practice correctly, following the principle faith manifests itself in daily life. The words of the Buddha contain no falsehood. Irrespective of the lies that issue forth from the priests who exploit the Buddha's teachings, Nichiren Daishonin's words are always true.

I suggest that you make a list of all of the representatives gathered here today. Why don't you keep track of the list and see what has become of each of you by May 3, Soka Gakkai Day, in 2001 and then every ten years after that?

No Prayer Will Go Unanswered

Nichiren Daishonin's Buddhism teaches that when we embrace faith in the Mystic Law, no prayer will go unanswered. Of course, it goes against the laws of reason to expect flowers and fruits to sprout tomorrow from seeds you just planted today. But if you continue to tend to the seeds of faith, you can be certain that in the end you will attain a state of life in which all your desires are fulfilled, just as you had wished.

The Mystic Law eradicates all offenses and is the source of all blessings. Moreover, it proves all righteousness. All these benefits of the Law manifest themselves in our lives, just as Nichiren declares in his writings.

Only with correct faith can we activate the power of this great

Law. However sophisticated an aircraft may be, it will not fly smoothly if its pilot is drunk. President Toda likened the Gohonzon to a happiness-manufacturing machine, but only when we have correct faith can we benefit from the infinite powers of the Law and the Buddha. And the SGI teaches this correct faith.

Those who chant Nam-myoho-renge-kyo throughout their lives, whatever may happen, are victors in life. As long as you remember this, your lives will be secure. Nichiren writes, "There is no true happiness for human beings other than chanting Nam-myoho-renge-kyo" (WND-1, 681), and I know this to be true from my own experience.

To Live Is To Move Forward

Not advancing is retreating — this is true not only of faith but also of study, work and all areas of our lives.

Students who do not study, workers who do not work — both are retreating. Living is moving forward, making progress on all fronts. If you stop trying to move forward, it means you are retreating from life itself.

And since faith is the driving force of our lives, retreating in faith is the cause of all unhappiness. That is why you must, with your fellow members and with the organization devoted to kosen-rufu, encourage one another and achieve victory in faith and in life.

Without the organization, it would be extremely difficult to carry through with correct faith on your own. The Buddhist Order comprising the followers of Nichiren in his time was, in modern terms, an organization for kosen-rufu. Shakyamuni Buddha also created an organization of believers (a Buddhist Order). Society is an organization, as is each human body. And the SGI organization exists to enable each member to freely carry out his or her mission.

Ideas and Philosophy Are the Heart of Society

In light of today's historic First SGI-USA Youth General Meeting, I would like to speak on a few more points.

Where in America, and in the world as a whole, can we find the key to revitalization? Although political and economic approaches are naturally very important, we must not forget that everything originates in the revitalization of the human spirit and eventually returns to that point.

In Buddhism, strife and chaos in a nation are perceived as arising from a decline in ideas and philosophy. Ideas and philosophy are the heart that makes a society and an age beat with life. When the heart weakens, healthy progress becomes impossible.

Where can we find new hope to open the door of the third millennium when most philosophies and ideas have lost their luster? I believe we have entered a stage when Nichiren's humanistic Buddhism will take its place on the grand stage of world history and demonstrate its worth there.

Thinking people here in America and around the world have discovered a new pulse of revitalization in Buddhism, and they have great hopes for it. Nichiren writes: "When the skies are clear, the ground is illuminated. Similarly, when one knows the Lotus Sutra, one understands the meaning of all worldly affairs" (WND-1, 376).

We can describe this principle of life that runs through the individual, society and the universe as a great sun that illuminates the darkness and chaos of the age.

I hope all of you, as young philosophers of the Mystic Law, will illuminate your homes, your regions, society and the entire world with rays of brilliant light.

THE POWER OF WISDOM PUTS KNOWLEDGE INTO ACTION

What the world urgently needs now is an age of wisdom. No matter how much information or knowledge we may have, it does not necessarily produce value or bring happiness. The power of wisdom effectively puts that knowledge and information to use, puts it into action.

Mr. Toda once told the following story:

In the Edo period (1600–1868), a certain Japanese scholar went to study Western medicine under Dutch physicians in Nagasaki, the only Japanese port open to the Western world at that time. He copied every word of the lectures into his notebooks, which amounted to an enormous number of words by the time he had completed his studies.

He then prepared to return home, but the ship on which he sailed sank, and his notes were lost. Though the scholar escaped with his life, his notebooks were all destroyed, and not a single word of them remained in his head.

Knowledge must be fully absorbed; you must make it a part of yourself. In that effort, you must develop your wisdom. You cannot attain wisdom without first walking through the door of knowledge. On the other hand, unless you acquire wisdom, you will drown in a flood of knowledge and lose sight of the right direction in life.

Buddhism enables us to tap the fundamental wisdom for correct living from the depths of our lives and to polish and cultivate that wisdom.

I hope that, in whatever situation you may find yourselves, you will always demonstrate a vigorous intelligence and engage reality with wisdom and cheer.

Especially for the members of the future division, now is the time when "faith equals study." Please make every effort to exercise and train your intellect.

At the same time, we SGI members must face the global problems confronting humanity and further widen the network of wisdom while continuing to take action to achieve harmony, peace and prosperity.

STRUGGLING WITH OUR SUFFERINGS

Tomorrow, I am scheduled to visit San Francisco's distinguished University of California, Berkeley, and meet with its renowned Chancellor Chang-Lin Tien. The SGI-USA has established a network of university groups, including a group at the University of California, Berkeley, and I have high hopes for their future activities.

Dr. Tien, who is carrying on the school's tradition of "a university for the people," makes a point of holding dialogues with students, infusing the campus with a new spirit of humanism. For these endeavors, he has won widespread respect and admiration.

The struggles that the Chinese-born chancellor went through in his youth are well known. His family was driven from their hometown in China by the invading Japanese army. Dr. Tien then made his way to the United States alone — a penniless youth. Despite many difficulties and racial discrimination, he tenaciously pursued his studies.

Here, let me quote from one of his speeches in which he offers the following words of encouragement to the youth he loves so well: "Many years ago, my father in China left me some words of advice. They have served me well over the years, so I want to share them with you: 'Do the best you can and worry later about what comes next.'

"My father, who relied heavily on Confucian wisdom, understood the pitfalls of ignoring problems. Instead, he believed the best course of action is meeting challenges head-on without getting bogged down in them.

"What is your surest path to success? Work hard. Test your limits. Push yourself to new heights. For if you strive for success, you will be ready for the future — no matter what it brings. 'Do the best you can now and worry later about what comes next.'"

Everyone's youth is a struggle with various problems. If you do your best to challenge your immediate problems with the vigor of youth, however, you will definitely find a way to overcome them. Moreover, it is often the case that what you thought at the time to be a major problem appears, in retrospect, quite insignificant.

Therefore, please be optimistic and enjoy your youth to your heart's content.

Thirty-five years ago on March 16, 1958 [the first Kosen-rufu Day], my mentor in life, Josei Toda, declared with a lion's roar, "The Soka Gakkai is the king of the religious world." This was at a time when most of the world had not yet even heard of the Soka Gakkai.

Nonetheless, embracing the cry of our mentor, we youth exerted ourselves unflaggingly; we took on one challenge after another. The mothers and fathers of many of you here today are among the nameless yet noble ordinary people who made history by dedicating their utmost to kosen-rufu. And today, thanks to their efforts, the SGI has become a pillar and mainstay of the world's people.

I am convinced that never in any other organization will we see such beautiful human solidarity as exists within the SGI.

On March 16, President Toda gathered the Soka Gakkai youth at the head temple for a ceremony to which Japan's prime minister had been invited. When the head of state canceled at the last minute [citing urgent business], my mentor was keenly disappointed.

As a direct disciple of President Toda, I am now forging ties of friendship with leaders throughout the world. I am sure this would make President Toda very happy.

I also have every confidence that you will follow in the path I have forged and go on to build a magnificent "Golden Gate Bridge of Human Victory." Nothing makes me happier than this thought.

A TRIBUTE TO THE IMPERISHABLE SPIRIT

In conclusion, let me recite a verse by the great American poet Walt Whitman:

> *O while I live to be the ruler of life, not a slave,*
> *To meet life as a powerful conqueror,*
> *No fumes, no ennui, no more complaints or scornful*
> *   criticisms,*
> *To these proud laws of the air, the water and the ground,*
> *   proving my interior soul impregnable,*
> *And nothing exterior shall ever take command of me.*

Wishing you all glory, success, victory and happiness, I close today's speech. Please give my very best regards to your families.

SGI President Ikeda with young women's division members at the
Soka University Los Angeles campus, in Calabasas, California,
February 25, 1990.

Encouraging young men's division members at Soka University Los
Angeles, February 25, 1990.

SGI President Ikeda at the Soka University Los Angeles campus,
February 1990.

With Harvard University students, Cambridge, Massachusetts,
September 26, 1991.

Speaking on "The Age of Soft Power" at Harvard University, September
26, 1991.

SGI President Ikeda greets members at the 1st SGI-USA General
Meeting, Santa Monica, California, September 29, 1991.

Viewing the SGI-USA "Ecology and Human Life" exhibition, Santa
Monica, California, September 18, 1993.

President and Mrs. Ikeda after morning exercises at the Miami
Community Center, February 3, 1993.

SGI President Ikeda greets children, Miami, February 3, 1993.

With the Miami skyline in the background, Miami, February 1993.

The SGI-USA Fife and Drum Corps performs "The Power of One," San Francisco, March 1993.

Greeting members of the future division outside the San Francisco Culture Center, March 14, 1993.

SGI President Ikeda plays the piano as Mrs. Ikeda looks on,
San Francisco, March 1993.

(Above) With members in the grand ballroom of the Boston Sheraton Hotel, the site of the SGI-USA New England Renaissance Conference, September 26, 1993.

(Left) In front of Ballou Hall, Tufts University, after President Ikeda received a certificate for his contributions to peace and culture from Tufts University President John DiBiaggio, September 22, 1993.

SGI President Ikeda greets members of President District, Brookline, Massachusetts, September 23, 1993.

At the 13th World Peace Youth Culture Festival, Paradise Cove, Hawaii, January 28, 1995.

Playing the piano for members during the 19th SGI General Meeting at the Hawaii Culture Center, Honolulu, January 30, 1995.

At the Soka University Los Angeles campus, Calabasas, California,
June 1996.

SGI President and Mrs. Ikeda arrive at the Denver Culture Center, June
9, 1996.

Thanking Bob Burch of Denver after the Rocky Mountain Joint
Territory General Meeting, Denver, June 9, 1996.

In the procession of
honorees, University of
Denver's commencement
ceremony, June 8, 1996.

Children greet SGI President Ikeda on his first visit to the New York Culture Center, June 15, 1996.

Encouraging Yo Kano, who is blind, at the New York Culture Center, June 15, 1996.

Members welcome President Ikeda to the Florida Nature and Culture Center, June 19, 1996.

Greeting elementary school division members at the Florida Nature and Culture Center, June 23, 1996.

SGI President and Mrs. Ikeda ride in a golf cart with a boy on the grounds of the Florida Nature and Culture Center, June 1996.

Looking out over Toda Lake at the Florida Nature and Culture Center, June 1996.

The Joy of Being Born
at the Time of Worldwide
Kosen-rufu

—⁂—

I AM TRULY DELIGHTED to take part in this convivial gathering of
the Soka family. A well-known Japanese author said, "How beautiful it is to be on harmonious terms with one another!"

A lone flower by itself may seem rather forlorn. But when many
fragrant flowers bloom in colorful profusion, the individuality of
each flower shines all the more vividly.

I hope that you, my beloved SGI-USA members, will widely
extend this garden of "human flowers" that blooms in unsurpassed
beauty and harmony.

GREAT PEOPLE ALWAYS LIVE FOR
THE FUTURE

Yesterday I had another unforgettable meeting with Linus Pauling,
the father of modern chemistry, who lives in the San Francisco Bay
Area. This is the fourth time we have come together for a discussion. Every time we meet, the Nobel Prize laureate burns with a
blazing passion for world peace and the health of humanity.

Despite having recently turned ninety-two, Dr. Pauling enjoys
vigorous good health and is still actively engaged in his endeavors.

In fact, he told me he had just given advice to three heart patients before departing for our meeting.

If he wanted to, he could easily sit back and rest on his truly illustrious achievements. But Dr. Pauling continues his unflagging efforts, with his eyes fixed firmly on the future of humankind.

Buddhism focuses on the present and the future. It is not the past, but the present and the future that are important. If we lose our passion for the future, life becomes merely a living death. Please advance with ever-youthful hearts, aiming for the hope-filled future of the SGI-USA in the twenty-first century.

THE JOY OF BEING BORN IN THIS AGE

The close friendship that existed between Linus Pauling and Albert Einstein is well known. The second Soka Gakkai president, Josei Toda, also cherished a special memory of Einstein [whose lecture he attended during the great physicist's visit to Japan in the early 1920s]. Mr. Toda said: "To meet and encounter an auspicious time, to be in rhythm with that time, makes having been born worthwhile.

"As an example in my own life, thirty-four years ago I had the opportunity, together with my mentor, Tsunesaburo Makiguchi, to hear Albert Einstein, one of the world's greatest physicists, who died just recently, lecture on his theory of relativity at the Keio University auditorium.

"It has been a long-standing source of pride for me, particularly as I was then making my living by teaching physics and chemistry, to have heard his lecture in person, even if I couldn't appreciate all the finer points of the theory of relativity.

"Another source of joy is that at that age of twenty-one, I encountered my mentor, President Makiguchi, and until forty-four, I received training from him and even accompanied him to prison. This is my great pride.

"Third, what gives me even greater joy than the first two is that I was born in the age of the Latter Day of the Law, right at the time of the seven-hundredth anniversary of the establishment of

Nichiren Daishonin's Buddhism, and received the Buddha's decree to accomplish kosen-rufu" (At the Nakano Chapter General Meeting in Tokyo, April 24, 1955).

Similarly, it is my eternal pride to have encountered my mentor, Josei Toda, to have served him and been trained by him, and to have inherited from him the mission for kosen-rufu.

I hope all of you, too, share in the joy of being born at the time of worldwide kosen-rufu and that you will advance together with me, filled with joy, good cheer and hope, on the path of kosen-rufu, the path of our mission, the golden path to happiness, the diamond path to world peace.

BENEFICIAL POWER OF THE MYSTIC LAW LIKE THE NOONDAY SUN

In the same guidance, President Toda continued: "The power of faith and the power of practice with which you pray to the Gohonzon — in other words, the power of faith when you believe in the Gohonzon and the power of practice when you make the Daishonin's heart your own — fuse to combine and manifest themselves in your lives as the power of the Law and the power of the Buddha. This is how happiness comes to permeate your daily lives.

"As long as you continue to practice faith in this way, you can progress naturally on the great path to kosen-rufu.

"If you maintain a pure-hearted attitude both in faith and in efforts to spread the Law, becoming models of faith to others through the great benefits you have manifested in your lives, then you can truly share this Buddhism through your example, even without actively telling others about the practice.

"When people start voicing their desire to practice faith of their own accord, kosen-rufu will naturally be attained. Moreover, since the time of kosen-rufu has arrived, the power of the Gohonzon is all the more great.

"Now someone may accuse me of making the contradictory statement that in the past the Gohonzon didn't have power, but now it does. Rest assured that there is no change in the Gohonzon.

But there has been a change in us who embrace the Gohonzon.

"After all, there's no difference in the sun that rises in the east and the sun that shines directly overhead at noon [but the intensity of the latter's rays are stronger]. Now we [have entered an age in which we] are receiving the direct 'sunlight' of the Gohonzon, just like the intense rays of the noonday sun.

"It's up to you whether you receive benefit in your daily lives. All I am teaching you is to practice strongly and receive great benefit.

"It's a great loss not to receive benefit. The only way to receive benefit is to practice vigorously. People ask me: 'Mr. Toda, I have no money. Is there any way to overcome this?' or 'I'm unwell; what can I do?' The only answer I have is to urge them to have faith and practice. That's all I can do."

President Toda had truly deep compassion for the members, who, in those days, had many earnest problems. To encourage them, to help them back on their feet, Mr. Toda would declare, "If, having practiced exactly as I told you, you don't experience benefit and your problems are not resolved, I'll give you my life." His guidance was always filled with such statements of conviction on which he was willing to stake his life.

Just as President Toda asserted, we have entered an age in which the benefit of the Mystic Law illuminates the entire world with the intensity of the noonday sun.

My desire is that all SGI members show brilliant actual proof of victory in society, as they bathe fully in the benefits of the Mystic Law. My constant prayer to the Gohonzon is that all of you become happy.

PATIENTLY CONSTRUCTING A SOLID SELF

The novel *Miyamoto Musashi* [an account of the seventeenth-century master swordsman of the same name] by the great Japanese author Eiji Yoshikawa, includes a passage where the protagonist, Musashi, gazing at Mount Fuji in the distance, counsels one of his young disciples as follows:"Rather than worrying about your future, thinking 'Perhaps I should become this. Perhaps I should become that,' first be still and build a self that is as solid and unmoving as Mount Fuji. Never court the favor of people in society. If you become someone who is looked up to by others, then the world will naturally accord you the value you merit."

For us, building a solid and unmoving self like Mount Fuji means doing our human revolution, elevating our state of life, based on our practice of faith. It means developing a solid self that is never defeated by our environment or circumstances and is capable of transforming everything into happiness and victory. True happiness shines in the lives of those who possess such an indomitable self.

When we summon forth a powerful life force to contribute to the welfare of people and society, we gather the admiration and trust of others, which testifies to the validity of the Mystic Law. Consequently, constructing a solid self equals advancing kosen-rufu.

In a letter to his follower Shijo Kingo, the Daishonin writes: "Bring forth the great power of faith, and be spoken of by all the people of Kamakura, both high and low, or by all the people of Japan, as 'Shijo Kingo, Shijo King of the Lotus school!' Even a bad reputation will spread far and wide. A good reputation will spread even farther, particularly if it is a reputation for devotion to the Lotus Sutra" (WND-1, 319).

Here the Daishonin instructs Shijo Kingo not just to establish his reputation as a samurai but to become a person who is praised by people as "Shijo Kingo of the Lotus school." This passage can be read to mean that the correct way of practice for those who embrace the Mystic Law is to show actual proof of victory based on faith and to win the respect and trust of others in society.

I hope all of you will be victors who are respected by many people as members of the SGI.

Establish Your Reputation Among the People

In another Gosho addressed to Shijo Kingo, the Daishonin writes: "Live so that all the people of Kamakura will say in your praise that Nakatsukasa Saburo Saemon-no-jo is diligent in the service of his lord, in the service of Buddhism, and in his concern for other people" (WND-1, 851).

In a modern context, this means that not only should we naturally develop strong faith, but we must also cultivate brilliant character and humanity so as to become indispensable people in our places of work and in our communities, thereby winning the praise and respect of others.

In the same Gosho, the Daishonin continues: "More valuable than treasures in a storehouse are the treasures of the body, and the treasures of the heart are the most valuable of all. From the time you read this letter on, strive to accumulate the treasures of the heart!" (WND-1, 851).

The "treasures of the heart" refers to those treasures stored up within our lives — such treasures as an expansive state of life, abundant good fortune, vigorous life force, inexhaustible wisdom and warm humanity. This richness of life that we establish through our practice of the Daishonin's Buddhism is the supreme treasure that will remain indestructible throughout the three existences of past, present and future.

When you accumulate the treasures of the heart, then the treasures of the body and the treasures of the storehouse will naturally follow.

TAKING RESPONSIBILITY FOR OUR OWN COMMUNITIES

In a letter to another of his followers, the lay priest Takahashi Rokuro Hyoe, the Daishonin writes: "I entrust you with the propagation of Buddhism in your province. It is stated that 'the seeds of Buddhahood sprout as a result of conditions, and for this reason they preach the single vehicle'" (WND-1, 1117).

The lay priest Takahashi lived in Kajima Village of the Fuji District of Suruga province (present-day Fuji City in Shizuoka Prefecture). In this passage, the Daishonin declares that he completely entrusts his lay follower with the propagation of Buddhism in this region.

To take personal responsibility for transforming your own

country, your own communities, into a Land of Eternally Tranquil Light (Buddha land) through your own efforts and for the sake of your own happiness — this is the correct course for the advancement of kosen-rufu. All the hard work and effort you put toward this end will become your eternal good fortune.

Accumulating Small Victories

There is a saying of which I am quite fond that goes: "Dig below your feet, and there you will find a wellspring." Taking care of the tasks at hand is important. The main thing is to make your goals clear and then set about achieving them one by one with steady and thorough efforts. Only through such continuous efforts can we open up the path before us. Also, we must never neglect the small details.

As you know, the first step I took here in San Francisco thirty-three years ago was indeed a most humble beginning. Today, however, a stream of capable people flows forth from this starting point of San Francisco as if from an inexhaustible spring. I hope all of you will enrich your regions and communities by tapping the spring of boundless benefit and good fortune as you go on to create your own proud pioneering history.

Buddhism expounds that Buddhahood is inherent and eternal within our lives and that therefore the Land of Eternally Tranquil Light always exists where we are right now. The Buddha land is not some far-off utopia. When we chant the daimoku of the Mystic Law and dedicate ourselves to the advancement of kosen-rufu, the place where we are becomes the Land of Eternally Tranquil Light, the Buddha land.

I hope each of you will brightly illuminate the land of mission where you live, with the powerful light of your determination.

Gratitude Leads to Happiness

Thank you so much for today's wonderful meeting. People who can express their gratitude are truly happy. A life that is always filled with appreciation is a bright and cheerful one — be it when you are meeting with people, when someone gives you a lift in his or her car, or when you are at home with your family. Sincerely offering thanks is a sign of living truly happy lives. Where people embody such a sense of appreciation, they send out waves of happiness that envelop both themselves and others.

To voice your appreciation, it is important to say "thank you" to your fellow members and to your friends. Leaders who take the members' sincere efforts for granted and assume a highhanded attitude toward them inevitably come to a deadlock because of their own arrogance. They bring bleakness and unhappiness to both themselves and others.

The expression *thank you* contains the essence of happiness. Those who appreciate the heart of these two words and use them generously are surely more eloquent than the most skilled of speakers.

Due to the warm sincerity of the members here in San Francisco and the rest of the United States, any exhaustion I might have felt from my long journey has completely evaporated.

I reiterate my humble appreciation to all those who worked so tirelessly behind the scenes during my visit. I close my speech, praying that all of you may enjoy immeasurable good fortune. Thank you so much.

The United Nations As the Crystallization of Twentieth-Century Wisdom

---

THE WAR MEMORIAL AND PERFORMING ARTS CENTER,
SAN FRANCISCO, CALIFORNIA, MARCH 18, 1993

I HAVE JUST RECEIVED from Thelma Shelley, managing director of the War Memorial and Performing Arts Center and the mother of this magnificent palace of culture, awards for contributing to world peace and promoting international cultural exchange. This is a great privilege, and I want to express my most humble appreciation.

I also offer my sincere appreciation to Mrs. Shelley; to her son, San Francisco City and County Supervisor Kevin Shelley; to the president of the U.N. 50 Committee, Patricia DiGiorgio, and to all those present today. In addition, I would like to convey my heartfelt gratitude for receiving a commendation from the San Francisco City Council and an invitation to attend the commemorative ceremonies for the United Nations' fiftieth anniversary.

I feel that I am truly undeserving of these honors. But, on behalf of all the SGI members who, both locally and worldwide, are struggling to build a network of peace, culture and education in 115 countries [now 192] through the solidarity of global citizens, I would like to accept these awards.

The words of one song say that "The winds of the future are waiting at the Golden Gate." San Francisco is a beautiful capital of hope that has always extended the frontiers of human history. The assembly of humankind, the United Nations, was also founded at this very center. This hall, the Green Room, is the historic site where the entire conference to establish the U.N. Charter was held. As I now stand here, what comes to mind are memories of my mentor.

In fact, at the time the United Nations was being formed, my mentor, Josei Toda, the second president of the Soka Gakkai, was released from prison and began to rebuild the organization. The U.N. Charter was established on June 26, 1945. President Toda's release from prison was on July 3, 1945.

My mentor emerged undefeated from two years of imprisonment by the Japanese military authorities and began a new humanistic movement for the common people. President Toda's ideals strongly paralleled the principles of the U.N. Charter. They were, indeed, expressions of President Toda's burning desire to bring a fundamental transformation to human history with its apparently ceaseless cycle of violence and war.

With the spirit of our mentor as our prime point, we have been strengthening the bonds among people throughout the world who are awakening to the principles of life and peace. President Toda's will was that we support the United Nations. The United Nations is the crystallization of twentieth-century wisdom. We must surely protect and nurture this fortress of hope for the coming century.

I agree with Patricia DiGiorgio, the president of the U.N. 50 Committee, that the upcoming fiftieth anniversary of the United Nations should not be an occasion to focus on the past. Rather, I would wish to enjoy a glorious celebration together with many young people, creating a powerful beginning of the next fifty years toward the hundredth anniversary.

My wish would be that, by pooling the diverse capabilities of nongovernmental organizations, the United Nations would more greatly emphasize the role of the common people. I hope to further my exchanges with your world-renowned center, a glorious castle of culture, broadening the current flowing toward the harmony of all people. It is my belief that, in this way, the drama of human victory will unfold.

This week, I went to see the bronze statue of San Francisco Mayor Jack Shelley, Mrs. Shelley's late husband. Mayor Shelley used to roll up his sleeves and work together with the people. I feel deeply moved at the work of such a champion of human rights, who devoted himself to unceasing dialogue for human dignity and equality. Jack Shelley is one of our predecessors who highly valued the United Nations.

In particular, we should never forget Mayor Shelley's humane actions when he stood firmly opposed to the confinement of Japanese Americans in internment camps during World War II.

This center is also where the peace treaty with Japan was signed. I would like to renew my determination to promote friendship between our countries.

I have heard that Mayor Shelley admired Goethe, a poet who anticipated a global culture. To end my address and to express my appreciation to you, I would like to recite a passage from one of Goethe's poems:

> *Be noble. Help others*
> *willingly and be*
> *good to others,*
> *because this*
> *behavior is what*
> *separates humans*
> *from other living*
> *beings.*
> *Only human beings can*
> *make the*
> *impossible*
> *possible.*
> *Only humans can make*
> *choices,*
> *differentiate, and*
> *make judgments.*

Humans also can, at the
spur of the
moment, grasp
infinity.

Again, thank you all very much.

Nichiren Daishonin's Buddhism Lives Only Within the SGI

—⟿—

AS YOU MAY KNOW, the SGI will henceforth confer upon members *okatagi* [woodblock print] Gohonzon based on a Gohonzon twenty-sixth high priest Nichikan transcribed in June 1720.

This has been made possible by the sincere offer of Chief Priest Sendo Narita of Joen-ji temple [in Tochigi Prefecture and founded in 1303] upon which this Gohonzon was originally bestowed.

Congratulations!

Okatagi Gohonzon based on a Nichikan-transcribed Gohonzon were also conferred on new members in the early days of the Soka Gakkai. It was a result of this Gohonzon being made widely available to members in those days that the kosen-rufu movement advanced so rapidly in Japan.

The conferral of Nichikan's Gohonzon by the SGI at this time indisputably marks the start of a new era for worldwide kosen-rufu.

A RESTORER OF THE SCHOOL AND A MODEL OF CHARACTER

Nichikan is regarded as one of the restorers of Nichiren Shoshu. He was a high priest known for his outstanding accomplishment in faith, practice and study.

Nichiko, the fifty-ninth high priest, discussing the reasons why Nichikan is so respected, said: "High Priest Nichikan's great achievement was in his practice even more than his scholarly attainment.... He was extremely conscientious. No doubt that is why his faith was so thoroughly communicated to the people in general."

Nichiko went on to say that Nichikan "perfectly and completely revealed the true teachings of Nichiren Daishonin in his writings, chiefly in his *Six-Volume Writings*."

Faith is revealed and demonstrated in the believer's life and actions. It is also evident in the believer's superior humanity, character and integrity. Precisely because Nichikan's everyday actions and his character were so excellent that they commanded universal respect, people could understand, accept and sincerely believe the doctrinal teachings he expounded.

In sharp contrast is someone like Nikken, whose base character and ignoble acts only destroy people's belief in Buddhism as a whole. His very existence is a threat to Buddhism.

Nichiren Daishonin wrote, "Another name for a devil is a robber of benefit...and because they [people] revere devils, they will fall into the hell of incessant suffering in [their next lifetime]" (WND-1, 87). Nikken destroys faith, robs others of benefit and depletes their life force. Just as the Daishonin instructs us, those who do not recognize Nikken for the devilish force he is, and who foolishly and uncritically revere him simply because he is the high priest, will in the end taste the terrible pains and punishments of the hell of incessant suffering.

Nichikan strongly upheld Nichiren Daishonin's teaching that we should base ourselves on the Gohonzon in all things. This is evident in many of his writings, including the *Six-Volume Writings* and his "Commentary on 'The Object of Devotion for Observing the Mind.'"

In his "Commentary on 'The Object of Devotion for Observing the Mind,'" Nichikan writes: "The blessings of the myriads of Buddhas and sutras of the ten directions and three existences, without a single exception, all return to this Gohonzon, which provides the seed of Buddhahood and is hidden in the sutra, just as a tree's hundreds and thousands of branches and leaves all return to the same root. This Gohonzon provides great and boundless benefits. Its mystic functions are vast and profound.... This [object of devotion] is the true purpose for which Nichiren Daishonin appeared in the world, the supreme and unsurpassed among the Three Great Secret Laws of Nichiren Daishonin's Buddhism, the true object of worship of the Buddhism of sowing in the Latter Day of the Law, and the brilliant mirror of Buddhist practitioners" (*The Commentaries of Nichikan*, p. 443).

The object of devotion for observing the mind contains the infinite benefit of all Buddhas. Nichikan wrote this in November 1721, just a year after he transcribed the Gohonzon that has been preserved at Joen-ji temple.

THE OBJECT OF DEVOTION IS FOUND ONLY IN FAITH

While making it clear that we should base ourselves on the Gohonzon, Nichikan also insisted that strong faith and practice are necessary to tap the infinite powers of the Buddha and the Law. He writes in the same commentary:

"One should understand that when one believes in the object of devotion [that is the embodiment of the Law of Nam-myoho-renge-kyo] hidden in the depths of the Lotus Sutra, and chants Nam-myoho-renge-kyo, one can, through the powers of the Buddha and the Law, perfect the practice of observing the mind and attain enlightenment. But if one is lacking in faith, the power of the object of devotion will not enable one to attain enlightenment" (*Commentaries*, 456).

Faith is crucial. Only with the actual practice of chanting daimoku and taking action for kosen-rufu does one's faith become true and correct and can one reap infinite benefit and blessings.

Nichikan also wrote: "The Gohonzon of three thousand realms in a single moment of life is not somewhere outside us. It resides within the faith of us ordinary people" (*Commentaries*, 465).

Of course, Nichikan's declaration is based on Nichiren Daisho-
nin's injunction: "Never seek this Gohonzon outside yourself.…
This Gohonzon also is found only in the two characters for faith"
(WND-I, 832).

Even though you may possess the Gohonzon, you will not
enjoy its true benefit unless you have faith and take action for
kosen-rufu.

Tsunesaburo Makiguchi spread the Law by teaching the concept of punishment. Believe it or not, there were priests who
opposed this, saying that it contradicted the teachings of Nichiren
Shoshu. Josei Toda decried this error on the part of the priests
and wrote: "In the upper right corner of the Gohonzon are the
words, 'If you slander this Law, you will have your head broken
into seven pieces.' Doesn't this signify the theory of punishment?
At the same time, in the upper left corner of the Gohonzon is an
inscription that reads, 'If you make offerings to the Law, you will
receive more good fortune than that derived from holding the ten
titles of the Buddha.' Doesn't this signify the promise the Gohonzon makes to us that we will receive benefits when we worship
it? Benefit, or value, and punishment, or anti-value, constitute the
reality of our daily lives. Some Nichiren Shoshu priests had forgotten that the power of the Gohonzon can be revealed in one's
daily life in either way until President Makiguchi discussed it. They
were astonished at what he brought out, and I am dumbfounded
that many of them have since pretended that they have known this
principle very well for quite some time.

"Also, some priests are not yet aware of this principle. I am saddened rather than surprised by their ignorance" ("The History and
Conviction of the Soka Gakkai," 1951).

How astonishing was the priests' ignorance of Buddhism, and
how little their faith in the Gohonzon! What is worse, they attacked
and criticized the Soka Gakkai, which was working hard to spread
the teachings in exact accord with the Daishonin's teachings while
demonstrating the power of the Gohonzon.

The Nichiren Shoshu priesthood today has not the least bit

of faith in the Gohonzon. To them, the Gohonzon is nothing more than a tool for controlling the believers and greedily plundering their offerings. They will inevitably face the Daishonin's condemnation.

Nichiren Daishonin said, "And even more valuable than reason and documentary proof is the proof of actual fact" (WND-I, 599). Nothing is more powerful than the proof of actual fact. Nothing is more convincing than the actual fact of benefit and victory. The purpose of our faith is to show actual proof of the benefit we derive.

Only the SGI has shown actual proof of the benefit of faith. It is an organization of believers overflowing with such proof, an organization that pulses with the lifeblood of faith.

NICHIKAN'S PASSIONATE DEVOTION TO KOSEN-RUFU

Nichikan Shonin strongly desired the realization of kosen-rufu. All of his writings, including the *Six-Volume Writings* and commentaries on various Gosho, were written solely for the sake of kosen-rufu. That is why he fiercely attacked the many aberrant teachings rampant throughout the land at the time and proclaimed the truth of the Daishonin's teachings. It was all an expression of his desire to accomplish kosen-rufu.

For example, in his introduction to the "Interpretations Based on the Law," one of the six treatises that comprise his *Six-Volume Writings*, he writes: "I have examined the passages [of the Lotus Sutra] that clearly indicate the Three Great Secret Laws, and, using them as proof that these principles represent the truth hidden in the depths of the Lotus Sutra, I humbly present this treatise to the disciples of later ages. It is entirely for the sake of accomplishing kosen-rufu."

Nichikan also criticized as slanderers of the Law those people who do not face the Gohonzon nor wish in their hearts to share Buddhism nor spread the teachings with their mouths.

In his "Commentary on 'On Practicing the Buddha's Teaching,'" Nichikan writes: "The minds of those who forget *shakubuku* and are not always mindful of the four dictums are identical to the minds of slanderers of the Law. If they are not practicing *shakubuku* with their mouths, it is the same as if their mouths are slandering the Law. If their bodies are not facing toward the Gohonzon with prayer beads in their hands, it is equal to their bodies slandering the Law" (*Commentaries*, 767).

No one can compare to SGI members when it comes to practicing the Buddha's teachings as Nichiren Daishonin instructs in the Gosho, for it is we who face the Gohonzon, do gongyo, chant daimoku, pray for the achievement of kosen-rufu and teach others of this Buddhism.

We have prayed, worked, taught others with all our might, faced and overcome one great persecution after another, and through it all, introduced many people to the Gohonzon. As a result, we have seen kosen-rufu develop on an unprecedented scale throughout the globe.

The Nichiren Shoshu priesthood does not do gongyo as it should; it does not do *shakubuku*. It excommunicated the SGI, which is faithfully practicing in accord with the Buddha's teachings; it obstructs kosen-rufu. It is in total and direct violation of the aforementioned injunction of Nichikan.

Nikken and his followers are committing great slander of the Law in all three categories of action — words, thoughts and deeds. To carry out Nichikan's teachings properly, we must strictly rebuke their slander of the Law.

The SGI will henceforth confer upon members *okatagi* Gohonzon produced from a Gohonzon transcribed by Nichikan, who clarified the correct way of faith and practice and who embraced a strong desire to accomplish kosen-rufu. This marks the start of a new phase in the advancement of kosen-rufu and is, I believe, a development in complete accord with the wishes of Nichiren Daishonin, Nikko Shonin and Nichikan. I am also confident that it would give them all the greatest joy.

EACH PERSON WILL BECOME THE BUDDHA
OF LIMITLESS JOY

Nichiren Daishonin's purpose in revealing the Gohonzon was to share with all people the heritage of the Law for becoming a Buddha, in other words, to enable them to attain enlightenment.

In the Gosho "The Heritage of the Ultimate Law of Life," the Daishonin states: "Nichiren has been trying to awaken all the people of Japan to faith in the Lotus Sutra so that they too can share the heritage and attain Buddhahood. But instead they have persecuted me in various ways and finally had me banished to this island" (WND-1, 217).

Nichikan also declared that when common mortals embrace the Gohonzon, their lives are transformed just as they are into the Buddha of limitless joy from time without beginning. This refers to the principle of the oneness of mentor and disciple.

In his "Commentary on 'The Object of Devotion for Observing the Mind,'" Nichikan wrote: "Everyone who receives and embraces this object of worship enters the way of the Buddha of time without beginning.... And we common mortals who have entered the way of this Buddha are entirely one with this Buddha of limitless joy. The Buddha of limitless joy is entirely one with us common mortals. How could this not indicate the oneness of mentor and disciple?" (*Commentaries*, 488).

The mission of followers of the Daishonin is to uphold the Gohonzon and to teach others about the Gohonzon and lead them to embrace faith so that they may attain Buddhahood. Nikko Shonin, the Daishonin's immediate successor, wrote, "Until kosen-rufu is achieved, propagate the Law to the full extent of your ability without begrudging your life" (GZ, 1618). This instruction is primarily addressed to priests. But in fact it is none other than the members of the SGI who are practicing without begrudging their lives to propagate the Gohonzon throughout the world in accord with Nikko Shonin's admonition.

Where within the Nichiren Shoshu priesthood have we seen anyone practice with the spirit of "not begrudging one's life"?

Nikken himself has schemed to destroy the SGI and disrupt the flow of kosen-rufu.

WE ARE THE DAISHONIN'S BELIEVERS

The previous high priest of Nichiren Shoshu, Nittatsu, told the priests: "Always remember that our believers are believers of the Daishonin. Our duty is simply to look after the believers and make it easier for them to pray to the Daishonin" (January 15, 1972). Nikken tried to usurp the believers of the Daishonin and make them believers of Nikken. This is a revolt against the original Buddha.

Nichiu, the ninth high priest, declared that when someone strays from the faith of the Daishonin, the heritage of the Law for attaining Buddhahood in this lifetime is severed.

In his treatise "On the Formalities of Nichiren Daishonin's Buddhism," Nichiu wrote: "When we remain true to the faith of the Daishonin, our bodies and minds are the bodies and minds of Myoho-renge-kyo, but when we stray from that faith, our bodies and minds are those of mere mortals, and as mere mortals, we cannot receive the heritage of the Law, which ensures the attainment of Buddhahood in our present form."

About this statement, the fifty-ninth high priest, Nichiko, said that when we deviate even in the slightest from faith as it is taught by Nichiren Daishonin and Nikko Shonin, falling into false faith that deviates from the Buddha's intent, we lose our claim to receive the heritage of the Law.

Nichiko wrote: "When we do not deviate in the least from the faith of Nichiren Daishonin, the founder of Nichiren Daishonin's Buddhism, and Nikko Shonin, the founder of Taiseki-ji, we, as their followers, though possessing lives that are vulgar, evil and impure, will exhibit the truth, goodness and purity of Myoho-renge-kyo in body and mind. . . . However, when our faith deteriorates into impurity and becomes mistaken and confused, thereby straying from the Buddha's intent, the path of the water of the Law will be clogged, and only our inherent baseness will be manifest in our body and mind, thus disqualifying us from receiving the heritage of the Law for attaining Buddhahood in our present form."

Nikken has excommunicated the SGI, an organization of believers that, in accordance with the Buddha's mandate and decree, is dedicated to the advancement of kosen-rufu. He is an aberrant priest who rebels against the Buddha's will. He has, as a result, disqualified himself from receiving the heritage of the Law for the attainment of Buddhahood in one's present form, just as Nichiko stated. It goes without saying that Nikken has lost all qualifications to transcribe the Gohonzon and confer it upon anyone. I want to make this fact perfectly clear.

APPEARING IN RESPONSE TO THE BUDDHA'S DECREE

In May 1951, soon after his inauguration as the second president, Mr. Toda declared that the time had come for a great propagation campaign, and he requested that the high priest transcribe a Gohonzon specially dedicated to the fulfillment of the Daishonin's vow to accomplish kosen-rufu.

Responding to the Soka Gakkai's request, the high priest at that time, Nissho, transcribed the Gohonzon, and down one side he wrote the following dedication: "For the Fulfillment of the Great Desire for Kosen-rufu Through the Compassionate Propagation of the Great Law." This Gohonzon clearly reveals the great significance and mission of the SGI, which made its advent to carry out the Buddha's mandate and decree to achieve kosen-rufu.

Now that Nikken has become an enemy of the Buddha, it is the mission and duty of the SGI to undertake the conferral of Gohonzon for the sake of people who seek it the world over, as well as for the sake of the ongoing advancement of kosen-rufu. This is an undertaking that accords with the time. It is also in perfect accord with the spirit of Nichiren Daishonin and Nikko Shonin.

As I have already discussed at length, there is profound

significance in the SGI's conferral of the Gohonzon transcribed by Nichikan, who was directly connected to the original Buddha, Nichiren Daishonin.

THE GOHONZON IN OUR HOMES
IS THE DAISHONIN'S LIFE

The Dai-Gohonzon, which Nichiren Daishonin bestowed upon all people of the world and which was the ultimate purpose for his advent in this world, is and will always be the basis of our faith. This will never change.

High Priest Nittatsu remarked: "The Daishonin has already died. His life, the life of Nichiren Daishonin, is the Dai-Gohonzon of the sanctuary of the essential teaching.... The Gohonzon enshrined in your altar is, itself, the life of Nichiren Daishonin. Your Gohonzon manifests the three enlightened properties of the Buddha — the property of the Law, the property of wisdom and the property of action — that is, Nichiren Daishonin himself" (September 7, 1962).

We should look upon the Gohonzon enshrined in each of our homes as the life of the Daishonin, the entity of the original Buddha. When we chant daimoku with that conviction, it is the same as if we are worshiping the Dai-Gohonzon itself right where we are.

Nittatsu also said: "Wherever the Gohonzon is enshrined, that place, in a broad sense, takes on the significance of the sanctuary of the essential teaching. The sincere daimoku you chant to that Gohonzon with a concentrated mind free of all extraneous thoughts is instantly received by the Dai-Gohonzon of the sanctuary of the essential teaching. The place where you chant Nam-myoho-renge-kyo is instantly transformed into Eagle Peak. And this is where you attain Buddhahood in your present form" (November 23, 1977).

Wherever you may be in the world, if you believe in the Gohonzon and chant daimoku with sincere faith, you are in contact with the Dai-Gohonzon at that moment and in that place. The claim that unless you visit the head temple you will not acquire true benefit is a great falsehood in violation of the teachings of Nittatsu.

Nichikan wrote of the benefit of the Gohonzon, "If only you take faith in this Gohonzon and chant Nam-myoho-renge-kyo even for a while, no prayer will go unanswered, no offense will remain unforgiven, all good fortune will be bestowed, and all righteousness proven" (*Commentaries*, 443).

Let us continue to advance confidently on the golden road to worldwide kosen-rufu, always basing ourselves on the Gohonzon and accumulating infinite benefit on our way.

GOJUKAI CEREMONY UNNECESSARY

Some of you may be concerned about what sort of ceremony will be conducted when the SGI begins conferring the Gohonzon. I have discussed the *gojukai* (lit. accepting the precepts) ceremony before, but since it is very important, I would like to touch upon it again here.

Briefly, in the Latter Day of the Law, to embrace the Gohonzon and be constant in one's faith and practice throughout one's life mean to uphold the precepts. This is called "embracing faith equals upholding the precepts." Thus, the true meaning of upholding the precepts in the Latter Day of the Law is to embrace the Gohonzon.

Nikko Shonin also wrote on the back of the "Orally Transmitted Teachings on the Three Great Secret Laws," a transcription of the Daishonin's statement, that "embracing [the Gohonzon] equals upholding the precepts."

No records show that the Daishonin, aside from the Tendai scholar-priest Sairen-bo, conferred the precepts on any of his other followers. Sairen-bo, as a priest of the Tendai school, had received the precepts of the theoretical teachings of the Lotus Sutra on Mount Hiei [where the head temple of the Tendai school is located]. It was probably on his own initiative that he requested the Daishonin to confer on him the precepts of the supreme teaching hidden in the depths of the essential teachings of the Lotus Sutra. With this exception, there are no records of Nichiren Daishonin having conferred the precepts on any of his disciples who were priests, much less records of lay followers having had the precepts conferred on them.

Commenting on this matter, Nichiko noted that in Nikko Shonin's time, there was no standard *gojukai* ceremony, and that we should therefore conclude that traditional Buddhist *gojukai* ceremonies were simply not held by Nichiren Shoshu [then known as the Fuji school] at that time. In fact, he notes, other Buddhist schools criticized the Fuji school for not having an established *gojukai* ceremony.

The *gojukai* ceremony conducted in more recent times was something that President Makiguchi asked the priesthood to initiate after the Soka Gakkai's establishment. President Makiguchi asked the priests to initiate a *gojukai* ceremony for the increasing number of people who came to embrace faith through the Soka Gakkai because he wanted something that would strengthen those new members' commitment to faith and to practicing throughout their lives. His main focus was on helping the members to consolidate their faith. He did not by any means believe that the ceremony, or ritual, of *gojukai* was necessary in and of itself.

Satoru Izumi, chairperson of the Soka Gakkai Executive Guidance Committee who practiced in the early days of the Soka Gakkai, says that "many of the new members at that time came to us from other religions. For this reason, the Soka Gakkai asked them to undergo the gojukai ceremony to make a fresh start, to cement their determination to uphold faith in Nichiren Daishonin's Buddhism, and to prevent them from falling away again."

Thus, Nichiren Shoshu's *gojukai* ceremony conducted in its more recent history was established as a result of the Soka Gakkai's great efforts in propagating the Daishonin's teachings.

From the perspective of the Daishonin's Buddhism, which

teaches that embracing the Gohonzon means upholding the precepts, when you embrace the Gohonzon, or when you arouse faith in the Gohonzon for the very first time, you have at that moment received the precepts of the Latter Day of the Law.

The essence of receiving the precepts is when those people who wish to take faith vow to uphold the precepts — in other words, to make the Gohonzon their object of devotion for the rest of their lives. This, too, is the idea behind the commemorative gongyo meetings that will be held at SGI community centers for those receiving the Gohonzon.

There are examples in the past where those receiving the bodhisattva precepts of Mahayana Buddhism made a personal vow before the Buddha to uphold the precepts. Nichiren Daishonin declares, "This is my vow, and I will never forsake it!" (WND-1, 281). You must never break a personal vow you have made.

The Daishonin teaches us this about faith: "To accept is easy; to continue is difficult. But Buddhahood lies in continuing faith" (WND-1, 471).

Never-regressing faith is what is important. To continue in faith is to truly uphold the precepts. In this sense, faith equals the precepts, and we of the SGI are the ones who in reality accept and uphold the precepts in the true spirit of Nichiren Daishonin's Buddhism.

PRACTICE AND STUDY BASED ON FAITH

When we analyze faith, we find that it can be divided into three essential components: faith, practice and study. Nichiko discussed the relationship between the three. Basically, he makes the analogy of faith being a general; practice, the first officer; and study, the second officer. He wrote: "The purpose of practice is to assist and support faith, and the purpose of study is to support practice.

"We can also say that practice is led by faith, and that study follows practice. Thus we must not practice in a way that contradicts our faith. And we must not engage in study in such a way that it obstructs our practice.

"In every case, faith is primary; its first lieutenant is practice; and its second lieutenant is study.

"When there is a gap in this relationship and it does not move smoothly, faith, practice and study fall out of synchronization. They die or wither, and they cannot function effectively.

"When faith, which is central, is not complete or true, a much larger danger arises, and both practice and study are destroyed.

"Even though not as drastic perhaps, we frequently see cases in which practice and study fail because they are led by an incomplete faith or the mere appearance of faith, without sincere spirit.

"For example, when a person without true faith in his heart preaches the Law to others, trying to force faith on them, all he does is toss about empty and futile notions. Though he may read from the Gosho and present them with time-honored passages, his words last only as long as he speaks to them and leave no impression on his listeners' hearts."

Nichiko made these comments in 1923, lamenting on the state of the priesthood, but it applies perfectly to the present-day priesthood as well. The priests of Nichiren Shoshu have completely lost their faith, while their practice and study have fallen into ruin. Faith, practice and study alike have perished there.

Nichiko's remark that those who lack true faith only toss about empty concepts and cannot make an impression on their listeners applies perfectly to Nikken. Nikken has defended himself against criticism that his lectures are so difficult to understand that they seem to be in a foreign language by asserting that the truth of Buddhism "can only be understood and shared between Buddhas" and that it would be far odder if his lectures were easy to understand.

"Without practice and study, there can be no Buddhism" (WND-1, 386), teaches Nichiren Daishonin. The three elements of faith, practice and study are the eternal standards for the practice of Buddhism as taught by the Daishonin. Only the SGI, directly connected to the Daishonin, has upheld correct faith, following the path of faith, practice and study. That is why the Buddhism of the Daishonin lives only in the SGI.

Nichijun, the sixty-fifth high priest, said: "Once you get deeply involved in doctrinal studies, you tend to be negligent in your practice. But when we ask what the core of religion, of religious faith is, the answer is practice. Doctrine is meant to be a support for practice. We must never forget that practice does not exist for the sake of doctrine but that doctrine exists for the sake of practice.

"I hope you will always remember that, if you forget practice and get carried away with doctrinal studies, you are just playing with Buddhism. Therefore, please devote yourselves to the study of doctrine as a support to practice" (May 3, 1956).

As these words of Nichijun indicate, the Nichiren Shoshu priesthood, which has forgotten about its practice for kosen-rufu yet continues to hold forth on the Gosho and Buddhist doctrine, is only playing with the Daishonin's Buddhism.

Mr. Toda always said our doctrinal studies must not lapse into an obsession with textual analysis but must always remain study based on faith, study for the sake of kosen-rufu.

THOSE "EMERGING FROM THE EARTH" WILL ACHIEVE KOSEN-RUFU

Nichijun also said: "When we speak of 'emerging from the earth,' the earth represents the place where all life dwells.

"The Great Teacher T'ien-t'ai interpreted this earth as 'the profound depth of the essential nature of the Law' or 'the ultimate state of enlightenment.' It is the state that is the source of all phenomena that constitute the world. It is the state of the secret and mystic powers of the Tathagata as described in the 'Life Span' chapter of the Lotus Sutra.

"Those who will propagate the Mystic Law gradually emerge from this earth. As the Daishonin described it, 'Then two, three, and a hundred followed, chanting and teaching others.

Propagation will unfold this way in the future as well. Does this not signify "emerging from the earth"?' (WND-1, 385).

"These individuals who emerge from the earth will protect the Daishonin's Great Mystic Law in the age of the Latter Day of the Law and propagate it in this defiled world, converting those slanderous people who will attain Buddhahood through a reverse relationship with the Law and accomplishing kosen-rufu.

"Whatever happens, the Mystic Law will not be extinguished in the world, and in the end everyone will take faith in it without fail. This is the wish of all Buddhas throughout the three existences and the ten directions" (*Dai-Nichiren*, January 1955).

Individuals who have "emerged from the earth" appear in the Latter Day of the Law to propagate the Buddhism of Nichiren Daishonin. This clearly refers to SGI members. Moreover, as Nichijun declared, the flow of kosen-rufu will not be disrupted, no matter what happens. The Buddhas of the three existences of past, present and future will never fail to protect the SGI, which is carrying out the Buddha's mandate. There can be no doubt that we enjoy the great protection of the original Buddha, Nichiren Daishonin.

The United States of America is the world leader and the model of worldwide kosen-rufu. Please advance cheerfully, confident that now is the time to achieve great progress and attain great benefit, full of pride as courageous champions of kosen-rufu who have "emerged from the earth."

Leaders must value and pray for the happiness of each member; they must also climb surely and steadily up the mountain of their own self-perfection.

Again, my congratulations to you all!

Become People
With Big Hearts

THIS IS A FAMILY GATHERING. Let's enjoy ourselves!

The SGI-USA has now entered a great second phase. I would like to congratulate all of you on this magnificent and solid development.

Big-hearted people are happy people. Faith enables us to become this kind of person. I hope all of you will become people who are generous and broad-minded.

The vast ocean is capable of encompassing anything; a small pond can only contain so much. The Buddhism of Nichiren Daishonin is as all-encompassing as the universe itself. We are its practitioners. Let us cherish those around us — family, friends and fellow members — embracing all with our big hearts and enjoying life together. Let us live truly great and wonderful lives.

Of course, we must be strict and uncompromising when it comes to fighting evil. Other than that, I hope you will be generous toward your friends and fellow members and have room in your hearts to think about the happiness of other people.

"Such-and-such is sick. So-and-so is suffering financially. I must do my best to give them encouragement." To think in this way, to offer prayers and take action for others' happiness — this is the behavior of a Buddhist.

Those who make efforts to bring joy to others even though they may be suffering themselves are bodhisattvas. "I know I'll be all right no matter what happens. I'm not worried about me. More important, I want to help such-and-such. I want to give hope to so-and-so." This is the kind of big-hearted person I would like you to become. This is the purpose of our Buddhist practice. When we climb the mountain of this practice, we accumulate solid good fortune in our lives without fail.

LEARNING FROM EVERYONE AROUND US

I also hope that you will have the willingness and open-mindedness to learn from everyone. You might admire a fellow member's sincere attitude toward faith or someone's happy and harmonious family. You can learn something from everyone, even if it is merely a person's good posture or the care and attention someone pays to her make-up or his grooming. To have the humility to always learn something is a measure of how big a person is.

Leaders, in particular, tend to become arrogant just because they hold high positions in the organization and think that they know everything. This is a common tendency. They put on airs and regard other truly upright people as being below them. This kind of behavior only alienates people. It also destroys the leader's own good fortune.

To leaders, I would like to say: The higher your position in the organization, the stronger should be your desire to learn from everyone around you. Viewed through the eyes of the Buddha and the eyes of the Law — in other words, through the eyes of faith — all members are Buddhas and heavenly deities.

GIVING OTHERS COURAGE AND CONFIDENCE

Leaders are people who bring joy to others. This is the most fundamental requirement of a leader.

In society at large, too, those who cause others grief and pain, who oppress the people, disqualify themselves as leaders. How much more this applies in the world of Buddhism. Leaders who have grown arrogant and haughty because of their position — not to mention a certain high priest who is given to sudden vociferous and violent outbursts of temper — are also disliked by those around them, and they themselves end up being miserable.

I would like leaders to make efforts so that people will say about them: "That person really put my mind at ease. I was convinced, reassured and encouraged. I now feel more confident and full of hope."

Leaders must never give orders or dictate to the members. I hope you will be gentle leaders who are generous in giving reassurance and peace of mind to fellow members. To be strict with oneself but gentle with others — this is the spirit of one who has strong faith.

Male leaders who scold women are the lowest of the low.

In any event, based on the reformation of leaders themselves, please make the new SGI-USA an even more splendid organization.

An Achievement of Active Intellects

The members of the SGI-USA culture department, a great force of active intellects, have published the first three volumes of a series titled *The Philosophy and Practice of the SGI*. This news was given top coverage in the *Seikyo Shimbun* in Japan and has drawn a response of great admiration from members around the world. No doubt these publications of the culture department will eventually find their way into libraries, not only in the United States but in countries throughout the globe as well.

Let me convey my deep respect to the chairperson of the culture department's publications committee, Dr. Eric Hauber, and to the authors of the first three booklets: Dr. Michael Hays, professor of cultural studies at Cornell University; Dr. Jay M. Heffron, associate professor of education at the University of Hawaii [as of 1996 at Soka University of America in Aliso Viejo, California]; and Dr. Kathleen H. Dockett, professor of psychology at the

University of the District of Columbia. I also wish to thank all those who are involved in this project for their efforts. Dr. Howard Hunter, professor of religion and chairman of the Department of Religion at Tufts University in Medford, Massachusetts, whom I met with the other day, spoke highly of the publications. [Dr. Hunter wrote the introduction for the series.]

This year marks the fiftieth anniversary of Tsunesaburo Makiguchi's imprisonment by the Japanese military authorities during World War II. On November 18 this year, it will also be the fiftieth anniversary of his death in 1944. [According to Japanese tradition, the actual date of a person's death is deemed the first anniversary; the second anniversary thus comes one year later, and so on.]

Mr. Makiguchi constantly called out to the members, "Let's treasure philosophy" and "We must leave behind a legacy of philosophy." How delighted Mr. Makiguchi would be at this wonderful project that the culture department members are now undertaking!

IN PRAISE OF DISTRICT LEADERS

Attending today's meeting are many district leaders who are fighting on the front lines of the kosen-rufu movement. You are truly noble people who possess a profound mission.

I was once placed in charge of a district myself, so I know what it is like. The amount of responsibility and hard work involved is truly great. Yet Buddhism teaches that earthly desires are enlightenment. All our hardships, therefore, will turn into brilliant treasures. This is what faith means.

I would like to express my sincere appreciation for your unflagging daily efforts. Thank you very much.

Josei Toda also highly treasured district leaders. Placing tremendous confidence in them, he cried, "Let's fight together, using our discussion meetings!"

President Toda said: "The Lotus Sutra states, 'If you see a person who accepts and upholds this sutra, you should rise and greet him from afar, showing him the same respect you would a Buddha' (LS, 324). Therefore, if you go to a discussion meeting and there are only, say, three people in attendance, you should be filled with joy and engage them in conversation. The same applies even if there is only one other person, for you can teach the truth of Myoho-renge-kyo to that one person.

"You should come home from a discussion meeting feeling happy and inspired from having shared in sincere conversation with fellow members — even with only one person or two. This is the kind of discussion meeting you should strive to hold — even if there is only one person who will listen to what you have to say. Just meeting that one person is important.

"'Today, I tried talking to an elderly woman. I did, and she went home full of joy and high spirits. I'm so glad.' This kind of spirit is important."

Compared to making such life-to-life contacts, talking eloquently in front of many people at big meetings and receiving their applause are relatively easy. If your efforts are solely inspired by your desire to receive applause, then you are only working for your own self-satisfaction. If you are only striving to win a popularity contest, you are using the organization. In contrast, to make efforts to instill a wholehearted sense of satisfaction in even one person represents the true spirit of our Buddhist practice.

Gathering Strength Through Suffering

The American writer Thomas Paine, who exerted a great influence on the American Revolution for Independence, wrote, "I love the man that can smile in trouble, that can gather strength from distress and grow brave by reflection."[1]

I, too, love such people. And I myself have lived in this way.

Paine continues: "It is the business of little minds to shrink; but he whose heart is firm, and whose conscience approves his conduct, will pursue his principles unto death."[2]

Conviction gives birth to courage. Faith is the highest conviction. For this reason, people of faith must possess the greatest courage.

USING ADVERSITY AS A SPRINGBOARD FOR CHANGE

Dr. Robert Jastrow, one of the world's leading astronomers and the director of the Mount Wilson Observatory in California, once referred to adversity and struggle in the context of the vast history of life's evolution on Earth. He said: "These terms, *adversity* and *struggle*, so negative in their connotations, describe the life force, for without adversity there is no pressure, and without pressure there is no change."[3]

The SGI has always challenged adversity head-on. This is the reason for its great development. This is why we have been able to lay an unshakable path for growth and advancement. Without adversity and struggle, we would never have been able to build the solid foundations that we have. This path of adversity and struggle is the law of evolution; it is the eternal path of the SGI.

The SGI-USA has developed and improved tremendously, and it continues to make steady progress. Please do not grow impatient but continue to advance slowly but surely, one step at a time.

The new Hawaii Culture Center will be completed by spring of next year [March 19, 1994]. And plans are now on the drawing board for a new facility for peace and culture in Boston. [The Boston Research Center for the 21st Century officially opened May 12, 1995.]

I will also do my utmost to support you in your endeavors in every way possible for the continued steady development of the SGI-USA.

RELIGION BECOMES OBSOLETE WITHOUT REFORM

The great American poet and philosopher Ralph Waldo Emerson, who had such close ties to Boston, wrote in his diary (in 1872): "One thing is certain: the religions are obsolete when the reforms do not proceed from them."[4]

The energy to bring about fresh and vibrant reform exists within a living religion. A living religion constantly routs out apathy and force of habit and stirs up a fresh, new breeze. In this respect, the

Nichiren Shoshu priesthood is completely obsolete, just as Emerson describes.

The great Buddhism of Nichiren Daishonin lives only in the SGI. Proclaiming this indisputable truth, I would like to conclude today's speech. Through our joint efforts, let's create a new SGI-USA!

Notes

1. Thomas Paine, *Political Writings*, edited by Bruce Kuklick (Cambridge: Cambridge University Press, 1989), p. 46.
2. *Political Writings*, p. 46.
3. Robert Jastrow, *Until the Sun Dies* (New York: W. W. Norton and Company, Inc., 1977), p. 14.
4. *The Journals and Miscellaneous Notebooks of Ralph Waldo Emerson: Volume XVI, 1866–1882*, edited by Ronald A. Bosco and Glen M. Johnson (Cambridge, Massachusetts: The Belknap Press of Harvard University Press, 1982), p. 262.

Five Guidelines Announced for a Model Organization

—ɷ—

SGI President Ikeda attended the second SGI-USA Executive Conference this evening. Out of his desire that the SGI-USA becomes a model for the rest of the world, the SGI leader gave the following five guidelines:

1) Let's value our health first and foremost.

We should never place unreasonable demands on ourselves and our fellow members. To overstrain oneself and to have strong faith are two different things.

Unless we are in good health, we cannot fully and unstintingly devote ourselves to activities for kosen-rufu. We should advance with wisdom and common sense and show actual proof of good health and longevity.

2) Let's relate our experiences.

One fact is more powerful than a million theoretical arguments. By promoting a movement to share with others our personal experiences in faith, we can spread the joy of faith and understanding toward Buddhism in our local communities, in society and throughout the United States.

3) Let's encourage others on the telephone.

It is important to use our wisdom. America is such a vast country that telephones serve as a valuable way of keeping in contact with, and giving encouragement to members with whom it may be difficult to meet regularly.

As is stated by Nichiren Daishonin, "The voice carries out the work of the Buddha" (OTT, 4). Your warm and friendly voices on the phone will greatly encourage your members.

4) Let's promote a "no-accidents" campaign.

Traffic accidents, in particular, bring suffering and sadness not only to those who are involved but to friends and loved ones around them. Through our strong prayers, we should strive to lead each day without any accidents.

5) Let's engage in joyful dialogue and hold happy discussion meetings.

There is no need to be hasty or impatient as we go about our efforts for kosenrufu.

Through our continuous and earnest devotion to such fundamentals as gongyo, personal guidance and discussion meetings, we can scale the mountain of attaining enlightenment and realizing kosen-rufu.

Also, as we continue to engage in joyful heart-to-heart dialogue with one another and conduct happy and cheerful discussion meetings, we will surely come to accumulate enduring good fortune in our own lives.

Embracing the Gohonzon
Is in Itself Enlightenment

—⚏—

THIRD SGI-USA EXECUTIVE CONFERENCE,

BOSTON, MASSACHUSETTS,

SEPTEMBER 21, 1993

I AM DELIGHTED to see you all again after two years. As members of one big family, let us again create a joyous and meaningful history together.

The day before yesterday (September 19), I met with Robert Jastrow, one of the world's leading astronomers and the director of the Mount Wilson Institute, which operates the Mount Wilson Observatory near Pasadena, California. I mentioned once again that there is no contradiction between Buddhism and reason. Buddhism is supported by an immense body of sutras and scriptures collectively called the eighty thousand teachings. It expounds the Law that is universal and all-pervading. In Buddhism, faith is an extension of reason, and faith inevitably manifests itself as the brilliance of reason.

The Buddhism of Nichiren Daishonin represents the very quintessence of Buddhism. "What is the meaning of my life? What is my mission? What is my relationship to the universe?" The Daishonin's Buddhism can help us find the answers to these questions. It can, in the words of Socrates, help one "know thyself."

If I may make rather broad generalizations, one might say the mission of scientists is to pursue truth, the prime concern of business people might be to make a profit, and that of politicians might be holding the reins of government.

Buddhism, however, fundamentally contains all spheres of learning and the entire spectrum of value. Consequently, those who embrace and practice the supreme sutra — the Lotus Sutra — are kings and queens of humanity.

In this respect, the SGI is a gathering of kings and queens, a gathering of Bodhisattvas of the Earth. In particular, all of you gathered here today are leaders of Buddhism. You are striving to lead people to happiness. There is no more noble or respectable mission than this.

Leading people to happiness is the responsibility of a leader. I would like you to be kings and queens of action and of seeking spirit toward Buddhism. I also hope you will become kings and queens of eternity, of happiness, of philosophy, of wisdom, of family harmony, of life and of society. Moreover, I am convinced that the members in Boston are kings and queens of intellect.

The truth is always found in our immediate reality. When I use the words *kings* and *queens*, it doesn't mean that you are going to become some kind of superhuman being. You are still and always will be a human being.

No matter what airs they may put on or how high a position they may rise to, human beings can never be anything more than human beings. Therefore, those who behave with the utmost humanity, who shine in the way that human beings really should, are true kings and queens.

For us SGI members, our immediate reality includes gongyo. It also includes personal guidance and discussion meetings. In our actual day-to-day efforts shine the brilliance of kings and queens and the light of Buddhism. I hope you will take note of this fundamental point.

WISDOM IS THE SOURCE OF CULTURE

Because this meeting is being held in Boston, the city of culture, I would like to talk a little about the subject of culture today.

At the Fifth Soka Gakkai Young Men's Division General Meeting in 1956, the sixty-fifth high priest, Nichijun, spoke of the relationship between Japanese culture and Buddhism. He referred to the cultural reform initiated by Prince Shotoku (574–622) [a devout follower of Buddhism who was instrumental in its spread in Japan], and the great cultural movement of the Heian era started by the Great Teacher Dengyo (767–822) [who established the Tendai school of Buddhism in Japan]. Nichijun observed that as both these examples indicate, a profound cultural movement ensues when the Mystic Law prospers and spreads in accordance with the time.

In the Latter Day of the Law, it is the Daishonin's Buddhism that has the power to constantly revitalize culture — keeping it fresh and alive. It is also the source for the creation of a vibrantly pulsing culture of humanism.

Josei Toda maintained that "culture represents turning wisdom into knowledge." He once said: "[Culture means] giving wisdom a concrete form, if you like; in other words, putting [wisdom] into a form in which it can be used by people. For example, something like a baby's diaper is a marvelous example of culture. Just because it is a diaper, that doesn't give one the right to denigrate it as a lowly form of culture. The person who invented the diaper must surely have possessed great wisdom, wouldn't you say? . . .

"True culture is the product of one's wisdom. Therefore, the greatest culture can derive only from the greatest wisdom.... I state unequivocally that today there is no greater wisdom than the Mystic Law. As long as this wisdom exists, humanity can avoid many crises and eventually develop a truly glorious culture. To do so, it is necessary to realize kosen-rufu — the only path, I believe, left to humankind.... In this respect, I feel I am perfectly justified in describing kosen-rufu as a cultural movement of the highest order."

We have earnestly pursued this path that President Toda indicated, and we have built a network of peace, culture and education throughout the world. Today, we stand on the brink of a great age of global exchange. We have launched a great cultural movement based on humanism, with the whole world as our stage.

Religion Is the Origin of Civilization

During my dialogue with the late British historian Arnold Toynbee, we discussed the relationship between civilization and religion. Dr. Toynbee said: "I believe that a civilization's style is the expression of its religion. I quite agree that religion has been the source of the vitality that has brought civilizations into being and has then kept them in being" (*Choose Life*, p. 309).

Dr. Toynbee also said that what he defined as higher religions "are the kind that modern man needs." [He defined higher religions as "those that bring an individual human being into direct contact with the ultimate spiritual reality instead of giving him only indirect contact with it through the medium of either a nonhuman natural force or an institution embodying collective human power."] And he agreed that "a universal system of laws of life, such as is presented in Buddhism, is likely to be a less misleading representation of ultimate spiritual reality [than either a pantheon or a unique god]" (*Choose Life*, 326).

Also, the former Soviet prime minister, Mikhail Gorbachev, said, "With respect to the role that religion will play in building a new civilization and a new world, I believe a world religion is indispensable for us to usher in such a new era."

With every passing moment, humanity is moving closer to a new age of world religion. In contrast, as you know, the Nichiren Shoshu priesthood denigrates and despises culture. To denigrate culture is to denigrate the fruits and achievements of human intellect and wisdom; it is an expression of contempt for human beings themselves.

Rebuking Slander of the Law

Decades ago, the fifty-ninth high priest, Nichiko, pointed out the corrupt state of Nichiren Shoshu priests: "[There are some priests of our school] who proclaim it is a virtue to put on a grand pretense of faith and move the believers to tears with their eloquence and then milk them of offerings. They say they acquire benefit from doing so because they satisfy the believers, even if just for a short time. They declare themselves to be fulfilling their duty to the head temple and performing a service to society. And their own pockets are satisfied as well, they say. What is more, they have the audacity to say that this way everyone is kept happy....

"Their attitude is highly immoral. By their behavior, they are harming both themselves and others. Many of those who betray Buddhism and degrade Nichiren Shoshu appear from among the ranks of priests such as these."

Corrupt priests who live off Buddhism and greedily devour the believers' offerings have been a constant in history.

The Nichiren Shoshu priesthood has become a truly corrupt and immoral school, while its priests, including Nikken, are nothing more than aberrant priests who transgress the teachings of Buddhism. When the correct teaching is endangered by an avalanche of heretical Buddhist teachings, the Daishonin instructs us: "At such a time, one must set aside all other affairs and devote one's attention to rebuking slander of the correct teaching. This is the practice of shakubuku" (WND-1, 126).

In light of this Gosho, to thoroughly rebuke the great slander of the Law that is being perpetrated by the Nichiren Shoshu priesthood is to practice Buddhism in a way that accords with the present time.

THE GREAT BENEFIT OF EMBRACING FAITH

As you know, it has recently been announced that the SGI will confer the Gohonzon — based on one transcribed by the twenty-sixth high priest, Nichikan — upon members around the world. This news has been greeted with great joy not only throughout the United States but in countries around the globe. Today, I would therefore like to talk a little about the significance of "embracing the Gohonzon."

In the Gosho "The Object of Devotion for Observing the Mind," the Daishonin writes: "Shakyamuni's practices and the virtues he consequently attained are all contained within the five characters of Myoho-renge-kyo. If we believe in these five characters, we will naturally be granted the same benefits as he was" (WND-1, 365).

This is a famous passage that elucidates the principle of "embracing the Gohonzon is in itself enlightenment." President Toda said the following about this Gosho passage: "'The five characters of Myoho-renge-kyo' refers to the Gohonzon of the Three Great Secret Laws. 'Shakyamuni's practices and the virtues he consequently attained' refers to all the practices and resulting virtues of Shakyamuni as described in the provisional [pre-Lotus Sutra] teachings, and in the theoretical and essential teachings [of the Lotus Sutra].

"One can attain the state of Buddhahood just through the benefit of embracing the Dai-Gohonzon, without requiring any meritorious deeds, the accumulation of any other benefit, or undergoing some kind of arduous practice.

"What then is the meaning of 'to embrace'? There are several ways in which this may be interpreted. But I feel that it is best viewed from the standpoint of the significance of the Three Great Secret Laws and of the three categories of action — thoughts, words and deeds. It goes without saying that the fundamental meaning of 'to embrace' is to believe in the Dai-Gohonzon of the Three Great Secret Laws and to simply and wholeheartedly chant Nam-myoho-renge-kyo....

"If you receive the Gohonzon and then merely enshrine it in your room, you are embracing the Gohonzon in outward form only.

"The daimoku of the Three Great Secret Laws has two aspects: one is faith and the other is practice. To carry out the daimoku of practice, you have to chant daimoku for yourself and for others. This is the daimoku of the Latter Day of the Law.

"If you simply have [the Gohonzon] enshrined in your room, then, even if you profess faith in it, you cannot be said to truly embrace the Gohonzon."

You SGI members who are diligently making efforts for kosen-rufu and assiduously performing gongyo and chanting daimoku are people who truly embrace and believe in the Gohonzon. The good fortune you possess, therefore, is immeasurable, and the fact that you will attain enlightenment is guaranteed.

REVERING THE MYSTIC LAW INHERENT IN OUR OWN LIVES

In another Gosho, Nichiren Daishonin writes, "When we revere Myoho-renge-kyo inherent in our own life as the object of devotion, the Buddha nature within us is summoned forth and manifested by our chanting of Nam-myoho-renge-kyo. This is what is meant by 'Buddha'" (WND-1, 887).

In regard to this passage, President Toda commented: "The body of the person who chants daimoku to the Gohonzon in itself becomes the entity of the object of devotion. This is clear. Surely this very action constitutes 'embracing the Gohonzon' in the truest sense."

The sixty-sixth high priest, Nittatsu, once remarked that the life of the Daishonin is in itself the Gohonzon. He said: "If we believe single-mindedly in this Gohonzon and chant Nam-myoho-renge-kyo, we ourselves become the Gohonzon. Furthermore, we become the noble entity of the life of the founder, Nichiren Daishonin. This is the true meaning of attaining Buddhahood in our present form.

"I therefore ask that all of you chant single-mindedly to this Gohonzon, harboring not the slightest doubt in your heart; and I ask that you establish the kind of profound faith where you can realize in the depths of your life that your mortal body itself becomes the entity of the life of the Daishonin and the Gohonzon."

In the Gosho "The Entity of the Mystic Law," the Daishonin writes on this principle: "In essence, the entity of Myoho-renge-kyo is the physical body that the disciples and followers of Nichiren who believe in the Lotus Sutra received from their fathers and mothers at birth" (WND-1, 420).

In his "Commentary on 'The Object of Devotion for Observing the Mind,'" Nichikan writes, "When one embraces and has faith in this Gohonzon and chants Nam-myoho-renge-kyo, one's life immediately becomes the object of devotion; it becomes the life of Nichiren Daishonin."

How worthy of respect then are the lives of those who pray for the realization of kosen-rufu day after day and who make painstaking efforts and chant daimoku for the sake of the Law and for the happiness of others!

The offense of the Nichiren Shoshu priesthood, in denigrating these noble members and excommunicating the SGI, is just as grave as the crime of persecuting the Daishonin himself. Those who respect and cherish the members of the SGI, the children of the Buddha, with all their heart are true followers of the Daishonin.

THE FUNDAMENTAL CAUSE OF CALAMITIES

Nichiren Daishonin writes: "Now, however, we have entered the Latter Day of the Law, and the medicines of these various schools no longer cure the people's illnesses. Moreover, all the Japanese have become icchantikas [people of incorrigible disbelief] and people of grave slander. Their offense is even worse than that of killing one's father or mother, fomenting a rebellion, or causing a Buddha to bleed. Japan is filled with individuals whose respective offenses exceed even those of one who were to gouge out the eyes of all the human beings of a major world system, or raze all temples and pagodas in the worlds of the ten directions. Consequently, the heavenly deities glare down furiously upon our nation day after day while the earthly deities tremble in continual rage" (WND-1, 414–15).

In a later passage of this same Gosho, the Daishonin goes on to state that when learned priests and those who observe the precepts slander the Law, their offense is especially grave, since they are the very ones who ought to be leading people toward the correct path.

THE GRAVE OFFENSE OF DISRUPTING THE UNITY OF BELIEVERS

Commenting on the phrase *fomenting a rebellion* mentioned in this Gosho, Nichikan said: "Even rebelling against the ruler of one's nation is deemed a grave offense. How much worse then is the offense of betraying the eternal rulers of the three existences, the Lotus Sutra and Nichiren Daishonin" ("Commentary on 'On Offering Prayers to the Mandala of the Mystic Law'").

The priests of Nichiren Shoshu, who have utterly betrayed the Daishonin's spirit, are guilty of the greatest treachery against the original Buddha.

Nittatsu said the following about the same Gosho: "This passage mentions 'fomenting a rebellion,' but this refers to the offense of disrupting the unity of believers, in other words, those who disrupt the harmoniously united body of believers — an offense classified as one of the five cardinal sins. . . .

"The unity of believers refers first and last to the body of believers who worship the Mystic Law. To disrupt their unity is the gravest offense of all.

"All those in the body of believers who embrace faith in the Mystic Law attain Buddhahood without exception. For this reason, any attempt to obstruct or hinder them constitutes a far graver crime than any in the secular world."

Those who attempt to destroy the SGI, the harmoniously united body of believers working to achieve the widespread propagation of the Mystic Law, are guilty of the serious offense of disrupting the unity of believers. Nittatsu's words clearly confirm this.

THE "ONE EVIL" OF THE PRESENT-DAY

Recently, the Daishonin's treatise "On Establishing the Correct Teaching for the Peace of the Land" has been translated into French, German, Spanish, Italian and Chinese. I would like to express my sincere appreciation to all those involved in this undertaking.

In this writing, the Daishonin states, "Rather than offering up ten thousand prayers for remedy, it would be better simply to out-law this one evil." (WND-1, 15).

Today, the "one evil" refers to the great slanderers of the Nichiren Shoshu priesthood. Please be assured, therefore, that the Daishonin would heartily applaud our efforts to establish the correct teaching for the peace of the land in the present day, that is, our efforts to carry out a noble religious reformation based on the Gohonzon and on the Gosho.

I conclude today's speech with my prayers for your vigorous endeavors and longevity as kings and queens of life blessed with great happiness and joy.

Contributions of Buddhism Toward a Humane Society

—⟋〰⟍—

ACCEPTING A COMMENDATION FROM
TUFTS UNIVERSITY, MEDFORD, MASSACHUSETTS,
SEPTEMBER 22, 1993

I WOULD LIKE to express my deepest appreciation on being presented today with this distinguished commendation from Tufts University, a great lighthouse of education that is open to the world. Thank you very much.

I am deeply moved to visit this university, which boasts a solemn and distinguished tradition. I am reminded of Charles Tufts, the university's namesake, and your first President Hosea Ballou II, whose shared aspiration was to make this institution "a source of illumination, as a beacon standing on a hill."

Upholding this beautiful founding spirit, your university made its debut with one building, four professors and a student body of seven. As the founder of Soka University, I understand the great difficulties that establishing a university entails. Tufts University, which currently has students from 110 countries, has now developed into a "global university" that produces a steady stream of capable people, including many diplomats, who go on to contribute to world peace in their respective fields. For your success in these endeavors, you have my deepest admiration.

Today, as an expression of my respect for the students of this university, I would like to present a gift of 145 books. Nothing could make me happier than for these books to be added to the collection of your prestigious library, which has been assembled with much loving care and painstaking effort.

In connection with the theme of "creating a humanistic society," I recall a highly memorable speech given by Tufts President DiBiaggio. In his inaugural address last year, President DiBiaggio said, "Ideas without humanity, innovation without concern for the human spirit, are nothing more than intellectual and technological egotism." His statement, while concise, offers penetrating insight into the essential nature of things.

As we saw the other day in the historic opening of the door to peace in the Middle East [Israel and the PLO signed a peace accord], humankind in today's post–Cold War era is earnestly struggling to find a path to peace. In the pursuit of this new order of mutual coexistence, attention must be given first and foremost to the needs and concerns of the human being.

At the beginning of this month, I met with Professor Howard Hunter in Tokyo. At that time we discussed how, whether it be in the area of religion or education, there is a tendency toward narrow-minded dogmatism once the human being is forgotten.

Humanism is the cornerstone of Buddhism, the crystallization of the wisdom of the East. Shakyamuni, the founder of Buddhism, describes the age in which he lived as follows: "Seeing people struggling, like fish, writhing in shallow water with enmity against one another, I became afraid" (*Suttanipata*). India, in what would seem to parallel conditions in the world today, was then at a chaotic turning point in its history and had yet to arrive at peace and stability. Spurred by impatience and animosity, people turned in vain to violence. It is said that not even at home could they feel safe without weapons.

Why do people fight? And why must they suffer? With his penetrating eye, Shakyamuni fixed his gaze on the true aspect of the human being, the unchanging reality that is concealed within the transient phenomena of life. He gave himself over to pondering the matter of how the luminance inherent in human life could be brought to shine forth in a radiation of peace, happiness and compassion. In this inquiry lies the starting point of Buddhism.

Shakyamuni waged a head-on struggle against dogmas that enchain and divide human beings. He strictly admonished, "The one who is full of rigid, fixed views, puffed up with pride and arrogance, who deems himself 'perfect,' becomes anointed in his own opinion because he holds firmly to his own view" (*Sutta-nipata*). Shakyamuni, who believed in continually seeking self-improvement, plunged into the realities of society as an "educator" in pursuit of a truly human way of life, not as an absolute being who looked down on the people.

The founder and first president of the Soka Gakkai, Tsunes-aburo Makiguchi, fought against Japanese militarism and died in prison as a result at age seventy-three. "We must never submit to inhumane authority," he cried. "Toward that end, we, each one of us, must awaken to the supremely precious brilliance that lies within the depths of human life. And we must enlarge the circle of solidarity for peace." With his heart thus ablaze, he persevered to the end in the struggle to bring about a human revolution in the depths of people's lives, with dialogue as his weapon.

It is my conviction that major progress in the development of a humane society may be realized by generating increasing trust in, and understanding for, humanism. In this respect, the educational values of Tufts University, which fosters leaders capable of contributing to society while placing importance on dialogue with students, seem to me to represent a brilliant light of hope.

To respond to your expectations, as symbolized by the great honor that you have bestowed upon me today, it is my intention to devote myself to further intensifying the light of humanism toward the twenty-first century, in solidarity with all of you.

While praying for the further prosperity of your distinguished university, I would like to conclude by reading a passage from the poem, "Song of the Universal," which Walt Whitman dedicated to your students:

Lo! keen-eyed towering science,
As from tall peaks the modern overlooking,
Successive absolute fiats issuing.

Yet again, lo! the soul, above all science,
For it has history gather'd like husks around the globe,
For it the entire star-myriads roll through the sky.

Thank you very much.

Mahayana Buddhism and Twenty-First-Century Civilization

—ɯɯ—

HARVARD UNIVERSITY, CAMBRIDGE, MASSACHUSETTS, SEPTEMBER 24, 1993

NOTHING COULD PLEASE ME more than to be back at Harvard University, to speak with faculty and students at this time-honored institution of unexcelled academic endeavor. To Professor Nur Yalman, Professor Harvey Cox, Professor John Kenneth Galbraith, and all the others who have made my visit possible, I extend grateful thanks.

THE CONTINUITY OF LIFE AND DEATH

It was the Greek philosopher Heraclitus who declared that all things are in a state of flux and that change is the essential nature of reality. Indeed, everything, whether it lies in the realm of natural phenomena or of human affairs, changes continuously. Nothing maintains exactly the same state for even the briefest instant; the most solid-seeming rocks and minerals are subject to the erosive effects of time. But during this century of war and revolution, normal change and flux seem to have been accelerated and magnified. We have seen the most extraordinary panorama of social transformations.

The Buddhist term for the ephemeral aspect of reality is "the transience of all phenomena." In the Buddhist cosmology, this concept is described as the repeated cycles of formation, continuance, decline and disintegration through which all systems must pass. During our lives as human beings, we experience transience as the four sufferings: the suffering of birth (and of day-to-day existence), that of aging, of sickness and, finally, of death. No human being is exempt from these sources of pain. It was, in fact, human distress, in particular the problem of death, that spawned the formation of religious and philosophical systems. It is said that Shakyamuni was inspired to seek the truth by his accidental encounters with many sorrows at the gates of the palace in which he was raised. Plato stated that true philosophers are always engaged in the practice of dying, while Nichiren, founder of the school of Buddhism followed by members of Soka Gakkai International, admonishes us to "first study death, then study other matters."[1]

Death weighs heavily on the human heart as an inescapable reminder of the finite nature of our existence. However seemingly limitless the wealth or power we might attain, the reality of our eventual demise cannot be avoided. From ancient times, humanity has sought to conquer the fear and apprehension surrounding death by finding ways to partake of the eternal. Through this quest, people have learned to overcome control by instinctual modes of survival and have developed the characteristics that we recognize as uniquely human. In that perspective, we can see why the history of religion coincides with the history of humankind.

Modern civilization has attempted to ignore death. We have diverted our gaze from this most fundamental of concerns as we try to drive death into the shadows. For many people living today, death is the mere absence of life; it is blankness; it is the void. Life is identified with all that is good: with being, rationality and light. In contrast, death is perceived as evil, as nothingness, and as the dark and irrational. Only the negative perception of death prevails.

We cannot, however, ignore death, and the attempt to do so has exacted a heavy price. The horrific and ironic climax of modern civilization has been in our time what Zbigniew Brzezinski has called the "century of megadeath." Today, a wide range of issues is now forcing a reexamination and reevaluation of the significance of death. They include questions about brain death and death with dignity, the function of hospices, alternative funerary styles and rites, and research into death and dying by writers such as Elisabeth Kübler-Ross.

We finally seem to be ready to recognize the fundamental error in our view of life and death. We are beginning to understand that death is more than the absence of life; that death, together with active life, is necessary for the formation of a larger, more essential, whole. This greater whole reflects the deeper continuity of life and death that we experience as individuals and express as culture. A central challenge for the coming century will be to establish a culture based on an understanding of the relationship of life and death and of life's essential eternity. Such an attitude does not disown death but directly confronts and correctly positions it within the larger context of life.

Buddhism speaks of an intrinsic nature (*bossho* in Japanese, sometimes translated as "Dharma nature") existing within the depths of phenomenal reality. This nature depends upon and responds to environmental conditions, and it alternates between states of emergence and latency. All phenomena, including life and death, can be seen as elements within the cycle of emergence and latency, or manifestation and withdrawal.

Cycles of life and death can be likened to the alternating periods of sleep and wakefulness. Just as sleep prepares us for the next day's activity, death can be seen as a state in which we rest and replenish ourselves for new life. In this light, death should be acknowledged, along with life, as a blessing to be appreciated. The Lotus Sutra, the core of Mahayana Buddhism, states that the purpose of existence, the eternal cycles of life and death, is to be "happy and at ease."[2] It further teaches that sustained faith and practice enable us to know a deep and abiding joy in death as well as in life, to be equally "happy and at ease" with both. Nichiren describes the attainment of this state as the "greatest of all joys."[3]

If the tragedies of this century of war and revolution have

taught us anything, it is the folly of believing that reform of external factors, such as social systems, is the linchpin to achieving happiness. I am convinced that in the coming century, the greatest emphasis must be placed on fostering inwardly directed change. In addition, our efforts must be inspired by a new understanding of life and death.

There are three broad areas where Mahayana Buddhism can help solve the problems suggested above and make a positive difference to civilization in the twenty-first century. Let us consider those aspects of Buddhism that offer workable, constructive guidance.

THE BUDDHIST EMPHASIS ON DIALOGUE

Since its inception, the philosophy of Buddhism has been associated with peace and pacifism. That emphasis derives principally from the consistent rejection of violence combined with stress on dialogue and discussion as the best means of resolving conflict. Descriptions of the life of Shakyamuni provide a good illustration. His life was completely untrammeled by dogma, and his interactions with his fellows stressed the importance of dialogue. The sutra, recounting the travels that culminated his Buddhist practice, begins with an episode in which the aged Shakyamuni uses the power of language to avert an invasion.[4]

According to the sutra, Shakyamuni, then eighty years old, did not directly admonish the minister of Magadha, a large country bent on conquering the neighboring state of Vajji. Instead, he spoke persuasively about the principles by which nations prosper and decline. His discourse dissuaded the minister from implementing the planned attack. The final chapter of the same sutra concludes with a moving description of Shakyamuni on his deathbed. As he lay dying, he repeatedly urged his disciples to raise any uncertainties that they might have about the Buddhist Law (Dharma) or its practice, so that they would not find themselves regretting unasked questions after his passing. Up until his last moment, Shakyamuni actively sought out dialogue, and the drama of his final voyage from beginning to end is illuminated by the light of language, skillfully wielded by one who was truly a "master of words."

Why was Shakyamuni able to employ language with such freedom and to such effect? What made him such a peerless master of dialogue? I believe that his fluency was due to the expansiveness of his enlightened state, utterly free of all dogma, prejudice and attachment. The following quote is illustrative: "I perceived a single, invisible arrow piercing the hearts of the people."[5] The "arrow" symbolizes a prejudicial mind-set, an unreasoning emphasis on individual differences. India at that time was going through transition and upheaval, and the horrors of conflict and war were an everpresent reality. To Shakyamuni's penetrating gaze, it was clear that the underlying cause of the conflict was attachment to distinctions, to ethnic, national and other differences.

In the early years of this century, Josiah Royce (one of many important philosophers Harvard University has given the world) declared that "Reform, in such matters, must come, if at all, from within.... The public as a whole is whatever the processes that occur, for good or evil, in individual minds, may determine."[6]

As Josiah Royce points out, the "invisible arrow" of evil is not to be found in the existence of races and classes external to ourselves but is embedded in our hearts. The conquest of our own prejudicial thinking, our own attachment to difference, is the necessary precondition for open dialogue. Such discussion, in turn, is essential for the establishment of peace and universal respect for human rights. It was his complete absence of prejudice that enabled Shakyamuni to expound the Law with such freedom, adapting his style of teaching to the character and capacity of the person to whom he was speaking.

Whether he was mediating a communal dispute over water rights, converting a violent criminal or admonishing someone who objected to the practice of begging, Shakyamuni attempted first to make others aware of the "arrow" of their inner evil. The power of his extraordinary character brought these words to the lips of one contemporaneous sovereign: "Those whom we, with weapons, cannot force to surrender, you subdue unarmed."[7]

Only by overcoming attachment to differences can a religion rise above an essentially tribal outlook to offer a global faith. Nichiren, for example, dismissed the shogunal authorities, who were persecuting him, as the "rulers of this little island country."[8] His vision was broader, directed toward establishing a religious spirit that would embody universal values and transcend the confines of a single state.

Dialogue is not limited to formal debate or placid exchange that wafts by like a spring breeze. There are times when, to break the grip of arrogance, speech must be like the breath of fire. Thus, although we typically associate Shakyamuni and Nagarjuna only with mildness, it was the occasional ferocity of their speech that earned them the sobriquet of "those who deny everything"[9] in their respective eras.

Similarly, Nichiren, who demonstrated a familial affection and tender concern for the common people, was uncompromising in his confrontations with corrupt and degenerate authority. Always unarmed in the chronically violent Japan of his time, he relied exclusively and unflinchingly on the power of persuasion and nonviolence. He was tempted with the promise of absolute power if he renounced his faith, and threatened with the beheading of his parents if he adhered to his beliefs. Nevertheless, he maintained the courage of his convictions. The following passage, written upon his exile to a distant island from which no one was expected to return, typifies his lionesque tone: "Whatever obstacles I might encounter, so long as men of wisdom do not prove my teachings to be false, I will never yield!"[10]

Nichiren's faith in the power of language was absolute. If more people were to pursue dialogue in an equally unrelenting manner, the inevitable conflicts of human life would surely find easier resolution. Prejudice would yield to empathy and war would give way to peace. Genuine dialogue results in the transformation of opposing viewpoints, changing them from wedges that drive people apart into bridges that link them together.

During World War II, Soka Gakkai, an organization based on the teachings of Nichiren, challenged head-on the forces of

Japanese militarism. As a result, many members were imprisoned, beginning with the founder and first president Tsunesaburo Makiguchi. Far from recanting, President Makiguchi continued to explain to his guards and interrogators the principles of Buddhism. They were the very ideas that had made him a "thought criminal" in the first place. He died at the age of seventy-three, still in confinement.

Josei Toda was heir to the spiritual legacy of President Makiguchi, and he became the second president of the organization. He emerged from the ordeal of two years' imprisonment declaring his faith in the unity of the global human family. He then preached widely among the population, who were lost and suffering in the aftermath of the war. Mr. Toda also bequeathed to us, his youthful disciples, the mission of building a world free of nuclear weapons.

With this as our historical and philosophical basis, Soka Gakkai International remains committed to the role of dialogue in the advancement of peace, education, and culture. At present, we are engaged in forging bonds of solidarity with citizens in 115 countries and regions around the world [now 192]. For my own part, I wish only to continue my efforts to speak with people all over the earth in order to contribute in some small way to the greater happiness of humankind.

RESTORING HUMANITY

What role can Buddhism play in the restoration and rejuvenation of humanity? In an age marked by widespread religious revival, we need always ask: Does religion make people stronger or weaker? Does it encourage what is good or what is evil in them? Are they made better and wiser by religion? While the authority of Marx as social prophet has been largely undermined by the collapse of socialism in Eastern Europe and the former Soviet Union, there is an important truth contained in his description of religion as the "opiate of the masses." In fact, there is reason for concern that more than a few of the religions finding new life in the twilight of this century are characterized by dogmatism and insularity, traits that run counter to the accelerating trend toward interdependence and cross-cultural interaction.

With this in mind, let us examine the relative weight that different belief systems assign to self-reliance, as opposed to dependence on powers external to the self. These two tendencies correspond roughly to the Christian concepts of free will and grace.

Broadly speaking, the passage from medieval to modern Europe coincided with a steady movement away from a theistic determinism, toward ever-greater emphasis on free will and human responsibility. Human abilities were encouraged, and reliance on external, abstract authority declined, making way for the great achievements of science and technology. More and more people began to believe in the omnipotence of reason and its scientific fruits. But to be blindly convinced of the power of technology can lead to the hubris of assuming that there is nothing we are unable to accomplish. It may be true that dependence on some external authority led people to underestimate both our potential and our responsibility, but excessive faith in our own powers is not the answer; it has, in fact, produced a dangerous overconfidence in ourselves.

We are now seeking a third path, a new balance between faith in ourselves and recognition of a power that is greater than we are. These words of Nichiren illustrate the subtle and richly suggestive Mahayana perspective on attaining enlightenment: "Neither solely through one's own efforts…nor solely through the power of others."[11] The persuasive argument of Buddhism is its conviction that the greatest good is derived from the dynamic fusion and balancing of internal and external forces.

Similarly, John Dewey, in *A Common Faith*, asserts that it is "the religious" rather than specific religions, that is of vital importance. While religions all too quickly fall into dogmatism and fanaticism, "that which is religious" has the power to "unify interests and energies" and to "direct action and generate the heat of emotion and the light of intelligence." Likewise, "the religious" enables the realization of those benefits that Dewey identifies as "the values of art in all its forms, of knowledge, of effort, and of rest after striving, of education and fellowship, of friendship and love, of growth in mind and body."[12]

Dewey does not identify a specific external power. For him "the religious" is a generalized term for that which supports and encourages people in the active pursuit of the good and the valuable. "The religious," as he defines it, helps those who help themselves.

As Dewey understood, and as the sad outcome of people's self-worship in modern times has demonstrated, without assistance we are incapable of living up to our potential. Only by relying on and merging with the eternal can we fully activate all our capabilities. Thus, we need help, but our human potential does not come from outside; it is, and always has been, of us and within us. How any given religious tradition handles the balance between interior and exterior forces will, I believe, decisively affect its long-term viability.

Anyone involved in religion must constantly work on keeping the balance, if we do not want to repeat history. For if we are not attentive, religion can enslave us to dogma and to its own authority just as easily as the religious impulse can serve as a vehicle for human restoration and rejuvenation.

Perhaps because our Buddhist movement is so human-centered, Harvey Cox of the Harvard Divinity School has described it as an effort to define the humanistic direction of religion. Indeed, Buddhism is not merely a theoretical construct; it helps us steer our lives, as we actually live them, moment by moment, toward the achievement of happiness and worth. Thus, Nichiren states: "When you concentrate the exertions of one hundred million aeons in a single life-moment, the three inherent properties of the Buddha will become manifest in your every thought and act."[13]

The expression *exertions of one hundred million aeons* refers to the ability to confront each of life's problems with our full being, awakening the total consciousness, leaving no inner resource untapped. By wholeheartedly and directly meeting the challenges of life, we bring forth from within ourselves the "three inherent properties of the Buddha." It is the light of this internal wisdom that constantly encourages and guides us toward true and correct action.

The vibrant tones of the drums, horns and other musical instruments that appear throughout the Lotus Sutra work metaphorically to encourage the human will to live. The function of the Buddha nature is always to urge us to be strong, good and wise. The message of the sutra is one of human restoration.

THE INTERRELATIONSHIP OF ALL THINGS

Buddhism provides a philosophical basis for the symbiotic coexistence of all things. Among the many images in the Lotus Sutra, a particularly compelling one is the merciful rain that falls everywhere, equally, moistening the vast expanse of the earth and bringing forth new life from all the trees and grasses, large and small. This scene, depicted with the vividness, grandeur and beauty characteristic of the Lotus Sutra, symbolizes the enlightenment of all people touched by the Buddha's Law. At the same time, it is a magnificent tribute to the rich diversity of human and all other forms of sentient and non-sentient life. Thus, each living thing manifests the enlightenment of which it is capable; each contributes to the harmony of the grand concert of symbiosis. In Buddhist terminology, dependent origination describes these relationships. Nothing and nobody exists in isolation. Each individual being functions to create the environment that sustains all other existences. All things are mutually supporting and interrelated, forming a living cosmos, what modern philosophy might term a *semantic whole*. That is the conceptual framework through which Mahayana Buddhism views the natural universe.

Speaking through Faust, Goethe gives voice to a similar vision. "Into the whole how all things blend, each in the other working, living!"[14] These lines are striking for their remarkable affinity with Buddhist thought. Although Johann Peter Eckermann criticized Goethe for lacking "confirmation of his presentiments,"[15] the intervening years have seen a steadily swelling affirmation of the deductive vision in both Goethe and Buddhist thought.

Consider, for example, the concept of causation. When viewed in terms of dependent origination, causal relationships differ fundamentally from the mechanistic idea of cause and effect that, according to modern science, holds sway over the objective natural world. In the scientific model, reality is divorced from subjective human concerns. When an accident or disaster takes place, for example, a mechanistic theory of causation can be used to pursue and identify how the accident occurred. It is silent, however, on other points, including the question of why certain individuals and not others should find themselves caught up in the tragic event. Indeed, the mechanistic view of nature requires the deliberate dismissal of existential questions.

In contrast, the Buddhist understanding of causation is more broadly defined and takes account of human existence. It seeks to directly address these poignant uncertainties, as in the following exchange that occurred early in Shakyamuni's career: "What is the cause of aging and death? Birth is the cause of aging and death."[16]

In a later era, through a process of exhaustive personal inquiry, Chih-i, the founder of the Chinese T'ien-t'ai school of Buddhism, developed a theoretical structure that included such concepts as the "three thousand realms in a single moment of life." It is not only sweeping in scope and rigorous in elaboration but is entirely compatible with modern science. While limitations of time prohibit discussion of his system, it is worth mentioning that many contemporary fields of inquiry — for example, ecology, transpersonal psychology and quantum mechanics — have some interesting points in common with Buddhism in their approach and conclusions.

The Buddhist emphasis on relatedness and interdependence may seem to suggest that individual identity is obscured. Buddhist scripture addresses this in the following passage: "You are your own master. Could anyone else be your master? When you have gained control over yourself, you have found a master of rare value."[17]

A second passage reads: "Be lamps unto yourselves. Rely on yourselves. Hold fast to the Law as a lamp, do not rely on anything else."[18]

Both passages urge us to live independently, true to ourselves and unswayed by others. The "self" referred to here, however, is not the Buddhist lesser self, caught up in the snares of egoism. Rather, it is the greater self, fused with the life of the universe through which cause and effect intertwine over the infinite reaches of space and time.

The greater, cosmic self is related to the unifying and integrating "self" that Jung perceived in the depths of the ego. It is also similar to Ralph Waldo Emerson's "The universal beauty, to which every part and particle is equally related; the eternal One."[19]

I am firmly convinced that a large-scale awakening to the greater self will lead to a world of creative coexistence in the coming century. Recall the lines of Walt Whitman, in which he sings the praises of the human spirit:

> *But that I,*
> *turning to thee O soul,*
> *thou actual Me,*
> *And lo,*
> *thou gently masterest the orbs,*
> *Thou matest Time,*
> *smilest content at Death,*
> *And fillest,*
> *swellest full the vastness of space.*[20]

The greater self of Mahayana Buddhism is another way of expressing the openness and expansiveness of character that embraces the sufferings of all people as one's own. This self always seeks ways of alleviating the pain and augmenting the happiness of others, here, amid the realities of everyday life. Only the solidarity brought about by such natural human nobility will break down the isolation of the modern self and lead to the dawning of new hope for civilization. Furthermore, it is the dynamic, vital awakening of the greater self that will enable each of us, as individuals, to experience both life and death with equal delight. Thus, as Nichiren stated: "We adorn the treasure tower of our being with the four aspects [of birth, aging, sickness and death]."[21]

It is my earnest desire and prayer that in the twenty-first century, each member of the human family will let shine the natural luster of their inner "treasure tower." Filling our azure planet with the chorus of open dialogue, humankind will move on into the new millennium.

Notes

1. Nichiko Hori, ed., *Nichiren Daishonin gosho zenshu* (Tokyo: Soka Gakkai, 1952), p. 1404.
2. J. Takakusu, ed., *Taisho Issaikyo* (Tokyo: Taisho Issaikyo Publishing Society, 1925), vol. 9, p. 43c.
3. *Nichiren Daishonin gosho zenshu*, p. 788.
4. J. Takakusu, ed., *Nanden daizokyo* (Tokyo: Taisho Shinshu Daizokyo Publishing Society, 1935), vol. 7, p. 27ff.
5. J. Takakusu, ed., *Nanden daizokyo*, vol. 24, p. 358.
6. Josiah Royce, *The Basic Writings of Josiah Royce* (Chicago: The University of Chicago Press, 1969), 2:1122.
7. J. Takakusu, ed., *Nanden Daizokyo*, vol. 11a, p. 137.
8. Philip B. Yampolsky, *Selected Writings of Nichiren*, trans. Burton Watson (New York: Columbia University Press, 1990), p. 322.
9. J. Takakusu, ed., *Taisho Issaikyo*, vol. 30.
10. *Selected Writings of Nichiren*, p. 138.
11. *Nichiren Daishonin gosho zenshu*, p. 403.
12. John Dewey, *A Common Faith* (New Haven: Yale University Press, 1934), pp. 50–52.
13. *Nichiren Daishonin gosho zenshu*, p. 790.
14. J. W. Goethe, *Faust A Tragedy*, trans. Bayard Taylor (New York: The Modern Library, 1967), pp. 17–18.
15. Johann Wolfgang von Goethe, *Conversations of Goethe with Eckermann* (London: J. M. Dent and Sons Ltd., 1930), p. 101.
16. J. Takakusu, ed., *Nanden Daizokyo*, vol. 13, p. 1ff.

17. J. Takakusu, ed., *Nanden Daizokyo*, vol. 23, p. 42.
18. J. Takakusu, ed., *Taisho Issaikyo*, vol. 1, p. 645c, 15b.
19. Ralph Waldo Emerson, *Essays and Poems of Emerson* (New York: Harcourt, Brace and Company, 1921), p. 45.
20. Walt Whitman, *Leaves of Grass* (Garden City: Doubleday & Company, 1926), p. 348.
21. *Nichiren Daishonin gosho zenshu*, p. 740.

Bringing Joy, Harmony and Happiness to the World

—~m~—

SGI-USA NEW ENGLAND RENAISSANCE CONFERENCE,
BOSTON, MASSACHUSETTS, SEPTEMBER 26, 1993

CONGRATULATIONS on this joyous Renaissance Conference! The music and singing and all of you gathered here today are the epitome of happiness, joy and harmony. It is truly wonderful to behold.

When I visited the United States earlier this year, a sudden change in my schedule for March prevented me from meeting SGI-USA members on the East Coast. I wish to offer my deepest apologies once again and, at the same time, celebrate with all of you today on meeting at long last.

An American philosopher stated his wish to stir up the winds of the American Renaissance from here in New England. I am confident that, in accord with this spirit, all of you will, from this same soil, stir up the winds of renaissance for the twenty-first century and spread it throughout the rest of the United States and the entire world.

THE PURPOSE OF KOSEN-RUFU IS TO SPREAD HARMONY AND JOY

First, I would like to state that leading a life filled with harmony and joy is the greatest happiness for human beings and is essential for true happiness — whether it be in a family, in an organization or in society. The purpose of all our efforts is so that everyone may savor happiness, harmony and joy. Nichiren Daishonin described the Mystic Law as "the greatest of all joys" (OTT, 212). The purpose of kosen-rufu is to spread this harmony and joy to all humankind.

We must never allow the slightest trace of discrimination to enter any aspect of our work. We are all equal as human beings. In the eyes of the Mystic Law, all members — those with or without leadership positions alike — are equal. This is the Buddhism of Nichiren Daishonin and the world of the Soka family.

The reason that the leaders are up here on the stage is not because they are in any way better than you are. It is simply to make it easier for everyone to see them!

The true world of the Daishonin's Buddhism is one where all advance in the spirit of "many in body, one in mind" as fellow members and friends. To do so, I hope you will respect one another.

Boston is a world capital of intellect. The eastern United States is renowned for the many illustrious people it has produced. Generally speaking, people who live in such a region tend to think that they are superior and look down on others. But such an atmosphere is not conducive to harmony and joy.

An environment of respect and trust produces harmony and joy. There are base and cowardly people who destroy others' harmony and joy. Some hate to see others happy and enjoying themselves and, out of jealousy, try to disrupt their pleasure. Such people are truly pitiful.

To take delight in destroying the happiness and enjoyment of others may perhaps be described as a spiritual sickness. Nikken is a prime example of such a person. The world such people inhabit is poles apart from the world of "the greatest of all joys" — the world of the Mystic Law.

True Buddhists always give the greatest thought and effort to how and what they themselves can do to steer everything in a direction of harmony and joy — to enable everyone to enjoy themselves and be happy.

I hope your families will also be happy and harmonious. Of course, wives may sometimes scold their husbands, and mothers may sometimes scold their children. This is only natural, I think. It is an unchanging drama that has existed since time without beginning! It is also perhaps part of the process for attaining even more solid harmony and joy.

In short, I hope you will treasure the kind of heart-to-heart communication that is based on an underlying spirit of trust and affection and a commitment to create an environment of harmony and joy.

The eastern United States is an area known for excellence in intellectual endeavors, culture and the arts. I hope that, on top of this, you will become known for your outstanding excellence in creating harmony and joy in everything that you do.

The Joy of Sharing Our Hopes With Others

Second, I would like you to live with hope. A person of hope can always advance. A person of hope lives an energetic and spirited life. They are always fresh and vibrant.

The desire to become healthier, obtain greater financial security, or become more beautiful — these things, too, are hopes we may cherish. So are the splendid development of one's children and the good health and long life of one's partner. "Let's work hard and accumulate more good fortune so that we can travel around the world one day." Families that can discuss and share these kinds of hopes and dreams are happy indeed.

At today's meeting there are also fellow members from Panama, Peru, Hong Kong, Korea and Japan in attendance. One might well be inspired by the idea of going to visit these countries one day and talking with the members there about the wondrousness of the Mystic Law. This is another magnificent hope to cherish.

As Buddhists, our greatest hope is the happiness not only of ourselves and those nearest and dearest to us but also of our friends and fellow members. "I want so-and-so to become happy. I want to enable all the members to enjoy themselves." There is no more lofty way of life than praying for and exerting ourselves for others' happiness.

In contrast, leaders who have lost the fresh and invigorating breath of hope, who have stopped growing and merely strut around arrogantly, are like a truck that has broken down on the highway. Rendered immobile, the truck blocks the entire lane of traffic, preventing the cars behind it from moving ahead. In the same way, leaders who stop growing obstruct the progress of their fellow members.

Please live with hope throughout your life. Right until the very end of your lives, I hope that you will not only cherish but also realize many great hopes and dreams and inspire others to do the same. Please proceed toward the glorious summit of your aspirations, sharing with one another your infinite hopes and dreams.

There are no deadlocks when you have faith. Through faith you can overcome any and all problems and eternally advance toward ever more expansive horizons of hope. This is the most wonderful way to live. Hope costs nothing; it is free. Yet at the same time, it is life's most valuable treasure.

Please cherish this treasure of hope, holding it close to your heart throughout your life. This in itself represents a life of victory, a life of glory.

THE IMPORTANCE OF DAILY EFFORTS

Third, I would ask that you pay attention to your daily lives. Faith manifests itself in daily life. Daily life, in turn, is the stage upon which we show proof of faith. True human victory and happiness are attained through the earnest and steady day-to-day efforts we make in our lives.

The sun silently follows a set course every day. Today, and again tomorrow, never resting, never pausing, the sun will rise brightly and illuminate the Earth before setting once again with magnificent splendor. This rhythm never changes.

The pattern of our lives, like that of the sun, may seem monotonous and routine, but there is nothing more profound than our daily endeavors. Achieving brilliant victory in our daily lives is what being victorious in faith is all about.

One kind of actual proof of victory in daily life is financial security. Therefore, I hope that as you accumulate bountiful treasures of the heart and much good fortune, you will also become secure financially.

Although we are currently experiencing a worldwide recession, I ask that you really put your wisdom to work and strive diligently so that you may enjoy peace of mind and a sense of security in your daily lives — and serve as an inspiration to others.

Though money isn't everything, without it, you can't even ride in a taxi! Some people might dismiss this and say that it is good exercise to walk, but when it comes to traveling overseas, walking there is simply out of the question!

As long as we are living and working in society, having a certain amount of financial security is an important element for happiness. Josei Toda used to say, even though your wallet may be empty, there is an abundance of money floating about in the world — it just hasn't come your way, that's all! But, he would continue, if you accumulate good fortune, using it to drill a hole into that vast reservoir of money and tap some for yourself, you will never be in want.

HEALTH FIRST

Fourth, I would like you to put your health first so that you can live long, productive lives. It is important to take whatever measures you feel necessary to protect your own "treasures of the body" and go about your activities brightly and cheerfully.

Try not to eat late at night, pay attention to nutritional balance, and when you're tired, make sure you get plenty of rest. The important thing is not to let fatigue accumulate.

Our daily gongyo should also be the source for living vibrant and exhilarating lives. Gongyo is beneficial to both our spiritual and physical health. What good will it serve, then, if pushing yourself to unreasonable limits, you feel totally exhausted after doing gongyo and, in the end, become ill! You are missing the whole point of doing gongyo if that happens!

As I am constantly saying, even if at times, because of various circumstances, you only recite the "Expedient Means" chapter and the verse portion of the "Life Span" chapter, or simply chant some daimoku, you still receive immeasurable benefit. The important thing is to continue doing the kind of gongyo that leaves you feeling invigorated, refreshed, positive and full of vitality afterward.

In addition, I hope that all of you will enjoy long and healthy lives, using your wisdom and making concrete efforts toward this end. Practical wisdom and common sense are the hallmarks of a Buddhist.

POLISHING OURSELVES AS HUMAN BEINGS

Last, I would like you to be people of solid character who possess rich common sense. To become people of magnificent character, upstanding citizens in society and loved and respected members of your families — this is the true goal of Buddhist practitioners.

Just because we practice the Daishonin's Buddhism, however, doesn't make us in any way special. Essentially we are in no way different from other people, except for the fact that we base ourselves on daimoku, that is, chanting to the Gohonzon. There is no such thing as a special kind of human being. To assume an elitist air is the behavior of fanatics. We have no room for such people in the SGI.

Human beings are just that — human beings. They can never be anything more. Consequently, the true purpose of faith is to enable human beings to polish and develop themselves as human beings.

In particular, we must ensure that we do not have leaders who, suffering from delusions of grandeur, become dictatorial, high-handed and oppressive toward the members. This is the exact opposite of what a leader should be.

THE ORGANIZATION EXISTS FOR OUR HAPPINESS

All of us started practicing the Daishonin's Buddhism to become happy. Our organization exists so that all may become happy. Neither our faith nor our organization exists to make us suffer.

Buddhism is reason; it is humanism. I hope that, with unsurpassed humanity, you will make this eastern region of the United States one that is pervaded by warmth, harmony, happiness and joy.

The United Nations and the governments of countries around the world all hold important conferences, but this conference we are holding here today is truly historic. It is a conference of the people, a conference of individuals of wisdom and intellect who embrace the Mystic Law.

With my congratulations to you on the great success of this Renaissance Conference, and with my prayers for your glory and victory, I close today's meeting. See you again.

1995

Peace and Human Security: A Buddhist Perspective for the Twenty-first Century

—⟋⟍—

UNIVERSITY OF HAWAII'S SPARK M. MATSUNAGA
INSTITUTE FOR PEACE, EAST-WEST CENTER,
HONOLULU, HAWAII, JANUARY 26, 1995

HAWAII DRAWS all people into the beautiful embrace of her nature. East and West meet here in friendship; diverse cultures mix and blend in harmony; there is a balance and fusion of the traditional and the modern. It is therefore an especially appropriate place to consider the issues of peace and security, issues of fundamental importance to humankind.

I myself began my travels to the world here in Hawaii in 1960, the year that this center was established. My earnest desire since youth had been somehow to help bring forth a brilliant dawn of global peace from here in Hawaii, stage of the tragic outbreak of the Pacific War, initiated by militarist Japan.

Looking back, we can say that the twentieth century has been stained by the all too common slaughter of humanity at human hands. Our century has been termed a century of war and revolution; aptly so, for with two world wars and countless revolutions, it has been an unprecedented and bloody torrent of conflict and upheaval.

Advances in science and technology have produced a dramatic increase in the lethality of our weapons; it has been estimated that a hundred million people died violent deaths during the first half of this century. Under the Cold War regime that followed, and since then, regional and internal conflicts have claimed more than twenty million lives.

At the same time, the income gap between the Northern and Southern hemispheres continues to grow, with some eight hundred million people living in hunger. We cannot turn a blind eye to the structural violence by which tens of thousands of precious young lives are lost daily to malnutrition and disease.[1]

Furthermore, many thinkers point with alarm to the spiritual impoverishment, rampant in both East and West, that demonstrates the vacuity of mere material prosperity.

What has twentieth-century humanity gained at the cost of this staggering sacrifice of human life? As we approach the end of this century amid deepening disorder, no one can suppress a sense of anguish at this question.

I am reminded of the following passage from the Lotus Sutra, which contains the essence of Mahayana Buddhism: "There is no safety in the threefold world; / it is like a burning house, / replete with a multitude of sufferings, / truly to be feared" (LS, 69). This passage gives voice to an unrestrained empathy for humanity, tormented by the flames of suffering and terror.

In the same sutra, his gaze fixed on this agonized panorama, Shakyamuni makes the following declaration: "I should rescue them from their sufferings and give them the joy of the measureless and boundless Buddha wisdom so that they may find their enjoyment in that" (LS, 59).

This determination is seminal in the thinking of Buddhism; from it flows a tradition of dynamic action toward the creation of an indestructible realm of security and comfort amid the stark realities of society. The foundation for this endeavor is always the inner reformation of the individual and the resultant renewal and invigoration of life and daily living. My mentor, the second president of the Soka Gakkai, Josei Toda, termed this *human revolution*.

Under the sway of the nineteenth-century cult of progress, we have feverishly devoted ourselves in this century to enhancing the structures of society and the state, laboring under the delusion that this alone is the path to human happiness. But to the extent that we have skirted the fundamental issue of how to reform and revitalize individual human beings, our most conscientious efforts for peace and happiness have produced just the opposite result. This, I feel, is the central lesson of the twentieth century.

I was greatly encouraged by the fact that [East-West Center] President Michel Oksenberg, a noted authority on security issues, holds similar views on this subject. When we met in Tokyo last autumn [October 9, 1994], he expressed himself thus: "If people live in a spiritual void, they will experience insecurity. They will not know stability. They will not feel at ease. The nations and states in which they live will therefore not be offering their people true security. Real security requires that we consider more than just the security of the state but that we also include in our considerations the security of cultures and individual human beings."

Our task is to establish a firm inner world, a robust sense of self that will not be swayed or shaken by the most trying circumstances or pressing adversity. Only when our efforts to reform society have as their point of departure the reformation of the inner life — human revolution — will they lead us with certainty to a world of lasting peace and true human security.

With this as my major premise, I would like to offer some ideas regarding three transformations that we face on our way toward the twenty-first century: from knowledge to wisdom; from uniformity to diversity; and finally, what I would term from national to human sovereignty.

FROM KNOWLEDGE TO WISDOM

The first transformation I would like to discuss is the need to move away from our present emphasis on knowledge toward a new emphasis on wisdom. Piercing to the heart of the matter, President Toda stated that confusing knowledge for wisdom is the principal error in the thinking of modern man.

Clearly, the volume of information and knowledge possessed

362 ■ MY DEAR FRIENDS IN AMERICA

by humanity has undergone an extraordinary increase compared to a hundred or even fifty years ago. It can hardly be said, however, that this knowledge has led to the kind of wisdom that gives rise to human happiness. Rather, the suffering generated by the grotesque imbalance between our knowledge and our wisdom is succinctly symbolized by the fact that the most sublime fruits of our science and technology have been nuclear weapons and the widening North–South development gap to which I referred moments ago.

With the advent of an increasingly knowledge-and-information-based society, it becomes all the more crucial that we develop the wisdom to master these vast resources of knowledge and information. The same communication technologies that can be used to incite terror and hatred in whole populations, for example, could just as easily produce a dramatic expansion of educational opportunity worldwide. The difference lies solely in the degree and depth of human wisdom and compassion.

The consistent intent of Buddhism is to develop the compassionate wisdom that is inherent in the depths of human life. Nichiren, founder of the Buddhism we uphold, wrote the following in a letter to one of his disciples: "Your practice of the Buddhist teachings will not relieve you of the sufferings of birth and death in the least unless you perceive the true nature of your life. If you seek enlightenment outside yourself, then your performing even ten thousand practices and ten thousand good deeds will be in vain. It is like the case of a poor man who spends night and day counting his neighbor's wealth but gains not even half a coin" (WND-I, 3).

A distinctive characteristic of Buddhism, and of Eastern thought in general, is the insistence that all intellectual activity be developed in intimate dialogue with such existential, subjective questions as "What is the self?" and "What is the best way to live?" The passage I quoted is representative of this style of reasoning.

There is growing concern that competition for water and other natural resources will be an increasingly frequent cause of regional conflicts. In this connection, I am reminded of the wisdom that

Shakyamuni demonstrated in response to a communal conflict over water in his native state.

When his peripatetic teaching brought Shakyamuni back to Kapilavastu, he found that a drought had depleted the waters of a river running between two ethnic groups in the region, bringing them into conflict. Neither group was prepared to yield, both had taken up arms and bloodshed seemed unavoidable.[2]

Stepping between the two factions, Shakyamuni admonished them: "Look at those who fight, ready to kill! Fear arises from taking up arms and preparing to strike."[3]

It is precisely because you are armed that you feel fear — this clear and simple reasoning reverberated in the hearts of the conflicting parties, awakening them to the folly of their actions. Everyone put down their weapons, and friend and enemy sat down together.

When Shakyamuni spoke again, he addressed not the rights and wrongs of the immediate conflict but the primal terror of death. He spoke with power and intimacy on overcoming the foremost fear — of our own inevitable death — and on living a life of peace and security.

Of course, compared to the fierce complexity of contemporary conflicts, this episode may appear all too simplistic in its outcome. The present war in the former Yugoslavia, to take but one example, has roots that reach back nearly two thousand years. During that time, the region has seen the schism between the eastern and western Christian churches, the conquests of the Ottoman Turks and, in this century, the atrocities of fascism and communism. The tangled animosities of race and religion are indescribably deep and powerful. Each group emphasizes its uniqueness; each group knows and draws upon its history for justification. The result is the deadly stalemate we see today.

It is for just these reasons that I find an urgent meaning in the pattern demonstrated by Shakyamuni's courageous dialogue. Our times demand an embracing wisdom that, rather than dividing, brings into view that which we share and hold in common as human beings.

The teachings of Buddhism offer a treasure trove of peace-oriented wisdom. Nichiren, for example, offers this pointed insight into the relationship between the basic negative tendencies within human life and the most pressing external threats to peace and security: "In a country where the three poisons [of greed, anger, and foolishness] prevail to such a degree, how can there be peace and stability?... Famine occurs as a result of greed, pestilence as a result of foolishness, and warfare as a result of anger" (WND-1, 989).

The wisdom of Buddhism enables us to break the confines of the lesser self, the private and isolated self held prisoner by its own desires, passions and hatreds. It further enables us to contextualize the deep-rooted psychology of collective identity as we expand our lives, overflowing with exuberance, toward the greater self, which is coexistent with the living essence of the universe.

This wisdom is not to be sought in some distant place but can be found within ourselves, beneath our very feet, as it were. It resides in the living microcosm within and wells forth in limitless profusion when we devote ourselves to courageous and compassionate action for the sake of humanity, society and the future. Through this kind of bodhisattva practice, we develop the wisdom to sever the shackles of ego, and the spheres of our disparate knowledge will begin to turn with vibrant balance toward a prosperous human future.

FROM UNIFORMITY TO DIVERSITY

The second transformation I would like to discuss is from uniformity to diversity. I deeply appreciate having the opportunity to discuss this theme here — in Hawaii, these "rainbow islands" that are a veritable symbol of diversity — and now, as we begin the United Nations Year for Tolerance.

The citizens of Hawaii are truly at the forefront of humanity in their efforts to harmonize and draw forth unity from diversity, and this will continue to be an issue of singular importance as we move into the future. Your invaluable pioneering endeavors can,

I believe, be likened to the *ohia* tree, which is the first to sink its roots into the barrenness of recent lava flows and sends forth lovely deep-red blossoms.

As exemplified by modes of economic development that aim exclusively at the maximization of profit, modern civilization tends to the elimination of difference — the subordination of both natural and human diversity to the pursuit of monolithic objectives. The result of this process is the grievous global *problématique* that confronts us today, of which environmental degradation is but one aspect. It is vital that we pursue a path of sustainable human development based on a profound sense of solidarity with future generations. A new appreciation of human, social and natural diversity is, in a sense, an inevitable reaction to the present crisis.

I am reminded of the wisdom of Rachel Carson, marine biologist and pioneer of the environmental movement. In 1963, one year before her death, she expressed her views in this way: "Now I truly believe that we in this generation must come to terms with nature, and I think we're challenged, as mankind has never been challenged before, to prove our maturity and our mastery, not of nature but of ourselves."[4]

The increasing attention focused on the Pacific Rim relates in no small way, I am convinced, to the hope that this "experimental sea," characterized by such remarkable ethnic, linguistic and cultural diversity, will play a leading role in bringing together the human family.

Hawaii is the crossroads of the Pacific and has a rich history of peaceful coexistence — accepting the contributions of many cultures and encouraging the mutual appreciation of diverse values. As such, I am convinced that Hawaii will continue to be a pioneering model for the emerging Pan-Pacific civilization.

The wisdom of Buddhism can also shed considerable light on the question of diversity. Because one central tenet of Buddhism is that universal value must be sought within the life of the individual, it works fundamentally to counter any attempt to enforce uniformity or standardization.

In the teachings of Nichiren we find the passage, "The cherry, the plum, the peach, the damson... without undergoing any change" (OTT, 200). This passage confirms that there is no need for everyone to become "cherries" or "plums" but that each should manifest the unique brilliance of his or her own character.

This simile points to a fundamental principle of appreciation for diversity that applies equally to human beings and to social and natural environments. As the concept of "revealing one's intrinsic nature" indicates, the prime mission of Buddhism is to enable all of us to blossom to the fullest of our potential. The fulfillment of the individual, however, cannot be realized in conflict with or at the expense of others but only through active appreciation of uniqueness and difference, for these are the varied hues that together blossom into the flower gardens of life.

Nichiren's teachings also contain the following imagery, "It is like the situation when one faces a mirror and makes a bow of obeisance: the image in the mirror likewise makes a bow of obeisance to oneself" (OTT, 165). I think this beautifully expresses the all-encompassing causality that is the heart of Buddhism. The respect we demonstrate for the lives of others returns to us, with mirrorlike certainty, ennobling our lives.

The Buddhist principle of dependent origination reflects a cosmology in which all human and natural phenomena come into existence within a matrix of interrelatedness. Thus we are urged to respect the uniqueness of each existence, which supports and nourishes all within the larger, living whole.

What distinguishes the Buddhist view of interdependence is that it is based on a direct, intuitive apprehension of the cosmic life immanent in all phenomena. Therefore, Buddhism unequivocally rejects all forms of violence as an assault on the harmony that underlies and binds the web of being.

The following words of Professor Anthony Marsella of the University of Hawaii are an excellent summation of the essence of dependent origination: "I intend to accept and to embrace the self-evident truth that the very life force that is within me is the same life force that moves, propels and governs the universe itself, and because of this I must approach life with a new sense of awe, humbled by the mystery of this truth, yet elated and confident by its consequences. I am alive! I am part of life!" (*Seikyo Shimbun*, January 1, 1995).

By focusing on the deepest and most universal dimensions of life, we can extend a natural empathy toward life in its infinite diversity. It is the failure of empathy, as that great pioneer of peace studies Johan Galtung notes, that in the end makes violence possible.

Professor Galtung and I are presently engaged in preparing a published dialogue. One subject of our discussion has been the education of children and youth and the need to instill a spirit of positive engagement with those whose very difference and "otherness" can extend and enrich us. This kind of open-ended empathy enables us to view human diversity as a catalyst for creativity, the basis of a civilization of inclusion and mutual prosperity.

I would like to note in passing that the SGI's efforts to promote cultural exchange and interaction around the world are based on this conviction and determination.

FROM NATIONAL TO HUMAN SOVEREIGNTY

The third transformation I would like to discuss is from national to human sovereignty. Undeniably, sovereign states and issues of national sovereignty have been the prime actors in much of the war and violence of the twentieth century. Modern wars, waged as the legitimate exercise of state sovereignty, have involved entire populations willy-nilly in untold tragedy and suffering. The League of Nations and later the United Nations, each founded in the bitter aftermath of global conflict, were in a sense attempts to create an overarching system that would restrain and temper state sovereignty. We must acknowledge, however, that this bold project today remains far from the realization of its original aims. The United Nations approaches its fiftieth anniversary [1996] laden with a trying array of problems.

It is my belief that, if it is to become a true "parliament of humanity," the United Nations must base itself on the so-called soft power of consensus and agreement reached through dialogue, and that the enhancement of its functions must be accompanied by a shift away from traditional, military-centered conceptualizations of security. As one suggestion, through the creation of a new environment and development security council, the United Nations would be empowered to engage the pressing questions of human security with renewed energy and focus.

In this effort, it is essential that we effect a paradigm shift from national to human sovereignty — an idea expressed powerfully by the words, "We the peoples..." with which the U.N. Charter opens. Concretely, we must promote the kind of grassroots education that will foster world citizens committed to the shared welfare of humanity, and we must foster solidarity among them.

As a nongovernmental organization, the SGI is engaged in developing effective activities on a global scale, focusing particularly on youth, to inform and raise the awareness of the world's citizens surrounding the unique opportunity presented by the fiftieth anniversary of the United Nations' founding.

From the viewpoint of Buddhism, the transformation from state to human sovereignty comes down to the question of how to develop the resources of character that can bravely challenge and wisely temper the seemingly overwhelming powers of official authority.

In the course of our dialogues held some twenty years ago, the British historian Arnold Toynbee defined nationalism as a religion, the worship of the collective power of human communities. This definition applies equally, I feel, to both sovereign states and to the kind of nationalism that, in its more tribal manifestations, is fomenting regional and subnational conflicts throughout the world today. Toynbee further required that any future world religion be capable of countering fanatical nationalism as well as "the evils that are serious present threats to human survival." In particular, I am unable to forget the profound expectation that Toynbee expressed with regard to Buddhism, which he termed "a universal system of laws of life" (*Choose Life*, 317–18).

Indeed, Buddhism possesses a rich tradition of transcending secular authority and making it relative through appeals to, and reliance on, inner moral law. For example, when Shakyamuni was asked by a Brahman named Sela to become a king of kings, a chief of men, Shakyamuni replied that he was already a king, a king of the supreme truth.

Equally striking is the drama of Shakyamuni halting the plans of the imperial state of Magadha to exterminate the Vajjian republics. In the presence of the minister of Magadha, who had come with brazen intent to inform Shakyamuni of the planned invasion, Shakyamuni asked his disciple seven questions about the Vajjians. With some elaboration, these are:

1· Do they (the Vajjians) value discussion and dialogue?

2· Do they value cooperation and solidarity?

3· Do they value laws and traditions?

4· Do they respect their elders?

5· Do they respect children and women?

6· Do they respect religion and spirituality?

7· Do they value people of culture and learning, whether they be Vajjian or not? Are they open to such influences from abroad?

The answer to each of these questions was "yes." Shakyamuni then explained to the minister of Magadha that so long as the Vajjians continue to observe these principles, they will prosper and not decline. Thus, he explained, it will be impossible to conquer them.

These are the famous "seven principles preventing decline," the seven guidelines by which communities prosper, expounded by Shakyamuni during his last travels (*Suttanipata*, 65).

It is interesting to note the parallels with contemporary efforts to establish security not through military might but through the promotion of democracy, social development and human rights.

This incident is also a vivid portrait of Shakyamuni's dignity and stature as a king of the supreme truth addressing secular authority.

It was in this same spirit that Nichiren issued his famous treatise "On Establishing the Correct Teaching for the Peace of the Land" in 1260, directed at the highest authorities in Japan at that time, admonishing them for remaining deaf to the cries of the people. From that time on, Nichiren's life was a series of unending, often life-threatening persecutions. He, however, expressed his sense of inner freedom in this way: "Even if it seems that, because I was born in the ruler's domain, I follow him in my actions, I will never follow him in my heart" (WND-1, 579); and elsewhere, "I pray that before anything else I can guide and lead the ruler and those others who persecuted me" (WND-1, 402); and also, "When one practices the Lotus Sutra under such circumstances, difficulties will arise, and these are to be looked on as 'peaceful' practices" (OTT, 115).

Relying on the eternal Law within to rise above the sway of evanescent authority in pursuit of nonviolence and humanity — it is in the course of this grand struggle that one experiences an indestructible life-condition of comfort and security. I am further confident that these declarations of soaring human dignity will resound strongly and deeply in the hearts of world citizens as they create the global civilization of the twenty-first century.

The three transformations I have outlined come together in the process of human revolution, the reformation of the inner life, its expansion toward and merger with the greater self of wisdom, compassion and courage. It is my firm conviction that a fundamental revolution in the life of a single individual can give rise to the kind of consciousness and solidarity that will free humanity from its millennial cycles of warfare and violence.

During World War II, Tsunesaburo Makiguchi, founder and first president of the Soka Kyoiku Gakkai (Value-Creating Education Society) engaged in a spirited confrontation with the military authorities of Japan. Even in prison, and until his death there at age seventy-three, he pursued principled debate, leading several among those who had judged and jailed him to appreciate and even take faith in Buddhism.

Seeking to live up to that spiritual inheritance, I began my own dialogue with the world's citizens here in Hawaii thirty-five years ago. It is my determination to devote the rest of my life to the endeavor, which I hope I will share with you, of marshalling the manifest wisdom of peace to create a new era of hope and security in the coming century.

In closing, I would like to share the following words of Mahatma Gandhi, whose lifetime devotion to the themes we have discussed today has long inspired my profound affection and respect: "You have to stand against the whole world although you may have to stand alone. You have to stare the world in the face although the world may look at you with bloodshot eyes. Do not fear. Trust that little thing in you which resides in the heart" (*All Men Are Brothers*, p. 49).

Notes

1. See Johan Galtung, *Peace and Development in the Pacific Hemisphere* (Honolulu: University of Hawaii Institute for Peace, 1989).

2. See V. Fausboll, ed., *The Jataka*, vol. 5, (London: Luzac and Company, Ltd., 1963), p. 412; H. Smith, *Sutta-Nipata Commentary II Being Paramatthajotika II*, 2 (London: Curzon Press, 1966), p. 566.

3. See "Attadanda Sutta," *The Suttanipata*, trans. H. Saddhatissa (London: Curzon Press, 1987), p. 109; Anderson, Dines and Helmer Smith, *Suttanipata* (London: Routledge & Kegan Paul), p. 182.

4. Paul Brooks, *The House of Life: Rachel Carson at Work* (Boston: Houghton Mifflin Company, 1972), p. 319.

Noble Are Those
Who Encourage Others

—⚍—

FIRST SGI-USA EXECUTIVE CONFERENCE,
HONOLULU, HAWAII, JANUARY 27, 1995

I AM DELIGHTED to see you, my beloved friends with whom I share so many fond memories. I regard all of you without exception as members of my own family.

Included in today's meeting are representatives of the Pioneer Group, who have been exerting themselves in faith since the early days of our movement. As for those Pioneer Group members whom I could not meet during this visit, I have carefully taken note of each of their faces in the photo albums they kindly sent me.

Over the years, we have fought together, side by side, as comrades and family; we share a truly profound connection. You will always be in my heart. Knowing that the members of the Pioneer Group in America and around the world are well and in high spirits is my greatest source of joy.

Yesterday, I was honored to receive the Aloha International Peace Award from the Spark M. Matsunaga Institute for Peace at the University of Hawaii, an academic institution respected for its commitment to peace. I want to share this joy and honor first and foremost with all of you, my comrades for peace, with whom I have shared so much — both joy and suffering — over the past thirty-five years.

This year marks the Soka Gakkai's sixty-fifth anniversary, the thirty-fifth anniversary of the start of the global kosen-rufu movement and the SGI's twentieth anniversary. I am happy and deeply moved to start this auspicious year with my beloved American friends here in Hawaii, the place where I took my very first step for worldwide kosen-rufu.

I also thank you for the warm welcome and hospitality you have extended to the members of various exchange groups visiting Hawaii in connection with the anniversary celebrations.

Motto: Above All Nations Is Humanity

The University of Hawaii motto is inscribed in both Hawaiian and English on the Founders' Gate at the Manoa campus:

MALUNA AE O NA LAHUI A PAU KE OLA KE KANAKA.
ABOVE ALL NATIONS IS HUMANITY.

What a splendid motto! This is, in fact, one of the points I stressed in the lecture I gave yesterday.

The SGI stands on the forefront of human history. Let's continue to advance together with even greater confidence and vigor on the grand path of humanism, reaching out to and forging ties of solidarity with people of goodwill throughout the world.

The University of Hawaii's seal features a torch and a book inscribed with the word *Malamalama* — meaning "Light of Knowledge" — set against a background of a circular map of the Pacific Ocean. Incidentally, one of President Makiguchi's favorite expressions was "Learning is light."

Many SGI-USA members study at the University of Hawaii. Among them are several exchange students and graduates from Soka University and the Soka Schools in Japan. The achievements of the Hawaii University Group members are impressive. Mr. Makiguchi would surely be overjoyed to see how diligently they are exerting themselves!

Young people of great promise and ability are emerging in

ever-increasing numbers. Now more than ever, I hope that you, the top leaders, will give your utmost energies to encouraging and raising capable people.

"A Voice That Is Tranquil and Refined"

Encouragement — offering encouraging words — is important. Nichiren Daishonin states, "A commentary [On 'The Profound Meaning,' volume one] says, 'The voice carries out the work of the Buddha'" (OTT, 4). Sincere words of encouragement have the power to give people hope and the courage to go on living.

Why was Shakyamuni respected? One reason lies in the power of his voice. A Buddhist scripture states: "Shakyamuni's voice is beautiful, like honey. He is endowed with a voice that is tranquil and refined.

"His voice is sonorous, his meaning clear and precise...."[1]

It also says: "Shakyamuni speaks and makes statements that are resonant and bright, he speaks elegantly and clearly, never in grating tones. He has the gift of eloquence to make his meaning understood."[2]

Throughout his life, Shakyamuni encouraged people with his clear, sonorous voice. The same Buddhist text describes how Shakyamuni warmheartedly welcomed everyone he met, expressing his joy at seeing them. He showed affection, joy and gentleness in all his interactions. He greeted everyone with courtesy and respect. He never scowled or grimaced. Moreover, to put others at ease and encourage them to speak up, Shakyamuni would always break the ice by initiating the conversation.[3] The power of Shakyamuni's eloquence and sincerity made it possible for Buddhism to gain wide acceptance among the people of his time, deeply penetrating their hearts and minds.

Applauding the Efforts of the Kansai Members

Following the recent devastating earthquake that hit the Kobe–Osaka area of Japan [on January 17, 1995], our indomitable Kansai members — true to their great tradition of faith — set aside their own personal concerns to travel to the affected areas and lend their support and offer encouragement to those in distress. We can well imagine the relief and courage their warm words have been bringing to the people they encounter. We continue to receive reports and thanks for the prompt and selfless efforts of our members.

All of you here today are experts in the art of offering guidance and encouragement. It is my sincere wish that you will bring your lives to fruition and complete them in the heartfelt endeavor of encouraging your fellow members with a voice that is warm and overflowing with compassion, a voice that is confident and rings with spirited energy, a voice that is clear and unequivocal, in order to defeat the devilish functions that lie at the root of people's suffering.

No one can hold a candle to those who have devoted themselves to caring for others, who have offered ceaseless encouragement to their friends. Such people lead the most noble and respectable lives — as magnificent as a Hawaiian sunset.

A Gentleman Who Fought To the End

As many of you know, Richard Causton, the general director of the SGI-United Kingdom, died recently [on January 13, 1995] at age seventy-four. His is a sublime example of the kind of life I have described. General Director Causton was truly an exemplary "gentleman of the Mystic Law" who fought to the very last moment for kosen-rufu, his fellow members and the youth who will inherit the future. I regard him as my eternal comrade.

Hawaii has profound ties with the United Kingdom — as is evident from the Union Jack that appears in the upper left-hand corner of Hawaii's state flag. Upon arriving here in Hawaii, I again offered sincere prayers in memory of Mr. Causton.

On January 28, our friends in the United Kingdom — heirs to Mr. Causton's noble legacy — will hold a meeting to embark on a fresh course with their new general director, Ricky Baynes. I hope that all the members in the United States will join me in wishing our friends in the United Kingdom all the best in their endeavors.

The University of Hawaii's seal is also engraved with the state motto in Hawaiian. It translates as: "The life of the land is perpetuated in righteousness." Broadly interpreted, these words echo the spirit of establishing the correct teaching for the peace of the land.

By felicitous coincidence, our global grassroots movement to create a lasting peace began here in Hawaii in the year that marked the seven-hundredth anniversary of Nichiren Daishonin writing his treatise "On Establishing the Correct Teaching for the Peace of the Land." Now, thirty-five years later, again here in Hawaii, let us mark a fresh beginning together, forging ahead with renewed commitment in our grand struggle for kosen-rufu in the United States and around the world in the twenty-first century.

As you aim toward this great objective, may each of you live joyfully and brightly and with a strong, resilient spirit.

Notes

1. *Nanden daizokyo*, vol. 6, ed. Junjiro Takakusu (Tokyo: Taisho Shinshu Daizokyo Publishing Society, 1935), p. 194.
2. *Nanden daizokyo*, vol. 6, p. 169.
3. *Nanden daizokyo*, vol. 6, p. 195.

Shaping a New History
With the Eloquence of Truth

—⚏—

SGI PAN-PACIFIC PEACE AND CULTURE CONFERENCE,
SECOND SESSION, HONOLULU, HAWAII,
JANUARY 29, 1995

ALOHA! I would like to reiterate my heartfelt congratulations to all of you on the great success of last night's thirteenth SGI World Peace Youth Culture Festival. It was truly magnificent!

The lively and vigorous performances of the youth division and boys and girls group members in particular filled me with hope; they confirm the bright and solid future that lies in store for kosen-rufu in Hawaii and the United States in the twenty-first century.

I cannot find enough words to express my profound appreciation to my dear fellow members of Hawaii for their great efforts and the warm hospitality they have extended to me and all those visiting in connection with the SGI twentieth-anniversary celebrations. I would like to take this opportunity to express my heartfelt *mahalo* (thank you) to all of you.

I also wish to extend my most sincere welcome to my beloved fellow members from the mainland United States, Asia and Oceania — the countries of the Pacific Rim — who are here as part of various exchange groups. The blue expanse of the Pacific Ocean extends from your shores to those on which Nichiren Daishonin spent his childhood. Beyond that vast horizon upon which he probably gazed every day lay Hawaii. How delighted the

Daishonin would surely be to see today's gathering for worldwide kosen-rufu! I hope that all of you will live your lives with hearts as expansive, buoyant, deep and bright as the Pacific.

IN PRAISE OF RESOLUTE FAITH

Nichiren Daishonin offers the following words of praise and encouragement to one of his lay believers, the lay nun Kubo: "Where strong winds cause the grasses to bend and flashes of lightning fill people with alarm—in a world such as ours, how wonderful it is that to this day you remain unshaken in your faith!

"They say that when roots are deep, the leaves will not wither; when there is a jewel in the heart of the fountain, its waters will never cease to flow. And how deep are the roots of your faith, how pure the jewel in your heart. How admirable, how admirable!" (WND-2, 755).

I cannot help reading these words of the Daishonin as praise for all of you who have fought so hard in your respective areas over the past two decades since the SGI's founding. The heavenly deities throughout the universe will surely bestow magnificent "leis of good fortune" upon each one of you.

We have received many congratulatory messages from fellow SGI members throughout the world to celebrate this gathering. The members in Russia, now in the midst of a bitterly cold winter, have also sent their heartfelt wishes. Last year's founding of an SGI organization in Russia, incidentally, can be traced back to the United States. [One of the first members in Russia began practicing Nichiren Daishonin's Buddhism after being introduced to the practice in the United States by a friend who is an SGI-USA member.] The United States has a truly mystic mission as the starting point for worldwide kosen-rufu.

Our friends from Russia also sent messages to Japan expressing their concern and support immediately after the Kobe–Osaka earthquake. They are holding chanting sessions even now to pray for the speedy recovery of the people in Kansai. I am truly moved by their noble spirit of compassion for their fellow members despite the confusion and difficulties they themselves are experiencing in Russia. As a tribute to their sincerity, I would like to share with you the words of the great Russian literary giant Leo Tolstoy.

A Change in Public Opinion Is Vital

Tolstoy declared: "No feats of heroism are needed to bring about the greatest and most important changes in the life of humanity; neither the arming of millions of men . . . nor barricades, nor dynamite outrages. . . . All that is necessary is a change of public opinion."[1]

Thus he concluded that the only way to bring about a fundamental change in society is to realize a change in public opinion, a change in people's minds.

How, then, can we change public opinion? Tolstoy asserted: "All that is necessary is to cease acquiescing in the public opinion of the past, now false and already defunct and only artificially induced by governments. It is only necessary for each individual to say what he really thinks and feels or at least to refrain from saying what he does not think."[2]

It is vital, in other words, not to be swayed by the opinions of others or by past ways of thinking or doing. Instead, each of us must become wise, possessing our own firm convictions. And, with courage and confidence, we must express and act in accord with those convictions. Tolstoy said: "If only men — even a few — would do that, the out-worn public opinion would at once and of itself fall away and a new, real, and vital public opinion would manifest itself. . . . It is only necessary to give up lying! Only let men reject the lie which is imposed upon them; only let them stop saying what they neither think nor feel, and at once such a change of the whole structure of our life will be accomplished as the revolutionaries would not achieve in centuries even if all power were in their hands."[3]

The SGI's great movement for kosen-rufu, which is propelled by the power of words and language, responds precisely to the expectations of Tolstoy; we are generating the kind of "new, real, and vital public opinion" to which he referred. This movement may appear inconspicuous and quiet, but the courageous voice of each individual daring to speak the truth is the surest force for shaping a new history for humanity.

PRAISEWORTHY ARE THOSE WHO SHARE BUDDHISM WITH OTHERS

In a letter to one of his loyal followers, Shijo Kingo, Nichiren Daishonin writes: "Moreover, following me, you, as a votary of the Lotus Sutra, have told others of this Law. What else could this be but the transmission of the Law?" (WND-1, 319). All of you are striving to tell people around the world about Nichiren Daishonin's Buddhism in accord with the original Buddha's wish. As such, you are contemporary votaries of the Lotus Sutra, the Bodhisattvas of the Earth in modern times.

Today, people of intellect and common sense throughout the world are seriously seeking the wisdom of Buddhism. Let us accomplish a great transformation in human history — opening people's hearts with "sincere and earnest eloquence"; crushing the forces of evil with "just and righteous eloquence"; paving the way toward victory with "bold and courageous eloquence."

Tolstoy also declared that "women make public opinion, and women are in our time particularly strong."[4] Were he to see the vibrant activities of the SGI women's and young women's divisions today, I feel sure he would definitely applaud them. Men must carefully listen to and respect the opinions of the women's and young women's division members. I would like to confirm with you that we must never scold or be arrogant toward women.

HUMAN DEVELOPMENT TOWARD COEXISTENCE

Already at the beginning of this century, President Makiguchi foresaw the importance of Hawaii as the center of what he termed "a Pacific civilization." These ideas are expressed in his book *The Geography of Human Life.* As I mentioned in my lecture at the

East–West Center [on January 26], Hawaii is a model of coexistence or symbiosis.

Mr. Makiguchi stressed the formation of the kind of human character that is conducive to coexistence with others and is not preoccupied solely with concerns of the self. A preeminent educator, he strove to develop people of intellect who could recognize their own weaknesses as well as see the strengths of others.[5] He also endeavored to foster people of generous and magnanimous character who would try to complement their own shortcomings with the strong points of others while at the same time ungrudgingly use their own strengths to make up for others' deficiencies.[6]

This is one of the underpinnings of Soka education; it is an important factor behind the joyful harmony of the Soka family. I hope that our members in each country or region around the world will always advance together in the beautiful unity of "many in body, one in mind."

FROM A DEPENDENT LIFE TO A CONTRIBUTIVE ONE

President Makiguchi also categorized the life of human beings into three different types: 1) a dependent life, 2) a self-reliant life and 3) a contributive life.[7]

Without going into a lot of detail, a dependent life is one in which we have no firm sense of purpose or mission, always being swayed by the opinions of others — a life, if you like, where we have no self-identity.

Many religions have demanded blind faith, taking away people's independence. President Makiguchi opposed such enslavement. What he called for instead was the solidarity of awakened common people. To achieve this, he proposed a self-reliant way of life in which we advance on the path of our choice with firm, independent character. He also stressed a contributive way of life in which we set our fundamental goal in life toward the realization of happiness for ourselves and others, casting aside arrogance and self-satisfaction to respect and benefit others. As each of us develops and elevates our life from a state of dependence to self-reliance and then to contribution to others, he maintained, we will be able to manifest our full splendor as human beings in everything we do.

The SGI is a noble organization of humanism, of people who live such a contributive life. Basing ourselves on the supreme Law of life, we dedicate ourselves untiringly for the happiness of humanity, the prosperity of society, the flourishing of culture and the realization of world peace.

The selfless actions of our fellow members in Kansai following the recent devastating earthquake in Kobe and Osaka display this spirit of humanitarian contribution.

THE JUSTICE OF THE SGI WILL SHINE LIKE THE SUN

Dr. N. Radhakrishnan, honorary president of the Bharat Soka Gakkai, the SGI organization in India, has traveled all the way to Hawaii to attend the culture festival and my lecture. I would like to introduce an Indian maxim that he shared with me: Earthworms, detesting the sunlight, stretch themselves to their full length just before the sun rises in an attempt to threaten and intimidate it. But they are actually powerless to do anything. Those who are attacking the SGI, he said, are like these earthworms. No matter how they may try to oppress us, the SGI is like the morning sun. He voiced his confidence that the SGI's justice will shine brilliantly in the end.

The true nature of the Nichiren Shoshu priesthood has been clearly revealed for all to see. Let us powerfully illuminate the world with the rising sun of hope for the twenty-first century.

I conclude my speech by offering my sincere prayers for the continued good health, longevity, happiness and security of all the members of Asia and Oceania and throughout the world. Please convey my very best regards to your families and fellow members in your respective regions and countries.

Notes

1. Leo Tolstoy, *The Kingdom of God and Peace Essays*, trans. Aylmer Maude (London: Oxford University Press, 1936), p. 530.

2. *The Kingdom of God and Peace Essays*, pp. 530–31.

3. *The Kingdom of God and Peace Essays*, p. 531.

4. Lev. N. Tolstoy, *What Shall We Do Then? — On the Moscow Census — Collected Articles*, trans. and ed. Leo Wiener (Boston: Dana Estes, 1904), p. 329.

5. Tsunesaburo Makiguchi, *Soka kyoikugaku taikei* (The System of Value-Creating Pedagogy) (Tokyo: Seikyo Shimbunsha, 1972), vol. 1, p. 217. See *Education for Creative Living: Ideas and Proposals of Tsunesaburo Makiguchi*, trans. Alfred Birnbaum, ed. Dayle M. Bethel (Ames: Iowa State University Press, 1989), p. 43.

6. *Soka kyoikugaku taikei*, p. 43.

7. *Soka kyoikugaku taikei*, vol. 1, p. 221. See *Education for Creative Living*, p. 45.

Shining With the Greatest Possible Brilliance

—ɷ—

NINETEENTH SGI GENERAL MEETING,
HAWAII CULTURE CENTER, HONOLULU, HAWAII,
JANUARY 30, 1995

ALOHA! Congratulations on holding the SGI General Meeting — and also on this wonderful weather! I am truly delighted to be here in this beautiful "castle of treasures" that is your new Hawaii Culture Center.

It is my fervent wish that the community and culture centers of the SGI always be sturdy and solid structures — like the indestructible royal palace of Rajagriha referred to in the Gosho[1] — for the safety and protection of the members, the children of the Buddha. Our centers in the Kobe–Osaka area of Japan, where the earthquake recently struck, have certainly proven to be so beyond a doubt.

All of the Soka Gakkai community and culture centers in the affected areas remained intact and were therefore immediately available as emergency shelters for the thousands left homeless in the disaster and as centers for the coordination of relief activities.

I also offer my heartfelt appreciation to all the members who have traveled great distances to attend this meeting — coming from throughout the United States, Japan and other areas of Asia and Oceania. Allow me also to reiterate my thanks to the members of Hawaii and the event staff, including all those who worked behind the scenes, for the warm welcome you have extended to your visiting fellow members and for treating us to an unforgettable culture festival.

In taking sincere actions for kosen-rufu, you are sowing the seeds for happiness in your lives. There is absolutely no doubt that all your efforts will blossom as beautiful flowers of boundless good fortune.

Kings and queens, for instance, possess tremendous treasures that enable them to lead lives of total ease and comfort, wanting for nothing. Likewise, as kings and queens of faith, you possess boundless treasures in your heart. You need only bring forth the treasure appropriate to the situation, and complete fulfillment will be yours. You will experience a state of life of total freedom. Such is the wondrous and inscrutable function of the Mystic Law.

Leaflet Announcing the Normandy Invasion

On this visit to Hawaii, the SUA staff presented me with a very rare and valuable leaflet — one of the many thousands that were addressed to the citizens of France and were scattered from the skies during the Normandy Invasion, the largest military operation in history. I understand that almost none of these leaflets remain today, so I sincerely thank the Soka University of America staff for a gift of such historic value.

The leaflet declares in bold print [in French], "The Allied Forces Are Landing." This was a dramatic announcement that the Allied Forces had arrived in Normandy to liberate the people of Europe from the grip of Nazi German forces. Copies of the leaflet were carried by Allied planes over enemy lines and dropped over the French countryside on that fateful day, June 6, 1944.

On the back of the leaflet is a message from General Dwight D. Eisenhower, supreme commander of the Allied Expeditionary forces, addressed to the valiant fighters of the French Resistance and the people of Western Europe: "All patriots — men and women, young or old — have to play a role in our march toward final victory....

"This landing is only the beginning of the campaign to free Western Europe. We are on the brink of great battles. I ask all people who love freedom to join us. Nothing must shake your faith — nothing must stop our advance — TOGETHER, WE WILL WIN!"

Though of course the SGI's nonviolent movement for peace is of an entirely different dimension from battles fought by military might, these words nevertheless strike a powerful chord with our own struggle.

June 6, 1944 — the day of the Normandy landing — was also the last birthday celebrated by President Makiguchi before his death. He was seventy-three, but he fought on with unremitting fervor against the forces of Japanese militarism even from his prison cell.

His disciple and successor, Josei Toda, was also in jail, confined to a solitary cell. From New Year's Day of that year, Mr. Toda embarked on a solemn quest to master the essence of the Lotus Sutra. No doubt he celebrated his mentor's birthday in solitude as he continued to plumb the depths of the Law of life, striving to find a way toward human revolution. He was fast approaching that profound insight and enlightenment that he attained in his prison cell and that would serve as a fundamental means of spiritual liberation for humanity. We of the SGI are proudly following in the footsteps of these two great champions of peace, human rights and freedom.

President Makiguchi vehemently denounced Japanese clergy who collaborated with the militarist authorities during World War II, declaring, "We must make a frontal assault on this enemy!" President Toda also left us the admonition "You must never let up in your struggle against evil."

Let us apply ourselves to this grand spiritual struggle with ever greater vigor so that we may usher in an era of the people in the twenty-first century.

A COUNTRY IS DISTINGUISHED
BY ITS PEOPLE

You are all Bodhisattvas of the Earth. How precious and indispensable each of you is to your country or region! This is expressed by the following Gosho passage: "Most important, one must understand that when the god of the sun rises at dawn in the east, he sends forth his rays of light, opens his heavenly eyes, and observes the southern continent of Jambudvipa. If there he sees a votary of the Lotus Sutra, he rejoices in heart. But if he sees a country that hates the votary, then his eyes flash with anger and he glares at that country" (WND-2, 653).

Let us continue to advance with the great conviction that to the degree we SGI members, the children of the Buddha, increase our vigor, energy and influence, our societies and countries will invariably prosper and flourish.

The great Indian poet Rabindranath Tagore voiced these thoughts on his seventieth birthday:

"A country is created by the people. It is made not from earth but people's hearts. Only through the brilliance of its people does a country distinguish itself."[2]

As I mentioned in my lecture at the East–West Center [on January 26], the Mystic Law — embodying the principle of "revealing one's intrinsic nature" — enables all human beings to shine with their greatest possible brilliance, to reveal their true and highest potential. This is one of the underlying principles of our SGI movement.

Our fellow members in Kansai have stood up with great energy and courage to begin reconstruction after the devastating earthquake. I am certain that as long as they continue to shine, keeping the flame of their "ever-victorious" spirit burning brightly, Kansai will always be filled with boundless hope.

"Don't Be Impatient; You Will Surely Become Happy"

My mentor, President Toda, was always a friend and ally of those who were suffering or in pain. He warmly embraced each person. Once, he offered the following words of encouragement to a member: "Don't be impatient. Since you have embraced the Gohonzon, your situation will definitely improve. There's no need to worry. Sure, there will be hard times, times when you feel like crying. But as long as you have the Gohonzon, your life will become bright and joyful.

"In the Gosho, it states: 'When the skies are clear, the ground is illuminated. Similarly, when one knows the Lotus Sutra, one understands the meaning of all worldly affairs' (WND-1, 376).

"Therefore, you will know and understand what it is you have to do, what is the best thing to do, with regard to your business or whatever your problem is. It will become clear what needs to be done, and you will surely become happy. So the only thing to do is have strong faith in the Gohonzon" (February 8, 1957).

As long as we persevere in faith, we will become happy. We must never doubt this, no matter what happens, but always advance resolutely, staunchly enduring all hardships and obstacles along the way. This is what true faith is.

The mission and responsibility of leaders is to give the members the kind of encouragement and hope that will enable them to keep moving forward, free of doubts.

The purpose of faith is to become happy. I hope all of you will take this sure path to happiness, never wandering onto byroads that lead to unhappiness. Please walk the great path of kosen-rufu with confidence and pride.

Chant Nam-myoho-renge-kyo in Times of Either Suffering or Joy

In a letter to one of his followers, Nichiren Daishonin writes: "When the world makes you feel downcast, you should chant

Nam-myoho-renge-kyo, remembering that, although the sufferings of this life are painful, those in the next life could be much worse. And when you are happy, you should remember that your happiness in this life is nothing but a dream within a dream, and that the only true happiness is that found in the pure land of Eagle Peak, and with that thought in mind, chant Nam-myoho-renge-kyo. Continue your practice without backsliding until the final moment of your life, and when that time comes, behold! When you climb the mountain of perfect enlightenment and gaze around you in all directions, then to your amazement you will see that the entire realm of phenomena is the Land of Tranquil Light. The ground will be of lapis lazuli, and the eight paths will be set apart by golden ropes. Four kinds of flowers will fall from the heavens, and music will resound in the air. All Buddhas and bodhisattvas will be present in complete joy, caressed by the breezes of eternity, happiness, true self, and purity. The time is fast approaching when we too will count ourselves among their number. But if we are weak in faith, we will never reach that wonderful place" (WND-1, 760–61).

Our lives are infinitely precious. To not attain a state of absolute happiness in this lifetime is a great loss. Our Buddhist practice exists so that we can attain indestructible happiness. We must fight to the fullest right now, not sometime in the future.

Please hold your heads high, thoroughly dedicating yourselves to the great goal of kosen-rufu, regardless of what may arise, always chanting daimoku with clear and resonant voices. In doing so, you are paving the way for a journey throughout the three existences endowed with the four noble qualities of eternity, happiness, true self and purity. This is the state of life in which you can experience both life and death with great joy.

In closing, I offer sincere prayers for your good health, first and foremost, as well as for your longevity, safety and happiness. These are my constant prayers. May this beautiful land of Hawaii, which I love so deeply, enjoy eternal peace, security and glory. Please have a wonderful day today.

Mahalo! Thank you very much. See you again.

Notes

1. Rajagriha is the capital of the ancient kingdom of Magadha, where King Bimbisara and his son Ajatashatru lived and where Shakyamuni often preached his doctrines. In the Gosho "The Royal Palace," it states: "Even though successive fires have destroyed the houses of the populace [within the city walls], they have never once engulfed the royal palace [because of the great good fortune of the king who dwells therein].... Therefore, if you name the entire city in which they dwell Rajagriha, 'the Royal Palace,' the god of fire will be afraid to burn their houses" (WND-1, 488).

2. Translated from Japanese: *Tagoru chosakushu* (Collected Writings of Tagore), trans. Kazuo Azuma et al. (Tokyo: Daisan Bunmeisha, 1987), vol. 10, p. 347.

A Sense of Responsibility
for People's Happiness:
The Hallmark of a True Leader

—⚍—

SECOND SGI-USA EXECUTIVE CONFERENCE,
HONOLULU, HAWAII, JANUARY 31, 1995

THE SGI-USA is realizing a magnificent rebirth. You have now begun to take off powerfully into the skies of the coming century. I would like to celebrate and offer heartfelt congratulations on this soaring flight.

Nichiren Daishonin states, "Employ the strategy of the Lotus Sutra before any other" (WND-1, 1001). The Mystic Law is the ultimate strategy. I therefore hope that each of you, who possess a profound mission, will polish your wisdom and insight as leaders, based on faith.

PREPARE FOR ANY SITUATION

Yesterday [January 30], I spoke about the message General Dwight D. Eisenhower sent to the citizens of France upon the Allied landing in Normandy. Immediately afterward, several American youth reported to me about an incident involving General Eisenhower. The incident offers an important insight into the responsibility of leaders, so I would like to share it with you here.

What was General Eisenhower's resolve when he gave the green light to what has been called the greatest military operation in history? The very day he gave the order, the American general prepared a press release, to be used if necessary: "Our landings [in Normandy]...have failed to gain a satisfactory foothold and I have withdrawn the troops. My decision to attack at this time and place was based on the best information available. The troops, the air and the Navy did all that bravery and devotion to duty could do. If any blame or fault attaches to the attempt it is mine alone."[1]

In point of fact, of course, his strategy was successful, and it was never necessary to release this statement. His thorough preparation and attention to detail — which planned even for the possibility of failure — might be given as one of the reasons for the operation's remarkable success.

All battles are determined by the quality of the preparations. It is only through the unseen efforts of the central figure, driven by the unflagging determination and sense of responsibility to be prepared for any situation, that people's safety can be assured and the path to victory opened.

Airplanes, for example, always carry enough fuel so that they can reach and land at an alternative airport or maintain a holding pattern for a long period in case of bad weather. On top of that they also carry an emergency fuel supply.

Those who fail to make such painstaking efforts and preparations and instead simply sit back complacently on their positions in the organization have disqualified themselves as leaders.

TRUSTING OTHERS AND BRINGING OUT THEIR FULL POTENTIAL

Eisenhower's statement conveys a sense of his sincere concern and consideration for his subordinates and his profound sense of responsibility as a leader.

Eisenhower was famous for his ability to delegate authority. Instead of concentrating power in his own hands, he trusted his commanders and took measures to make it easier for them to be effective. He always made the effort to listen to their opinions. He was uninterested in gaining credit for himself but pushed his commanders forward so that they could accept praise. Because he let his subordinates take credit while courageously accepting full responsibility for any failures, those under his command could fight to their fullest. The soldiers were unified in their desire to respond to his trust and expectations. We must not overlook the fact that behind the Normandy landing was the leadership of this great general.

These kinds of leaders have become rare. The trend for leaders to be egotistical, irresponsible and concerned only with protecting themselves is truly regrettable. My mentor, Josei Toda, once said: "In becoming president, I well understood the responsibility I would be taking on. Why then should I have any cause to grieve or lament? I offer myself to you, determined to wage a struggle as a great warrior for kosen-rufu."

He also said: "Bound as we are by profound ties of mentor and disciple, I will take complete responsibility for any transgressions committed by my disciples. So I would like you to concentrate on becoming happy."

I hope you will be humanistic leaders who have a deep sense of responsibility to ensure that your precious fellow members, children of the Buddha, become happy without exception. With this determination, may you create a new and unprecedented history of American kosen-rufu.

After World War II, Eisenhower retired from the army to become president of America's renowned Columbia University. Speaking of Columbia University, I had the opportunity to hold a discussion with Robert Thurman, chairman of the Department of Religion at the university's Center for Buddhist Studies, during my stay here in Hawaii. One of the subjects we touched on was education.

I have decided that education is the most important undertaking of my final years, and I am putting my fullest efforts into that field. I am therefore delighted by the expectations and hopes that many scholars and intellectuals around the world have voiced with regard to Soka education.

The University of Hawaii's Richard Dubanoski, dean of the College of Social Sciences, and Anthony Marsella of the Department

of Psychology seem to have truly fond memories of their visit to
the Soka Schools in Kansai [in September 1994]. They are among
the many scholars who have asked me to convey their sympathy and concern to the brave young students of the Kansai Soka
Schools following the devastating earthquake in that region.

SINCERE COMMUNICATION IS THE KEY
TO RAISING YOUTH

Secretary General Rajender Singh Varma of the International Cultural Development Organization of India also sent his condo-
lences to the students. When he visited the Kansai Soka Schools
last year [in December 1994], he shared the following thoughts
on Soka education: "The esteemed Mr. Makiguchi left this world
under unfortunate circumstances [dying in prison] with the dream
of founding Soka University and the Soka Schools in his heart....
Why did President Makiguchi dream of education? Why didn't he
dream of becoming a king or emperor? Because he knew that
through education he would be able to enlighten many, many
lives. Youth are a nation's future. A nation that does not care for
its youth does not care for its future."

To foster youth is to foster the future. In the nineteenth century here in Hawaii, Princess Pauahi devoted her life to opening
the way for the education of youth, leaving a truly noble legacy.
I hope that SGI-USA members will continue to spread the warm
light of humanistic education throughout American society.

Only when leaders have a strong inner determination to find
and raise people, to sow seeds for the future, will talented and
capable individuals emerge and develop. The important thing
is to maintain contact and communication with people. The
warmth and sincerity of our interactions will caress others like
a gentle rain and warming sunlight, nurturing their growth and
development. For that reason, I avail myself of every opportunity
to meet with young people and personally strive to foster their
growth and ability.

Leaders who allow their position to go to their heads and grow arrogant, who use others to make themselves look good, will bring ruin not only upon themselves but upon the younger members whom they are striving to raise. Leaders who are intent only on exploiting others for their own benefit cannot possibly grow themselves or help others do so. On the other hand, leaders who have the spirit to fight for everyone's sake will grow, as will all around them. This subtle difference in inner commitment and resolve leads to vastly different outcomes.

OILING THE WHEELS OF A HEAVY CART

In the Gosho it states: "Teaching another something is the same as oiling the wheels of a cart so that they turn even though it is heavy, or as floating a boat on water so that it moves ahead easily" (WND-1, 1086).

We must ask ourselves: "What can I do to make that person's wheels begin to turn?" "What can I do to get the boat moving in the right direction?" It is our responsibility as leaders in Buddhism to give constant consideration to how we can make it easier for others to do their best so that they can advance with hope and joy, and for us to take practical steps toward this end.

The SGI-USA enjoys one of the world's most diverse gatherings of talented and capable people. "Build a fortress of capable people!" was President Toda's ardent appeal to Soka Gakkai members. I hope you will keep these words alive in your heart and forge ahead to expand the network of wonderfully warmhearted people here in Hawaii, creating a solid foundation that will last for all eternity. I am determined to support the endeavors of the SGI-USA to the very fullest.

In closing, I would like to reiterate my appreciation to all those who have worked so hard to make this visit so enjoyable and successful. Please give my very warmest regards to all those I was unable to meet this time, to all those who, with beautiful hearts, have been looking after things in your absence and earnestly sending us their sincere daimoku.

Notes

1. "D-day's Fiftieth Anniversary Celebrated Duty and Sacrifice," *Insight on the News,* June 20, 1994, vol. 10, no. 25, p. 40.

1996

Convey the Message of Peace Throughout the World

—ﾊﾙ—

SGI-USA EXECUTIVE CONFERENCE,
LOS ANGELES, CALIFORNIA, JUNE 1, 1996

MY MOST HEARTFELT congratulations on this SGI-USA Executive Conference. I'm delighted that all my beloved American friends are in such high spirits. You are all extremely precious individuals who have devoted yourselves to your endeavors with unchanging passion and commitment. With the humblest respect and appreciation, I commend all of you from the bottom of my heart.

Earlier today, a development planning committee meeting for the Soka University of America, Aliso Viejo campus in Orange County, California, was convened. The SGI-USA is advancing dynamically! With hope and vigor, you are moving forward, leading the way toward a new century of peace, culture and education. Congratulations!

"HOME" IS THE WORLD OF THE SGI

On the grounds of the SUA Calabasas campus, there is an avenue of eucalyptus trees said to have been used in filming scenes for the famous movie *Gone With the Wind*. Whenever I walk along this picturesque path, I recall the novel's final scene, where the heroine, Scarlett, weary and desolate, vows: "I'll go home to Tara

to-morrow.... I'll think of it all to-morrow, at Tara. I can stand it
then.... After all, to-morrow is another day."[1]

Tara was Scarlett's childhood home. The thought of her home
gave her the courage to fight on when she was left alone, with
no one to whom she could turn, at the end of a turbulent period
in her life.

She had seen the chaos of the American Civil War, the death of
her beloved child and, finally, her husband Rhett's abrupt departure. Life is a series of changes, a succession of ups and downs.
But those who possess a prime point, a home to which they can
return, no matter what happens, are strong.

To always come home to the world of friendship of the SGI,
to talk things over and prepare for a fresh beginning — this is the
way I hope all of you will live. When you do, you will advance
upon a fundamentally unerring path to happiness.

THE LIGHT OF THE FULL MOON

Tonight, a full moon is shining in the sky. Nichiren Daishonin
writes: "The Lotus Sutra is like the moon. For those who have
faith in the Lotus Sutra, but whose faith is not deep, it is as though
a half moon were lighting the darkness. But for those who have
profound faith, it is as though a full moon were illuminating the
night" (WND-1, 94).

Faith is light. The hearts of those with strong faith are filled with
light. A radiance envelops their lives. People with unshakable conviction in faith enjoy a happiness that is as luminous as the full
moon on a dark night, as dazzling as the sun on a clear day.

I hope that all of you, as top leaders of the kosen-rufu movement in the United States, will work with all your might to ensure
that each member comes to shine with a happiness as bright and
complete as the full moon. Please pursue sincere and patient dialogue that will both encourage your members and deeply touch
their hearts. With warm concern and kindness, please treasure
each person with all your heart and make your organization shine

with an even greater harmonious unity as sublime as the full moon itself.

TREASURING OTHERS' HEARTS IS THE KEY
TO GROWTH

The SGI organization is a gathering of people. So it is essential that we mix and interact with others, that our hearts are united and in rhythm with one another. As the Daishonin says, "It is the heart that is important" (WND-I, 949).

Orders do not make an organization strong. Far from it. The spirit to treasure each person is what touches and moves people. Behaving with a spirit of genuine concern, respect and courtesy toward each person is the greatest driving force for the organization's development.

Leaders must study continually. Once a leader stops growing, those who look to him or her for guidance and support will suffer. Therefore, today, I will share with you a few points on leadership from some Chinese classics.

First, let's look at *The Analects*, a compilation of the words and deeds of the great Chinese philosopher Confucius: "The man of wisdom is never in two minds;[2] the man of benevolence never worries;[3] the man of courage is never afraid."[4]

In other words, a person of wisdom, possessing good sense and reason, never wavers. A person of benevolence, having abundant compassion for others and few personal desires or ambitions, never frets or worries. A person of courage, possessing boldness, never trembles in fear.

Leaders need to have immense wisdom, compassion and courage. Nonetheless, each person is different. There are some who may have an outstanding intellect, others who may possess deep compassion for others, and still others who are filled with courage. Through the Mystic Law, the different strong points of each person are used to the fullest to create the greatest possible value.

A GENUINE LEADER REJOICES IN PEOPLE'S HAPPINESS

Mencius, another great Confucian philosopher, observes: "The people will delight in the joy of him who delights in their joy."[5] That is, if a leader rejoices in the happiness of the people, the people, in turn, will rejoice in the leader's happiness.

To strive not only for one's own happiness but to constantly think and pray about how you can contribute to the happiness of others and to take joy in doing so — this is the SGI spirit. This also parallels the spirit of American democracy. In our organization, there is no one above or below; everyone is equal. The higher our leadership position, the more humbly we must work for the happiness of the members. This is how genuine Buddhist leaders behave.

In *The Analects*, Confucius says: "Only a well-balanced admixture of these two [native substance and acquired refinement] will result in gentlemanliness."[6]

"Native substance" refers to a person's unadorned inherent qualities, while "acquired refinement" refers to the learning and cultural polish that a person acquires. Confucius declares that an outstanding leader possesses a harmonious balance of both those attributes.

I hope that, as leaders, you will study ceaselessly and strive to deepen your character and refinement. At the same time, I would like you to be brimming with a genuine and unpretentious humanity.

GANDHI: A TIRELESS SPEAKER AND WRITER

In honor of the full moon tonight, I turn now to the Land of the Moon, India. The father of India's movement for independence, Mohandas K. (Mahatma) Gandhi, was a person of action who literally walked from one corner of the nation to the other. He was also a tireless speaker and writer. Not only did he warmly encourage the people with his voice, but his pen was never still. His lifetime writings are said to number more than ten million words. He kept writing even in prison, where he spent nearly six years.

What was one of Gandhi's great weapons in his struggle to communicate his ideas to the people? It was publishing his own newspaper. He believed that a newspaper's sole purpose is to serve the people. Through his newspaper, he called for nonviolent resistance and rallied the people to this cause. The autobiography he began to write in prison was also serialized in the paper and tens of millions of Indians across the land waited eagerly to read each installment. In the meantime, it was ordinary, nameless youth who spread Gandhi's message — conveyed to them via the pages of his newspaper — widely among the populace.

The gallant youth division members of the SGI-USA are also exerting themselves admirably.

With newspaper in hand, the youth of India boldly set off to rural villages and spoke of Gandhi's spirit of nonviolence. And in what must have been a moving sight to behold, they read out Gandhi's writings for those who were illiterate, transmitting his ideals orally. Millions across the land learned in this way. Through the selfless efforts of these courageous yet unrecognized youth, Gandhi's spiritual message permeated every corner of Indian society and inspired the people to unite and take action.

All of you, my dear friends of America, are spreading the message of Nichiren Daishonin. You are immeasurably noble and precious emissaries of the Buddha. I press my palms together in fervent reverence and appreciation for your sincere and dedicated efforts. You are truly to be commended.

I also take this opportunity to voice my unceasing gratitude for our uncrowned friends in Japan who each day deliver the Soka Gakkai newspaper, the *Seikyo Shimbun*, to members' homes.

The purpose underlying all of Gandhi's writings and speeches was to make the people wise and strong. Once when Gandhi was traveling around the country, a peasant threw a sheet of paper into his car. On it was written a poem by a renowned ancient Indian poet. Gandhi was moved to declare that no other peasantry in the world was as cultivated as India's, and he cited the piece of paper as ample proof.[7] Nothing delighted Gandhi more than seeing the people become enlightened.

Genuine leaders personally take on the most demanding challenges, work the hardest and rejoice when people grow wise and become happy.

Equipped with the new awareness Gandhi had given them, the Indian people joined in the struggle for independence one after another. Their strength came from correctly understanding the significance of his movement. Women, who for centuries had been confined to the home, now marched in demonstrations shoulder to shoulder with men, liberating themselves from the chains that had long bound them. The power of the awakening masses gave rise to a vast groundswell toward independence.

Gandhi declared, "Unwearied ceaseless effort is the price that must be paid for turning faith into a rich infallible experience."[8] In the final analysis, faith not accompanied by action is merely an abstraction. Ceaseless effort is what makes our faith a living and breathing part of us. And making our faith in the Daishonin's Buddhism an active and indivisible part of our lives is what it means to attain Buddhahood.

Tireless and unflagging effort — this is the spirit of the American members who are making all-out efforts at the forefront of the SGI movement.

In the year 2000, we will celebrate the fortieth anniversary of the kosen-rufu movement in America. Let us take good care of our health and strive to create a momentous history of the people by boldly carrying on our movement for peace through speech and the written word.

THE HUMAN SPIRIT:
A WELLSPRING OF INEXHAUSTIBLE HOPE

There is no pessimism in Buddhism — not in the past, present or future. There is only optimism. Therefore, let us advance eternally with hope and optimism, come what may.

The great Norwegian folk poet Arnulf Overland, who fought against the Nazis during World War II, writes:

> *A people can be conquered,*
> *But their freedom of spirit can never be destroyed*
> *Nor their thoughts ever bound!*
> *Only those without weapons*
> *Possess an inexhaustible wellspring;*
> *Only the spirit triumphs!* [9]

The power of the human spirit, of thought and philosophy, is indestructible. With this power, let us advance joyfully and confidently toward an age of peace in the twenty-first century.

For the eternal future of all humankind, I am determined to keep striving tirelessly to plant the seeds of peace here in America and throughout the world.

I conclude with my prayers for your ever-greater vitality and good health, and freedom from illness and accidents.

Notes

1. Margaret Mitchell, *Gone With the Wind* (London: Pan Books Ltd., 1974), pp. 1010–11.
2. About right and wrong.
3. About the future.
4. Confucius, *The Analects*, trans. D.C. Lau (London: Penguin Books, 1979), p. 100.
5. *Mencius*, trans. D.C. Lau (London: Penguin Books, 1970), p. 63.
6. *The Analects*, p. 83.
7. Martin Green, *Gandhi: Voice of a New Age Revolution* (New York: The Continuum Publishing Company, 1993), p. 310.
8. *Quotes of Gandhi*, compiled by Shalu Bhalla (New Delhi: UBS Publishers' Distributors Ltd., 1991), p. 172.
9. Translated from the Japanese version of the Norwegian poem "Morklagt by"; Arnulf Overland, *Warera wa Subete o Ikinuku — Senjichu no shi*, trans. Joji Hayashi (Tokyo: Heibonsha, 1967), p. 144. The book's Norwegian title is *Vi Overlever Alt!: Dikt Fra Krigsarene* (We Will Survive All: Poems of the War Era).

Tsunesaburo Makiguchi's Lifelong Pursuit of Justice and Humane Values

—ⱴ—

FIRST LECTURE IN THE "TSUNESABURO MAKIGUCHI HUMAN RIGHTS LECTURE SERIES," SIMON WIESENTHAL CENTER, LOS ANGELES, CALIFORNIA, JUNE 4, 1996

IN JANUARY 1993, just before its official opening, I had the opportunity to visit the Museum of Tolerance. The history of the Holocaust must be termed the ultimate tragedy wrought by human hatred and intolerance. Viewing the exhibits, I was powerfully moved. More than that, however, I was profoundly outraged. Exceeding either of these emotions was the intensity of the determination that welled up within me: the determination that we must never allow this tragedy to be repeated — in any age, in any country.

Taking to heart the words of Simon Wiesenthal, that "hope lives when people remember," and with the unstinting support and cooperation of the Simon Wiesenthal Center, Soka University was proud to organize the exhibition "The Courage To Remember" at venues throughout Japan beginning in May 1994.

At the initial opening of the exhibit at the Tokyo Metropolitan Government Office, Rabbi Abraham Cooper led a distinguished delegation from the center, and we were honored by the attendance of U.S. Ambassador Mondale as well as diplomatic representatives from twenty countries.

On August 15 of last year, the fiftieth anniversary of the end of World War II, the exhibition opened in Hiroshima. At that time, Rabbi Marvin Hier represented the center at an opening ceremony attended by many prominent figures. "The Courage to Remember" later traveled to Okinawa and to date has been shown in nineteen Japanese cities.

The exhibition has had an average of five thousand visitors per day and thus far has been seen by approximately one million Japanese citizens. Many of the visitors are children and teenagers, and we frequently see them moved to tears by the courageous example of their fellow teen Anne Frank, whose life is portrayed in the exhibit. There has also been an endless succession of parents visiting the exhibition with their children. I am gratified to report that "The Courage to Remember" is serving as a site of learning where people are being awakened to an invaluable sense of justice.

At the initial opening, I could not help but recall the words of my mentor, Josei Toda —"One must learn from the indomitable spirit of the Jewish people." Indeed, I feel that there is much to learn from the strength and courage that have enabled the Jewish people to overcome endless persecutions and tragedies over the centuries.

As they have risen above each of the trials that have beset them, the Jewish people have learned, have remembered and have passed on their wisdom and spiritual strength to succeeding generations. The courage to remember is at the same time the compassion to teach. Hatred is learned; tolerance must therefore be taught.

Buddhism asserts that anger can function both for good and for evil. Needless to say, anger that serves self-absorbed emotionalism or greed is of an evil nature. Anger driven by hatred brings only conflict and confrontation to human society.

Anger, however, that is directed at great evil, against the desecration of humanity and the abusive disregard for human life, is anger of great good. This kind of anger reforms and rejuvenates society, opening the way to a world of humanism and peace.

Indeed, the emotion that "The Courage to Remember" inspires in viewers is none other than this feeling of righteous anger.

One of the most important issues facing humankind in the wake of the Cold War is that of how to bridge the chasms of mistrust and hatred between different peoples, cultures and religions. I was deeply struck by the following words spoken by Dr. Wiesenthal when he addressed the Fiftieth Session of the United Nations General Assembly last November, in a culminating event of the U.N. Year for Tolerance. He stated: "Tolerance is the prerequisite for the peaceful coexistence of all people on this earth and the only alternative to the hatred that led to the horrible crimes against humanity. Hatred is the evil opposite of tolerance."[1]

It should be noted here that, like anger, tolerance also has its passive and its active modes, its helpful and its harmful forms.

The indifference and apathy that are so prevalent in modern societies could be cited as an example of passive tolerance. Earlier in this century, the Japanese tendency to confuse unprincipled compromise for tolerance created the spiritual conditions that led to the growth of militarism — and to the bitter historical experience that followed.

In contrast, active tolerance is inseparable from the courage to resolutely oppose and resist all forms of violence and injustice that threaten human dignity. It is a way of life based on empathy, seeing the world through other people's eyes, feeling their sufferings and joys as one's own.

The Simon Wiesenthal Center provides a model of positive tolerance, actively seeking to create opportunities for dialogue between cultures, promoting shared learning and mutual understanding. A person of true tolerance is at the same time a courageous person of action who works to encourage the bonds of empathy and appreciation among people.

It is an unparalleled honor to have this opportunity to speak about the life of Tsunesaburo Makiguchi, the teacher of my teacher and first president of the Soka Gakkai, here at the Simon Wiesenthal Center — a fortress dedicated to the noble mission of protecting peace and human rights. I would like to share with you the convictions for which Mr. Makiguchi gave his life, focusing on the two themes of "righteous anger" and "active tolerance."

The following quotes from Mr. Makiguchi's writings will suffice to indicate the degree to which his thinking ran counter to that of Japanese militarism — the prevailing mood of his times.

> Rebuking and removing evil is part and parcel of embracing and protecting good.

> If you cannot be a courageous enemy of evil, you cannot be a friend to the good.

> One must not be satisfied with passive goodness; one must be a person of courage and mettle who can actively strive for good.[2]

Mr. Makiguchi opposed Japan's role in World War II and the restrictions the military government imposed on freedom of religion. As a consequence, he was jailed, abused and died in prison at seventy-three.

Tsunesaburo Makiguchi was born in 1871 in a small village on the Sea of Japan in Niigata Prefecture. The name of the village was Arahama, which might be translated as "beach of rough seas." June 6, the day after tomorrow, will mark the one hundred twenty-fifth anniversary of his birth.

Mr. Makiguchi proudly referred to his humble origins, his birth in an impoverished fishing village. The poverty of his family and the need to support them forced him to give up further study after elementary school. Nevertheless, he utilized every opportunity for reading and learning and showed great talent for teaching. Because of his scholarly disposition, a small sum of money was contributed by those with whom he worked so that he could go to a teachers' college, from which he graduated at age twenty-two.

Mr. Makiguchi poured his youthful energy and passion into the task of expanding educational opportunity for his underprivileged students. Many who were taught by Mr. Makiguchi have left grateful descriptions of his efforts as a teacher.

It was during Mr. Makiguchi's days as a young teacher that

Japan began pursuing a national policy expressed by the slogan "national wealth and military strength" — the path of imperial expansion. In the field of education, highest priority was likewise accorded to national aims, and all efforts were made to instill a blind, unquestioning patriotism.

Tsunesaburo Makiguchi, by contrast, expressed this view: "What then is the purpose of national education? Rather than devise complex theoretical interpretations, it is better to start by looking to the lovely child who sits on your knee and ask yourself: What can I do to assure that this child will be able to lead the happiest life possible?"[3]

Mr. Makiguchi's focus of interest was never the state, but always people, individual human beings. This reflects his strong sense of human rights, which inspired him to declare, in an era when the priorities of state sovereignty were being forcefully emphasized, that "the freedom and rights of the individual are sacred and inviolable."[4]

In 1903, at age thirty-two, Tsunesaburo Makiguchi published his thousand-page work, *The Geography of Human Life*. This publication came on the eve of the Russo-Japanese war. The tenor of the times is symbolized by the fact that seven of Japan's most famous scholars from Tokyo Imperial University petitioned the government to take a hard-line stance against Russia, heightening public enthusiasm for war. In contrast, Mr. Makiguchi, an unknown school teacher, was promoting an awareness as global citizens who, while rooted in the local community, avoid the pitfalls of narrow-minded nationalism.

At forty-two, Mr. Makiguchi was appointed principal of an elementary school in Tokyo. For the next twenty years, he served in this capacity, developing some of Tokyo's most outstanding public schools.

One important influence on Mr. Makiguchi's thinking was the American philosopher John Dewey, whose philosophy he sought to use to create change in the Japanese educational system. An outspoken advocate of educational reform, Mr. Makiguchi found himself under the constant scrutiny and pressure of the authorities. Among his controversial proposals was a call for the abolition of the system of official inspection through which representatives of the central bureaucracy could directly interfere in the running of local schools.

He also refused to give in to the prevailing custom of granting special treatment to the children of influential families. This eventually resulted in the involvement of a leading national politician, who lobbied for Mr. Makiguchi's ouster. Students, teachers and parents all rallied to Mr. Makiguchi's defense and sought to have the transfer order stayed, even staging a boycott of classes. At the school to which Mr. Makiguchi was transferred, he met with similar harassment. This time, before he was transferred, he demanded as a condition that the educational authorities renovate a playground.

Mr. Makiguchi's endeavors bring to mind the great love of humanity demonstrated by his contemporary, the extraordinary Jewish Polish educator Janusz Korczak, who fought to the very end to protect the lives of his students, dying together with them in the Holocaust.

In 1928, Tsunesaburo Makiguchi encountered Buddhism. Buddhism, in that it recognizes and seeks to develop the wisdom inherent in all human beings, can be considered a philosophy of popular education. Mr. Makiguchi felt that in Buddhism he had found the means by which to realize the ideals he had pursued throughout his life — a movement for social reform through education. Mr. Makiguchi was already fifty-seven when he embraced Buddhism — an event that commences the dramatic final developments of his life.

Two years later, on November 18, 1930, together with his disciple and fellow teacher, Josei Toda, Mr. Makiguchi published the first volume of *The System of Value-Creating Pedagogy*, and it is from this day that we date the establishment of our organization.

Soka is Japanese for "value creation." From Mr. Makiguchi's viewpoint, the most fundamental and central value is that of life itself. Taking into account John Dewey's pragmatism, Mr. Makiguchi stated that "the only value in the true sense is that of life itself.

All other values arise solely within the context of interaction with life."[5] The fundamental criterion for value, in Mr. Makiguchi's view, is whether something adds to or detracts from, advances or hinders, the human condition.

The ultimate goal of Soka, or value-creating, education is to foster people of character who continuously strive for the "greatest good" of peace, who are committed to protecting the sanctity of life and who are capable of creating value under even the most difficult circumstances.

In 1939, what was in effect the first general meeting of the Soka Kyoiku Gakkai (Value-Creating Education Society) was held. Needless to say, this was the year in which World War II began with the Nazi invasion of Poland. Japan's armies were also on the move, committing horrible barbarities in China and Korea.

Deeply disturbed by these developments, Mr. Makiguchi launched a frontal critique of militarist fascism. At the time, most religions and religious organizations in Japan lent their support to State Shinto, which provided the philosophical and spiritual underpinnings for the prosecution of the war. Mr. Makiguchi, however, opposed this trampling underfoot of the freedoms of conscience and belief, refusing to permit his religious convictions to deviate from their orientation toward peace.

He was also outraged by the attempt to impose on the peoples of Asia belief in Japanese Shinto, writing "The arrogance of the Japanese people knows no bounds."[6] His stern and uncompromising attitude in this regard stemmed from a profound spirit of tolerance toward the cultural and religious heritage of other peoples.

In December 1941, Japan's forces made a surprise attack on Pearl Harbor, thus initiating the war in the Pacific. Five months later, the periodical of the Soka Kyoiku Gakkai, *Kachi Sozo* (Value Creation), was forced to cease publication at the order of the domestic security authorities.

Having deprived the Japanese people of their freedoms of conscience and religion, it was a simple task for the fascist military powers to suppress freedom of speech. By depriving people of their fundamental freedoms, the military authorities sought to create an obedient, sheeplike mass. Mr. Makiguchi expressed his firm conviction that "a single lion will triumph over a thousand sheep. A single person of courage can achieve greater things than a thousand cowards."[7] Mr. Makiguchi's stance squarely confronting all forms of evil and injustice made his ideas a potent threat to the powers that be. He was considered a thought criminal, and his activities were subject to constant surveillance by the secret police.

Nevertheless, Mr. Makiguchi continued to organize small discussion meetings where he openly expressed his religious and moral convictions. According to his written indictment, he attended over the course of two wartime years more than two hundred forty such meetings. In the presence of the police during these meetings, Mr. Makiguchi continued to criticize military fascism. Often his speech would be cut short by the police.

Where even the priests who professed to share his Buddhist faith capitulated to government pressure to pray to the Shinto talisman, Mr. Makiguchi refused to the very last. In July 1943, Mr. Makiguchi and Mr. Toda were arrested by militarist Japan's equivalent of the Gestapo. They were charged with violations of the notorious Peace Preservation Act[8] and with lèse-majesté, disrespect for the emperor. Mr. Makiguchi was already seventy-two and spent the next year and four months, a total of five hundred days, in solitary confinement.

Mr. Makiguchi, however, never retreated a step. It is said that he used to call out from his solitary cell, asking the other prisoners if they were bored, offering to engage them in debate about such questions as whether there is any difference between not doing good and actually committing wrong.[9] He was an unrestrained master of humanistic education who always sought equal and unqualified dialogue with others.

He even explained, patiently and clearly, the principles of Buddhism to his guards and interrogators. The official deposition records his view that a way of life in which people are "so sensitive to the praise or censure of society that, while not doing evil, they fail to do good" runs, in the final analysis, counter to the teachings of Buddhism.[10]

There is a famous Buddhist aphorism that if you light a lamp for another, your own path will be brightened.[11] Indeed, Mr. Makiguchi was to the very end an example of a life of positive contribution, bringing forth the brilliant light of hope for himself and for others.

Elsewhere in the record of his interrogations, we find him declaring Japan's invasion of China and the "Great East Asian War" a "national catastrophe" brought on by the fundamental spiritual misorientation of the Japanese nation. At a time when Japan's invasions were described as a "sacred war," and the press and opinion-makers were vying to glorify this undertaking, Mr. Makiguchi's words reflect a singular courage and determination.

His prison letters to his family have survived, and in them we find such passages as these:

> For the present, aged as I am, this is where I will cultivate my mind.
> I can read books, which is a pleasure. I want for nothing. Please watch over the home in my absence and don't concern yourselves about me.
> Being in solitary confinement, I can ponder things in peace, which I prefer.[12]

His letters are filled with concern and consideration for his family; in them one senses composure, even optimism. "Even hell has its enjoyments, depending on one's outlook," he wrote in a passage scratched out by the prison censors.

The hell of the four walls of his stifling solitary cell, its heat and cold, took a steady toll on Mr. Makiguchi's aged frame. But he was never despondent; in his heart, the brilliant sun of his beliefs rose and remained high. Burning with righteous anger, Mr. Makiguchi continued his struggle against the forces of a state authority that refused to respect human rights. His anger, however, was never tainted with hatred.

Eventually, age and malnutrition brought the inevitable physical decline, and Mr. Makiguchi finally agreed to be transferred to the infirmary. Donning his formal clothes, he straightened his hair and walked there unaided, with frail yet determined stride. The following day, on November 18, 1944, the anniversary of the founding of the Soka Gakkai, Tsunesaburo Makiguchi died peacefully.

Even the terror of death was unable to force Mr. Makiguchi into submission.

For human beings, nothing is perhaps more universally dreaded than the prospect of one's own demise. It could even be said that fear of death forms the basis for instinctual aggression. Yet Buddhism speaks of the indivisible unity of life and death, asserting that these are both integral aspects of an eternal continuum. For one who lives with just and unwavering conviction and has a penetrating understanding of the essential nature of life and death, both life and death can be experienced as joys.

In the frigid confines of prison, Mr. Makiguchi proved the truth that by living with utter dedication to humane and noble ideals, it is possible to greet death without a trace of fear, regret or loathing. Unknown to anyone, he brought to completion the life he had made great by his actions and his spirit.

His quiet passing was at the same time a new start, a new departure.

Josei Toda spoke of the unbearable grief and outrage that seized him when, two months later, one of the judges bluntly informed him, "Mr. Makiguchi's dead." He spoke of moaning in solitude, of crying until his tears ran dry.

But from the depths of this despair, a new hope was born. Mr. Toda the disciple emerged alive from the prison where his mentor had died. Anger at the authoritarian forces that had robbed his mentor of life was transformed into a pledge and determination to create a new popular movement for peace.

In *The System of Value-Creating Pedagogy*, Mr. Makiguchi wrote: "Driven by their instinct for self-preservation, evil-minded people band together, increasing the force with which they persecute the good. In contrast, people of goodwill always seem to be isolated and weak.... There is no alternative but for people of goodwill to unite."[13] This was his penetrating insight based on personal experience.

As a disciple sharing profound unity of purpose with his mentor, Josei Toda began, amid the postwar devastation, to construct a movement based on the solidarity of ordinary citizens of goodwill. Again, his methodology was grassroots — one-on-one dialogue and small-scale discussion meetings.

Grounded on the principle of the sanctity of life as expounded in Buddhism, this is a movement that seeks to empower people, to awaken their inner wisdom, thus creating a world in which justice and humane values are accorded universal respect.

In his theory of value, Mr. Makiguchi states that the existence of religion is justified by the degree to which it relieves suffering and brings happiness to individuals — the value of gain — and to societies — the value of goodness. In his unalloyed humanism, he asserted that people do not exist to serve religion; religion exists to serve people.

This past April, a cherry tree was planted on the Tokyo campus of Soka University, an institution that takes as its founding spirit the philosophy of President Makiguchi. Seeking to eternalize the memory of the late Prime Minister Yitzhak Rabin, who consecrated his life to the realization of Middle East peace, this tree was planted in a ceremony attended by Vice President Moshe Arad of the Hebrew University of Jerusalem, which recently concluded agreements for academic and student exchanges with Soka University.

Prime Minister Rabin left us these unforgettable words: "There is no greater victory than peace. In war there are the victors and the vanquished. But in peace, everyone is a victor."[14]

I am profoundly confident that as each spring brings new and fuller bloom to the Rabin Cherry Tree, we will see emerge new generations committed to the same vision of peace that was his pursuit. Truly, education represents the light of hope and new life.

Tsunesaburo Makiguchi's life was an all-out struggle against fascist authority, never retreating a single step. His message of courage and wisdom will continue to echo and resound, awakening people's conscience in the coming centuries. He realized that, no matter how noble the principle or belief, it can only be realized through a concerted grassroots effort. It is in this spirit that the SGI Charter[15] calls for dialogue and cooperation among people of different faiths toward the resolution of the fundamental issues facing humankind. This spirit of the first president, Tsunesaburo Makiguchi, lives on within the Soka Gakkai and takes concrete form in the activities of the SGI. We will always remain firm and unbending before any form of authoritarianism and in this way will carry on Mr. Makiguchi's beliefs and convictions far into the future. It is our determination to continue to develop and expand a people's movement of peace, education and culture into the coming millennia, in accordance with the vision of Nichiren, the founder of the school of Buddhism we practice.

For my own part, I am determined, for as long as I live, to act with courage toward the realization of an era of peace in the twenty-first century, for the peace that will signal victory for all. And I trust that I will have the pleasure and privilege of sharing that journey with our distinguished friends and colleagues gathered here today.

In closing, I dedicate today's talk to President Makiguchi, and to all those who have given their lives for justice and humane values, and to the youth of our world who live each day with a profound determination toward the future.

> *It is my belief —*
> *that a person, a people,*
> *who embrace a noble philosophy,*
> *people upholding sublime faith —*
> *that only a person, a people,*
> *who, amidst raging storms,*
> *live out the drama*
> *of reality and grand ideals,*
> *subjected to and enduring*
> *limitless persecution —*

that only such a person,
only such a people,
will be bathed in the sunlight
of perpetual joy, glory and victory.

Thank you very much.

Notes

1. Statement by Simon Wiesenthal as an Austrian delegate to the United Nations General Assembly, Fiftieth Session, November 20, 1995.
2. *Collected Works of Tsunesaburo Makiguchi* (in Japanese) (Tokyo: Daisan Bummeisha, 1988, 1983), vol. 9, p. 97; vol. 6, pp. 71, 180.
3. *Collected Works of Tsunesaburo Makiguchi* (1981), vol. 4, p. 27.
4. Tsunesaburo Makiguchi, *The Geography of Human Life* (in Japanese) (Tokyo: Seikyo Shimbunsha, 1980), vol. 5, p. 16.
5. *Collected Works of Tsunesaburo Makiguchi* (1982), vol. 5, p. 232.
6. *Collected Works of Tsunesaburo Makiguchi* (1987), vol. 10, p. 84.
7. *An Anthology of Tsunesaburo Makiguchi's Works* (in Japanese), ed. Takehisa Tsuji (Tokyo: Daisan Bummeisha, 1994), pp. 26–27.
8. The Peace Preservation Act of 1925 was one of the prime legal tools used to suppress all forms of dissident expression. The Religious Organizations Act of 1940 consolidated all religious organizations in Japan under Shinto leadership.
9. *Collected Works of Josei Toda* (in Japanese) (Tokyo: Seikyo Shimbunsha, 1988), vol. 8, p. 463.
10. *Collected Works of Tsunesaburo Makiguchi*, vol. 10, pp. 209–10.
11. "The Three Virtues of Food," *Complete Works of Nichiren Daishonin* (in Japanese), ed. Nichiko Hori (Tokyo: Soka Gakkai, 1952), p. 1598.
12. *Collected Works of Tsunesaburo Makiguchi*, vol. 10, pp. 276–78, 85.
13. *Collected Works of Tsunesaburo Makiguchi*, vol. 6, p. 69.
14. Yitzhak Rabin, preface to *The Rabin Memoirs* (in Japanese), ed. Tetsuo Sagara, trans. Junko Takeda (Tokyo: Mirutosu, 1996), p. 19.
15. The SGI Charter has been reprinted in the SGI Quarterly magazine, January 1996.

Related Reading

Korczak, Janusz. *King Matt the First.* Translated by Richard Lourie. New York: The Noonday Press, 1988. The Introduction, by Bruno Bettelheim, profiles Korczak's lifelong endeavors on behalf of children. The story of King Matt parallels Korczak's own life.

Bethel, Dayle M., ed. *Education for Creative Living: Ideas and Proposals of Tsunesaburo Makiguchi.* Translated by Alfred Birnbaum. Ames: Iowa State University Press, 1989.

Allam, Cheryl Marie. "The Path to Surrender: Nichiren Buddhism and Roman Catholicism Confront Japanese Nationalism, 1912-1945." Master's thesis, University of Hawaii, 1988.

SGI President Ikeda Holds
Question-and-Answer Session

—⚊—

SIMON WIESENTHAL CENTER, LOS ANGELES,
JUNE 4, 1996

IMMEDIATELY FOLLOWING his lecture titled "Makiguchi's Lifelong Pursuit of Justice and Humane Values" at the Simon Wiesenthal Center, SGI President Ikeda answered questions from members of the audience.

The first question fielded was "Why did Soka University, among the many universities and other institutions in Japan, decide to cosponsor 'The Courage to Remember—Anne Frank and the Holocaust' exhibition?"

President Ikeda, the university's founder, began by explaining that part of the reason for establishing Soka University (in 1971) was the desire to find a way out of the educational deadlock in which Japan found itself in the late 1960s and early 1970s—a situation thrown into sharp relief by the often violent student demonstrations that took place at that time. Embracing the motto "Be the fortress of peace for humankind," Soka University has maintained a strong antiwar stance and an unwavering commitment to peace and human rights since its founding. The decision to cosponsor the Holocaust exhibition, he said, derives from this pledge. The SGI leader voiced his determination to keep making efforts to transform the fundamental karma of humankind so that such a tragedy would never be repeated.

The second question sought President Ikeda's opinion on the similarities between Judaism and Buddhism.

The SGI leader said he believes that the two religions have many points in common. He cited, for example, their shared desire for peace and human happiness, their respect for education and the family, their commitment to empowering people through knowledge and their humanistic spirit.

Noting that both Judaism and Buddhism aspire for peace and have a history of religious persecution by the powers that be, Mr. Ikeda remarked that a great conviction in faith is a powerful driving force for great contributions to the realization of global peace.

As he had mentioned in his speech, Mr. Ikeda said, his mentor, second Soka Gakkai president Josei Toda, had intuitively grasped the common ground between the two religions and urged Soka Gakkai members of his day to learn from the experiences of the Jewish people.

The third question was posed by an educator involved in high school education: "How should we teach tolerance at the primary, secondary and tertiary levels?"

President Ikeda referred to the serious problem of schoolyard bullying in Japan, at which root lies intolerance. The need for tolerance, he observed, has become a pressing issue around the world. Teaching tolerance requires a multipronged approach. In the actual classroom situation, he stressed that the key is, first and foremost, the growth and development of the teachers themselves. If teaching professionals do not put their heart into their job and just regard it as something to be done with as little effort as possible, this will be communicated to the students who are very much aware of their teachers' attitudes. Mr. Ikeda emphasized that teaching is a sacred vocation and suggested that the best way for teachers to teach tolerance to their students is through their own sense of responsibility and compassion, their concern for the students' welfare and their committed efforts to help them grow.

Mr. Ikeda noted that another important factor in nurturing tolerance is having contact with different cultures. For this reason, he said, he wishes to promote even greater exchange between the Soka Schools in Japan and academic institutions in America. He also mentioned plans for the establishment of a new campus of Soka University of America in Aliso Viejo, California. It was his desire, the SGI leader said, to energetically pursue the sacred undertaking of education and thereby contribute in some meaningful way to American society.

Anchoring Our Faith Firmly in Our Daily Lives

———✺———

EXECUTIVE CONFERENCE,
LOS ANGELES, CALIFORNIA, JUNE 5, 1996

WE ARE ALL A FAMILY, a fine family of the people, bound together by deep karmic ties through past, present and future. Let us all live wonderful lives together!

Please allow me to congratulate all of you on this conference. Los Angeles has been the power source of kosen-rufu in the United States and an important cornerstone in our worldwide movement. Los Angeles's victories have also been the SGI's victories.

Tomorrow, June 6, is the one hundred twenty-fifth anniversary of the birth of the first Soka Gakkai president, Tsunesaburo Makiguchi. I would like to celebrate and pay fitting tribute to this momentous event with you, my precious friends, here in my beloved Los Angeles.

THE KISHINEV MASSACRE

Yesterday, I spoke about Mr. Makiguchi at the Simon Wiesenthal Center. To commemorate my address, Soka alumni living in America — graduates of the Soka Schools and heirs to Mr. Makiguchi's legacy — presented me with a handwritten manuscript by the great Russian writer Leo Tolstoy, whom I so admire. It is a draft of a letter he wrote to Czar Nicholas II, protesting the 1903

Kishinev pogrom,[1] the massacre of Jews by Russians in the city of Kishinev.

In 1903 also, as I mentioned in my address, Mr. Makiguchi published *The Geography of Human Life*. In this work, he called out for the people to develop an awareness as global citizens and stressed the importance of human rights and morality, peace and coexistence.

Going back to the Kishinev pogrom, some fifty people were killed and more than five hundred injured in riots perpetrated against the city's Jewish residents by anti-Semitic forces. This is an indescribably tragic chapter in the history of the Jewish people.

Why did this violence occur? One reason is that the civil and religious authorities fanned the flames of hatred and resentment against the Jews. False reports vilifying the Jews were published in newspapers, rumors were spread, and the Russian people were encouraged to commit acts of violence against them — all of which led to the ultimate atrocity, the massacre.

Mr. Tolstoy was enraged by what happened. In another letter, he declared that he loved the Jews as his brothers and had met many excellent Jewish people. He expressed deep sadness at the fate of innocent people who became targets of the barbaric mob, and he had the strongest condemnation for the so-called educated people who had stirred up the violence.[2]

The Russian author declared that the entire responsibility for the tragedy lay at the feet of the government and the clergy, who worked so hard to keep the masses in a state of ignorance and fanaticism.

Mr. Tolstoy wrote with great force, saying of the Jews: "They should fight the Government not by violence — that weapon should be left to the Government — but by virtuous living to the exclusion not only of all violence towards their neighbors but of all participation in violence."[3]

In his compassion for humanity, his anger at the authorities and his trust of the people, Mr. Tolstoy was identical to Mr. Makiguchi.

I am very pleased at the spirit with which the Soka alumni presented me the manuscript of Mr. Tolstoy's letter of protest— out of their respect for Mr. Makiguchi's message and a feeling of deep solidarity with the Jewish people.

I am also gratified to see the Soka alumni's wonderful growth and development. To raise and nurture people younger in faith or experience so that they can surpass even your own achievements — that is the prayer of a senior in faith, the most heartfelt desire of a mentor.

The Meaning of Benefit

The SGI-USA has struggled against the tyranny of the priesthood. The benefit you have achieved as a result is immeasurable.

Nichiren Daishonin discusses the meaning of the Chinese characters for the word *benefit* (Jpn *kudoku*), as follows: "The element *ku* in the word *kudoku* means good fortune or happiness. It also refers to the merit achieved by wiping out evil, while the element *toku* or *doku* refers to the virtue one acquires by bringing about good" (OTT, 148).

We fight against those who try to destroy the correct teaching. That struggle purifies us and brings forth benefits in our lives. Justice or happiness without a battle is just an illusion. Thinking that happiness means a life free of hard work and effort is a fantasy.

Only by struggling against the extremes of evil can we live a life of extreme good. That effort will help us create lives that can transcend any obstacle or difficulty with ease and dignity. I hope that all of you, my dear friends in America, will lead lives as champions of justice and happiness.

True Happiness Is Not Built on the Misfortune of Others

Dr. Johan Galtung, the founder of peace studies and a dear friend of my wife and mine, is giving a series of special lectures at Soka

University. On May 18, Dr. Galtung and his wife, Fumiko, both gave a talk to students at the Kansai Soka Junior and Senior High Schools, after which they opened the floor for a friendly discussion with the students and teachers. I'll share with you some of the remarks Dr. Galtung made.

He said he feels a deep accord with the Soka Schools' underlying tenet that true happiness is not built on the misfortune of others. He noted that it is a universal principle that has implications in all spheres of human endeavor. For instance, in the realm of economics, it means that we should not grow rich on the poverty of others, and in the realm of government, that it is wrong to seize the reins of power by force and hold dictatorial authority.

He also said that while teachers are doing their best to educate children, it is important that they step back from time to time and ask themselves whether what they are doing is really for each child's good. I would add that the same applies to leaders as well.

There were two students, a boy and a girl, who each asked a question during the discussion, and Dr. Galtung expressed his wish to keep informed on their progress, saying he would like to meet them again in ten years. All in all, Dr. Galtung was delighted to have the opportunity to meet the students and talk with them. Both he and his wife treasure each encounter with others. I sense their profound integrity and fine character in this trait.

As a committed proponent of peace studies, Dr. Galtung says that he wishes to raise peace workers for the future. These, he stresses, are not political leaders or administrators; they are, as we say in Buddhism, people with empathy, people who understand and feel the sufferings of others as their own. Since war and violence destroy human culture and human hearts, it is vital that we educate people who can heal that damage.

Dr. Galtung has high praise for the SGI as a grassroots movement that shares those same goals. Let us advance with bright hope for the future, spreading peace and friendship — valuing old friends and making new ones — all around the world.

WOMEN'S STRENGTH POWERS SOCIETY'S PROGRESS

June 10 is Women's Division Day in Japan. I'd like to say a few words to commemorate this event.

In our dialogue *Choose Peace*, Dr. Galtung and I concurred that women, in general, have a natural tendency toward pacifism. In the course of that discussion, we also touched upon Henrik Ibsen, who wrote the play *A Doll's House* and was one of the first to take up the theme of greater freedom for women.

Ibsen is Norwegian, like Dr. Galtung. *A Doll's House* was among the many works of world literature that members of the youth division studied under President Toda.

Even now I fondly remember Mr. Toda declaring that it wasn't enough for men just to be strong. Instead of strutting around arrogantly, he said, they would be better advised to spend their time occasionally reading fine works such as Ibsen's famous play.

About a hundred years ago, Ibsen and his wife were invited to attend a banquet of the Norwegian League for Women's Rights. In his speech on that occasion, Ibsen said: "The task always before my mind has been to advance our country and to give our people a higher standard. To achieve this, two factors are important."[4]

What were these two factors? Culture and discipline — in other words, cultivating character and making diligent efforts to firmly acquire something of meaning and lasting value.

Further, Ibsen stated his belief that women make the most ceaseless efforts to guide others toward developing culture and discipline. He ends his speech by declaring: "It is the women who shall solve the human problem.... My thanks! And success to the League for Women's Rights!"[5]

I praise our women's division members in the same spirit, for it is truly you who are working to "solve the human problem." Because of your presence, the happiness and progress of women everywhere are made possible. Only when women enjoy happiness and progress is it possible for men to enjoy the same. Moreover, I declare, with great respect and admiration for each of you, that your very existence ensures the joy and advancement of all humankind.

STEADY COMMITMENT TO "FAITH EQUALS DAILY LIFE"

Prayer is the foundation. But at the same time, if we fail to make concrete efforts, no matter how much daimoku we chant, our prayers will not be answered. Buddhism is reason. If we just chant without doing any work, we cannot succeed in our jobs; if students do not study, it will be reflected in their grades.

We must make steady and persistent efforts firmly grounded in daily life. If we travel in the orbit of faith equals daily life, all our prayers will definitely be answered. We can then lead lives in which all our desires will be fulfilled.

Should all our prayers be answered without our having to make any effort, we would grow lazy. Should all our desires be achieved without our ever having to experience suffering or hardship, we could not understand the pain and struggles of others, and our compassion would gradually wane.

The real benefit of the Mystic Law is inconspicuous. Just as trees grow taller and stronger year after year, adding growth rings that are imperceptible to the human eye, we, too, will grow toward a victorious existence. For this reason, it is important that we lead tenacious and balanced lives based on faith.

THE IMPORTANCE OF LEADERS

The role of leaders is important. Everything is determined by the leaders' behavior. A passage in the famous Chinese novel *The Romance of the Three Kingdoms* explains that only those who possess genuine wisdom and virtue win the highest regard from people. It all comes down to you. You have to polish and develop yourselves. Should there be a leader or leaders in faith whom you do not like, all you have to do is determine not to become like them. All you have to do is decide that you will become leaders who will make everyone feel comfortable and at ease.

My dear friends of Los Angeles, let's advance with a cheerfulness, unity and joy unsurpassed anywhere in the world! Filled with eternal hope, let's build a magnificent SGI-USA!

Notes

1. Pogrom: organized persecution or massacre, often officially prompted, of a minority group, especially of Jews (as in czarist Russia). (ref. *Webster's New World Dictionary*, New York: Prentice Hall, 1991), p. 1042.
2. See Michael Davitt, *Within the Pale: The True Story of Anti-Semitic Persecutions in Russia* (New York: Arno Press, 1975), pp. 268–72.
3. *Within the Pale*, p. 272.
4. *Ibsen: Letters and Speeches*, ed. Evert Sprinchorn (Massachusetts: MacGibbon and Kee, 1964), p. 337.
5. *Ibsen: Letters and Speeches*, p. 338.

Advancing With Optimism and Joy

—❧—

ROCKY MOUNTAIN JOINT TERRITORY CHERRY BLOSSOM
GENERAL MEETING, DENVER CULTURE CENTER,
DENVER, COLORADO, JUNE 9, 1996

THANK YOU ALL for traveling such long distances to attend this meeting. I am truly delighted to have the chance to meet all of you at last.

I think you must be very tired after your long journeys. Today let's have a relaxed general meeting where everyone can get refreshed. All your efforts in traveling will turn into benefit. In the world of faith, absolutely no effort is wasted; there is no sacrifice. This is the profound working of the Mystic Law.

In the Gosho, Nichiren Daishonin teaches the benefit of traveling a long way to seek Buddhism, writing, "The great distances these persons traveled are indicative of their devotion" (WND-2, 1030).

Here are three *waka* I composed to commemorate this day:

> *At long last*
> *Visiting Denver,*
> *A city aflame*
> *With pioneering spirit,*
> *I clasp the hands of friends.*
> • • •

Denver today
Is a bright land
Embodying the history
Of kosen-rufu in America
And the world.

. . .

Nichiren Daishonin,
With smiling countenance,
Protects and praises
My radiant friends
In Denver.

Also, I propose the following five-point motto for the Rocky Mountain Joint Territory:

1. Everyone in harmony.

2. Everyone cheerful.

3. Everyone safe from mishap.

4. Everyone healthy.

5. Everyone happy.

"WONDROUS GIFTS" OF THE "GOLDEN WEST"

Denver is a wonderful city. The streets are broad, and the air is clean and fragrant — like your pure hearts. Gazing at the Rocky Mountains in the distance, I am struck by the vivid contrast between the white snow-covered peaks and the bright green slopes.

Denver, situated at the western edge of the Great Plains, is known as the "Queen City of the Plains." The American poet Laura DuVall beautifully sings of Denver:

There's education, culture rare,
In schools the very best;
Oh, come the wondrous gifts to share,
Of this far Golden West!

Once here in Denver, you will stay
For Colorado's air;
To bring you wealth along your way
And health beyond compare.

"Queen City of the Plains," proclaim:
For all delight to dwell
In Denver of illustrious fame —
Beneath her magic spell![1]

All of you practicing in this wonderful region of wide open spaces are most fortunate. I am overjoyed to meet you, who are working so energetically alongside Joint Territory Leader Brian Matsuo and Women's Division Leader Rita Risom.

I also have fond memories of my many friends from Denver. These include the late Alton Eastman and Ted Osaki, who made tremendous efforts to lay the foundation for our movement here, as well as Eileen Eastman, who currently lives in Dallas, and Alvah Allison, who is now at the SGI-USA Headquarters in Los Angeles.

Your joint territory leader, Mr. Matsuo, is fifty-two and a graduate of Hiroshima University. He has worked diligently over the years. Mr. Matsuo was previously in Los Angeles and Arizona, and he came to Denver eight years ago. He has a fine personality and is well respected. He is committed to dedicating the rest of his life to working for kosen-rufu here with all of you. I ask that you continue to support Mr. Matsuo as joint territory leader and to advance in harmonious unity.

To Lead Victorious Lives Is the Purpose of Buddhism

Prayers based on the Mystic Law will definitely be answered. The twenty-sixth high priest, Nichikan, writes: "If you take faith in this Gohonzon and chant Nam-myoho-renge-kyo even for a short while, no prayer will go unanswered, no offense unexpiated, no good fortune unbestowed and no righteousness unproven."[2]

"No prayer will go unanswered." We practice this Buddhism

to make our prayers and dreams come true and to achieve the greatest possible happiness. The purpose of Nichiren Daishonin's Buddhism is to enable us to realize victory. The fact that our prayers are answered proves the correctness of this teaching.

When we plant the seed of happiness that is faith and carefully tend its growth, it will produce fruit without fail. We have to bear in mind, however, that we cannot plant a seed today and expect it to bear fruit tomorrow. That's not reasonable, and Buddhism is reason. If we persevere in the practice of faith equals daily life in accord with reason, then our prayers will definitely be answered. This is Nichiren Daishonin's promise to us, and his words are true beyond any doubt.

"No offense unexpiated." Any offense or slander will be cleansed from our lives through the power of the Mystic Law. It will disappear and turn into benefit.

"No good fortune unbestowed." Good fortune will be attracted to our lives in ever-increasing abundance, and in time we will definitely enter the path of life in which all wishes are fulfilled.

"No righteousness unproven." All correct reason and principles will be clearly manifested and verified in our lives. We will definitely see actual proof and become experts of human existence and masters of daily life.

I would like each of you to show glowing proof of these four points in your own lives.

THE POWER OF DAIMOKU

"Nam-myoho-renge-kyo is like the roar of a lion" (WND-I, 412), the Daishonin says. It is by chanting powerful daimoku, like a lion's roar, that we can move the Buddhist deities, the protective forces of the universe.

The voice is very important — it has profound power. If a wife is scolding her husband, for example, her words won't have any effect if she speaks in a weak voice. To get his attention, she has to shout, "Hey, you!" with a voice that reverberates throughout the house.

While naturally being careful not to disturb your neighbors, I hope you will try to chant cheerful and powerful daimoku that reaches all the Buddhist deities and Buddhas throughout the ten directions.

The purpose of life is to be happy. We should not be pessimistic. Let us always be optimistic — joyful, strong and bright. That is why we practice the Daishonin's Buddhism.

A CELEBRATION IN THE GREAT OUTDOORS

Yesterday, I was privileged to receive an honorary doctorate of education from the University of Denver, an institution of higher learning that abounds with a great pioneering spirit. No award is of more universal nature than one in education. This honor is shared by all of you who are great pioneers of *soka*, or value creation.

The presentation took place at the university's graduation ceremony, which was held outdoors in an informal yet dignified atmosphere. The sun shone brilliantly, and the moon was also faintly visible in the sky. The sun symbolizes passion; the moon, intellect. The Rocky Mountains evoked firm conviction; the wind, a respite from hard work; and the trees, the place of learning. The outdoor venue of the ceremony, meanwhile, was fittingly symbolic of young men and women poised to take their places on the forefront of society.

The academic gown and cap of the University of Denver that I wore are steeped in profound tradition. The gown symbolizes the egalitarian character of learning. When people don this gown, the clothes worn underneath and the differences in social status that they signify are covered up. This is symbolic of how, in the pursuit of learning, everyone is equal.

The significance of the cap goes back to Roman times. When slaves were liberated under Roman law, they gained the right to wear hats. Thus, the graduation cap symbolizes the responsibility and sanctity of learning, as well as intellectual freedom.

Regarding the significance of robes worn by priests, Nichikan says that they are "work clothes for carrying out Buddhist practice" and "active clothing for kosen-rufu." Somewhere along the way, however, they became symbols of authority indicating superiority over lay believers.

But the academic gown and cap of the university are not symbols of authority. On the contrary, they are permeated with a wonderful tradition bespeaking the ideals of democracy, freedom and equality.

Chancellor Daniel Ritchie of the University of Denver is a rare individual who refuses all remuneration for his work in education. When the SGI-USA's ecology exhibition was held at the University of Denver two years ago, Chancellor Ritchie attended the opening and delivered a warm speech of praise. At the graduation ceremony yesterday, he remarked: "We know that the best way to live a healthy, happy and satisfying life is to have a purpose in your life more important to you than yourself. Self-centeredness isn't healthy, and it isn't much fun....

"My charge and wish for each one of you is to find your passion, if you haven't already — and go for it!"

The chancellor's words no doubt made a deep impression in the hearts of the graduates. In the same spirit, I again express my praise for all of you who are devoting yourselves to lives of service.

Chancellor Ritchie and I had a warm, informal exchange following the graduation ceremony. He has said: "Students' lives are not changed by lectures but by people. That is why it is important to have a faculty that constantly interacts with students." This is the spirit of the University of Denver.

MENTOR IN LEARNING

Dr. Ritchie was himself fortunate to have had a good mentor during his youth. When he was studying at Harvard University, he knew a student who had come from Asia. Sympathetic to the human rights activities of that student, he threw himself into the human rights movement. Filled with passion for this cause, he stopped attending classes and almost had to drop out.

An advising professor who was worried about the young Ritchie's situation gave him guidance based on his wealth of experience, telling him, "Right now is the time for you to study!" In addition, every day the professor tutored him. As a result, he caught up in his studies.

That he did not drop out of school and instead went on to play an important role in society he attributes to the dedicated concern of that professor. Because of this powerful experience, Chancellor Ritchie is a strong believer in the need for young people to have mentors with broad life experiences. In his present dedication to education, he is motivated by the desire to repay his debt of gratitude to the mentors he has had. This is Chancellor Ritchie's conviction.

Human beings are raised by human beings. Only people can help other people become happy. I hope that all of you, as outstanding humanistic educators, will also raise many fine individuals.

Denver, famous for the Gold Rush, is now experiencing the start of a "gold rush" of capable people for kosen-rufu.

You are all children of Nichiren Daishonin. You are all children of the original Buddha. You are incomparably noble and worthy of respect. As long as I live, I will continue to pray for your happiness and victory, your health and longevity. The infinite sky above the Rocky Mountains is the symbol of your infinite hope.

I hope that you, my friends in the Rocky Mountains, will always be optimistic, and that you will be the happiest and most harmonious people in the world.

Please convey my warmest regards to all those whom I could not see today. Until we meet again, please remain healthy and in high spirits.

Notes

1. Laura S. DuVall, "Denver: 'Queen City of the Plains'" (1928), from *Colorado in Verse and Picture*, 1916–1928.
2. "Commentary on 'The True Object of Worship,'" *Fuji shugaku yoshu*, vol. 4, p. 213.

Leading a Sublime Life in Accord With the Gosho

—〰—

THANK YOU for all the efforts you have made and the long distances you have traveled to attend today's meeting. I am overjoyed to meet with all of you, who possess such beautiful hearts, here in the lovely city of Denver. May all of you live long, long lives. Please cherish hopes for the future and strive to realize all your dreams as you live each day with courage and tenacity.

The Gosho serves as the foundation of our Buddhist practice. With the desire that you advance brightly and harmoniously and with abundant good fortune, I will share some passages of Nichiren Daishonin's writings with you today.

In *The Record of the Orally Transmitted Teachings*, he talks of "the great joy that one experiences when one understands for the first time that one's mind from the very beginning has been the Buddha. Nam-myoho-renge-kyo is the greatest of all joys" (OTT, 211–12).

People who possess strong faith are fearless; they can overcome anything. There is no obstacle or adversity they cannot surmount. In the very depths of their lives, no matter what happens, they live with "the greatest of all joys."

RESPECT COMES FROM RESPECTING OTHERS

In another passage of *The Record of the Orally Transmitted Teachings*, the Daishonin observes, "When one faces a mirror and makes a bow of obeisance: the image in the mirror likewise makes a bow of obeisance to oneself" (OTT, 165). People who respect others are respected by others in turn. Those who are unstinting in their compassion and concern for others are also protected and supported by others. Our environment is essentially a reflection of ourselves.

In "On Attaining Buddhahood in This Lifetime," the Daishonin writes: "A mind now clouded by the illusions of the innate darkness of life is like a tarnished mirror, but when polished, it is sure to become like a clear mirror, reflecting the essential nature of phenomena and the true aspect of reality. Arouse deep faith, and diligently polish your mirror day and night. How should you polish it? Only by chanting Nam-myoho-renge-kyo" (WND-1, 4).

No one can match a person who earnestly chants daimoku. Those who chant abundant daimoku, dedicating their lives to kosen-rufu, are people who enjoy the greatest glory.

In "Letter to Akimoto," the Daishonin states, "If the mind of faith is perfect, then the water of wisdom, the great impartial wisdom, will never dry up" (WND-1, 1015). If you have faith, wisdom wells forth. Wisdom is proof of faith. As the expression *great impartial wisdom* indicates, impartiality and fairness are requirements of a Buddhist leader.

In "The Blessings of the Lotus Sutra," Nichiren Daishonin writes: "The more gold is heated in the flames, the brighter will be its color; the more a sword is whetted, the sharper it will become. And the more one praises the blessings of the Lotus Sutra, the more one's own blessings will increase" (WND-1, 673).

The heart matters most. A heart that praises the Mystic Law brings forth boundless benefit, and the heart that praises those who spread the Mystic Law elicits still greater benefit. I hope all the leaders in the SGI will have the spirit to praise others and put everyone at ease, creating a warm and pleasant atmosphere. Kosen-rufu expands where people feel a true sense of pleasure and enjoyment.

There is truly no more sublime way of life than living in accord with the golden words of Nichiren Daishonin.

COURAGE AT A CRUCIAL MOMENT

Nothing gives me greater pleasure than to be here creating a momentous page in history with you, my dear friends in Denver.

Margaret Tobin (Molly) Brown, a native of Denver, was on board the *Titanic* when it tragically sunk in 1912. Although she knew the ship was taking on water, she shouted to a panic-stricken fellow passenger: "There's no danger. It simply can't go down, because I'm on it and I'm unsinkable." Her bantering words, which rang out with the determination never to be defeated and never to give in to despair, are said to have given courage to her fellow passengers as she assisted them into the lifeboats.

Those who stand up at a crucial moment demonstrate genuine greatness. They are people who leave behind an immortal history. May each of you in the Rocky Mountain Joint Territory lead truly victorious existences. May your lives be as majestic as the soaring Rocky Mountains.

Please convey my very warmest regards to all the members whom I couldn't meet on this visit. I am praying with all my heart that you will enjoy even greater good health and happiness. Thank you for your warm hospitality.

Thoughts on Education
for Global Citizenship

—ᴍ—

LECTURE PRESENTED AT TEACHERS COLLEGE,
COLUMBIA UNIVERSITY, NEW YORK CITY,
NEW YORK, JUNE 13, 1996

JUST AS THE CURRENTS of the Hudson River move ceaselessly, with power and grandeur, Teachers College is producing an unbroken flow of youthful leaders who will create a magnificent new era in the coming century. It is an unparalleled honor to speak here today at the premier institute for graduate study in education in the United States, a monarch in the world of education, whose crown sends forth brilliant beams that light the future.

I offer my heartfelt gratitude to President Arthur Levine and all those whose support has made this event a reality. I would also like to thank in advance our distinguished commentators who will later be sharing with us their enlightening views.

In 1975, twenty-one years ago, it was my privilege to visit Columbia University. Four years earlier, in 1971, we had established Soka University in Tokyo. The warm encouragement and invaluable advice we received at that time for a university still in its infancy is something that I will never forget. Thank you very much.

It is with profound emotion that I speak today at the college where the world-renowned philosopher John Dewey taught. The first president of the Soka Gakkai, Tsunesaburo Makiguchi, whose thinking is the founding spirit of Soka University, referenced with great respect the writings and ideas of Dewey in his 1930 work *The System of Value-Creating Pedagogy*.

My own interest in and commitment to education stem from my experiences during World War II. My four elder brothers were drafted and sent to the front; the eldest was killed in action in Burma. During the two or so years following the end of the war, my three surviving brothers returned one after another from the Chinese mainland. In their tattered uniforms, they were a truly pathetic sight. My parents were already aged; my father's pain and my mother's sadness were searing.

To the end of my days, I will never forget the disgust and anger with which my eldest brother, on leave from China, described the inhuman atrocities he had seen committed there by the Japanese army. I developed a deep hatred for war, its cruelty, stupidity and waste. In 1947, I encountered a superb educator, Josei Toda. Mr. Toda, together with his mentor, Tsunesaburo Makiguchi, was jailed for opposing Japan's wars of invasion. Mr. Makiguchi died in jail. Mr. Toda survived the two-year ordeal of imprisonment.

When, at nineteen, I learned of this, I instinctively knew that here was someone whose actions merited my trust. I determined to follow Mr. Toda as my mentor in life.

It was President Toda's constant and impassioned plea that humanity could be liberated from horrific cycles of war only by fostering new generations of people imbued with a profound respect for the sanctity of life. He therefore gave the highest possible priority to the work of education.

Education is a uniquely human privilege. It is the source of inspiration that enables us to become fully and truly human, to fulfill a constructive mission in life with composure and confidence.

The end point in the development of knowledge isolated from human concerns is the weaponry of mass destruction. At the same time, it is knowledge also that has made society comfortable and convenient, bringing industry and wealth. The fundamental task of education must be to ensure that knowledge serves to further the cause of human happiness and peace.

Education must be the propelling force for an eternally unfolding humanitarian quest. It is for this reason that I consider education the final and most crucially important undertaking of my life. This is also the reason I deeply concur with the view expressed by President Levine that while education is perhaps the slowest means to social change, it is the only means.

Global society today faces a myriad of interlocking crises. These include the issues of war, environmental degradation, the North–South development gap and divisions among people based on differences of ethnicity, religion or language. The list is long and familiar, and the road to solutions may seem all too distant and daunting.

It is my view, however, that the root of all these problems is our collective failure to make the human being — human happiness — the consistent focus and goal in all fields of endeavor. The human being is the point to which we must return and from which we must depart anew. What is required is a human transformation — a human revolution.

There are many areas of commonality in the thinking of Tsunesaburo Makiguchi and John Dewey, and this is one of them. They shared an immovable conviction in the need for new modes of people-centered education. As Dewey put it, "Everything which is distinctly human is learned."[1]

John Dewey and Tsunesaburo Makiguchi were contemporaries. On opposite ends of the Earth, amid the problems and dislocations of their newly industrializing societies, both wrestled with the task of laying a path toward a hope-filled future.

Greatly influenced by the views of John Dewey, President Makiguchi asserted that the purpose of education must be the life-long happiness of learners. He further believed that true happiness is to be found in a life of value creation. Put simply, value creation is the capacity to find meaning, to enhance one's own existence and contribute to the well-being of others, under any circumstances. Mr. Makiguchi's philosophy of value creation grew from the insights on the inner workings of life his study of Buddhism afforded him.

Both John Dewey and Mr. Makiguchi looked beyond the limits of the nation-state to new horizons of human community. Both, it could be said, had a vision of global citizenship, of people capable of value creation on a global scale.

What then, are the conditions for global citizenship? Over the past several decades, I have been privileged to meet and converse with many people from all walks of life, and I have given the matter some thought. Certainly, global citizenship is not determined merely by the number of languages one speaks or the number of countries to which one has traveled. I have many friends who could be considered quite ordinary citizens but who possess an inner nobility; who have never traveled beyond their native place, yet who are genuinely concerned for the peace and prosperity of the world.

I think I can state with confidence that the following are essential elements of global citizenship:

○ The wisdom to perceive the interconnectedness of all life and living.

○ The courage not to fear or deny difference, but to respect and strive to understand people of different cultures and to grow from encounters with them.

○ The compassion to maintain an imaginative empathy that reaches beyond one's immediate surroundings and extends to those suffering in distant places.

The all-encompassing interrelatedness that forms the core of the Buddhist worldview can provide a basis, I feel, for the concrete realization of these qualities of wisdom, courage and compassion. The following scene from the Buddhist canon provides a beautiful visual metaphor for the interdependence and interpenetration of all phenomena.

Suspended above the palace of Indra, the Buddhist god who symbolizes the natural forces that protect and nurture life, is an enormous net. A brilliant jewel is attached to each of the knots of the net. Each jewel contains and reflects the image of all the other jewels in the net, which sparkles in the magnificence of its totality.

When we learn to recognize what Henry David Thoreau refers to as "the infinite extent of our relations,"[2] we can trace the strands of mutually supportive life and discover there the glittering jewels of our global neighbors. Buddhism seeks to cultivate wisdom grounded in this kind of empathetic resonance with all forms of life.

In the Buddhist view, wisdom and compassion are intimately linked and mutually reinforcing. Compassion in Buddhism does not involve the forcible suppression of our natural emotions, our likes and dislikes. Rather, it is the realization that even those whom we dislike have qualities that can contribute to our lives and can afford us opportunities to grow in our own humanity. Further, it is the compassionate desire to find ways of contributing to the well-being of others that gives rise to limitless wisdom.

Buddhism teaches that both good and evil are potentialities that exist in all people. Compassion consists in the sustained and courageous effort to seek out the good in all people, whoever they may be, however they may behave. It means striving, through sustained engagement, to cultivate the positive qualities in oneself and in others. Engagement, however, requires courage. There are all too many cases in which compassion, owing to a lack of courage, remains mere sentiment.

Buddhism calls a person who embodies these qualities of wisdom, courage and compassion, who strives without cease for the happiness of others, a bodhisattva. In this sense, it could be said that the bodhisattva provides an ancient precedent and modern exemplar of the global citizen.

The Buddhist canon includes the story of a contemporary of Shakyamuni, a woman by the name of Srimala, who dedicated herself to education, teaching others that the practice of the bodhisattva consists in encouraging, with maternal care, the ultimate potential for good within all people. Her vow is recorded thus: "If I see lonely people, people who have been jailed unjustly and have lost their freedom, people who are suffering from illness, disaster or poverty, I will not abandon them. I will bring them spiritual and material comfort."[3]

In concrete terms, her practice consisted of the following:

○ Encouraging others by addressing them with kindness and concern through dialogue (Skt *priyavacana*).

○ Giving alms, or providing people with the things they require (Skt *dana*).

○ Taking action on behalf of others (Skt *arthacarya*).

○ Joining with others and working together with them (Skt *samanartha*).

Through these efforts she sought to realize her goal of bringing forth the positive aspects of those she encountered.

The practice of the bodhisattva is supported by a profound faith in the inherent goodness of people. Knowledge must be directed to the task of unleashing this creative, positive potential. This purposefulness can be likened to the skill that enables one to make use of the precision instruments of an airplane to reach a destination safely and without incident.

For this reason, the insight to perceive the evil that causes destruction and divisiveness — and that is equally part of human nature — is also necessary. The bodhisattva's practice is an unshrinking confrontation with what Buddhism calls the fundamental darkness of life.[4]

"Goodness" can be defined as that which moves us in the direction of harmonious coexistence, empathy and solidarity with others. The nature of evil, on the other hand, is to divide: people from people, humanity from the rest of nature. The pathology of divisiveness drives people to an unreasoning attachment to difference and blinds them to human commonalities. This is not limited to individuals but constitutes the deep psychology of collective egoism, which takes its most destructive form in virulent strains of ethnocentrism and nationalism.

The struggle to rise above such egoism and live in larger and more contributive realms of selfhood constitutes the core of the bodhisattva's practice. Education is, or should be, based on the same altruistic spirit as the bodhisattva.

The proud mission of those who have received an education must be to serve, in seen and unseen ways, the lives of those who have not had this opportunity. At times, education may become a matter of titles and degrees and the status and authority these confer. I am convinced, however, that education should be a vehicle to develop in one's character the noble spirit to embrace and augment the lives of others.

Education should provide in this way the momentum to win over one's own weaknesses, to thrive in the midst of society's sometimes stringent realities, and to generate new victories for the human future.

The work of fostering global citizens, laying the conceptual and ethical foundations of global citizenship, concerns us all. It is a vital project in which we all are participants and for which we all share responsibility. To be meaningful, education for global citizenship should be undertaken as an integral part of daily life in our local communities.

Like John Dewey, Tsunesaburo Makiguchi focused on the local community as the place where global citizens are fostered. In his 1903 work *The Geography of Human Life,* which is considered a pioneering work in social ecology, Mr. Makiguchi stressed the importance of the community as the site of learning.

Elsewhere Mr. Makiguchi wrote: "The community, in short, is the world in miniature. If we encourage children to observe directly the complex relations between people and the land, between nature and society, they will grasp the realities of their homes, their school, the town, village or city, and will be able to understand the wider world."[5]

This is consonant with John Dewey's observation that those who have not had the kinds of experience that deepen understanding of neighborhood and neighbors will be unable to maintain regard for people of distant lands.[6]

Our daily lives are filled with opportunities to develop ourselves and those around us. Each of our interactions with others — dialogue, exchange and participation — is an invaluable chance to create value. We learn from people, and it is for this reason that the humanity of the teacher represents the core of the educational experience.

Mr. Makiguchi argued that humanistic education, education that guides the process of character formation, is a transcendent skill that might best be termed an art. His initial experience as a teacher was in a remote, rural region of Japan, where he taught in the Japanese equivalent of a one-room schoolhouse. The children were poor; the manners they brought from their impoverished homes, rough. Mr. Makiguchi, however, was insistent: "They are all equally students. From the viewpoint of education, what difference could there be between them and other students? Even though they may be covered with dust or dirt, the brilliant light of life shines from their soiled clothes. Why does no one try to see this? The teacher is all that stands between them and the cruel discrimination of society."[7]

The teacher is the most important element of the educational environment. This creed of Tsunesaburo Makiguchi's is the unchanging spirit of Soka education.

Elsewhere, he writes: "Teachers should come down from the throne where they are ensconced as the object of veneration to become public servants who offer guidance to those who seek to ascend to the throne of learning. They should not be masters who offer themselves as paragons but partners in the discovery of new models."[8]

It is my abiding conviction that it is the teacher dedicated to serving students, and not the inanimate facility, that makes a school.

I recently heard an educator offer this view: students' lives are not changed by lectures but by people. For this reason, interactions between students and teachers are of the greatest importance.

In my own case, most of my education was under the tutelage of my mentor in life, Josei Toda. For some ten years, every day before work, he taught me a curriculum of history, literature, philosophy, economics, science and organization theory. On Sundays, our one-on-one sessions started in the morning and continued all day. He was constantly questioning me — *interrogating* might be a better word — about my reading.

Most of all, however, I learned from his example. The burning commitment to peace that remained unshaken throughout his imprisonment was something he carried with him his entire life. It was from this, and from the profound compassion that characterized each of his interactions with people, that I most learned. Ninety-eight percent of what I am today, I learned from him.

The Soka, or value-creating, education system was founded out of a desire that future generations should have the opportunity to experience this same kind of humanistic education. It is my greatest hope that the graduates of the Soka Schools will become global citizens who can author a new history for humankind.

The actions of such citizens will not be effective unless coordinated, and in this regard we cannot ignore the important potential of the United Nations system.

We have reached the stage where the United Nations can serve as a center not only for "harmonizing the actions of nations"[9] but also for the creation of value through the education of global citizens who can create a world of peace. While states and national interests have dominated debate at the world organization to date, increasingly, the energy of "we the people..." has been making itself felt, particularly through the activities of nongovernmental organizations.

In recent years, global discourse on such critical issues as the environment, human rights, indigenous peoples, women and population has been held under U.N. auspices. With the participation of both governmental and nongovernmental representatives, conferences on world issues have furthered the process of shaping the kind of global ethic that must undergird global citizenship.

In coordination with ongoing efforts of the United Nations in this direction, I would hope to see these issues incorporated as integral elements of education at all levels. For example:

○ Peace education in which young people learn the cruelty and folly of war — to root the practice of nonviolence in human society.

○ Environmental education — to study current ecological realities and means of protecting the environment.

○ Developmental education — to focus attention on issues of poverty and global justice.

○ Human rights education — to awaken an awareness of human equality and dignity.

It has long been my belief that education must never be subservient to political interests. To this end, I feel that education should be accorded a status within public affairs equivalent even to that of the legislative, executive or judicial branches of government. This proposal grows out of the experiences of my predecessors, the first and second presidents of the Soka Gakkai, who fought consistently against political control of education.

In the coming years, I would hope that there could be held a world summit not of politicians but of educators. This is because nothing is of greater importance to humanity's future than the transnational solidarity of educators.

Toward that end, we are determined to continue our efforts to promote educational exchange among young people, following the example of Teachers College, which I understand at present has a student body drawn from some eighty countries.

As Mr. Makiguchi stated: "Educational efforts built on a clear understanding and with a defined sense of purpose have the power to overcome the contradictions and doubts that plague humankind, and to bring about an eternal victory for humanity."[10]

I pledge my fullest efforts to working, together with my distinguished friends and colleagues gathered here today, toward fostering the kind of global citizens who alone can produce this "eternal victory for humanity."

Notes

1. John Dewey, "Search for the Great Community," *The Public and Its Problems: An Essay in Political Inquiry* (Chicago: Gateway Books, 1946), p. 154.

2. Henry David Thoreau, "The Village" in *Walden, The Selected Works of Thoreau,* ed. Walter Harding, Cambridge ed. (Boston: Houghton Mifflin Company, 1975), p. 359.

3. See Alex Wayman and Hideko Wayman, trans., *The Lion's Roar of Queen Srimala: A Buddhist Scripture on the Tathagata-garbha Theory* (New York: Columbia University Press, 1974), p. 65.

4. See *The Writings of Nichiren Daishonin,* vol. 1, p. 223.

5. *An Anthology of Tsunesaburo Makiguchi's Works* (in Japanese), ed. Takehisa Tsuji (Tokyo: Daisan Bummeisha, 1994), p. 40.

6. John Dewey, "The Problem of Method," *The Public and Its Problems,* p. 213.

7. *Collected Works of Tsunesaburo Makiguchi* (in Japanese) (Tokyo: Daisan Bummeisha, 1982), vol. 7, p. 183.

8. *Collected Works of Tsunesaburo Makiguchi* (1983), vol. 6, p. 289.

9. Charter of the United Nations, Article I.

10. *Collected Works of Tsunesaburo Makiguchi* (1984), vol. 8, p. 365.

The Buddhism of the Sun
Breaks Through the Darkness
of Suffering

—ɱ—

GONGYO MEETING WITH REPRESENTATIVES OF THE NEW YORK
JOINT TERRITORIES, NEW YORK CULTURE CENTER,
NEW YORK CITY, NEW YORK, JUNE 15, 1996

MY FRIENDS IN NEW YORK, you have grown magnificently. Your organization today is truly outstanding. You have won over everything! Congratulations! And thank you for all your tireless efforts.

To commemorate this occasion, I dedicate the following *waka* to you:

> *New York,*
> *serene and at last triumphant,*
> *you have created a record*
> *invincible and immortal.*
> • • •
> *New York,*
> *deep in faith,*
> *deep in camaraderie,*
> *is watched and praised*
> *by friends the world over.*
>
> *The Daishonin will*
> *protect you without fail.*

Therefore, New York,
enjoy each day
with courage and hope.

Why do we practice faith? So that we may live the most wonderful lives. So that we may serenely surmount the sufferings of birth, aging, sickness and death that are an inescapable part of the human condition.

A LOFTY WAY OF LIFE

Birth — we have been born, and life is made for living. It is important that we strive to live tenaciously to the very end, no matter what happens. Faith in the Mystic Law supplies us with the immense life force we need to live strongly and confidently each day so that we can overcome the various kinds of suffering and hardship we encounter.

Life lived without purpose or value, the kind in which we don't even know the reason why we are born, is joyless and lackluster. To just live, eat and die without any real sense of purpose surely represents a life pervaded by the world of Animality. On the other hand, to do, create or contribute something that benefits others, society and ourselves, and to dedicate ourselves as long as we live to that challenge — that is a life of true satisfaction, a life of value. It is a humanistic and lofty way to live. Faith in the Mystic Law is the driving force that enables us to create the greatest possible value for both ourselves and others.

LIKE A GOLDEN AUTUMN

Aging — life passes by in an instant. In the twinkling of an eye, we grow old. Our physical strength wanes and we begin to suffer various aches and pains. We practice Nichiren Daishonin's Buddhism so that instead of sinking into feelings of sadness, loneliness and regret, we can greet aging with deep inner richness and maturity as round and complete as the ripe, golden fruit of autumn. Faith exists so that we can welcome, smiling and without regrets, an aging that is like a breathtaking sunset whose dazzling rays color heaven and earth in majestic hues.

THE BUDDHIST DEITIES NEVER FAIL TO PROTECT US

Sickness — we are all mortal flesh and blood. Everyone at some time suffers from illness in one form or another. The power of the Mystic Law enables us to bring forth the strength to overcome the pain and suffering of sickness with courage and determination. The Daishonin writes: "Nam-myoho-renge-kyo is like the roar of a lion. What sickness can therefore be an obstacle?" (WND-1, 412).

Moreover, irrespective of our health or our circumstances, if we dedicate our lives to kosen-rufu, we will always be protected by the original Buddha, Nichiren Daishonin. Indeed, all the Buddhas, bodhisattvas and heavenly deities throughout the universe will unite without fail to protect us. This the Daishonin promises. He writes: "A woman who takes this efficacious medicine will be surrounded and protected by these four great bodhisattvas at all times. When she rises to her feet, so too will the bodhisattvas, and when she walks along the road, they will also do the same. She and they will be as inseparable as a body and its shadow, as fish and water, as a voice and its echo, or as the moon and its light" (WND-1, 415).

As this Gosho indicates, we will definitely be protected — not only in this lifetime but throughout all eternity.

SOARING FREELY THROUGH THE SKIES OF BUDDHAHOOD

Death — this is uncompromising. Everyone has to face death. At that time, those who walk the path of the Mystic Law will make their way serenely to Eagle Peak aboard the great white ox cart described in the Lotus Sutra. They will merge with the universal Buddhahood. The dimensions of the great white ox cart are truly colossal and its entire surface is adorned with gold, silver and innumerable precious gems.

I would say it is a far cry from the taxicabs that race around New York City! Nor are there any traffic jams to worry about!

Nichiren Daishonin states: "These large carriages drawn by white oxen are able to fly at will through the sky of the essential nature of phenomena.

Those persons who come after me will ride in these carriages and journey to Eagle Peak. And I, Nichiren, riding in the same kind of carriage, will come out to greet them" (WND-2, 976).

The Daishonin's words are never false; they always speak the absolute truth. We can therefore have the utmost confidence in them.

Even the most sophisticated rocket cannot compare to the great white ox cart. Riding on this wondrous vehicle of the Law, we can soar freely toward the destination where our next mission lies. As the Lotus Sutra indicates when it says those who uphold the Law "freely choose where they will be born" (LS, 163), we can be reborn wherever and in whatever form we desire.

It does not have to be on Earth. There are countless planets throughout the universe where intelligent life is bound to exist. Many scientists and astronomers also endorse this view.

If we attain the state of Buddhahood in this lifetime, that state will forever pervade our lives. Throughout the cycle of birth and death, in each new lifetime, we will be endowed with good health, wealth and intelligence, along with a supportive and comfortable environment, and will lead lives that overflow with good fortune. Each of us will also possess a unique mission and be born in an appropriate form to fulfill it.

This state of life is everlasting, and it can never be destroyed. It is precisely so that you may enjoy such eternal happiness that I continually urge you to apply yourselves to your Buddhist practice and firmly consolidate the state of Buddhahood in your lives. This is not just a matter of personal sentiment; it is the teaching of Nichiren Daishonin.

Therefore, it is important that we do not wander from the path leading to the attainment of enlightenment. Please advance ever forward with patience and persistence along the path of kosen-rufu and Buddhist practice.

Doing gongyo every day is a challenge. Introducing others to the practice is a challenge. Getting people to subscribe to our organizational newspaper is a challenge. Attending meetings is a challenge. Sometimes it can all become too much and leave one feeling negative and wanting to take a break! Since we are human beings, it's only natural that we might feel this way on occasion.

The important thing, however, is not to spin out of the orbit of faith. I hope you will continue to pursue the path of Buddhahood steadily and patiently, encouraging one another on your journey.

If a plane flies off course or a car wanders carelessly over the center divider, an accident can easily happen; they won't be able to reach their destinations. Similarly, if our lives go off course, they too will crash, plunging us into misery.

Life proceeds along a path, though it is invisible. There is definitely a path for human beings that leads to absolute happiness — the path of the Mystic Law. If we continue to advance along this road without abandoning our faith, we will definitely come to savor a state of life in which all our desires are fulfilled both spiritually and materially.

INCONSPICUOUS BENEFIT

It is important to take a long-range view. No great achievement is accomplished overnight or without difficulty. Should benefit be obtained easily without making any efforts in Buddhist practice, we'd probably just as easily abandon our faith and end up miserable as a consequence.

Because it isn't easy to get into a top-ranked school, students study with all their might, gaining an abundance of knowledge and ability as a result. Faith follows basically the same formula: practice is essential to attaining Buddhahood.

This is my first visit to New York in fifteen years. President Toda often used to cite fifteen years as one milestone for showing actual proof in faith. He would say that even a small bud grows into a great tree after fifteen years. Someone who had not seen the bud sprout and grow during those fifteen years would be amazed by its growth; this is called an inconspicuous benefit. On the other hand, he observed, a great tree may also wither away during a fifteen-year period; this is an example of inconspicuous punishment or loss.

The young people I spoke with on those June days fifteen years ago have grown splendidly, actively engaging themselves in their activities as the core of the SGI-USA. This itself is proof of their remarkable human revolution.

President Toda used to say that even the seeds of simple plants take ten to twenty days to sprout; it does not happen overnight. And he maintained that it is only after we have been practicing this Buddhism for about fifteen years that things really start improving in a profound way. For this reason, he urged us to devote ourselves in faith and practice with patience and determination.

New York is known as the Big Apple. An apple tree must also take root first, grow branches and bear fruit. It is only natural that this should take time. There is no reason to be impatient or in a hurry. As long as one wins in the end, that's what matters. Those who do so are the true victors.

THE NOBLE SPIRIT OF THE STATUE OF LIBERTY

The mention of New York immediately conjures the image of the Statue of Liberty, her torch lighting the way to a future of freedom for not only the United States but the entire world. The statue, formally titled "Liberty Enlightening the World," was presented as a token of friendship by the people of France to the United States in commemoration of the centennial of this country's independence.

Who designed the Statue of Liberty? It was the French sculptor Frédéric-Auguste Bartholdi. A design sketch of the statue bearing Mr. Bartholdi's signature is among the important treasures of Soka University in Japan.

It is said that the face of the Statue of Liberty is modeled after Bartholdi's mother. We may speculate that this is an expression of his gratitude for his mother, who had raised him with self-less devotion. A mother's face may appear the most beautiful and noble of all to her child.

In her right hand, the statue holds aloft a torch symbolizing the light of freedom, and in her left, a tablet of law inscribed with the date of the Declaration of Independence — July 4, 1776. It is said this pose was inspired by a young woman Bartholdi had seen in his youth.

During a popular uprising against the powerfully ambitious ruler Louis Napoleon in 1851, people shrank in fear before an army barricade. Suddenly, out of the darkness, a young woman appeared, carrying a torch. "Advance!" she cried, jumping nimbly over the barrier. In that instant, gunshots rang out and the young woman fell to the ground. But the flames of her torch set the barricade on fire, her courageous act opening a way forward.

The spirit of this anonymous yet noble young woman now soars regally in the Statue of Liberty.

A HOPE-FILLED VISION FOR THE FUTURE

Today's world, too, is sorely lacking in hope, a positive vision for the future and a solid philosophy. There is no bright light illuminating the horizon. Everything stands at an impasse — economics, politics, environmental issues and humanitarian concerns. Human beings — the driving force behind all these activites — are also at a loss as to how to move forward.

That is precisely why we, the Bodhisattvas of the Earth, have appeared. That is why Nichiren Daishonin's Buddhism of the sun is so essential. We have stood up, holding high the torch of courage in one hand and the philosophy of truth and justice in the other. We have begun to take action to boldly break through the darkness of the four sufferings — birth, aging, sickness and death — as well as the darkness of society and of the world.

I hope that all of you, my friends of New York, one of the

world's pivotal cities, will strive to become exemplary models of such courage and justice.

The very careful historical research done by some of our bright and gifted New York members revealed something of great interest. In the early years of this century, this building, the New York Culture Center, was the home of the Rand School of Social Science, which served as an institution for adult education. On the side of this building was the truly marvelous slogan "The People's House." As it turns out, the American philosopher and educator John Dewey came to this building to lecture many times.

Incidentally, the director of the Center for Dewey Studies at Southern Illinois University has sent a very warm letter of congratulations.

In one of the lectures Dewey delivered here, he said: "Genuine culture stimulates the creative powers of imagination, of mind and of thought. It includes not merely free access to things of mind and taste already in existence, but a positive production of them, so that the waters of knowledge and of ideas are kept really fresh and vital."[1]

Culture is a stimulus. Culture means to produce things. Culture enriches life. And culture belongs to the people. I look forward to the future of this New York Culture Center, which I am certain will function as a place where genuine culture flourishes and as a house that contributes to people's happiness.

INTRODUCING TSUNESABURO MAKIGUCHI'S IDEAS TO THE WORLD

As you all know, the day before yesterday, I delivered a lecture at Columbia's Teachers College, a "castle of education" and one of the most important institutions of higher learning in the United States. This event, along with my speech at the Simon Wiesenthal Center in Los Angeles [June 4], has made this trip to the United States, in a sense, a journey to introduce to the world the life and ideals of the first Soka Gakkai president, Tsunesaburo Makiguchi. This is a source of the greatest joy.

At the start of this century, President Makiguchi was quick to foresee that, as he put it, "the United States of America is the land that will synthesize and unite civilizations in the future." Our founding president must truly be rejoicing at what, together, we have achieved here.

President Toda once said: "The tenth anniversary[2] of President Makiguchi's passing is drawing near and I would like to commemorate this occasion by making his theory of value known to universities throughout Japan. Whether or not there is any response, thirty or fifty years hence there will definitely be people who appreciate and show great admiration and respect for his ideas.

"This is because his theory of value is seriously focused and based on the realities of society. A person of insight will never fail to understand its greatness. It is enough if even one person understands. That person will tell others, who in turn will spread that understanding to countless more. I am confident that his theory of value will definitely spread globally."[3]

Everything that I am doing now is to actualize this earnest wish of President Toda.

Incidentally, I understand that the room number of the lecture hall at Columbia University where the address took place is 125. This seems a mystic coincidence, celebrating the one hundred twenty-fifth anniversary of President Makiguchi's birth on June 6.

PUBLICATION OF A NEW VOLUME OF THE GOSHO IN ENGLISH

Furthermore, the prestigious Columbia University Press has just published a second volume of selected Gosho, titled *Letters of Nichiren*. It contains seventy-three writings, most of which are letters that Nichiren Daishonin sent to his followers. These include "On the Buddha's Prophecy," "On Practicing the Buddha's Teachings" and "Letter from Sado."

I offer my gratitude to Dr. Burton Watson for his work on these translations, as well as Professor Philip Yampolsky of Columbia University and all concerned parties who edited this volume.

After the Daishonin's death, the five senior priests destroyed many of the letters their mentor had written in the phonetic script that was easy for people to read [rather than in Chinese characters, the script of scholarly texts]; they either burned the letters or reprocessed the paper on which they were written so that they could use it to write other things. These treacherous disciples despised the precious letters that the Daishonin had written for the sake of ordinary people — letters containing enduring messages for all humanity in the Latter Day of the Law — spurning them as "a stain on the reputation of our late teacher."

By contrast, Nikko Shonin, who was one in spirit with the Daishonin as his successor, designated all of these letters *Gosho*, or "Esteemed Writings," and resolutely moved to preserve them for later generations. He declared with dignity to the five senior priests who had turned against their mentor that when the time of kosen-rufu comes these letters written in ordinary, phonetic Japanese would be translated and communicated to the world (see GZ, 1613).

Seven hundred years later, just as Nikko Shonin confidently foresaw, an English translation of the Daishonin's letters has been published by Columbia University, a great center of learning and intellect. I would like to share with all of you the joy of vindicating here in New York the integrity and truth of Nichiren Daishonin and Nikko Shonin, who were joined by an inseverable bond of mentor and disciple.

LETTER TO THE LAY NUN SENNICHI —
RESPECT FOR DIVERSITY

To continually read the Gosho and take action in accord with the Daishonin's teachings is the eternal path of the SGI. Today, I'd like to read a famous passage from one Gosho. It is from a letter that the Daishonin wrote to the lay nun Sennichi, a woman who was an active follower on distant Sado Island: "All living beings in the nine worlds and the six paths differ from one another in their minds. For example, two persons, three persons, a hundred, or a thousand people all may have faces about a foot in length, but no two look exactly alike. Their minds differ, and therefore so do their faces. How much greater still is the difference between the minds of two persons, of ten persons, and of all the living beings in the six paths and the nine worlds! So it is that some love the cherry blossoms and some love the moon, some prefer sour things and some prefer bitter, some like little things and some favor big. People have varied tastes. Some prefer good and some prefer evil. There are many kinds of people.

"But though they differ from one another in such ways, once they enter into the Lotus Sutra, they all become like a single person in body and a single person in mind. This is just like the myriad different rivers that, when they flow into the ocean, all take on a uniformly salty flavor, or like the many kinds of birds that, when they approach Mount Sumeru, all assume the same [golden] hue" (WND-I, 1042).

The Lotus Sutra embodies a philosophy that most highly respects, fosters and harmonizes human diversity. The Mystic Law is the source that enables us to manifest our unique brilliance against a backdrop of mutual understanding and appreciation of one another's differences; to create a lush garden of "cherry, plum, peach and damson" blossoms.

With its rich diversity, New York is the world in miniature. In such a setting, you New York SGI members are taking on a challenging and crucially important issue for humankind — respecting and creating harmony amid diversity. Without doubt, Nichiren Daishonin is watching over and protecting this solidarity of the Buddha's children in New York.

FORGE BONDS WITH TRUE COMRADES

President Makiguchi said: "It isn't the number of people that matters. Even if we are small in number, we should continue to seek out true comrades." The Soka Gakkai's founding president cherished true comrades, likening them to "gold unearthed from sand," "lotus flowers blooming in muddy water" and "diamonds." I would therefore like the organization in New York to be a gathering of lions — each one a person of truly outstanding ability and caliber.

Each individual is important. Everything starts from treasuring just one person. This is the eternal formula for the development of kosen-rufu. The great American poet Walt Whitman, who was born in New York, wrote:

> Each of us inevitable,
> Each of us limitless — each of us with his or her right
>   upon the earth,
> Each of us allow'd the eternal purports of the earth,
> Each of us here as divinely as any is here.[5]

The Lotus Sutra is also a teaching of the highest filial piety. The Daishonin deeply praised the faith of the lay nun Sennichi, whom I mentioned earlier, in offering prayers for her deceased father, and he sent her a precious gift of a copy of the Lotus Sutra in ten volumes.

Through our practice of the Mystic Law, we can bring the greatest imaginable benefit to our parents, whether they practice or not, whether they are still alive or have died. Please be confident of this point.

"WHAT IS THERE THAT CANNOT BE ACHIEVED?"

We all face various problems and obstacles. But Nichiren Daishonin writes: "Kyo'o's misfortune will change into fortune. Muster your faith, and pray to this Gohonzon. Then what is there that cannot be achieved?" (WND-1, 412).

The first thing is to pray. From the moment we begin to pray, things start moving. The darker the night, the closer the dawn.

From the moment we chant daimoku with a deep and powerful resolve, the sun begins to rise in our hearts.

Hope — prayer is the sun of hope. To chant daimoku each time we face a problem, overcoming it and elevating our life-condition as a result — this is the path of "cearthly desires are enlightenment" taught in Nichiren Daishonin's Buddhism.

Suffering and undergoing hardships for the sake of friends and for spreading the Law are manifestations of the great sense of responsibility of a genuine leader and the behavior of a bodhisattva. There is no suffering or hardship that a Bodhisattva of the Earth cannot surmount. So no matter what happens, I would like you to advance steadily, one step at a time, always chanting Nam-myoho-renge-kyo with a vibrant voice.

Expanding the Network of Understanding

Nichiren Daishonin wrote to one of his lay followers: "I entrust you with the propagation of Buddhism in your province. It is stated that 'the seeds of Buddhahood sprout as a result of conditions, and for this reason they preach the single vehicle'" (WND-1, 1117). Forming connections with other human beings is important. For each of us, everything starts with developing ties with others, forging bonds of friendship and winning trust.

Buddhism stresses the importance of the present and the future. There is little point in dwelling on the past. Far more constructive is looking to the future and moving forward. What is vital is that we achieve a bright and glorious future through our current efforts and perseverance. Things are just starting for the SGI members in New York. I hope you will join me in creating another exhilarating drama of victory and joy.

John Dewey, whom President Makiguchi held in such high esteem, also finds freedom within growth and development. He stated: "We are free not because of what we statically are, but inasfar as we are becoming different from what we have been."[6] People of genuine freedom are those who continue to grow and develop, who continue to keep themselves fresh and new. In that respect, I heartily rejoice at the hope-filled future in store for the members of the new New York.

I conclude my speech with my heartfelt prayers for your continued development, good health, happiness and safety. Please also convey my warmest regards to all the precious members whom I could not meet today.

New York, congratulations! And my deepest thanks. I look forward to seeing you all again soon.

Notes

1. John Dewey, "Politics and Culture," a lecture at the Rand School of Social Science, New York City, March 14, 1932, published in the May 1932 issue of *Modern Thinker*.

2. This actually indicates nine years after Mr. Makiguchi's death, since according to the Japanese tradition, the date on which the person dies is counted as the first anniversary.

3. Remarks made on June 23, 1953. *Toda Josei zenshu* (Collected Works of Josei Toda) (Tokyo: Seikyo Shimbunsha, 1989), vol. 4, p. 64.

4. Walt Whitman, "Salut au Monde!" from *Leaves of Grass and Selected Prose*, ed. John Kouwenhoven (New York: The Modern Library, 1950), p. 117.

5. John Dewey, *The Political Writings*, ed. Debra Morris and Ian Shapiro (Indianapolis/Cambridge: Hackett Publishing Company, Inc., 1933), p. 136.

"The Sublime Flowering
of Art and Artistry"

—⚏—

DEDICATED TO THE PARTICIPANTS OF THE FIFTEENTH WORLD
PEACE YOUTH CULTURE FESTIVAL HELD AT CARNEGIE HALL,
NEW YORK, ON JUNE 18, 1996

New York!
New York!
Such a splendid and glorious
culture festival.

Such a magnificent and superb
culture festival.

This culture festival
has been the pinnacle
the most sublime flowering
of art and artistry.

The venue—
Carnegie Hall
renowned throughout
the world.

I offer my wholehearted applause
to these unparalleled,
these matchless performers and producers
both on the stage and off.

Excitement ran electric
through the hall
bringing forth
a concerto of
praise and pure tears.

The glistening sweat
and sparkling eyes of
these lofty performers,
your lovely voices and dance
are certain to be praised
by all the forces of nature
by all the Buddhas of the universe.

How much your dance today
resembles your performance then—
the remotest past
of Eagle Peak.

This culture festival
held here in New York,
this city of the world,
on June 18, 1996,
your voices, the resonant applause—
has surely created
a ceaseless succession of waves,
an eternal, undying path
that will illuminate the twenty-first century
and will resound for ten thousand years and more.

468 ■ MY DEAR FRIENDS IN AMERICA

Bravo!
The new New York.
Bravo!
My magnificent New York friends!
Thank you very much.

Great Leaders in Lifetime
After Lifetime

—⚇—

SGI REPRESENTATIVES CONFERENCE,
FLORIDA NATURE AND CULTURE CENTER,
FORT LAUDERDALE, FLORIDA, JUNE 22, 1996

I WISH TO EXPRESS my profound respect for you, the leaders of kosen-rufu of countries around the globe. In light of the Gosho and the Lotus Sutra, you are all incomparably noble and precious individuals. You are great leaders far surpassing any leader of great renown or power in society.

Moreover, you are accumulating the causes in your lives to become outstanding leaders of the societies into which you will be born in your next existence and indeed throughout eternity. And this is not just limited to Earth. In lifetime after lifetime, you will be reborn as leaders of great honor and esteem on the countless planets that fill the universe.

In this lifetime, to demonstrate the power of faith in the Mystic Law to others, some of you may have been born into poverty so that you could show actual proof by gaining secure and comfortable lives, or some of you may have been born with ill health so that you could show proof by growing strong and healthy. Irrespective of your situations, however, the light of faith in the depths of your beings will continue to shine on eternally with diamond-like brilliance.

Humanity today lacks hope and vision for the future. It is

for precisely this reason that the Bodhisattvas of the Earth have appeared. Without your presence, the future of humanity would be bleak and spiritual decline its destination. That is why you have been born in this age and are now playing an active role in society. This is the meaning of "emerging from the earth." Consequently, each of you will definitely become happy. Please be confident that you will lead lives overflowing with good fortune throughout the three existences of past, present and future.

Conversely, those who slander and persecute the noble Bodhisattvas of the Earth will receive strict retribution in terms of the Buddhist law of cause and effect. Of this there is no doubt.

A LIFE OF GREAT FULFILLMENT

Truly praiseworthy are those who resolve to work hard for kosen-rufu and the SGI within the lofty realm of Nichiren Daishonin's Buddhism. They are genuinely capable people, and they will definitely attain a life-condition of complete fulfillment.

By contrast, those who abuse the SGI organization, who exploit the members for their own selfish reasons and aims, are committing the gravest slander of the Law.

The SGI is the sun and the pillar of humanity. Each of you is a leader of this noble organization. I conclude my remarks with my sincerest prayers for your excellent health and further great works.

Pioneer a Leadership
Revolution

—⚌—

TWENTY-FIRST SGI GENERAL MEETING,
FLORIDA NATURE AND CULTURE CENTER,
FORT LAUDERDALE, FLORIDA, JUNE 23, 1996

CONGRATULATIONS on today's SGI General Meeting! Together with members around the world, I truly rejoice at the opening of this wonderful Florida Nature and Culture Center. Once again, my sincerest congratulations.

Every inch of the center's vast grounds sparkles with the members' beautiful sincerity. I wish to express my heartfelt thanks to all those who devoted so much time and energy to preparing the center for this opening and general meeting.

I wholeheartedly welcome all of you who have gathered today — praiseworthy leaders of kosen-rufu from fifty-two countries and territories around the world. Thank you for traveling such long distances. I also express my deepest appreciation to all of our American friends for their warm welcome and hospitality.

A SELFLESS SPIRIT OF COMPASSION

Yesterday, the World Women's Peace Conference was held, signaling another landmark in the history of our movement. My congratulations to the women's and young women's division members throughout the world.

Today, I would like to talk a little about Gabriela Mistral, the Chilean poet who is widely praised for her great humanism and renowned as the first woman in Latin America to receive the Nobel Prize for Literature (1945). She also taught for a time at Columbia University and was well respected as a humanistic educator dedicated to teaching the children of her homeland. Indicative of the great spirit of compassion and caring with which she interacted with her students is her "Teacher's Prayer": "Let me be more mother than the mother herself in my love and defense of the child who is not flesh of my flesh. Help me to make one of my children my most perfect poem, and leave within him or her my most melodious melody from that day when my own lips no longer sing."[1]

With this same spirit, let us care for and nurture the members of the youth and future [2] divisions. My prayer is that you will foster your juniors to become even more capable than yourselves, while striving ceaselessly for your own self-improvement so that you may bring your lives to a wonderful completion.

All of you are chanting for the happiness of the many members — children of the Buddha — in your respective communities; you support and encourage them and work tirelessly on their behalf as if they were your own children. Your actions are truly those of great bodhisattvas; your state of life, that of noble Buddhas.

In the Gosho, we find Nichiren Daishonin citing the words "the truer the teaching, the lower the stage [of those it can bring to enlightenment]"[3] (WND-1, 785–86). Similarly, the deeper a leader's faith, the more humbly he or she respects others and works for their happiness.

Viewed in light of the causal Law of Buddhism, the great good fortune you are now accumulating by looking after and treasuring many people predestines you to a state of being where you will be supported and protected by many people in each successive lifetime. Our Buddhist practice in this life is our training for becoming great leaders throughout all future existences.

RESOLVING TO WORK WITH AND LEARN
FROM OTHERS

In his *System of Value-Creating Pedagogy*, founding president Makiguchi called for a "leadership revolution" — a revolution in our understanding and practice of leadership. He stressed the need for humanity to bring a close to an age where those in power and authority use people to fulfill self-serving ends. It is imperative, he said, that we produce a steady stream of new leaders who will contribute selflessly to people's happiness and welfare.

According to this perspective, a leader is not one who stands above others, much less one who declares "I am special" and regards others with contempt. The moment we resolve to join in and work alongside everyone, to respect everyone and have the spirit to humbly learn from them, we embark on the road to becoming great leaders. This was also an essential point of the "leadership revolution" of which President Makiguchi spoke.

AN ORGANIZATION WHERE ALL TAKE
RESPONSIBILITY

Some very interesting thoughts have been published in the United States using the image of a herd of buffalo to describe outdated modes of organization.[4]

In a buffalo herd, all the individuals follow the lead buffalo; they go where he wants to go and do what he wants to do. In other words, they merely wait for the instructions of the leader. When human organizations follow this model, they become an unthinking herd. Unable to adapt to changing times, such organizations travel a course to inevitable decline.

As a far more successful type of organization, the book's authors propose a model based on the image of a flock of geese. The flock they envisage flies in a V formation, with the role of lead goose changing frequently as different geese take turns. It is a model in which everyone takes responsibility, everyone is equal and everyone unites solidly for a shared objective. An organization of this kind, the authors argue, will succeed in the changing times in which we live.

Based on their conclusions, we can summarize the following as some important guidelines for leaders:

○ Create an environment where each person wants to take leadership and responsibility.

○ Learn yourself and encourage others to do the same. This process of continual learning by all parties is the key to success.

○ Realize that constructive change in your organization begins with you, the leader, changing first.

THE LEADER'S COMMITMENT

Is a leader taking action for the members' happiness and for kosen-rufu or is he or she using the SGI and the members for selfish ends? The difference in commitment may not be visible, but with the passing of time, it will manifest with unmistakable clarity.

President Toda once said: "All of you gathered today are Soka Gakkai leaders. I am sure that as leaders you are giving a great deal of thought to the fact that those whom you are serving must become happy as well as yourselves.

"Becoming happy yourself is no great challenge; it's quite simple. Working for the happiness of others in addition to your own happiness, however, is the foundation of faith. I think that unless you honestly pray to the Gohonzon to do this, strengthen your faith and really devote yourself to faith with a spirit of seeking nothing for yourself, then you cannot be called a true leader."[5]

I hope that as leaders you will maintain a passionate pledge to do all in your power to ensure that everyone becomes happy and victorious.

As a specific point for leaders to bear in mind, it is also important that you praise and encourage your fellow members. You must never direct your anger toward others out of emotion, shouting at or abusing them. In the Gosho, the Daishonin cites the words of the Great Teacher Dengyo, who said, "Those who praise him will receive blessings that will pile up as high as Mount Calm and Bright, while those who slander [a practiioner of the Lotus Sutra] will be committing a fault that will condemn them to the hell of incessant suffering" (WND-2, 559).

Viewed from the perspective of the Buddhist principle of cause and effect, those who harass and torment the children of the Buddha are destined to meet with great suffering themselves. The law of cause and effect is strict and uncompromising. On the other hand, those who praise the children of the Buddha can construct lives of great and enduring good fortune as lofty and indomitable as the peaks of the Himalayas.

The Daishonin also says: "The more one praises the blessings of the Lotus Sutra, the more one's own blessings will increase. Bear in mind that the twenty-eight chapters of the Lotus Sutra contain only a few passages elucidating the truth, but a great many words of praise" (WND-1, 673).

It is most important to offer praise. Being human, people experience ups and downs in their emotional state. So I'd like to see leaders offering encouragement and heartfelt praise to those they encounter — even simply remarking brightly, "Thank you!" or "I really appreciate all your efforts!" Both parties will then feel cheered and refreshed. Ripples of joy will spread out to others and all will enjoy that much more benefit.

A GLOBAL FAMILY

People of many different linguistic, ethnic and cultural backgrounds are gathered in this hall. This is truly a beautiful family gathering whose members come from all around the world. Today's meeting is itself actual proof of the ideal of a global family that was advocated by President Toda many decades ago.

The late Professor David Norton of the University of Delaware worked tirelessly to realize the publication of *Education for Creative Living: Ideas and Proposals of Tsunesaburo Makiguchi*.[6] In his posthumously published work, *Imagination, Understanding, and the Virtue of Liberality*, which he kindly dedicated to me, Dr. Norton writes, "By the virtue of 'liberality,' I refer to the cultivated disposition to recognize and appreciate truths and values other than one's own."[7]

He also says, "Ignoring others is no longer possible when besetting human problems are global in scope and will require interactive cooperation if they are to be promisingly addressed."[8] Dr. Norton had profound expectations for the solidarity of ordinary people that we in the SGI are working to create.

On the occasion of my address at Columbia University [on June 13], my wife and I were delighted to meet again with Mary Norton, Dr. Norton's widow, and to find her in such high spirits. When we form bonds of friendship with someone, we treasure those ties forever.

The English words *culture* and *cultivate* share the same linguistic root. Buddhist practice is also an undertaking to cultivate our inner lives and spirit. In that sense, Buddhism and culture are intrinsically related. As members of the SGI, let us continue to vigorously carry out our great cultural movement in the pursuit of cultivating "fertile plains of peace" and "flower gardens of friendship" for the benefit and prosperity of all humanity.

CONTRIBUTING TO SOCIETY

To date, the members of the Florida Joint Territory have engaged in many forms of cultural interaction and contributed greatly to their local communities. I have been kept informed of your activities and commend you all most highly for these admirable endeavors.

As I also mentioned in my address at the Simon Wiesenthal Center in Los Angeles [on June 4], President Makiguchi defined the value of good as benefitting society and maintained that this is also the raison d'être of religion. Social contribution is the fundamental spirit of the SGI.

Therefore, I propose that we come up with an alternate name for the SGI to make it more accessible and familiar to a large number of people both inside and outside the organization. For example, we might use the organization's initials to create a catch phrase like "Social Good Institution." The dynamic pulse of kosen-rufu lies in our energetic efforts to contribute greatly to society and to expand our network of trust and friendship.

Bring Forth
the Radiance Within

The great German poet and author Friedrich von Schiller wrote: "As soon as it becomes light inside Man, there is also no longer any night outside him; as soon as it is calm within him, the storm in the universe is also lulled, and the contending forces of Nature find rest between abiding boundaries."[9]

Though the world around us deepens in confusion as we approach the turn of the century, the SGI represents a brilliant light of hope.

Everything begins from the human revolution of one person. It is important first and foremost that all of you win in life and in society. I also hope that with your brilliant presence, you will each illuminate all around you — the people you encounter, your local community, your country and all of humanity.

A Full and Satisfying Life
Is the Touchstone of Happiness

In the Gosho, Nichiren Daishonin writes, "You must not spend your lives in vain and regret it for ten thousand years to come" (WND-1, 622).

How should we live our lives? What is the most valuable and worthwhile way to live? A well-known Japanese poem goes: "The life of a flower is short / Sufferings only are there many."[10] The meaning of these lines is that flowers suddenly come into bloom and then, just as suddenly, their petals fall and scatter; ultimately, the only thing that lasts for a long time is suffering. Life, indeed, may be like that in some ways.

A philosopher once remarked that it was perhaps only possible to determine happiness or unhappiness in life by adding up at the end of one's days all the joys and all the sorrows one had experienced and basing one's final evaluation on whichever figure was larger.

Despite illustrious positions in society or great material wealth, there are many people who fail to become happy. Despite enjoying wonderfully happy marriages or relationships, people must ultimately be parted from the person they love through death. Being separated from loved ones is one of the sufferings inherent in the human condition. Despite gaining great fame and popularity, there are many who die after long, agonizing illnesses. Despite being born with the seeming advantage of rare and exceptional beauty, there are not a few people whose lives have been made a misery instead.

HAPPINESS IS NOT DETERMINED BY OUTWARD APPEARANCES

Where on earth is happiness found? How can we become happy? These are fundamental questions of life, and human beings are no doubt destined to pursue them eternally. The teachings of Buddhism, faith in the Mystic Law, provide fundamental answers to these questions.

Ultimately, happiness rests on how we establish a solid sense of self or being. Happiness based on such externals as possessing a fine house or a good reputation is "relative happiness." It is not a firm, unchanging "absolute happiness." One can be in apparently the most fortunate circumstances, but if that person feels only emptiness and pain, then he or she cannot be considered happy.

Some people live in truly splendid houses yet do nothing but fight in them. Some people work for famous companies and enjoy a prestige that many envy yet are always being shouted at by their superiors, left exhausted from heavy workloads and rendered sick and weary of life.

Happiness does not lie in outward appearances nor in vanity. It is a matter of what you feel inside; it is a deep resonance in our lives. I would venture that the first condition for happiness is fulfillment.

To be filled each day with a rewarding sense of exhilaration and purpose, a sense of tasks accomplished and deep fulfillment — people who feel this way are happy. Those who have this sense of satisfaction even if they are extremely busy are much happier than those who have free time on their hands but feel empty inside.

THE DAWN OF LIFE

As practitioners of the Daishonin's Buddhism, we get up in the morning and do gongyo. Some perhaps may do so rather reluctantly! Nevertheless, doing gongyo is itself a truly great and noble thing. Gongyo is a solemn ceremony in which we are, in a manner of speaking, looking out and over the universe; it is a dialogue with the universe.

Doing gongyo and chanting daimoku before the Gohonzon represents the dawn, the start of a new day, in our lives; it is the sun rising; it gives us a profound sense of contentment in the depths of our being that nothing can surpass. Even on this point alone we are truly fortunate.

Some people appear to be happy but actually start off the day feeling blue and depressed. A husband might be admonished by his wife in the morning and begin his day dejected, wondering, "How on earth did I get into such a marriage?" He will savor neither happiness nor contentment. Just by looking at our mornings, it is clear that we in the SGI lead lives of profound worth and satisfaction.

In addition, each of you is striving to do your best in your job or other responsibilities and to win in all areas of life while using your spare time to work for the Law, for kosen-rufu, for people's happiness and for the welfare of society. In this Latter Day of the Law teeming with perverse individuals, you are exerting yourselves energetically, often amid many hardships and obstacles, chanting daimoku for others' happiness, traveling long distances to talk with friends and show them warm concern and understanding.

You are truly bodhisattvas. There is no nobler life, no life based on a loftier philosophy. Each of you is translating this unsurpassed philosophy into action and spreading its message far and wide. To possess a philosophy of such profound value is itself the greatest fortune.

Accordingly, the second condition for happiness is to possess a profound philosophy.

HOLDING FAST TO ONE'S CONVICTIONS

The third condition for happiness is to possess conviction. We live in an age in which people can no longer clearly distinguish what is right or wrong, good or evil. This is a global trend. If things continue in this way, humanity is destined for chaos and moral decay. In the midst of such times, you are upholding and earnestly practicing Nichiren Daishonin's Buddhism, a teaching of the highest good.

In "The Opening of the Eyes," the Daishonin writes: "This I will state. Let the gods forsake me. Let all persecutions assail me. Still I will give my life for the sake of the Law" (WND-1, 280). In this same Gosho, he instructs his believers not to be swayed by temptations or threats, however great — such as being offered the rulership of Japan or being told that one's parents will be beheaded (see WND-1, 280).

The important thing is to hold on resolutely to one's convictions, come what may, just as the Daishonin teaches. People who possess such unwavering conviction will definitely become happy. Each of you is such an individual.

VIEWING EVERYTHING IN A POSITIVE LIGHT

The fourth condition is living cheerfully and vibrantly. Those who are always complaining and grumbling make not only themselves but everyone else around them miserable and unhappy. By contrast, those who always live positively and filled with enthusiasm, who possess a cheerful and sunny disposition that lifts the spirits and brightens the hearts of all they meet are not only happy themselves but are a source of hope and inspiration for others.

Those who are always wearing long, gloomy expressions whenever you meet them — who have lost the ability to rejoice and feel genuine delight or wonder — live a dark, cheerless existence.

On the other hand, those who possess good cheer can view even a scolding by a loved one, such as a spouse or partner, as sweet music to their ears; or they can greet a child's poor report card as a sign that there is great potential for gradual improvement in the future. Viewing events and situations in this kind of positive light is important. The strength, wisdom and cheerfulness that accompany such an attitude lead to happiness.

To regard everything in a positive light or with a spirit of goodwill, however, does not mean being foolishly gullible and allowing people to take advantage of our good nature. It means having the wisdom and perception to actually move things in a positive direction by seeing things in their best light, while all the time keeping our eyes firmly focused on reality.

Faith and the teachings of Buddhism enable us to develop that kind of character. The acquisition of such character is a more priceless treasure than any other possession.

COURAGE AND TOLERANCE

The fifth condition for happiness is courage. Courageous people can overcome anything. The cowardly, on the other hand, because of their lack of courage, fail to savor the true, profound joys of life. This is truly unfortunate.

The sixth condition for happiness is tolerance. Those who are tolerant and broad-minded make people feel comfortable and at ease. Narrow and intolerant people who berate others for the slightest thing, or who make a great commotion each time some problem arises, just exhaust everyone and inspire fear.

Leaders must not intimidate or exhaust others. They must be tolerant and have a warm approachability that makes people feel relaxed and comfortable. Not only are those who possess a heart as wide as the ocean happy themselves, but all those around them are happy, too.

GREATEST OF ALL JOYS

The six conditions I have just mentioned are all ultimately expressed in the word *faith*. A life based on faith is a life of unsurpassed happiness.

The Daishonin writes, "[Chanting] Nam-myoho-renge-kyo is the greatest of all joys" (OTT, 212). I hope all of you will savor the truth of these words deep in your lives and show vibrant actual proof of that joy.

I thank everyone who traveled long distances from their respective countries to take part in this general meeting. You have my profoundest respect and appreciation. The original Buddha, Nichiren Daishonin, and the Buddhas, bodhisattvas and heavenly deities throughout the universe are surely praising you. Please convey my very best regards to all the members back home in your countries.

With the chairperson's permission, and reiterating my deepest thanks to all of you, I'll now conclude today's meeting. Thank you very much.

Notes

1. William J. Castleman, *Beauty and the Mission of the Teacher* (Smithtown, New York: Exposition Press, 1982), p. 111.
2. Future division: Shortly after this announcement, the name of the group was expanded and changed to reflect its focus: junior high school division and high school division. Several months later, the SGI-USA boys and girls

group was established, which later was renamed the elementary school division.

3. From Miao-lo's commentary on T'ien-t'ai's *Great Concentration and Insight*, titled *Annotations of Great Concentration and Insight.* This passage consists of six Chinese characters in the original.

4. James A. Belasco and Ralph C. Stayer, *Flight of the Buffalo: Soaring to Excellence, Learning To Let Employees Lead* (New York: Warner Books, 1993), pp. 16–23.

5. Josei Toda, *Toda Josei zenshu* (Collected Writings of Josei Toda) (Tokyo: Seikyo Shimbunsha, 1984), vol. 4, p. 378.

6. Translation in summary of Tsunesaburo Makiguchi's *System of Value-Creating Pedagogy.*

7. David L. Norton, *Imagination, Understanding, and the Virtue of Liberality* (Lanham, Maryland: Rowman & Littlefield Publishers, Inc., 1996), p. 81.

8. *Imagination, Understanding, and the Virtue of Liberality*, p. 114.

9. Friedrich von Schiller, *On the Aesthetic Education of Man*, trans. Reginald Snell (London: Routledge & Kegan Paul Ltd., 1957), p. 120.

10. By Japanese author Fumiko Hayashi (1903–51).

"To the Great Pioneers of Kosen-rufu of El Paso"

DEDICATED TO THE SGI-USA MEMBERS
IN EL PASO, TEXAS, ON JUNE 29, 1996

O El Paso!
where the Rio Grande flows powerfully
and the vast sky stretches endlessly
In this city too
are courageous pioneers
valiant and respectworthy
blazing the trail of kosen-rufu

In rhythm
with my inauguration
as third Soka Gakkai president
you stood up
pioneering friends
your sweat, tears and hardship
crystallizing today
in a beautiful garden
of human flowers

In a land of vast distances
you have prayed with all your heart
taken action with all your being
spoken with all your life

and you have won
your victory undisputed

Like the timeless Rio Grande
beginning from a single drop
from the peaks of Colorado
the great river of El Paso kosen-rufu
flows boldly and serenely
growing ever wider and higher
toward a new century of humanism

El Paso—
your lovely name
has the meaning of "path"

Birds have a path in the sky
fish have a path in the sea
And though invisible to the eye
there exists without a doubt
an unsurpassed path for human beings
continuing eternally
throughout three existences

Along that path
we are traveling!
In accord with the unchanging
and indestructible Law
encouraging friends who are suffering
guiding those who feel sad
we proceed
one step and then another
along the great path of hope

Cheerfully
exuberantly
our sights on the distant future
we advance!

Poet Laureate

Mentor and Disciple: Giving Positive Direction to Humanity

—⟋𝔪⟍—

SGI-USA COMMEMORATIVE TRAINING SESSION,
LOS ANGELES, CALIFORNIA, JULY 3, 1996

I AM DELIGHTED to meet with my friends in the United States on this significant day, the fifty-first anniversary of July 3, the Day of Mentor and Disciple. On this day in 1945, at seven in the evening, my mentor, Josei Toda, was released from prison. Alone, he courageously initiated a struggle to prove the righteousness, truth and greatness of his mentor, Tsunesaburo Makiguchi, who had been unjustly incarcerated and humiliated by those in power and who had died in prison.

On the same day, twelve years later, July 3, 1957, also at seven in the evening, I was jailed on entirely groundless charges. I went to jail to protect President Toda and the sincere and courageous Kansai members. [SGI President Ikeda, then Soka Gakkai youth division chief of staff, was arrested on trumped-up charges of violating the election law filed by the Osaka District Prosecutors Office. He was later cleared of any wrongdoing.]

When one is completely dedicated to the path of mentor and disciple, he or she experiences no doubt or confusion, no uncertainty or fear.

During the reconstruction of Japanese society following World

War II, President Toda appreciated more deeply than anyone the debt the Japanese owed the United States for introducing freedom of religion and other democratic institutions to Japan. Out of my desire to repay this debt, I founded Soka University of America.

THE EXPANSION OF KOSEN-RUFU BEGINS WITH STRONG PRAYER

Like the indomitable lion seeking no companion, President Toda launched a new struggle for kosen-rufu on July 3. He relied on no one but himself. Physically he was extremely weak. His businesses were in complete ruin. And in the majority of cases, the whereabouts of the former Soka Gakkai members were unknown. Under these adverse circumstances, President Toda started anew, based on strong and earnest prayer.

Nichiren Daishonin says: "I am praying that, no matter how troubled the times may become, the Lotus Sutra and the ten demon daughters will protect all of you, praying as earnestly as though to produce fire from damp wood, or to obtain water from parched ground" (WND-1, 444). Such was the prayer of the Daishonin, determined to resolutely protect his followers while exiled on Sado Island.

It's not up to others — everything depends on ourselves. As leaders of kosen-rufu, we should first pray ourselves. Being a leader is not a matter of getting others to do things; it is to become an engine and set oneself in motion. This is the key to victory in all endeavors.

It is important that youth, in particular, actively seek challenges to forge and strengthen themselves. Those who enjoy material luxury from a young age and do not work hard cannot become people of outstanding character. They cannot become great leaders who protect the people.

I hope you will work hard, sparing no effort, and develop yourselves as indomitable champions whom nothing can shake or dishearten.

YOUTH, LIVE VIGOROUSLY

Today, a commemorative youth division gathering is taking place at the SGI-USA Headquarters in Santa Monica. I am delighted to see the growth of so many strong successors in the U.S. youth division.

I praise them for their strenuous efforts in creating another momentous page in the history of our movement with the New York culture festival and the SGI general meeting in Florida. It is my sincere wish that, in the workplace, at home and in the community, the youth will fully and freely manifest all that they have gained from this valuable training.

During an air raid not long after his release from prison, President Toda wrote to his wife's younger brother: "Chanting daimoku develops the state of Buddhahood. And developing the state of Buddhahood means devoting yourself confidently to your work while leading the most reasonable, sound and cheerful daily life. This sounds easy enough, although putting it into practice is difficult. But it is possible! If this practice did not enable us to, it would not be a genuine faith. I would like you to be a person who can succeed in this. A young person's life, in particular, should manifest the true power of faith. I, your older brother, have awakened to an eternal life, blazing with a vibrant, youthful spirit, and I am living vigorously and cheerfully."

Practicing Buddhism means being victorious. In advancing one step at a time amid the realities of daily life while showing concrete actual proof and in becoming victors and successes — people who enjoy abundant good fortune — we demonstrate with our very beings the validity of Nichiren Daishonin's Buddhism and serve as a source of hope and inspiration for those who will follow us on the path of faith.

I hope that the youth division members, while encouraging and supporting one another, will work courageously and cheerfully to realize the great American dream of the twenty-first century.

SEEKING BENEFIT FOR ONESELF AND OTHERS

Tomorrow, July 4, is America's Independence Day. Two hundred and twenty years have passed since the signing of the Declaration of Independence, which upholds the ideals of liberty and equality.

Tsunesaburo Makiguchi and Josei Toda both recognized the humanism that pulses in America. President Makiguchi discerned a need for humanity to move beyond military, political and economic competition and toward what he termed "humanitarian competition." His perceiving this in his *Geography of Human Life* as early as 1903 shows remarkable foresight.

Regarding both individual and international relations, Mr. Makiguchi asserted: "The purpose of interaction or exchange should not be simply to promote self-interest but to protect and enhance the lives of both ourselves and others. We have to choose a way to bring benefit to ourselves while working for the welfare and benefit of others."[1]

Where did Mr. Makiguchi find the seeds of this humanitarian formula of seeking the happiness of oneself and others? In America.

GIVING ONE'S ALL FOR THE MEMBERS' HAPPINESS

All my American friends are cheerful. They have a good sense of humor and are warmhearted and hard-working. In these qualities, I, for one, perceive the ideal characteristics of the human being. I deeply respect and treasure my American friends, who possess such pure and beautiful hearts.

As leaders, please strive to be great pilots of kosen-rufu who guide all of your fellow members without exception toward health, prosperity and happiness. The members are central. Their happiness has to be the prime concern and objective.

"If you see a person who accepts and upholds [the Lotus Sutra], you should rise and greet him from afar, showing the same respect you would a Buddha" — this, as the Daishonin says in *The Record of the Orally Transmitted Teachings,* is the "foremost point [the Buddha] wished to convey" (OTT, 192). We must never lose the spirit to respect and trust one another.

It is vital for leaders to bravely take action at the forefront, ready to bear the brunt of any onslaught. It is the role of leaders to unfailingly provide courage, hope and peace of mind to the Buddha's children. Only by advancing with a stand-alone spirit — no matter what happens — and resolutely leading the way toward victory can we fulfill our mission. This is the spiritual flame that infuses July 3.

BRINGING ONE'S LIFE TO A BEAUTIFUL CONCLUSION

Please make every effort to find and raise capable people. My wish is that you construct a wonderful organization here in the United States, joyfully building ever-expanding circles of friendship and a solidarity of people who cherish hope for life and the future. Please lead the most wonderful of lives.

In closing, I present to you, my beloved and esteemed friends, these short poems I composed:

> *What great joy!*
> *What profound significance!*
> *To celebrate*
> *this noble day of July here in America.*
> • • •
> *My friend,*
> *as a disciple,*
> *please bring your life*
> *to a magnificent completion*
> *by working*
> *for American kosen-rufu.*

Note

1. Tsunesaburo Makiguchi, *Jinsei chirigaku* (Tokyo: Seikyo Shimbunsha, 1980), vol. 5, p. 183.

SGI President Ikeda Participates in Los Angeles Representatives Conference

—w—

SGI PRESIDENT IKEDA joined Los Angeles representatives for a conference this evening. At the meeting, he expressed his deep appreciation for the tremendous hospitality he and his party had been shown throughout the duration of their stay in the United States. He then made the following remarks:

○ You have become a truly wonderful SGI-USA. The organization in America is now like the rising sun of a brilliant new dawn. Everything is determined by people. Because the number of fine people has increased, you have developed into a fine SGI-USA.

If the organization in America is solid both in terms of its movement for kosen-rufu and its position in society, the world can rest at ease. Please have the awareness, therefore, that your very existence is the hope of all humankind. I pray that you will become the world's most harmonious SGI-USA, where members unite together in a spirit of mutual trust and respect.

○ I would like each of you to enjoy your life to the fullest. In light of the Buddhist principle that "earthly desires are enlightenment," all our hardships, efforts and challenges are causes for rejoicing. Let us strive to live our lives with this spirit.

Each of you is working for peace in accordance with the teachings of Nichiren Daishonin. Each of you is working for kosen-rufu, for the sake of the Law and people's happiness, and for a better world. There is no doubt, therefore, that you enjoy Nichiren Daishonin's warm accolades and protection. With that great conviction, please advance with lion-like courage and vigor.

Glossary

—⚭—

Abutsu-bo Abutsu-bo Nittoku, a lay follower of Nichiren Daisho-nin. Nittoku is his Buddhist name, but he was commonly called Abutsu-bo. When Nichiren Daishonin was exiled to Sado, Abutsu-bo visited him at Tsukahara to confront him in debate, but was himself converted. He and his wife, the lay nun Sennichi, earnestly served the Daishonin during his exile, supplying him with food and other necessities for more than two years until he was pardoned and left the island in 1274.

benefit (Jpn *kudoku*) *Ku* means to extinguish evil and *doku* means to bring forth good.

bodhisattva (Skt) A being who aspires to attain Buddhahood and carries out altruistic practices to achieve that goal. Compassion predominates in bodhisattvas, who postpone their own entry into nirvana in order to lead others toward enlightenment.

Bodhisattvas of the Earth Those who chant and propagate Nam-myoho-renge-kyo. *Earth* indicates the enlightened nature of all people. The term describes the innumerable bodhisattvas who appear in the "Emerging from the Earth" chapter of the Lotus Sutra and are entrusted by Shakyamuni with the task of propagating the Law after his death. In several of his writings, Nichiren Daishonin identifies his own role with that of their leader, Bodhisattva Superior Practices.

Brahma (god) A god said to live in the first of the four meditation heavens in the world of form above Mount Sumeru and to rule over the *saha* world. In Buddhism, he was adopted as one of the two major tutelary gods, together with Shakra.

Buddhahood The state that a Buddha has attained. The ultimate goal of Buddhist practice. The highest of the Ten Worlds. The word *enlightenment* is often interchangeable with Buddhahood.

Buddhism of Nichiren Daishonin That Buddhism which plants the original seed of Buddhahood or enlightenment in people's lives.

Buddhist deities In Buddhism, nature and people who protect and cherish all life, especially those who chant Nam-myoho-renge-kyo to the Gohonzon.

bushido The Way of the Samurai. From the early seventeenth through the nineteenth centuries in Japan, *bushido* shaped the spiritual development of the Japanese people.

Chih-i The founder of the Chinese T'ien-t'ai school of Buddhism. See also *T'ien-t'ai*.

conspicuous benefit Benefit that appears in clearly recognizable form.

Dai-Gohonzon The object of devotion that Nichiren Daishonin inscribed on October 12, 1279, as the ultimate purpose of his advent in this world. *See also* Gohonzon.

daimoku (Jpn) Literally, "title." 1) The title of a sutra, in particular the title of the Lotus Sutra, Myoho-renge-kyo. 2) The invocation of Nam-myoho-renge-kyo in Nichiren Daishonin's Buddhism.

Daishonin (Jpn) Literally, "great sage." In particular, this honorific title is applied to Nichiren to show reverence for him as the Buddha who appears in the Latter Day of the Law to save all humankind.

Dengyo The founder of the Tendai sect in Japan.

dependent origination Also dependent causation, conditioned co-arising. A fundamental Buddhist doctrine of the interdependence of things. It teaches that all beings and phenomena exist or occur only because of their relationship with other beings or phenomena.

Devadatta A disciple of Shakyamuni Buddha who later turned against him.

Eagle Peak A small mountain located northeast of Rajagriha, the capital of Magadha in ancient India. Eagle Peak is known as a place frequented by Shakyamuni, where he is said to have expounded the Lotus Sutra and other teachings. According to *The Treatise on the Great Perfection of Wisdom* by Nagarjuna, Eagle Peak derived its name from its eagle-shaped summit and the many eagles or vultures inhabiting it. "Eagle Peak" also symbolizes the Buddha land or the state of Buddhahood, as in the expression "the pure land of Eagle Peak."

"earthly desires are enlightenment" The principle that teaches that one can attain Buddhahood by transforming illusions and earthly desires into enlightened wisdom rather than by extinguishing them.

eight sufferings Eight kinds of universal suffering mentioned in the Nirvana and other sutras. They are the four sufferings of birth, aging, sickness and death, as well as the suffering of having to part from those whom one loves, the suffering of having to meet with those whom one hates, the suffering of being unable to obtain what one desires, and the suffering arising from the five components that constitute one's body and mind.

eternity, happiness, true self and purity *See* four virtues.

external deity Godlike or divine nature outside one's own body or mind.

five senior priests Five of the six senior priests, excluding Nikko, designated by Nichiren Daishonin as his principal disciples shortly before his death. They are Nissho, Nichiro, Niko, Nitcho and Nichiji. While the Daishonin was alive, they devoted themselves earnestly to the propagation of his teachings, but after his death, they refused to follow Nikko even though Nichiren had formally appointed him as his successor. They gradually departed from the orthodoxy of the Daishonin's teachings.

four noble qualities *See* four virtues.

four powers In Nichiren Daishonin's Buddhism, the power of the Buddha, the power of the Law, the power of faith and the power of practice. Four powers of the Mystic Law whose interaction enables one to have his or her prayers answered and attain Buddhahood. The power of the Buddha is the Buddha's compassion to save all people. The power of the Law indicates the boundless force of the Mystic Law to lead all people to enlightenment. These two powers are present in the Dai-Gohonzon of the Three Great Secret Laws, the embodiment of the oneness of the Person and the Law. The power of faith is to believe in this Gohonzon, and the power of practice is to chant Nam-myoho-renge-kyo for the sake of oneself and others. To the extent that one brings forth his powers of faith and practice, he can manifest the powers of the Buddha and the Law embodied in the Gohonzon.

four sufferings The four universal sufferings of birth, aging, sickness and death. Shakyamuni's quest for enlightenment is said to have been motivated by a desire to find a solution to these four sufferings.

four virtues Four noble qualities of the Buddha's life expounded in the Nirvana Sutra — eternity, happiness, true self and purity. Because common mortals possess the Buddha nature, they too can develop the four noble qualities when they attain Buddhahood by fulfilling the Buddha's teaching.

fourteen slanders Fourteen attitudes that believers should avoid in their practice of the Mystic Law: (1) arrogance, (2) negligence, (3) arbitrary, egotistical judgment, (4) shallow, self-satisfied understanding, (5) attachment to earthly desires, (6) lack of seeking spirit,

(7) not believing, (8) aversion, (9) deluded doubt, (10) vilification, (11) contempt, (12) hatred, (13) jealousy and (14) grudges.

Gohonzon (Jpn) *Go* means "worthy of honor" and *honzon* means "object of fundamental respect." The object of devotion in Nichiren Daishonin's Buddhism and the embodiment of the Mystic Law permeating all phenomena. It takes the form of a mandala inscribed on paper or on wood with characters representing the Mystic Law as well as the Ten Worlds, including Buddhahood. Nichiren Daishonin's Buddhism holds that all people possess the Buddha nature and can attain Buddhahood through faith in the Gohonzon.

gongyo (Jpn) Literally, "assiduous practice." In Nichiren Daishonin's Buddhism, it means to chant Nam-myoho-renge-kyo and recite portions of the "Expedient Means" and "Life Span" chapters of the Lotus Sutra. It is performed morning and evening.

Gosho (Jpn) Literally, "honored writings." The individual and collected writings of Nichiren Daishonin.

heavenly deities *See* Buddhist deities.

Hennentai Gosho A compilation of the writings of Nichiren Daishonin in Japanese and arranged in chronological order.

Hinayana Buddhism One of the two major streams of Buddhism, the other being Mahayana. Hinayana literally means lesser vehicle.

human revolution A term first used by the Soka Gakkai's second president, Josei Toda, to indicate the self-reformation of an individual — the strengthening of life force and the establishment of Buddhahood — that is the goal of Buddhist practice.

ichinen-sanzen *See* "three thousand realms in a single moment of life."

inconspicuous benefit Benefit that accumulates over a period of time and is not immediately recognizable.

jiyu (Jpn) Literally, "emerging from the earth."

kalpa (Skt) An extremely long period of time. Sutras and treatises differ in their definitions, but *kalpas* fall into two major categories, those of measurable and immeasurable duration. There are three kinds of measurable *kalpas*: small, medium and major. One explanation sets the length of a small *kalpa* at approximately sixteen million years. According to Buddhist cosmology, a world repeatedly undergoes four stages: formation, continuance, decline and disintegration. Each of these four stages lasts for twenty small *kalpas* and is equal to one medium *kalpa*. Finally, one complete cycle forms a major *kalpa*.

karma Potential energies residing in the inner realm of life which manifest as various results in the future. In Buddhism, karma is interpreted as meaning mental, verbal and physical action, that is, thoughts, words and deeds.

kosen-rufu (Jpn) Literally, to "widely declare and spread [Buddhism]." Nichiren Daishonin defines Nam-myoho-renge-kyo of the Three Great Secret Laws as the Law to be widely declared and spread during the Latter Day. There are two aspects of kosen-rufu: the kosen-rufu of the entity of the Law, or the establishment of the Dai-Gohonzon, which is the basis of the Three Great Secret Laws; and the kosen-rufu of substantiation, the widespread acceptance of faith in the Dai-Gohonzon among the people.

ku (Jpn) A fundamental Buddhist concept, variously translated as nonsubstantiality, emptiness, void, latency, relativity, etc. The concept that entities have no fixed or independent nature.

Kumarajiva (344–413 CE) Translator of the Lotus Sutra into Chinese.

Latter Day of the Law Also, the Latter Day. The last of the three periods following Shakyamuni Buddha's death when Buddhism falls into confusion and Shakyamuni's teachings lose the power to lead people to enlightenment. A time when the essence of the Lotus Sutra will be propagated to save all humankind.

Lotus Sutra The highest teaching of Shakyamuni Buddha, it reveals that all people can attain enlightenment and declares that his former teachings should be regarded as preparatory.

Mahayana Buddhism The teachings that expound the bodhisattva practice as the means toward the enlightenment of both oneself and others, in contrast to Hinayana Buddhism, or the teaching of the Agon period, which aims only at personal salvation. Mahayana literally means greater vehicle.

Many Treasures Also referred to as Taho (Jpn) Buddha. A Buddha who appears, seated within the treasure tower, at the Ceremony in the Air to bear witness to the truth of Shakyamuni's teachings in chapter 15 "Emerging from the Earth" of the Lotus Sutra.

mentor-and-disciple relationship *See* oneness of mentor and disciple.

Miao-lo The sixth patriarch in the lineage of the T'ien-t'ai school in China, counting from the Great Teacher T'ien-t'ai (Chih-i). Miao-lo reasserted the supremacy of the Lotus Sutra and wrote commentaries on T'ien-t'ai's three major works, thus bringing about a revival of interest in T'ien-t'ai Buddhism. He is revered as the restorer of the school.

"mutual possession of the Ten Worlds" The principle that each of the Ten Worlds contains all the other nine as potential within itself. This is taken to mean that an individual's state of life can be changed, and that all beings of the nine worlds possess the potential for Buddhahood. See also Ten Worlds.

Mystic Law The ultimate law of life and the universe. The Law of Nam-myoho-renge-kyo.

Nam-myoho-renge-kyo The ultimate Law of the true aspect of life permeating all phenomena in the universe. The invocation established by Nichiren Daishonin on April 28, 1253. Nichiren teaches that this phrase encompasses all laws and teachings within itself, and that the benefit of chanting Nam-myoho-renge-kyo includes the benefit of conducting all virtuous practices. *Nam* means "devotion to"; *myoho* means "Mystic Law"; *renge* refers to the lotus flower, which simultaneously blooms and seeds, indicating the simultaneity of cause and effect; *kyo* means sutra, the teaching of a Buddha.

Nichiren The thirteenth-century Japanese Buddhist teacher and reformer who taught that all people have the potential for enlightenment. He defined the universal Law as Nam-myoho-renge-kyo and established the Gohonzon as the object of devotion for all people to attain Buddhahood. Daishonin is an honorific title that means "great sage." Also referred to as Nichiren Daishonin.

ninth consciousness One of nine kinds of discernment. The ninth consciousness or *amala*-consciousness is defined as the basis of all spiritual functions and is identified with the true entity of life.

nirvana Enlightenment, the ultimate goal of Buddhist practice.

"oneness of life and its environment" The principle stating that the self and its environment are two integral phases of the same entity.

oneness of mentor and disciple This is a philosophical as well as a practical concept. Disciples reach the same state of Buddhahood as their mentor by practicing the teachings of the latter. In Nichiren Daishonin's Buddhism, this is the direct way to enlightenment, that is, to believe in the Gohonzon and practice according to Nichiren's teachings.

shakubuku (Jpn) A method of propagating Buddhism by refuting another's attachment to heretical views and thus leading him to the correct Buddhist teaching.

Shakyamuni Also, Siddhartha Gautama. Born in India (present-day southern Nepal) about three thousand years ago, he is the first recorded Buddha and founder of Buddhism. For fifty years, he expounded various sutras (teachings), culminating in the Lotus Sutra.

soka (Jpn) Literally, "value creation."

Soka Gakkai International A worldwide Buddhist association that promotes peace and individual happiness based on the teachings of the Nichiren school of Buddhism, with more than twelve million members in 192 countries and territories. Its headquarters is in Tokyo, Japan.

Tatsunokuchi Persecution An unsuccessful attempt to execute Nichiren Daishonin at Tatsunokuchi on the western outskirts of Kamakura on the night of September 12, 1271.

Ten Worlds Ten life-conditions that a single entity of life manifests. Originally the ten worlds were viewed as distinct physical places, each with its own particular inhabitants. In light of the Lotus Sutra, they are interpreted as potential conditions of life inherent in each individual. The ten are: (1) hell, (2) hunger, (3) animality, (4) anger, (5) humanity, (6) heaven, (7) voice-hearers, also known as learning, (8) cause-awakened ones, also known as realization, (9) bodhisattvas and (10) Buddhahood.

three existences Past, present and future. The dimension of time. The three aspects of the eternity of life, linked inseparably by the law of cause and effect. "Throughout the three existences" means throughout eternity.

Three Great Secret Laws The core principles of Nichiren Daishonin's Buddhism, the object of devotion, the invocation or daimoku of Buddhism and the sanctuary of the essential teaching. These three constitute the core of Nichiren Daishonin's Buddhism.

three obstacles and four devils Various obstacles and hindrances to the practice of Buddhism. The three obstacles are: 1) the obstacle of earthly desires; 2) the obstacle of karma, which may also refer to opposition from one's spouse or children; and 3) the obstacle of retribution, also obstacles caused by one's superiors, such as rulers or parents. The four devils are: 1) the hindrance of the five components; 2) the hindrance of earthly desires; 3) the hindrance of death, because untimely death obstructs one's practice of Buddhism or because the premature death of another practitioner causes doubts; and 4) the hindrance of the devil king.

three poisons Greed, anger and foolishness. The fundamental evils inherent in life that give rise to human suffering.

"three thousand realms in a single moment of life" Also, *ichinen sanzen* (Jpn). A philosophical system set forth by T'ien-t'ai in his *Great Concentration and Insight*, clarifying the mutually inclusive relationship of the ultimate truth and the phenomenal world. This means that the life of Buddhahood is universally inherent in all beings.

Thus Come One One of the ten honorable titles for a Buddha, meaning one who has arrived from the world of truth. That is, the Buddha appears from the world of enlightenment and, as a person who embodies wisdom and compassion, leads other beings to enlightenment.

T'ien-t'ai Also called Chih-i. The founder of the T'ien-t'ai school, commonly referred to as the Great Teacher T'ien-t'ai.

Index

—∽—

99–100; life based on, 482; manifesting, 78; meaning of, 164;
mind(s) of, 99, 235–36, 240; never-
regressing, 309; Nichiren Daishonin
describes the mind of, 220; Nichiren
Daishonin teaches, 309; orbit of,
456; path of correct, 266; people of,
317; place to manifest, 159; power
of, 26–27, 221, 234, 239, 353, 481;
power of having correct, 279–80;
power of the mind of, 157; proof of,
439; purpose of, 22, 26, 90, 103,
246, 266–67, 301, 313; purpose of
practicing, 265, 453; and reason,
322; sincere, 254; spreading the joy,
320; stage upon to show the proof
of, 353; strong, 234, 299; true, 60,
355; victory in, 353–54; and wisdom, 246; world of, 4, 430
faith equals daily life, orbit of, 428;
practice of, 433
faith manifesting itself in daily life, actualizing principle of, 109. See also
faith equals daily life
family, 78; attitude of SGI members
toward, 266–67; appreciating, 313;
global, 475
fanatics, behavior of, 355; psychological
foundation of, 153
fanaticism, 153
Faust (Goethe), 345
fear, foremost, 363
Fifteenth World Peace Youth Culture
Festival, poem dedicated to the participants of, 466–68
filial piety, three types of, 62
financial security, 354
First Lecture in the "Tsunesaburo
Makiguchi Human Rights Lecture
Series," 406–19
First SGI All-America General Meeting,
67–73
First SGI-USA Boston Gongyo
Meeting, 133–46; announcement of
"Humanity in Education" at, 137
First SGI-USA Executive Conference,
52–59, 372–82
First SGI-USA General Meeting, 147–
59, 280
First SGI-USA Training Meeting, 3–5
First SGI-USA Women's Division
Meeting, 92–103

First SGI-USA Youth Division Training
Session, 10–14
First SGI-USA Youth General Meeting,
274, 276
five senior priests, destructive actions,
461
Florida, 268
Florida Joint Territory, activities
of, 476
Florida members, appreciation toward,
471
Florida Nature and Culture Center,
opening of, 471; plans for, 269
Flower Garland Sutra, 261
forbearance, Nichiren Daishonin states
the requirement for, 272. See also
tolerance
foresight, 94
formality, 220, 265; Josei Toda and, 19
formenting a rebellion, Nichikan's
"Commentary on 'On Offering
Prayers to the Mandala of the Mystic
Law'" describes, 330; Nittatsu's com-
ment about, 330
fortune, greatest, 480
four powers, 71; Josei Toda explains
the workings of, 287
four sufferings, 26, 277–78, 337, 453–
56, 458; Josei Toda on the, 179;
overcoming the, 26–27, 278. See
also eight sufferings
four virtues, 40, 47, 178, 278; establishing the, 69, 389
fourth of July, 489
Franklin, Benjamin, 33, 127, 216–17
freedom, gaining, 26; obstructions to
secure eternal, 26; people of genuine, 464; true, 85
French Revolution, 24
friends, appreciate, 313
friendship, 253; bonds of, 464
fulfillment, sense of, 479
fundamental darkness, of life, 446
Fushi kaden (The Transmission of the
Flower Acting Style) (Zeami), 257
future, 286, 464
future division members, nurturing, 472

Galbraith, John Kenneth, 336
Galtung, Fumiko, 426
Galtung, Johan, 367, 425, 427; and
peace studies, 426; and SGI, 426;

interdependence, scene from the Buddhist classics provides a metaphor for, 444–45
International Cultural Development Organization of India, 394
international order, search for a vision to a new, 222–23
international relations, Tsunesaburo Makiguchi view of, 489
interpenetration of all phenomena, scene from the Buddhist classics provide a metaphor for, 444–45
interpersonal relationships, rejuvenating, 131
intimidate, 482
intolerance, 481–82
Iroquois League, role of women in, 272
Izumi, Satoru, 308

James, William, 257
Japan, 352, 385; advancement of the kosen-rufu movement in, 297; Mother's Day in, 61; reason for the development of the kosen-rufu movement in, 57; spiritual history of, 126–28
Japanese American relations, 127–29
Jarvis, Anna M., 61–62
Jastrow, Robert, 318, 322
jealousy, 188
Jefferson, Thomas, 25–26; death, 27
Jewish people, Josei Toda on, 407
job, 78
John F. Kennedy School of Government, 122
Joint Conference for Leaders of the SGI Organizations, 160–76
joy, 46, 253; destroying, 351; Nichiren Daishonin explains the greatest, 438; path to, 66; producing, 351–52. *See also* Nam-myoho-renge-kyo
July 3, spirit of, 490
Jung, Carl Gustav, 347
justice, 425; prerequisite for upholding, 239

Kaigai Shimbun (Overseas News), 220
Kaneko, Kentaro, 128
Kansai, Josei Toda on, 199; role of, 202
Kansai members, greetings to, 200
Kansai Soka Schools, students, 394
Keller, Helen, 23, 139

Kennedy, John F., 23, 30, 54
Khrushchev, Nikita, 171
Kierkegaard, Søren, 188
killing, Shakyamuni on, 129
King, Martin Luther, Jr., 243
Kishinev pogrom (in Russia), 424
Kissinger, Henry, 23
knowledge, 446
Kobe-Osaka earthquake, 374; remarks about Kansai members efforts after the, 387; Russian SGI members concern about the, 378–79; selfless actions of Kansai members to the victims of the, 374–75, 382
Korczak, Janusz, selflessness of, 411
Korea, 352, 412
kosen-rufu, accomplishing worldwide, 237; action for, 299–300; admonition about, 187; basis for advancing, 106; benefits of committing to, 69; benefits on lives dedicated to, 454; benefits of taking action for, 41–42, 385; cornerstone of the worldwide, 233, 423; Daisaku Ikeda's commitment to worldwide, 70; eternal formula for the development of, 462–63; first steps for worldwide, 373; guidelines for finding the place of worldwide, 146; identifying the time of, 11; Josei Toda on, 9, 324; Josei Toda highlights the basis for attaining, 287; model of worldwide, 312; new phase in the advancement of worldwide, 297–302; protecting the movement of, 172–73; power source of, in the United States, 423; pulse of, 477; purpose of, 351; realizing, 240; realm of, 253; second stage of worldwide, 4; signally the advent of worldwide, 117–18; spreading, 18, 73; starting point of worldwide, 263; takes root, 440; working for, 470; worldwide, 4
kosen-rufu movement, 40; foundation of, in the United States, 6; future leaders of the worldwide, 76; growth and development of worldwide, 25; role of, 80; thirty-fifth anniversary of worldwide, 373
Kübler-Ross, Elisabeth, 338
Kubo (the lay nun), Nichiren Daishonin's praise and encouragement to, 378

New York members, appreciation toward, 201; hopes for, 458, 464–65; and humankind, 462; *waka* poem to, 452–53

Nichigen-nyo (wife of Shijo Kingo), 65

Nichijun, "Democracy and Religion," remarks in, 116–17; Fifth Soka Gakkai Young Men's Division General Meeting and, 324; and the Gohonzon, 46; the standard for the practice of Buddhism, remarks about, 311

Nichikan, 297, 326; "Commentary on "The Object of Devotion for Observing the Mind,"" 298, 329; desired, 301; "Interpretation Based on the Law," 301; Nichiko's view of, 298; on "The Object of Devotion for Observing the Mind," 98; *Six-Volume Writings*, 298, 301

Nichiko, 305; mistaken views of Niko, comments on, 186; the standard for the practice of Buddhism, remarks about, 310

Nichiren Daishonin, 130, 173, 417; "On Attaining Buddhahood in This Lifetime," 95, 439; "The Blessings of the Lotus Sutra," 15, 439; "On the Buddha's Prophecy," 460; cites *Profound Meaning of the Lotus Sutra*, 174–75; cites *"The Words and Phrases of the Lotus Sutra,"* 174; describes " The Entity of the Mystic Law," 328; discovery of, 39; "The Essentials for Attaining Buddhahood," 50; "On Establishing the Correct Teaching for the Peace of the Land," 182, 184–85, 330, 370, 376; example of profound compassion of, 267; execution, 231; "The Fourteen Slanders," 49; "The Farther the Source, the Longer the Stream," 18; fulfilling the mandate of, 242; and Hawaii, 377–78; "The Heritage of the Ultimate Law of Life," 303; humanistic actions in, 198–99; humanity of, 64–66; Josei Toda on, 179; "Letter from Sado," 460; "Letter to Akimoto," 71, 439; "Letter to Niike," 48; letters of, 15, 261; mandate of, 121; and Nikko Shonin, 461; "The Object of Devotion for Observing the Mind,"

97, 327; "On Offerings for Deceased Ancestors," 48–49; "Offering Prayers to the Mandala of the Mystic Law," 265; "opening the door of Buddha wisdom," 220; "The Opening of the Eyes," 480; original teacher in "Reply to Sairen-bo" refers to, 175; "On Practicing the Buddha's Teachings," 460; promise, 433; reason for the advent of, 306; "Reply to Sairen-bo," 48; sincerity, 64–66; vow, 309

Nichiren Daishonin's Buddhism, 14, 69; American people's hopes for, 281; correct method of propagating, 188; correct practice of, 111; demonization of, 151; demonization of religion in, 155; enemies of, 119; era of, 281; events marking the seven-hundredth anniversary of, 68; existence of, 84; "Holy Peak" in, 111; measuring the value of, 88; object of devotion in, 45–46; observe one's own mind in, 34; purpose of, 85; purpose of practicing, 453; realizing the greatness of, 59; Shakyamuni's Buddhism versus, 34–35; teachings of, 37, 69, 117, 119, 144–45, 242, 254, 279, 313, 351, 455, 480; the ultimate (the Gohonzon) in, 151

Nichiren Shoshu priesthood, issue with, 120, 151, 164, 167, 170, 183–84, 186–87, 189, 199, 217, 237, 241–42, 265, 267–68, 279, 300–05, 311, 318–19, 326, 329–31, 382, 425; Nichiko describes the corrupt state of the, 325–26; restorers of the, 297; significance of the issue of the, 149, 156, 186

Nicholas II, 423

Nietzsche, Friedrich Wilhelm, "Last Man," 225

Niko, 182–83; slanderous acts of, 170

Nikken Abe, 305, 326, 351; character of, 298; great slander of, 302; remarks of, 165; SGI women's decisive actions against, 272

Nikko Shonin, 173, 302, 307; Article Eight of "The Twenty-six Admonitions" of, 186; charge against, 170; dedication of, 164; leaving Mount Minobu, reason for, 167; 181–83; Niko's accusation against,

Other Books
by Daisaku Ikeda

———ɯ———

The following titles can be purchased from your local
or online bookseller, or go to the Middleway Press Web site
(www.middlewaypress.com).

Buddhism Day by Day: Wisdom for Modern Life
by Daisaku Ikeda
This treasury of practical information and encouragement will
appeal to those seeking a deeper understanding of how to apply
the tenets of Nichiren Daishonin's Buddhism in their day-to-day
lives.
(Paperback: ISBN 978-0-9723267-5-9; $15.95)

Buddhism for You series
In this oasis of insight and advice on the power of Nichiren Daishonin's Buddhism—which holds that everyone has a Buddha
nature of limitless power, wisdom and compassion—readers will
learn how to live a life filled with courage, determination, love
and prayer to achieve their goals and desires.

(Courage Hardcover: ISBN 978-0-9723267-6-6; $7.95)
(Determination Hardcover: ISBN 978-0-9723267-8-0; $7.95)
(Love Hardcover: ISBN 978-0-9723267-7-3; $7.95)
(Prayer Hardcover: ISBN 978-0-9723267-9-7; $7.95)

Choose Hope: Your Role in Waging Peace in the Nuclear Age
by David Krieger and Daisaku Ikeda
"In this nuclear age, when the future of humankind is imperiled by irrational strategies, it is imperative to restore sanity to our policies and hope to our destiny. Only a rational analysis of our problems can lead to their solution. This book is an example par excellence of a rational approach."
—Joseph Rotblat, Nobel Peace Prize laureate
(Hardcover: ISBN 978-0-9674697-6-8; $23.95)

The Living Buddha: An Interpretive Biograpy
by Daisaku Ikeda
An intimate portrayal of one of history's most important and obscure figures, the Buddha, *The Living Buddha* chronicle reveals him not as a mystic, but a warm and engaged human being that was very much the product of his turbulent times. This biographical account traces the path of Siddhartha Gautama as he walked away from the pleasure palace that had been his home and joined a growing force of wandering monks, ultimately making his way toward enlightenment beneath the *bodhi* tree, and spending the next forty-five years sharing his insights along the banks of the Ganges. The Buddhist canon is expertly harvested to provide insight into the Buddha's inner life and to grant a better understanding of how he came to play his pivotal role as founder of one of the world's largest religions.
(Paperback: ISBN 978-0-9779245-2-3; $14.95)

Planetary Citizenship: *Your* Values, Beliefs
and Actions *Can* Shape a Sustainable World
by Hazel Henderson and Daisaku Ikeda
"*Planetary Citizenship* is a delightful introduction to some of the most important ideas and facts concerning stewardship of the planet. I cannot think of any book that deals with more important issues."
—Mihaly Csikszentmihalyi, author of *Flow: The Psychology of Optimal Experience,* California
(Hardcover: ISBN 978-0-9723267-2-8; $23.95)

Unlocking the Mysteries of Birth & Death...
and Everything In Between, A Buddhist View of Life
(second edition) by Daisaku Ikeda
"In this slender volume, Mr. Ikeda presents a wealth of profound information in a clear and straightforward style that can be easily absorbed by the interested lay reader. His life's work, and the underlying purpose of his book, is simply to help human beings derive maximum meaning from their lives through the study of Buddhism."
—ForeWord Magazine
(Paperback: ISBN 978-0-9723267-0-4; $15.00)

The Way of Youth: Buddhist Common Sense
for Handling Life's Questions
by Daisaku Ikeda
"[This book] shows the reader how to flourish as a young person in the world today; how to build confidence and character in modern society; learn to live with respect for oneself and others; how to contribute to a positive, free and peaceful society; and find true personal happiness."
—Midwest Book Review
(Paperback: ISBN 978-0-9674697-0-6; $14.95)

The following titles can be purchased at SGI-USA bookstores nationwide or through the mail order center: call 800-626-1313 or e-mail mailorder@sgi-usa.org.

Faith into Action: Thoughts on Selected Topics
by Daisaku Ikeda
A collection of inspirational excerpts arranged by subject. Perfect for finding just the right quote to encourage yourself or a friend or when preparing for a meeting.
(World Tribune Press, mail order #4135; $12.95)

The Human Revolution boxed set
by Daisaku Ikeda

"A great human revolution in just a single individual will help achieve a change in the destiny of a nation, and further, can even enable a change in the destiny of all humankind." With this as his main theme, the author wrote his twelve-volume account of Josei Toda's life and the phenomenal growth of the Soka Gakkai in postwar Japan. Published in a slightly abridged two-book set, this work paints a fascinating and empowering story of the far-reaching effects of one person's inner determination. Josei Toda's awakening and transformation, his efforts to teach others the unlimited power of faith, his dedication in leading thousands out of misery and poverty, the efforts of his devoted disciple, Shin'ichi Yamamoto—within these stories we find the keys for building lives of genuine happiness.

(World Tribune Press, mail order #4182; $45.00)

Kaneko's Story: A Conversation with Kaneko Ikeda

Kaneko Ikeda shares thoughts and stories of her youth, marriage and family and of supporting her husband of more than fifty-five years, SGI President Daisaku Ikeda. Also included are four messages written to the women of the SGI.

(World Tribune Press, mail order #234302; $9.95)

My Dear Friends in America
by Daisaku Ikeda

This volume brings together for the first time all of the SGI president's speeches to U.S. members in the 1990s.

(World Tribune Press, Hardcover: mail order #4104; $19.95)

My Path of Youth
by Hiromasa Ikeda

This book presents a selection of essays by Hiromasa Ikeda that were published in Japanese in the *Koko Shimpo*, the Soka Gakkai's high school division newspaper. In them, he conveys his message to youth by way of recounting childhood memories,

his experiences as a young teacher at Kansai Soka High School and episodes from his travels around the world representing his father, SGI President Daisaku Ikeda. Hiromasa Ikeda also shares his views on the spirit of the mentor-disciple relationship in Buddhism, the significance of his father's work and mission, and the importance of living based on a resolve for peace.
(World Tribune Press, mail order #234476; $9.95)

The New Human Revolution
by Daisaku Ikeda
An ongoing novelized history of the Soka Gakkai, which contains not only episodes from the past but guidance in faith that we can apply as we grow our movement here in the United States.
(World Tribune Press; $12.00 each volume)
Volume 1, mail order #4601
Volume 2, mail order #4602
Volume 3, mail order #4603
Volume 4, mail order #4604
Volume 5, mail order #4605
Volume 6, mail order #4606
Volume 7, mail order #4607
Volume 8, mail order #4608
Volume 9, mail order #4609
Volume 10, mail order #4610
Volume 11, mail order #4611
Volume 12, mail order #4612
Volume 13, mail order #4613
Volume 14, mail order #4614
Volume 15, mail order #275446
Volume 16, SKU #275447

The Wisdom of the Lotus Sutra, vols. I–VI
by Daisaku Ikeda, Katsuji Saito, Takanori Endo and Haruo Suda
A captivating dialogue on the twenty-eight-chapter Lotus Sutra that brings this ancient writing's important messages into practical application for daily life and for realizing a peaceful world.

(World Tribune Press, $10.95 per volume)
Volume I, mail order #4281
Volume II,mail order #4282
Volume III, mail order #4283
Volume IV, mail order #4284
Volume V, mail order #4285
Volume VI, mail order #4286

The World of Nichiren Daishonin's Writings, vols 1–4
by Daisaku Ikeda, Katsuji Saito and Masaaki Morinaka
These books bring to life the teachings and major life events of
Nichiren Daishonin through an ongoing discussion between SGI
President Ikeda, Soka Gakkai Study Department Leader Katsuji
Saito and Study Department Vice Leader Masaaki Morinaka. Revi-
talize our pursuit of creating happiness and peace with this four-
volume series.
(SGI Malaysia, $7.95 per volume)
Volume 1, mail order #1891
Volume 2, mail order #1892
Volume 3, mail order #1893
Volume 4, mail order #1894

A Youthful Diary: One Man's Journey From the
Beginning of Faith to Worldwide Leadership for Peace
by Daisaku Ikeda
Youthful inspiration for people of all ages. Through the tale of the
ever-deepening relationship between the young Daisaku Ikeda
and his mentor-in-life, Josei Toda, *A Youthful Diary* is a compelling account of both triumphs and setbacks on the road to establishing the foundation of today's Soka Gakkai.
(World Tribune Press, Paperback: mail order #4120; $15.00